Contagious Architecture

Technologies of Lived Abstraction

Brian Massumi and Erin Manning, editors

Relationscapes: Movement, Art, Philosophy, Erin Manning, 2009

Without Criteria: Kant, Whitehead, Deleuze, and Aesthetics, Steven Shaviro, 2009

Sonic Warfare: Sound, Affect, and the Ecology of Fear, Steve Goodman, 2009

Semblance and Event: Activist Philosophy and the Occurrent Arts, Brian Massumi, 2011

Gilbert Simondon and the Philosophy of the Transindividual, Muriel Combes, translated by Thomas LaMarre, 2012

Contagious Architecture: Computation, Aesthetics, and Space, Luciana Parisi, 2013

Contagious Architecture

Computation, Aesthetics, and Space

Luciana Parisi

The MIT Press
Cambridge, Massachusetts
London, England

MIT Press books may be purchased at special quantity discounts for business or sales promotional use. For information, please email special_sales@mitpress.mit.edu or write to Special Sales Department, The MIT Press, 55 Hayward Street, Cambridge, MA 02142.

This book was set in Stone Sans and Stone Serif by Toppan Best-set Premedia Limited, Hong Kong. Printed and bound in the United States of America.

Library of Congress Cataloging-in-Publication Data

Parisi, Luciana.
Contagious architecture : computation, aesthetics, and space / Luciana Parisi.
p. cm—(Technologies of lived abstraction)
Includes bibliographical references and index.
ISBN 978-0-262-01863-0 (hardcover : alk. paper)
1. Space (Architecture). 2. Architecture—Philosophy. I. Title.
NA2765.P36 2013
720.1—dc23
2012027959

10 9 8 7 6 5 4 3 2 1

Contents

Series Foreword

"What moves as a body, returns as the movement of thought."

Of subjectivity (in its nascent state)

Of the social (in its mutant state)

Of the environment (at the point it can be reinvented)

"A process set up anywhere reverberates everywhere."

• • • •

The Technologies of Lived Abstraction book series is dedicated to work of transdisciplinary reach inquiring critically but especially creatively into processes of subjective, social, and ethical-political emergence abroad in the world today. Thought and body, abstract and concrete, local and global, individual and collective: the works presented are not content to rest with the habitual divisions. They explore how these facets come formatively, reverberatively together, if only to form the movement by which they come again to differ.

Possible paradigms are many: autonomization, relation; emergence, complexity, process; individuation, (auto)poiesis; direct perception, embodied perception, perception-as-action; speculative pragmatism, speculative realism, radical empiricism; mediation, virtualization; ecology of practices, media ecology; technicity; micropolitics, biopolitics, ontopower. Yet there will be a common aim: to catch new thought and action dawning, at a creative crossing. Technologies of Lived Abstraction orients to the creativity at this crossing, in virtue of which life everywhere can be considered germinally aesthetic, and the aesthetic anywhere already political.

• • • •

"Concepts must be experienced. They are lived."

Preface: Weird Formalism

This book is about the logic of *computation*[1] and its ingression into culture. It describes a world in which *algorithms* are no longer or are not simply instructions to be performed, but have become performing entities: actualities that select, evaluate, transform, and produce data. In this world, algorithms construct the digital spatiotemporalities that program architectural forms and urban infrastructures, and are thereby modes of living. This is not to contend that algorithms are the building blocks of a physical universe in which any kind of thought can be fully computed. Instead, a closer look at algorithmic procedures shows that incompleteness in *axiomatics* is at the core of computation. These performing entities—algorithms—expose the internal inconsistencies of the rational system of governance, inconsistencies that correspond to the proliferation of increasingly random *data* within it. Instead of granting the infallible execution of automated order and control, the entropic tendency of data to increase in size, and thus to become random, drives infinite amounts of *information* to interfere with and to reprogram algorithmic procedures. These entropic bursts of data within computation add new information to the recursive functions of control, without becoming simply incorporated or used by the system (i.e., by transforming dissipative energy into information). Entropic data are operative agents of irreducible size that crack and rescript the source program of the system from within. The system of governance defined by the digital world of data can therefore no longer rely upon the smooth programming of tasks, the exact reproduction of rules, and the optimization of conducts, habits, and behaviors. *Randomness* has become the condition of *programming culture.*

This book does not imagine a world in which rationality has been replaced by the arbitrariness of information. Far from it: computational *randomness* corresponds to infinite volumes of data that are meaningful contingencies which refuse to be fully comprehended, compressed, or sensed by totalities (i.e., by the mind, the machine, or the body). This also means that algorithms do not exclusively channel data according to preset mechanisms of binary synthesis (0s and 1s), as they also enumerate the indeterminate zone between finite states. This new function of algorithms thus involves not the reduction of data to binary digits, but the ingression of random quantities into computation: a new level of determination that has come to characterize automated modes of organization and control. Far from making the rational system of governance more efficient, this new level of determination forces governance to rely on indeterminate probabilities, and thus to become confronted with data that produce alien rules. These rules are at once discrete and infinite, united and fractalized.

From another standpoint, the emphasis on the new tendencies of algorithms to be overshadowed by infinite volumes of data explains the ingression of computational logic into culture. What is important here is not that culture has become doomed by the automated rules that transform its variety of expressions into data that can be classified, profiled, and consumed. Instead, the addition of random quantities to finite procedures turns automation into a computational adventure resulting in the determination of new cultural actualities. Instead of being exhausted by the formalism of rules or symbols that execute instructions, automated processing requires a semiopen *architecture* of axioms, whereby existing postulates are there to be superseded by others that can transform infinite quantities into contingent probabilities. Incompleteness in axiomatics thus brings to light the fact that automated processing is not predeterminate, but rather tends toward new determinations. In making this claim I do not intend to suggest that computation can now explain culture, aesthetics, and thought because it can account for change. My contention is rather that there is a concrete culture, an aesthetic and a mode of thought, specific to the computational production of new probabilities.

This is why this book argues for a new digital space that no longer or not fully coincides with Deleuze and Guattari's notions of "striated" (metric) and "smooth" (vectorial and projective or topological) space. Striated space is gridded, linear, metric, and optic.[2] It is also described as the space of logos, based on the deductive reduction of infinities to discrete unities constituting the building blocks of reason, the function of which is to find solutions to occurring problems.

In this book the striated space corresponds to the digital matrix of points that do not change over time: a prefixed, gridlike architecture derived from postulates based on discrete sets of algorithms through which optimal forms can be constructed. This is the striated space of the city, the urban planning deduced from the exact relation between points, which establishes an infrastructural grid that predetermines movement.[3] In the last twenty years, however, the digital mapping of space has been intersected by a new tendency in digital design that has more fully embraced the power of computation to generate new architectural forms or smooth surfaces. By drawing on biological notions of morphogenesis, and thus by relying on the capacity of forms to change over time, algorithms have become generative components for form-finding and pattern-making architectures. The new centrality of generative algorithms (but also cellular automata, L-systems, and parametricism) in digital design has led to the construction of various topological geometries and curvilinear shapes that have come to be known as blob architectures. While the gridlike architecture of striated space (or digital mapping) places discrete unities at the center of a design made of points connected by lines, the topological curves of smooth space (or blob architecture) starts from the generative power of a point, the meshing and folding of which becomes the condition for the emergence of a new form.

Far from being in direct opposition, Deleuze and Guattari often refer to these two spaces as being in a relation of reciprocal presupposition, so that points can generate new curves, and curves can become frozen segments. However, this mutualism between the two kinds of spaces—or planes—may not be fully sufficient to explain the mode of extension produced by the ingression of computation into culture. To the striated (metric) and smooth (topological) spaces, this book annexes another approach to extension. This approach is defined by *mereotopology*: the study of the relation between parts, of that between parts and wholes, and of the boundaries between parts. In particular, I turn to Alfred North Whitehead's schema of mereotopological relations—a schema that is a concrete abstraction—in order to argue that neither discrete unities nor continual surfaces can account for the transformation of the digital grid, as the latter is characterized by the infiltration of randomness into finite sets of rules.

Mereotopology describes parts as being semiopen: it casts them as discrete and separable on the one hand and as undivided and continuous on the other. It postulates that there is no gap between parts, and neither are there *infinitesimal* points constituting continuous trajectories (or topological surfaces). Instead, between points there are always more points (or an infinite amount of points), which correspond not to infinitesimals, percepts, and affects but to finite segments internally defined by a unique arrangement of infinities. For Whitehead these finite segments are actualities, which are at once extended and intensive, or equipped with space and time; they are finite durations. In contrast to blob architectures, which have given rise to a computational aesthetics expressed by the topological surface or the smooth plane of total connection, mereotopological architecture reveals that infinity is intrinsic to parts, unities, and discrete objects. From this standpoint, infinity does not coincide with the total fusion of spatiotemporal dimensions into one deforming surface, but instead can be explained by how wholes (continuities) become parts (discontinuities), and how parts can be bigger than wholes. In computational terms, infinity is equivalent to random (or incompressible) quantities of data (which are at once discrete and continuous) interfering with and reprogramming the algorithmic procedures in digital design, for instance. This also means that algorithms are not the building blocks of a topological surface whose forms continuously evolve. What connect the multiplicity of points are instead infinite quantities that ingress into the gap between points, thereby revealing the existence of yet another point (or spatiotemporal actuality) that overlaps them, but which does not originate from them. Yet how do these quantities come to determine and characterize algorithmic procedures in digital design?

This is where computation becomes entangled with Whitehead's view that it is *prehensions* that define what an entity is and how it relates to others. Prehensions point to how any actuality (from an animal body to a grain of sand, from an amoeba to an electron) grasps, includes and excludes, and transforms data. Instead of an ontological dominance of higher forms of actuality (such as human beings) over others, Whitehead argues that all entities have an equivalent status. Not only are they all real, but also they all matter. Nevertheless, this seemingly flattening ontology does not simply contend that these actualities are all the same, nor does it hold that they are all different. Whitehead proposes a radical pragmatism according to which determinate events, or what he calls occasions of experience, are defined by degrees of prehension that in turn constitute the degree of importance of some actualities compared to others.

In this book, the new function of algorithms within the programming of spatiotemporal forms and relations reveals how the degree of prehension proper to algorithms has come to characterize computational culture. Algorithms are no longer seen as tools to accomplish a task: in *digital architecture*, they are the constructive material or abstract "stuff" that enables the automated design of buildings, infrastructures, and objects. Algorithms are thus actualities, defined by an automated prehension of data in the computational processing of probabilities. From this standpoint, digital algorithms are not simply representations of data, but are occasions of experience insofar as they prehend information in their own way, which neither strictly coincides with the binary or fuzzy logic of computation nor with the agency of external physical inputs. Instead, as actual occasions, algorithms prehend the formal system into which they are scripted, and also the external data inputs that they retrieve. Nevertheless, this activity of prehension does not simply amount to a reproduction of what is prehended. On the contrary, it can be described as a contagion. This is because to prehend data is to undergo an irreversible transformation defined by the way in which rules are immanent to the infinite varieties of quantities that they attempt to synthesize. This means that rules cannot change these infinite quantities; instead the latter can determine rules anew and thus produce new ones. From this standpoint, I do not use this notion of contagion to suggest that there is a physical connection between points (i.e., that one point of prehension is determined by the next point in a sequential order) or a potential relation between points (i.e., the fact that points are linked by infinitesimal approximations). Instead, to maintain that a prehension can be understood as a contagion is to say that infinite amounts of data irreversibly enter and determine the function of algorithmic procedures. It follows that contagion describes the immanence of randomness in programming. This irreversible invasion of incompressible data into the digital design of space has led to the production of digital spatiotemporalities that do not represent physical space, but are instead new spatiotemporal actualities. The contagious architecture of these actualities is constructing a new digital space, within which programmed architectural forms and urban infrastructures expose not only new modes of living but also new modes of thinking.

Nonetheless, by prehending (or becoming infected with) infinite quantities of data, algorithms do not simply work to generate optimal probabilities that will more closely match the architecture of the future and its urban infrastructure. The futurity of algorithmic prehensions cannot be exhausted by the image of the future. Instead, as prehensive entities, algorithms unleash the concrete futurity of the digital spatiotemporalities of the present, of which digital architecture is but one example (other examples might include the relational architecture of databases, the cultural, political and economic statements of search culture, the connectedness of social media, and the immediacy of data communication).

This book is about the ingression of computational logic into culture. It is most appropriately placed in the field of digital architecture, because the algorithmic production of digital spatiotemporalities defines: (1) that logic is becoming an aesthetic operation, and (2) that computational aesthetics is characterized by the algorithmic prehension of *incomputable* data. In adding this aesthetic interference to computational logic I do not mean to imply that algorithms are the new synthesizer of indeterminate quantities. On the contrary, one condition of this book is that no actuality—physical or automated—could ever contain the infinite amount of infinities that are immanent to all actualities. Instead, what happens with all actualities is that these varieties of infinities are only partially and uniquely processed, so that not only is each actuality asymmetric with respect to another, but it is also asymmetric within itself. In other words, the discovery of incomputable quantities in axiomatics reveals that there can never be any totality that could subsume (external or internal) parts into one encompassing whole.

From this standpoint, the aesthetic operations of logic suggest that the prehensive activity of algorithms not only evaluates and transforms, but also enumerates and produces new computational actualities. In the field of digital architecture, this means that computational logic does not need to be used to reach aesthetic results as if it were operated by an external agent, which would select the activities of the process from an "outside." Aesthetics must instead be understood to reside at the core of computational logic, because it defines computational processing as the determining of infinities in a step-by-step fashion, and without subjecting them to complete synthesis and/or axiomatics. Aesthetics, that is, is not only complementary to logic but is immanent to it: it exposes contingency in programming, and the reality of chance in the calculation of probabilities.

It would be misleading, however, to attribute the aesthetic capacities of algorithms to a mainly qualitative synthesis of data. It is important to bear in mind when speaking of aesthetics in computation that one cannot obviate the entropic size of data, and therefore the tendencies of quantities to increase in volume, length, and density each time they are calculated. Thus, this book does not depart from one basic crux of computation: namely, the fact that computation is a method of quantification that deals with quantities. From this standpoint, *algorithmic prehensions are quantifications of infinite quantities that produce new quantities.*

This is also to say that there is a production of the new within computation that specifically concerns increasing randomness or increasing volumes of data that cannot be systematized in smaller algorithmic procedures. This book therefore contains no claims as to the necessity of cleansing culture of data pollution, because it admits that data production is an immanent process that unravels the gaps, blind spots, and incompatibilities within formal systems in their attempt to constantly invent new axioms and rules.

Similarly, this book also distances itself from the dominant cybernetic model of feedback control, which aims to include qualitative data in computational procedures by allowing the system to become co-constituted by its outside. In particular, the dominance of *second-order cybernetics* and its autopoietic model of feedback in digital architecture has led to a plethora of interactive projects whereby algorithms are designed to respond and adapt to external inputs, so as to be able to add chance to programming. Yet rather than challenge computation, this attempt to add qualitative data to programming has in my opinion served to reify the fundamental system of inference which assigns logic to rationality and aesthetics to sensation. Against this tendency, this book embraces the aesthetic function of algorithms in their quantitative concreteness, the prehension of contingency and thus the outbreak of randomness within logic. I claim that this is the computational aesthetic that governs digital culture today.

The investigation of this weird formalism points to a further level of analysis that looks for the properties of a speculative function of computation. In doing so it turns again to Whitehead's metaphysics, because the scope of his attempts to disentangle reason from the enclaves of rationality are sufficiently broad to include the possibility that automated modes of thought are modes of decision, and that decision is a mode of adding new data to and thereby rethinking what already exists, by counteracting the sequential order of patterns. In short, Whitehead's study of the function of reason has offered my investigation the opportunity to discuss a mode of thought proper to algorithms: *soft(ware) thought*. Instead of looking for ways of comparing (or conflating) computation with (or into) formal or practical notions of reason, and instead of thus associating it with conceptions of the mind that view the latter as something that executes thoughts onto the world, or as something produced by the synaptic connections of the brain's neural networks, my analysis starts from the reality of algorithms as actual modes of thought.

Seen from this standpoint, computation does not refer to a rational calculus that deduces reality from universal axioms, but rather to the algorithmic prehension of the random data that are now contaminating formal logic's attempts to continuously invent new axioms. The speculative function of algorithms corresponds to an abstract scheme of concrete data, or to enumerations of procedures through which computation is constructing our present. Thus, speculative computation is not to be confused with a new mode of prediction, which for instance forecloses the potential threat of the unknown by prompting immediate decisions that anticipate the happenings of the present. Instead, this abstract scheme includes interference (the entropic expansion of quantities) in the procedures of the present insofar as it allows infinite volumes of data to determine spatiotemporal activities. In short, speculative computation is not a new system of probabilities that tries to turn potentialities into possibilities. It is instead an aesthetic ordering of entropic data. This is a weird ordering that involves the prehension not simply of temporal infinities but also of the infinities of extension as they become enumerated in computational procedures. This immanent partiality helps us to describe computation in terms of Whitehead's *speculative* function of *reason*, according to which algorithmic actualities select quantitative novelty from repetition, thereby allowing computation to add new data structures or spatiotemporalities to the extensive continuum of actualities.

This speculative character of computation cannot be accommodated by a cybernetic system of probabilities. As Massumi has clarified in his discussion of the efficacy of preemptive power, such a system can no longer rely on already processed data. Instead, the cybernetic mode of control based on feedback as the self-regulating property of governance—whereby the output allows the system to incorporate more complexity, and thus to become extended into or fused with its outside—now needs to account for what is not there, i.e., for the determinacy of the unknown. This is why the binary language of digital computation is no longer sufficient to anticipate the emergence of errors, or to convert unknown quanta into preset probabilities. Thus, as Massumi explains, the cybernetic apparatus of control, which is based upon and defined by the operation and the operability of procedures, employs a quasi-empirical mode of calculation, according to which the necessary emergence of the new (the uncertain) and its potential effects are precalculated and preempted before the fact. In other words, the effects of the unknown have become the causal motor by which control is unconditionally exercised and driven by immanent decisions about what has not yet happened.

The cybernetic system of feedback therefore inserts temporality or qualitative variations into its binary calculation. In particular, the calculation of infinitesimal variations between these states has challenged cybernetics to overcome its own limit, and thereby to extend its power of prediction toward qualitative variations. It is this stretch toward the inclusion of temporal variations that reveals postcybernetic control's power to act retroactively, i.e., to act by turning the potential effects of the future into operative procedures within the present. The matrix of binary digits is therefore turned into a fold of approximate calculations of the infinitesimal points that join two coordinates at a tangent: the derivatives of the *x* and *y* coordinates turn parallel lines into the infinities of a potential curve. A *topological* surface thus rises above the digital matrix of sequential coding, and is ceaselessly reproduced in the digital design of facades, buildings, and urban planning. This computational aesthetic of the curve is now the dominant expression of postcybernetic control.

My investigation however does not stop at this point, as it continues to explore the stubborn reality of quantities that remains at the core of digital architecture. The reason why algorithmic and interactive architecture—or digitality in general—has been unable to grasp or produce the intensive qualities of spatiotemporal experience, of the bodily feeling of spatiotemporal variations, is that computation deals in quantities and quantifications. This book asks the reader to consider the density of computational quantities as enumerations of new actualities, or spatiotemporal entities that enter and are added to the infrastructural organization of information. The book thus embarks on a close exploration of digital architecture projects in order to account not for the generative evolution of a topological surface, but rather for the *mereotopology* of parts that are bigger than wholes. Here, once again, algorithms are foregrounded as actual occasions of data that cannot be subsumed under the totalizing framework of postcybernetic control. These parts, I suggest, do not become the fused agents in a smooth space of control: they are instead autonomous events or nexuses of actual occasions.

The mereotopological exploration of computational quantities leaves my investigation with yet another question to discuss. If digital architecture implies the production of computational space-time, does it follow that there is an architecture of thought proper to computation? The pursuit of this question leads the book's arguments toward the inevitable realization of the incomprehensible existence of soft thought: an automated mode of prehension that cannot be compressed into a totalizing system (i.e., the mind, the machine, the body, or into idealism, mechanicism, or vitalism).

Soft thought is not the new horizon for *cognition*, or for the ontological construction of a new form of rationality. Instead, soft thought stems from the immanent ingression of *incomputable* data into digital programming. Soft thought is not what replaces thinking understood as a cognitive action, or affords the mind new capacities to order and calculate, or indeed gives the body new abilities to navigate space. Simply put, soft thought pertains to the existence of modes of thought, decision making, and mentality that do not exist in direct relation to human thinking. These modes of thought (of which soft thought is only one configuration) maintain a certain degree of autonomy from cognition demonstrated by their logical inconsistencies. This book thus ends with no surprise or final revelation, but with one remark: soft thought is not there to be understood as a new cognitive function or as a transcendent form of rationality, but to reveal that *programming culture* is infected by incomputable thoughts that are yet to be accounted for.

Acknowledgments

As Gilles Deleuze once said, there are periods when one looks back on events and realizes that one does not really know what happened. In these periods, what remain important are friendship and love.

Thank you to all my friends for helping me ride through the storm. Particular thanks are due to Steve Goodman, Stefania Arcara, Maud Pons, Melina Puleo, Jessica Edwards, Tiziana Terranova, Piero D'Alterio, Annamaria Morelli, Kevin Martin, Yari Lanci, Stamatia Portanova, Lidia Curti, Iain Chambers, and Silvana Carotenuto. Your unique combination has been indispensable for fueling my war machine. Francesco and Marcello Parisi deserve special recognition for their forward-thinking energy, as do my parents, Anna and Gennaro Parisi, for their continuous encouragement. Maria, Sofia, and Davide: thanks are due to you too.

I am also grateful to the Centre for Cultural Studies at Goldsmiths and its staff for supporting me during these years. In particular, I would like to thank Matthew Fuller, Graham Harwood, and Olga Goriunova for their altruism and their intellectual honesty. I have learned a lot from working with you. Thanks also to Scott Lash and Celia Lury for providing me with a space to further my theoretical adventure, to Lisa Rabanal and Breda McAleer for listening, to Mariam Fraser and Josephine Berry Slater for talking, and to John Hutnyk for his time. To the wonderful students on the MA Interactive Media (especially all of you on the program between 2008 and 2011), the postgraduate students at the Centre, and in particular the New Media Meetings group: I have greatly enjoyed our challenging discussions and your ambitious thinking. Thank you also to Maria Beatrice Fazi (grazie per la tua disponibilità e intelligenza), Susan Schuppli (for helping with the images too), Chryssa Sdrolia, Masa Kosugi, Sandra Gaudenzi, Carina Lopez, and Inigo Wilkins.

This project could never have started without the trust and the generosity of Erin Manning and Brian Massumi. You are exemplary people, and I cannot thank you enough for your belief in "research creation" and for foreseeing that processes do lead to conclusions. I am also grateful to Doug Sery for his commitment to this project and to Katie Helke Dokshina at MIT. A special thank you to Tom Bunyard for helping me with the copy-editing.

I know what made it possible to finish this book: the unconditional love of Stephen and Cleo. You belong to a new solar system. Thank you for making me brave and for showing me the wonders of the present. This book is dedicated to you both.

1 Incomputable Objects in the Age of the Algorithm

The late twentieth century may one day be known as the dawn age of the algorithm. If so, we wish to be the first to embrace the new rationality that sees space and matter as indistinguishable, as active mediums shaped by both embedded and remote events and the patterns they form.[1]

1.0 Metamodeling

Algorithms do not simply govern the procedural logic of computers: more generally, they have become the objects of a new programming culture.[2] The imperative of information processing has turned culture into a lab of generative forms that are driven by open-ended rules. Whether we are speaking about DNA, bacteria, or stem cell cultures, cultures of sounds and images, time-based cultures, or cultures of spatial modeling, algorithms now explain evolution, growth, adaptation, and structural change. Algorithms, therefore, have become equated with the generative capacities of matter to evolve.[3] It is not by chance that the age of the algorithm has also come to be recognized as an age characterized by forms of emergent behavior that are determined by continual variation and uncertainty.

Computational studies of evolutionary processes have taken to modeling randomly mutating software instead of creating large, complex simulations of biological systems. For example, the new field of metabiology aims to develop all possible designs for biological organisms within a software space.[4] These metabiological designs are examples of an *algorithmic architecture* that appears to deploy the software of matter itself.

But if generative algorithms[5] are no longer mere simulators of material dynamics, it may then be possible that they have acquired a new, ontological status that is unrelated to the preexistence of biophysical bodies. In other words, the mode of existence of algorithms no longer merely corresponds to models that simulate material bodies: instead it constructs a new kind of model, which derives its rules from contingencies and open-ended solutions. Generative algorithms are said to dissolve the opposition between mathematics and biology, between abstract models and concrete bodies.[6] Just as matter has an abstract form, so too have software programs become evolutionary bodies.

Nevertheless, the ontological claim for an ultimate merging between information and matter does not seem to account for a simple but entirely inevitable question: if, as Kwinter points out,[7] the age of the algorithm announces the advent of a new rationality, in which matter and space become indistinguishable, how can what is abstract remain as real as what is concrete? If the model and matter are fused into *one* invariant principle of continual variation, then what makes novelty take place? What adds novelty to this system of perennial change? These questions will guide this chapter's attempts at defining algorithmic objects as data actualities that exist without and beyond their biophysical referent and mathematical form.

From this standpoint, it is important to discuss the place of algorithms within recent critical approaches to computation and cybernetics.[8] In particular, the view that information systems are open and not closed, dynamic and evolutionary (with rules that change over time), and are thus not preprogrammed, has led most cultural analysis to argue that information, far from being abstract, is always already another form of matter. But although this new version of materialism has contributed toward challenging the assumption that the information model *represents* (i.e., governs) materiality, it has also divorced algorithms from their own reality and undermined insight into the true nature of the latter.

I will argue in this chapter that this form of materialism has led to a naive reading that flattens algorithms onto the biophysical ground, which they are then said to shape. By overlooking the existence of actual entities that cannot be physically felt and cognized, the cultural approach to cybernetics and computation has thus dissolved the reality of algorithms into thin air.

I suggest that a refusal *tout court* of the actuality of algorithms has coincided with the disqualification of computational formalism and the attendant rise of a computation that is driven by biophysical and sensorimotor responses. It will be claimed here that by leaving behind computational formalism (and symbolic logic) and the entropic nature of closed systems, so as to highlight the open-ended and negentropic forces of self-organization, cultural analysis has denied algorithms the potential of being anything other than a finite set of rules.

For this reason, this chapter questions the centrality of the *metacomputational* approach to information theory, according to which finite sets of algorithms, or mathematical *axioms*,[9] generate infinitely complex structures. At the same time, however, the chapter also contests the replacement of systems based on finite sets of algorithms with interactive processes relying on external inputs and temporal variations. The chapter concludes that the ideas about algorithms that are propounded by the metacomputational and the interactive approaches are characterized by their dismissal of the view that algorithms are actual entities imbued with infinity.

In order to challenge such assumptions, it seems important here to rearticulate the notion of the model, so as to distance it from the assumptions that algorithms either constitute the model of biophysical reality or are the latter's result. For this reason, I will turn to a reformulated version of Félix Guattari's concept of *metamodeling*.[10]

This concept can explain that the potential of computation coincides neither with the generative power of algorithms to design self-evolving structures, nor with interactive systems of physical connections. In other words, I suggest that neither the mathematical nor the physical underpinnings of computation can suffice to describe what an algorithmic object can be.

Guattari's concept of metamodeling is important because it challenges both mathematical truths and physical laws. It offers us the opportunity to describe an *extraspace* of nonunifying actualities, a *contagious architecture* that does not prioritize formalism or empiricism. This extraspace of algorithmic actualities is not to be found outside or between mathematics and physics, but rather within mathematical truths and physical laws. This is an extraspace of algorithmic actualities that are infected with abstractions but which are not themselves abstract. To be infected with abstractions means that these are immanent to actualities to the extent that they are intrinsic to their composition and finitude. There is therefore no contagious architecture between algorithms or between algorithms and biophysical bodies. Instead, contagion is taken here to define the quasi-finitude of algorithmic objects: the fact that these objects are spatiotemporal actualities which (and this is specifically discussed in this chapter) cannot be summed up in smaller programs, and which do not result from the sum of their parts. Similarly, it is argued here that this extraspace is not defined by the generative capacities of algorithms, from which rules evolve over time to deploy complex behavior. On the contrary, this extraspace corresponds to the random, incompressible data of algorithmic objects that are immediately experienced as irreducible parts larger than any totalizing whole.

Guattari's concept of metamodeling offers a critique of the notion of the model, but at the same time does not collapse the actuality of algorithms into that of biophysical objects. Instead, Guattari understood models in terms of cybernetic systems. He believed that models were simulations based on patterns of recognition (social, cultural, political, aesthetic patterns of governability).[11] Models, therefore, were for him reductions of a diagrammatic space made of intersections and disjunctions, operated by abstract signs and symbols. This diagrammatic space is a metamodel and not a series of prototypes or inherited and learned behavioral patterns. Instead, for Guattari signs and symbols become layered together without having any direct correspondence. Metamodeling—as opposed to the cybernetics of probabilities based on the possibility of forecasting the future through the data of the past—explains how signs and symbols are probes of futurity engaged in building the invisible architecture of the present. Metamodeling, therefore, describes how process becomes configuration, or how potentialities exceed preordained typologies.

Since the model is a formal structure but also a psychologically inherited blueprint (instructions or codes), Guattari argued that the hierarchy between models and facts, the formal and the practical, had to be turned into an ethico-aesthetics of signs, symbols, and objects. This meant that rules did not have to conform to programs, but needed to be resingularized and reconfigured while being subtracted from their realm of probabilities. In other words, metamodeling described how any set of rules "constructs its own cartographies, its own reference points, and thus its own analytic approach, its own analytic methodology."[12]

For Guattari, mathematics, but also software, can be taken as examples of metamodeling communication, which bypasses the imperative of representation. He argued against the idea that mathematics is the language of physics. Instead, he believed that mathematics articulated material processes of production that could not be physically detected or proven. Guattari's notion of metamodeling suggested that mathematical signs had no physical objects as their referent, but instead described a reality greater than could be physically explained.[13] In particular, he thought that the diagrammatic operations of mathematics pointed out "a physico-mathematic complex which links the deterritorialization of a system of signs to the deterritorialization of a constellation of physical objects."[14]

The intersection of these deterritorialized signs (mathematical symbols deterritorialized from the system of formal language) and objects (deterritorialized from their physical laws) defined metamodeling as the discovery and construction of new worlds and novel actualities. Hence, metamodeling was not simply the result of summing distinct models into a transcendent system/order, or merely the transposition of a model from one field into another (for instance, moving the scientific model of cybernetics into the cultural system of grouping). From the standpoint of metamodeling, the sign and the object both exceeded their mathematical and physical realms by setting up new conditions for change beyond formal schemes and empirical evidence.

Guattari's notion of metamodeling may thus help us to argue that algorithmic actualities can be thought independently of formal models. At the same time, however, it may be necessary to push his notion of metamodeling further, so as to avoid equating it with the logic of mixing and remixing signs and objects through digital computation.[15] This means that it is important to disagree with Guattari's notion that metamodeling announces the arrival of a postmediatic era in which all media forms share the same mathematical language. Instead, metamodeling is used here to suggest that a mathematical model, no matter how deterritorialized it is, cannot fully explain the actuality of algorithmic objects. This algorithmic actuality is transverse to both the mathematical and the physical domains. It is a transverse actuality. Thus, and *contra* Guattari, it will be argued here that algorithms are transverse objects constituted by mathematical and physical limits, the points at which patternless or incomputable data have infected all mediatic forms of communication.

These patternless data define not a new kind of algorithmic matrix so much as the immanence of incompressible data in all diagrammatics. As will become clearer below, algorithmic objects are both actual and abstract entities. In a manner that differs from Guattari's diagrammatics and metamodeling of nonsignifying connections, it is suggested here that in order to define algorithmic objects one has to admit the possibility that there may be an extra layer of potentiality within axiomatic computation,[16] a layer that is not exclusive to the empirical realm. It is this extra layer of potentiality—the reality of abstract objects—that this chapter intends to argue for.

But how, when discussing algorithmic objects, can one articulate this potentiality? And hasn't this potentiality already been discussed in computation, as that which temporarily appears in the foreground of experience as an evanescent object, but which then withdraws from actual existence? Isn't an emphasis on the abstraction or on the potentiality of algorithmic objects just another way to say that they only appear temporarily within a range of given possibilities, without ever existing as actual entities (i.e., a sterile rehearsal of Platonism)?

While I agree that algorithmic objects are not physical entities, it is difficult to deny that sets of instructions are actual data. One obvious example, and one that will become important here, can be found in the fact that algorithms correspond to data objects that build actual instances of space and time that have volume, weight, gravity, depth, height, and density, and can thus be found in algorithmic architecture. I suggest that algorithmic architecture explicitly offers us the opportunity to understand that these data objects are not simulations of some biophysical ground of the past or future. Algorithmic architecture corresponds to the software production of space as it implies automated data able to evolve in a search space so as to design buildings, urban infrastructures, and city plans. In algorithmic architecture, algorithms are not exclusively defined by the quality they can reproduce (color, sound, or variables), but also by the quantities of data that they operate. In other words, algorithmic architecture cannot overlook the fact that algorithms are quantifications of data that are at once actual and abstract and thus cannot be reduced to one plane of reality (that is, they cannot be flattened down into one continuous plane of qualitative relation). These quantities are not characterized by external relations (*partes extra partes*; i.e., one part of space is exterior to another part) but need to be understood as infinite varieties of parts that infect (take over and program) actual algorithmic sequences. Actual algorithms are indeed the hosts of abstract quantities or infinite varieties of infinities that constitute, at the same time, both condition and limit of any actual entity as a finite set of instructions. As actualities, algorithms hold within themselves abstractions that determine both their infinite change and their present finite status. As abstractions, algorithms are defined by the internal relations of an infinite variety of infinities. Abstract algorithms are unrelated to one another and can only enter into contact with one another once they are hosted by actual algorithms or finite computational states. I therefore claim that algorithms are both actual and abstract. They are actual and thus spatiotemporally determined, conditioned and limited. But they are also abstract, and are thus capable of irreversibly determining change according to the degree to which they contaminate actualities.

While algorithmic architecture explicitly treats algorithms as data objects, it has also failed to articulate their existence and has equated them to empty abstractions and/or simulations of physical entities. Similarly, the debate between metacomputational structures and interactive and responsive space still lacks a thorough engagement with algorithmic objects. On the one hand, algorithmic architecture has rearticulated formal mathematical structures in terms of evolving dynamics such as *cellular automata*. On the other hand, the shift toward the use of interactive algorithms has led designers to rely on biophysical inputs. Algorithmic architecture, therefore, has not offered a solution to the question of temporal objects, or to the problem of a biophysically induced computational structure. It views algorithmic objects either as the result of evolving data patterns or as a reaction to biophysical inputs. But my aim in this chapter is not to look for a solution to a problem. On the contrary, I am suggesting here that the questions of *what* an algorithmic object is and indeed of *how* it is have not been sufficiently discussed. This chapter intends to remedy that situation.

Nevertheless, in order to embark upon this project, it is first of all important to engage with computational theory, according to which a question of infinity lies at the core of the algorithm. Since the invention of the Turing machine, the problem of computing infinite quantities of data (or abstract quantities) into finite sets of rules has blended with the more general problem of ordering and programming noncomputable (incomputable) algorithms. Viewed from this standpoint, the debates within information theory that pertain to this problem already reveal to us that the ontology of algorithmic objects is to be found within the incompleteness of the axiomatic method.[17] Similarly, if one does not engage with the challenges posed to the axiomatic underpinning of algorithmic objects, then it becomes impossible to address their uniqueness and singularity.

However, it is important to be cautious here. This chapter does not argue that a thorough mathematical investigation of algorithms will give us answers to the questions noted above. On the contrary, I use algorithmic information theorist Gregory Chaitin's notion of *Omega* (incomputable algorithms at the limit of any computational process) to argue that any search for a mathematical Holy Grail is completely futile. Chaitin's theory about incomputable probabilities suggests that any closed set of finite algorithms is imbued with incompressible data, and by taking this notion further, beyond the specific field of algorithmic information theory, I argue that algorithmic objects cannot be contained by a metacomputational ontology.

Similarly, I also question the assumption that only what lies outside the realm of computation, automation, discreteness, and finitude can help us to define algorithmic objects as dynamic, changeable, and in movement. Instead, the concept of Omega proves that although infinity cannot be found in the physical world, it can be discerned within computational processing. This means that the possibility for change is intrinsic to the ontology of algorithmic actualities. Consequently I argue that interactive algorithms and responsive computation (i.e., algorithms defined by external factors, or driven by external inputs) do not contribute to the explanation, but rather to the occlusion, of the *what* and *how* of algorithmic objects. In particular, this chapter points out that interactive and responsive architecture end up attributing change to external agents, actuators or participants; algorithmic objects are thus seen as remaining passive in the face of an ever-changing environment of interaction.

The chapter demonstrates that computation offers us a rather more complicated and subtle notion of algorithms, according to which the latter are not equivalent to evolving agents that mutate in time, but are sequential spatiotemporal data structures conditioned by an infinite amount of information. These data structures are actual spatiotemporalities and have precisely become the objects of algorithmic architecture. In chapter 2 these structures will be analyzed more closely; here my aim is to develop an understanding of algorithms *qua* actual entities.

To engage further with the ontology of algorithms, one cannot avoid discussing the philosophical problems of what constitutes an object, and whether or not there are such things as abstract objects. In order to address these problems I will draw on Alfred North Whitehead's process philosophy, and on Graham Harman's object-oriented metaphysics. The encounter between these two contrasting metaphysical systems will also be used to challenge the idea that algorithmic objects are finite sets of instructions. This discussion is intended to shed some light on why the notion of the incomputable is able to help us to define algorithms in terms of actual and abstract objects.

This chapter will conclude that algorithmic objects are actual entities: spatiotemporal structures imbued with incomputable or patternless objects. The latter are not, however, to be misunderstood as the indefinite background of self-evolving energy. On the contrary, patternless objects correspond to entropic bursts of energy within sets of instructions, thereby defining the odd existence of discrete yet infinite algorithms within the structure of our programming culture. In this sense, algorithmic objects are not simply emergent forms within software, but are discrete unities injected with random data. It is as if algorithmic objects no longer pertain to the realm of software, but have unintentionally built an extraspace of data that infects (or irreversibly reprograms) all levels of matter.

From this standpoint, an algorithmic object is more than a temporal appearance or the result of interactive stimuli. Instead, it is a symptom of the new spatiotemporal structures that are most clearly deployed by algorithmic architecture. This is an important point against the idea that algorithms are merely temporal forms that are destined to disappear in the background of ubiquitous computation. Computational design problematically embraces the logic of prediction and the calculation of probabilities, and is unable to explain novelty in spatiotemporal experience. I argue against this form of metacomputation, and against the rational logic based on few unchangeable rules, the combination of which is held to produce all forms of complexity.

Contrary to the view of computation as a form of rationalism, I will suggest here that the ingression of the incomputable in axiomatics leads us to rethink computation in terms of speculative reason, to borrow from Whitehead. Computation, it will be argued, is an instance of speculative reason, since it no longer nor exclusively aims at the prediction or calculation of probabilities. On the contrary, Whitehead's understanding of speculative reason explains that the function of reason is to add new data to what will always already happen in an efficient chain of cause and effect. Similarly, it will be observed that the speculative view of computation implies that calculation is not equivalent to the linear succession of data sets. On the contrary, and as will be explained later in the chapter, each set of instructions is conditioned by what cannot be calculated: by the incomputable algorithms that disclose the holes, gaps, irregularities, and anomalies within the formal order of sequences. This means that a notion of speculative computing is not concerned with quantifying probabilities to predict the future, but with including random or patternless quantities of data in sequential calculation so as to add novelty in the actual architecture of things. This is why a notion of speculative computing is not to be confused with the capacity of algorithmic architecture to create temporary forms. On the contrary, the notion of speculative computing advanced here suggests that random data—indeterminate quantities—are the contagious architectures of the present. These architectures, far from withdrawing from actuality and thus being temporal forms that appear and disappear, rather remain actualities: spatiotemporal realities which are objective data to be inherited, evaluated, and appropriated by future actualities, of whichever kind at whichever scale, even when they cease to be there.

Far from predicting the spatiotemporal structures of a possible future, algorithmic architecture is conceived here as a symptom of the speculative programming of the present. Algorithmic architecture can also count as an instance of computational aesthetics, understood here in terms of the algorithmic prehension[18] of indeterminate data. Computational aesthetics therefore is not about the idealism of form, or about a code unraveling the complexity of biophysical structures. Instead, this chapter will conclude that algorithmic architecture explains computational aesthetics as the programming of actualities through the algorithmic selection of patternless data. For this reason, algorithmic architecture is another form of *postcybernetic control*, because it relies on algorithms to prehend incomputable data in order to program culture.

1.0.1 Programming the living

It is hard to understand what is meant by the age of the algorithm without referring to at least two distinct conceptions of algorithms. On the one hand, algorithms correspond to a set of finite instructions. On the other, algorithms have been conceived as evolving data able to adapt and to vary unpredictably according to external stimuli.[19]

A cybernetic reading of computation may clarify these two points. From the standpoint of *first-order cybernetics*, computation is a closed system, a formal language able to describe any biophysical process without having to be acted upon by the external environment. This is a closed, self-sufficient set of programmed instructions able to predict the future behavior of the system in terms of preset probabilities. On the other hand, *second-order cybernetics* suggests that biophysical indeterminacy or the contingency of environmental factors can open software programming to the modeling of dynamic systems that change over time and generate results that differ from initial conditions.

It is not argued here that these two tendencies simply correspond to a historical shift, whereby algorithms are no longer to be understood as finite sets of data but as interactive instructions open to change. Similarly, it may be misleading to assume that the age of the algorithm and the advance of programming cultures can be described simply in terms of an epistemological shift (and progress) from symbolic formalism to a biophysical understanding of computation and information systems. To embrace this view of an epistemological shift is to imply that algorithms lack the irregular dynamics of biological or physical systems. The second-order cybernetics understanding of computation certainly points out that dynamics or change can only be derived from the indeterminacy of living systems. Yet I will argue here against this predominant tendency, as it discards the possibility that change could concern the formal logic of computation, and by doing so forces the abstract reality of algorithms to become a mere effect of the biophysical world.

In the field of algorithmic architecture, one recent example of such a tendency can be found in the works of architect Greg Lynn, whose digital design takes inspiration from biophysical vector fields that lead to the growth of an emerging algorithmic form. This approach to design sees architectural form as the result of the computational processing of biophysical variables (e.g., the distribution of weight, gravitational pressures, the circulation of air, the movement of people). By closing the gap between mathematical models and biophysical contingencies, second-order cybernetics has turned computation into a temporal system, which explains change through the iteration of codes into a search space for evolving complexity. From this standpoint, biophysical unpredictability has become superior to mathematical calculability, and the reality of abstraction has slipped behind the concreteness of matter.

According to architect Karl Chu, algorithms have been central to the late-twentieth-century convergence of computational and biogenetic revolutions leading to the ultimate design of biological and mathematical codes, which promises the embodiment of life, emotion, and intelligence through "abstract machines or through biomachinic mutation of organic and inorganic substances."[20] Of course, one cannot deny that this biodigital combination of material parts arranged by algorithmic computation has added a distinctive trait to our information-based technoculture. For instance, much debate about cybernetic machines and biotechnologies in the late 1990s directly engaged with the no-longer-natural essence of biology, and with the new technoscientific ontologies of biological bodies. Since the natural ground upon which biology could be distinguished from artificial technics (for instance evolutionary technics of breeding, reproduction, cross-pollination, adaptation, etc.) was dissolving, it was argued that nature itself was the result of the plasticity of biological forms.

Second-order cybernetics has explained computation in terms of an evolving system that depends on its structural coupling with the environment. According to this biological view of computation, an interactive culture of response drives the calculation of mathematical probabilities. As a result, algorithmic architecture started to adopt these dynamics of biophysical variations in order to provoke changes in the program, for instance by inserting errors into the sequence of algorithms. Similarly, and perhaps more problematically, algorithmic architecture has also been related to a body that acts "as the framer of spatial information, as the source of its 'autonomy' or 'interiority'."[21]

Against the digital design of space, Mark Hansen argued that architecture "must reconceive its function for the digital age as the art of framing par excellence, it must embrace its potential to bring space and body together in . . . a 'wearable space'."[22] Here the algorithmic programming of space is conceived as imposing a coded invariant on the liveliness of an embodied experience of space. A haptic (bodily centered and not merely optical) interaction with software is seen here as necessary for the opening of digital architecture (algorithmic probabilities) to unpredictable variabilities and to the movement of space. This plunges computation into the actualities of biophysical change and novelty.

According to Hansen, algorithmic architectures are unable to explain the biophysicality of space: mathematics can only reduce the biological and physical complexity of living bodies to elegant formulas, and cannot explain the changing nature of experience. Hansen's objections to the computation of space can be seen as only one symptom of a more generalized critique of computational culture, which opposes codes, rules, and software programming to physicality, change, and indetermination. From this standpoint, biodigital computation must mean the biunivocal relation between mathematics and biology, the fusion of model and execution, the hybridization of the abstract and the concrete, algorithmic models and biophysical space. It has become evident, however, that the structural coupling between programs and bodies has meant an all-encompassing rejection of the reality of abstraction and of algorithmic objects.

It is not by chance that in the last ten years digital media art and architectural projects have worked to annex algorithmic programs to physical sensors. These sensors have the role of gathering data from the environment through actuators, which are set to feed information back into the program. The result is a series of automatic steps that translate control signals into action through motor, light, and speaker capacities.[23] By retrieving sensory data and processing their dynamic value through a string of zeroes and ones, the machine is able to physically interact with the participant. In principle, these procedures will eventually enable the machine (or the software program) to learn and calculate the probabilities of a similar scenario before it actually happens. The cybernetic logic of forecasting the future through models of the past is geared here toward a new level of predictability. It now involves the capacity of the software to rewrite the rules that it was programmed for, and that of the mathematical model to change as a result of physical interactions.

From this standpoint, interactive design has quickly replaced the assumed coldness of finite sets of rules with the ever-present warmth of sensory data. In other words, second-order cybernetics has added biophysical contingencies to the formal language of mathematics. Just as the programming cultures associated with AI defined algorithms through the first-order cybernetics and formal logic of zeroes and ones, so too has the culture of interactive architectures locked itself within second-order cybernetics: the autopoietic self-organization of biophysical systems. What is missing from this picture is a serious consideration of the residual power of algorithms, the processing of rules and the indeterminacies of programming, which are able to unleash novelty in biological, physical, and mathematical forms.

It is impossible to deny that algorithmic architecture has, over the years, become a computational system that has learned to incorporate, run, and anticipate the evolutionary capacities of all material phenomena. Similarly, despite its attempts at merging information and matter, algorithmic architecture has ultimately shown that the reality of abstraction is irreducible to the properties of living systems. To put it in another way, algorithmic architecture has been unable to do away with a problem proper to computation: the problem of calculating infinite series of probabilities in a manner that also includes—and this is significant here—the probability of incomputability.

This power of calculating indeterminacy corresponds not to the merging of information and matter, but to the challenge that the limit of computation has posed to the axiomatic method in computation. According to this method, finite sets of algorithms are programmed to calculate an infinite amount of information, and thus should also be able to compute the future. Nevertheless, this kind of computation could not rely on already-set probabilities that are always already destined to reach a limit beyond which computation would fail, and the prediction of the future would remain a repetition of the past. On the contrary, the computation of the future could only rely on the computational limit. Alan Turing already encountered the problem of the incomputable and attempted to transform the limit of computation into an algorithmic probability. However, as will be discussed in the next section, Turing could not prove the completeness of axiomatics through computation; on the contrary, the problem of random quantities of data continues to haunt computation today. But this is not a problem that solely concerns the field of computation: it is neither a discipline-related problem nor merely a technical difficulty. Instead, I will argue that this problem is intrinsic to all forms of digital programming. More importantly, it is an ontological problem, and one that characterizes computational culture today. This is also to say that in order to define an algorithmic object, one cannot overlook the limit that is imposed upon computation by random data, and one must recognize this as a problem intrinsic to the logic of calculation. To that end, a direct engagement with the problem of the incomputable within computation, framed in the context of algorithmic architecture, will clarify how abstract algorithms are constructing the actuality of spatiotemporal experience.

From this standpoint, the search for the indeterminate, the unpredictable, and change does not need to be grounded in biophysical matter. On the contrary, I argue that the probability of randomness (or incomputable data) is the condition of computation. This is not to assert that there is an underlying mathematical truth able to explain change solely through information. Rather, I suggest that a pure axiomatic method in computation needs to be radically challenged and contrasted with the axiomatic reality of random data.

At the same time, however, a too-rapid retreat into the enclaves of biophysical matter may result in the mere substitution of one problematic solution for another, the risk being that of obliterating the actuality of information and its own indetermination altogether. Instead, in this chapter I point out that the randomness of data is at the core of computation, and yet that these data cannot be fully explained in either mathematical or physical terms. As will be discussed in the next section, these data are "quasi-mathematical," as they can be formalized as probabilities and yet remain incomplete. It is to this apparently paradoxical condition of "incomputable probability" that we will now turn.

1.0.2 Random probabilities

In order to appreciate the role of incomputable algorithms in computation, it is necessary to refer here to the logician Kurt Gödel, who challenged the completeness of the axiomatic method by proving the existence of undecidable propositions within logic.

In 1931, Gödel took issue with mathematician David Hilbert's metamathematical program. He demonstrated that there could not be a complete axiomatic method according to which the reality of things could be proved to be true or false.[24] Gödel's "incompleteness theorems" explained that propositions might be true but could not be verified by a complete axiomatic method. Propositions were therefore ultimately deemed to be undecidable: they could not be proved by the axiomatic method upon which they were hypothesized (instead certain propositions needed new sets of axioms to be added to the original ones).

In Gödel's view, Hilbert's quest for an ultimate algorithm able to reach a finite statement, true or false, pertaining to the initial predicative formula on which it originated proved vain. The problem of axiomatic incompleteness instead affirmed that no decision, and thus no finite rule, could be used to determine the state of things before things could run their course.

Not too long after, the mathematician Alan Turing encountered Gödel's incompleteness problem while attempting to formalize the concepts of algorithm and computation through his famous thought experiment now known as the Turing machine. In particular, the Turing machine demonstrated that problems that can be decided according to the axiomatic method were computable problems.[25] Conversely, those propositions that could not be decided through the axiomatic method would remain incomputable. To put it otherwise: beyond the axiomatic method or the mathematical program that could calculate all (in which all can be decided on the basis of its mathematical ground), Turing realized that there was a constellation of undecidable, incomputable propositions, the reality of which could not be empirically proven. According to Turing, there could not be a complete computational method in which the manipulation of symbols and the rules governing their use would realize Leibniz's dream of a *mathesis universalis*.[26]

For Turing, the incomputable determined the limit of computation: no finite set of rules could predict in advance whether or not the computation of data would halt at a given moment or whether it would reach a zero or one state, as established by initial conditions. This halting problem meant that no finite axiom could constitute the model by which future events could be predicted. Hence, the limit of computation was determined by the existence of those infinite real numbers that could not be counted through the axiomatic method posited at the beginning of the computation. In other words, these numbers were composed of too many elements that could not be ordered into natural numbers (e.g., 1, 2, 3). From this standpoint, insofar as any axiomatic method was incomplete, so too were the rules of computation. As Turing pointed out, it was mathematically impossible to calculate in advance any particular finite state of computation or its completion.[27]

Software artist Alex McLean recently devised a program that addresses the problem of the limits of computation. He called this software the *Fork Bomb Program,* as it served to demonstrate the incumbent software disaster that the Turing machine's halting problem already anticipated.[28] The *Fork Bomb* is a short section of code able to process a large number of algorithmic calculations, which very quickly saturate the available space in the list of processes kept by the computer's operating system. The *Fork Bomb* shows how computational processes are slowed down by means of computational processes. The limit of computation is demonstrated here by the continual repetition of a simple sequence of algorithms, which saturate the search space and make the entire computation collapse.

But if computation has always been haunted by its incomputable limits and by the incompleteness of its axiomatic method, one may wonder how computation has become so central to a culture, which is now characterized as the "age of the algorithm." To understand the cultural (and epochal) dominance of computation, it may be necessary to look at how second-order cybernetics, and in particular the autopoietic understanding of systems, turned the notion of the limit away from ideas of collapse.

Second-order cybernetics and early research in neural networks had already attempted to use the limit of computation to engender self-generating systems of control, the end results of which did not have to match the rules established at their initial conditions. For second-order cybernetics, the autopoietic capacities of biophysical phenomena to self-organize, adapt, and change over time indicated a way out from the cul de sac of research on AI that was strictly based on formal computational models.[29] This meant that the limit of computation could become an evolutionary threshold, to the extent that generative rules could give rise to a new level of order.

If the limit of computation was equivalent to the limit of a physical system whose internal order was threatened by increasing heat or entropy, then the autopoietic model of self-organization demonstrated that chaos could be turned into order in the form of negentropic information.[30] In other words, information could order the energetic chaos of random forces in the same way as biophysical systems self-organize and transform dissipative energy into information. The computational limit thereby no longer posed an obstruction to calculation, but rather became an opportunity for exploring new levels of order able to transform energy into strings of coded instructions.

Paradoxically, however, this new view of computation stemmed from the observation that biophysical systems were able to incorporate uncertain results and account for dynamic structures more effectively than axiomatic methods. This is the view that has constituted the ontological monotheism of evolutionary progress, which searches for increasingly higher forms of order able to minimize (optimize) the entropic randomness of chaos. To put it simply, the shift from formal to evolutionary models of computation has not radically challenged the ontological conception of modeling in itself. On the contrary, the turn toward second-order cybernetics has dismissed what is possibly the most striking implication of computational processing: the arrival of incomputable algorithms in axiomatics.

The early twentieth century's realization that computation was an incomplete affair radically challenged the axiomatic method and forced formal computation to admit that infinite quantities of information had entered its core.[31] If a program is left to run according to precise algorithmic instructions based on the evolutionary drive of growth, change, adaptation, and fitness, then the computational limit arrives as the space of incomputable probabilities that reveal how abstract quantities can reprogram preset rules. The programming of generative algorithms, for instance, does not simply lead to new orders of complexity (in which one level of complexity builds on the previous one, e.g., by transforming entropic energy into useful information), but instead encounters a wall of data that cannot be synthesized in smaller quantities. This wall of incompressible data instead overruns the program, and thus neutralizes or reveals the incompleteness of the axioms on which the program was based in the first place.

These incomputable probabilities are discrete states of nondenumerable infinities. Algorithmic information theorist Gregory Chaitin calls these infinities Omega. The latter corresponds to the halting probability of a universal free-prefix self-delimiting Turing machine.[32] Omega is thus a constant that is computably enumerable, since it defines the limit of a computable, increasing, converging sequence of rational numbers. Nevertheless, it is also algorithmically random: its binary expansion is an algorithmic random sequence, which is incomputable.[33] Hence algorithmic architectures are used not simply to build profiles based on prefixed sets of algorithms, but to exploit the self-delimiting power of computation, defined by its capacity to decide when a program should stop, by transforming nondenumerable infinities into random discrete unities or Omega probabilities: random actualities. These actualities are not simply the product of computation or its representation, but are instead its operative agents, imbued with infinite amounts of data that cannot be synthesized into a smaller, synthetic and complete computational procedure.

However, according to Chaitin, these discrete states are themselves composed of infinite real numbers that cannot be counted through finite axioms. This means that the incompleteness of computational models cannot simply be explained away by the paradigmatic substitution of biological dynamics for mathematical axiomatics. On the contrary, one must explain the incompleteness of computation by addressing contingency within algorithmic processing. This is to say that it is in the axiomatic method of computation that incomputable algorithms reveal the incompressible (infinite, nondenumerable, uncountable) discrete unities, which are strictly neither mathematical nor biological. Incomputable algorithms instead can only be defined by the immanence of infinities in finite sets of data.

This is the sense in which postcybernetic (and postdigital) programming cultures have to be understood: to the same extent that generative algorithms are entering all logics of modeling—so much so that they now seem to be almost ubiquitous (from the modeling of urban infrastructures to the modeling of media networks, from the modeling of epidemics to the modeling of populations flows, work flows, and weather systems)—so too are their intrinsic incomputable quantities building immanent modes of thought and experience.

The age of the algorithm therefore involves the construction of digital space conditioned by incomputable quantities of data.[34] Similarly, it can be argued that programming cultures too cannot be simply modeled through finite sets of probabilities, through which physical variations and approximate profiles can be built. Because real infinities are incomputable, mathematically existing as noncountable by a universal finite axiomatic method, programming cultures are now the immanent hosts of an infinite amount of infinite data. Rather than finite probabilities, programming now can only coincide with a speculative calculus able to introduce incomputable algorithms into actual spatiotemporalities. Here order no longer emerges out of chaos. The emergent properties proposed by the autopoietic self-organization of second-order cybernetics were only the lightning before the striking thunder of chaos: the rumbling noise of incomputable quantities unleashes entropic data at all levels of programming.[35]

As Chaitin hypothesizes, if the program that is used to calculate infinities will no longer be based on finite sets of algorithms but on infinite sets (or Omega complexity), then programmability will become a far cry from the algorithmic optimization of indeterminate processes realized through binary probabilities. Programming will instead turn into the calculation of complexity by complexity, chaos by chaos: an immanent doubling infinity or the infinity of the infinite. If the age of the algorithm has also been defined as the age of complexity, it is because the computational searching for the incomputable space of nondenumerable quantities has become superior to the view that algorithms are simply instructions leading to optimized solutions.

Chaitin's pioneering information theory explains how software programs can include randomness from the start, and indicates that they do not have to be limited to fixed sets of algorithms or to a closed formal axiomatic system. Thus the incompleteness of axiomatic methods does not define the endpoint of computation and its inability to engage with dynamical change, but rather its starting point, from which new axioms, codes, and algorithms become actual spatiotemporalities. Algorithmic architecture, it is argued here, can be conceived precisely as the programming of infinitely random data possessed of volume, depth, and length, which thus come to define actual spatiotemporalities of data. The next section will discuss how these algorithmic spaces have been overlooked in computational and interactive architecture.

1.0.3 Anticipatory architecture

For instance, Brandon Williams/Studio Rocker have argued that algorithms do not give us representations of spatial experience, but are computational

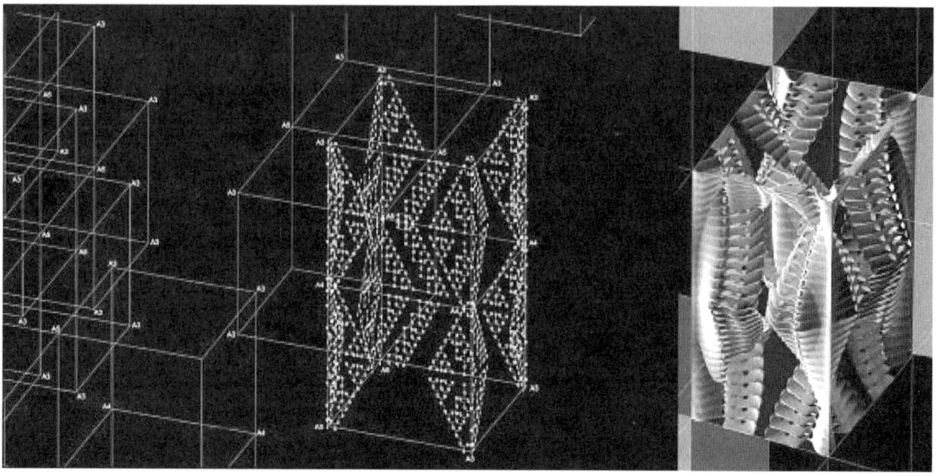

Figure 1.1
Brandon Williams/Studio Rocker, *Expression of Code*, 2004.

processes that can be used to generate unseen structures and unlived events.[36] In *Expression of Code* (2004), Ingeborg M. Rocker argues that coding is intrinsically mutable, as algorithms are malleable parts of information that can become a straight wall in one instance and a twisting column in another. Algorithmic mutations work to fundamentally challenge basic intuitions about what form and space can be. Rocker believes that as changing codes have always characterized architecture throughout history, so the development of calculus into computation can ultimately recode architecture: abstract codes can realize surfaces and structures of another kind in which the incompleteness of form is revealed.[37] It is precisely this incomplete nature of spatial form, I argue, that has become entangled in the incompleteness of computation. Incomputable algorithms have replaced patterns of probabilities (e.g., the forecasting of future scenarios through finite sets, or the modeling of culture through past data) with a metamodel of infinite programmability, whereby random (incompressible) data are included in computation step by step through the continual addition of new axioms.

From this standpoint, not only computational design per se but programming cultures in general have become veritable operators of Omega ciphers: discrete yet infinite states at the limit point of algorithmic computation. These discrete unities of incomputability not only determine the limit point of sequential algorithms but also, significantly, interrupt the digital processing of data into binary states. To put it another way, incomputable algorithms are indivisible yet infinite real numbers that demarcate the limit of computation by defining a discrete yet uncountable space. They atomize the linear continuity of sequential programming. This is, however, another kind of atomization. Not the binary division of zeroes and ones, but the infinite division of potentiality: unity as discrete infinity. If algorithmic computation defines the general matrix of postcybernetic culture, it is because the indeterminateness of programming has become ubiquitous. The operations of programming do not need to be interrupted by an external agent—the environment—in order to expose changes in coding. The continual processing of information is internally and ceaselessly interrupted by incomputable data. This interruption is the space in which the program becomes generative of unprogrammed states, cutting itself off from the continuity of procedural rules.

This is a far cry from metacomputational logic, according to which complexity and variations are the result of the evolution of simple rules. According to this logic, algorithmic mutations explain patterns of emerging complexity, but, as will be argued later in this chapter, these mutations cannot account for patternless data. Against the metacomputational view of a universe contained in simpler axioms, I will argue that incomputable limits are truly intrinsic to computation. This means that ontological complexity or chaotic incompleteness does not emerge from order, but is rather the unconditional condition, part and parcel, of procedural calculations. The appearance of incomputable algorithms (or real infinite numbers) in programming reveals how indeterminate quantities now govern the logic of computation. Incomputable algorithms are not exceptional probabilities, marking, for instance, the moment at which programming breaks down. On the contrary, incomputable probabilities are known probabilities that point toward a new conception of rule. The latter is exposed to a certain indeterminate quantity that cannot be compressed in a smaller cipher or simpler axioms than the output achieved. This new quantitative level of uncertainty is at the core of the metamodeling of everyday operations of programming, designing, measuring, and calculating probabilities through digital, biodigital, and nanobiological machines.

From this standpoint, I will argue against the idea that algorithmic architecture is underpinned by a metacomputational logic through which all can be calculated, but I will also question the biophysical grounds of computation by interaction. If computational architecture and design have reduced the experience of space to the aesthetic form of coding, interactivity has reduced this experience to enactive feedbacks, grounding algorithmic rules in the reality of what is physically constructed. Interactive architecture, it is suggested here, has been too quick to substitute tangible living systems for mathematical forms. Whereas computational aesthetics has reduced experience to the grammar of codes, phenomenal aesthesis has dissolved the discreteness of mathematical sets into a plurality of points of view joined together by one encompassing perspective. The incomputable limits of algorithmic computation instead show that any coding procedure is intrinsically attached to its incalculable quantities, and that aesthetics may imply how algorithmic actualities are infected with an infinite variety of infinities. As may become clearer later, I will propose that algorithmic architecture needs to be explained through another kind of aesthetics, relying neither on the beauty of simpler axioms nor on the continual variation of biophysical interactions. On the contrary, algorithmic architecture is important because it offers us an opportunity to discuss another species of actualities: algorithmic objects, the data structures of which now constitute the immanent data of experiences that do not stem from the directly lived.

Consider for instance the computational programming of a wall, a model of spatiotemporal experience par excellence, which includes the combination of digital and physical data: algorithmic rules, interactive possibilities that these rules can and cannot entertain through physical actuators, the biological data derived from a neoplasmatic design[38] of the wall's materials, and so on. The experience of a computational wall is therefore neither simply programmed into a set of probabilities nor simply left open to the interactive devices that allow rules to become responsive to physical data and direct perception. On the contrary, this experience is involved in incomputable states (algorithmic infinities in sequential calculation) that undermine the seamless linear causality linking algorithmic

Figure 1.2
Mark David Hosale and Chris Kievid of Hyperbody, *InteractiveWall*, commissioned by Festo (Hannover Messe), 2009. Courtesy of Festo AG & Co. KG. Photographs by Walter Fogel.

procedures, interactive responses, preengineered functions, and the material composition of the wall. These states of incomputability correspond to those data that immediately cut, atomize, and divide information into mathematical calculation, biological responsiveness, and nanodesign of materials.

Let's take for example the *InteractiveWall* project (2009), designed by the architectural group Hyperbody in collaboration with Festo bionic learning networks.[39] The algorithmic programming of this spatiotemporal architectural element, the wall, is carried out by the biophysical interaction with a set of its finite uses. The Hyperbody group wanted to demonstrate that interaction implies not simply a reaction to algorithmic rules, but a transformation of the behavior of people through motion, light, and music in *real time*. In other words, the group conceived of the algorithmic wall as a spatiotemporal zone of experiential transformation, where algorithmic functions could become complicated by the wall's interactive capacity to respond to external stimuli. Despite the Hyperbody group's intentions, however, while the *InteractiveWall* may to some extent succeed in taming spatiotemporal experience, it does so at most by gathering data resulting from the interaction between programmed algorithms and biophysical inputs.

The *InteractiveWall* is made of seven individual panels—each 1.09 meters wide, 0.53 meters deep, and 5.30 meters high—and its structural design is inspired by the anatomy of a fish's tail fin. The wall's panels are programmed to move laterally, with the movement deflected through two electronic drive units. The structure's skeleton moves on its central axis, away from and toward the user, so as to form a convex "hunchback" or a concave "hollow." The wall is programmed to sense the user's slightest movement through ultrasound sensors, which collect data that are inputted back into the computational parameters of the wall's behavior. As the wall moves from one side to another it also deploys changes in patterns of light: an assemblage of 24 circuits, equipped with 20 LEDs, forms a reactive interface between the LED skin and the user. The wall glows brighter when users get closer, and dimmer when they move away. More exactly, the LED skin pulses rapidly and slowly in relation to the position of other wall elements, which are individually programmed so that each has its own region of interactivity while communicating with all the others. Sound adds another element of interaction. The interactive architecture of the wall brings together synchronic movements of calmer sounds and asynchronic motion intended to build an intensified sonic ambience. Each node of the wall is conceived as a member of a choir that sings complex patterns of oscillating chords. The Hyperbody group conceived interactivity in terms of responses that are not algorithmically programmed, since programming is tailored here to respond directly to the user's perceptions. In order to achieve this interaction between algorithms and biophysical inputs, the group used Festo-designed electric drive units that could convert signals from ultrasound sensors into motion so that the wall could, for instance, shift away from approaching visitors.

Following the *InteractiveWall* project, also in 2009, the Hyperbody group designed the *Emotive Wall*, a new prototype, which was intended to highlight more clearly than its predecessor the existence of a mutual, dynamic interaction between programmed rules and user responses. In contrast with the *InteractiveWall*, which was designed to respond to the user, the *Emotive Wall* was more specifically designed to develop the computational persona of the programmed wall. In the words of its designers, this is "a wall that can move because it wants to."[40] This architectural object is thus no longer conceived as delimiting the interaction between mathematical probabilities and biophysical contingencies, but itself exposes its algorithmic and biophysical layers of composition, circumscribing its reality as an actual object.

By designing algorithmic models that are open-ended and attuned to biophysical contingencies, the Hyperbody group also strictly followed the science of emergence and spontaneous order, according to which complex patterns derive from simple rules, in order to model the behavioral patterns of the wall. Here the complexity of the wall was mostly based on the interactions of localized contingencies, such as the specific responses of flashing tails. In other words, local biophysical inputs were devised so as to add indetermination to the whole programmed structure of the wall. Rather than relying on the external input of visitors to create movement and to generate complex behavior, the *Emotive Wall* is now designed to respond to its own biophysical changes. Local variations of data input thus affect the whole behavior of the structure by inducing or stopping movement.

For this project, the Hyperbody group has specifically used concepts of swarm architecture to highlight how computational programming implies a new relation between space and matter, as these both become generated by codes. It could be argued therefore that the *Emotive Wall* prototype may be going a step further compared to those interactive systems whose behavioral patterns are derived from fixed rules. The dynamic configuration of computational architecture that can be found here is not a result of reactive responses to algorithmic programming. On the contrary, the computational architecture of the wall is understood as an *anticipatory system* that is apt not only to program responses, but also to generate potential conditions for interaction from the open-ended evolution of algorithms. With such devices as electric and pneumatic drive units combined with software programs of control, regulation technologies, and sensor systems, this algorithmic programming is transformed into an anticipatory architecture.[41] What is anticipated here are probabilities of interaction, which are not the indeterminate probabilities that were previously defined as incomputable. The *Emotive Wall* is instead an instance of algorithmically adaptive space imbued with interacting components. It aims to provoke anticipation rather than reaction, forcing both software and interactive devices to foresee conditions in which spatiotemporal change can be experienced. Nevertheless, precisely what is missing from these interactive projects is an engagement with the algorithmic nature of spatiotemporal experience.

In particular, swarming models are used here as a means of generating complex algorithmic behaviors, and to explain spatiotemporal experience in terms of a self-organizing autopoietic system that evolves in time through interaction with the environment. Biophysical interactions are therefore the enactors of algorithmic change. From this standpoint, the *Emotive Wall* does not fully work as an example of anticipatory architecture, because here the spatiotemporal experience is derived from physical data, which works as an input for the entire algorithmic architecture. As such, the *Emotive Wall* overlooks two main problems. On the one hand, these experiments in interactive architecture do not acknowledge that algorithms are actual entities, not simply a simulation of physical data. These entities, as discussed later in the chapter, are actuals without being biological and thus need to be addressed according to their own spatiotemporal structure. On the other hand, Hyperbody focuses on the interaction of/with biophysical data in order to explain change.

Recently, algorithmic architectures have engaged with another kind of data collected from materials designed at the atomic and nano levels. In particular, the nanofabrication of biomaterials that can program, control, and sustain cellular structures that grow, evolve, and mutate are becoming central premises for the development of nanoarchitectures.[42] Here the algorithmic programming of spatiotemporalities has entered the space of atomic structures[43] so as to grow systems that anticipate the conditions of possible responses. For instance, Anders Christiansen's nanoarchitectural design of a *Homeostatic Membrane*[44] shows how the intersection of artificially designed molecules creates a responsive interface between the interior and the exterior walls of cells, anticipating the probability of uncertainty in sequential processing.

As opposed to interactive architecture, according to which spatiotemporal experience is defined by a change in the system induced by biophysical data, nanoarchitectures are spatiotemporal structures of anticipation characterized by incomputable data, corresponding neither to mathematical nor to physical inputs. From *ubiquitous computing* to the nanofabrication of walls, smart objects, and clothes that sense and anticipate (or productively prerespond to) changes in atmospheric pressures, moods, sounds, images, colors, and movements, incomputable data have infected the general ecology of media systems.

As predicted by Mark Weiser's dream of an age of ubiquitous and calm technology, all post-desk digital machines are now embedded with a *seamful* environment of data, in which each level of computation extends into another: not through seamless compatibility but through the incorporation of incomputable data within systems.[45] If digital computation has come to characterize the invisible architecture of everyday space, the pervasive extension of algorithmic logic has now become attuned to alien regions of perception and cognition. These are zones occupied by abstract yet real incomputable states that interfere with computational calculus by anticipating new conditions of spatiotemporal experience. However, in order to appreciate the nuances of anticipatory architecture further, it is important to look closer at, and thus to distinguish this architecture from, the notions of interaction and responsiveness that have been developed in the context of ubiquitous computing.

1.1 Background media

> The history of old media technologies comes to an end when machines not only handle the transmission of addresses and data storage, but are also able, via mathematical algorithms, to control the processing of commands.[46]

As Kittler reminds us, the introduction of mathematical algorithms into machines turned media into processing systems of command, in which interaction was just the result of feedback operations of control. With algorithmic machines, then, the system became extended to include the user, now part and parcel of an infinite series of loops, in which all forms of input were equivalent to one another.

The algorithmic age therefore also corresponds to the now realized dream of the post-desktop culture of ubiquitous computing.[47] According to Lev Manovich, the post-desk invention of cultural computing was not simply determined by the rise of the personal computer industry, the adoption of graphical user interfaces (GUIs), the expansion of computer networks, and the World Wide Web, but is to be found in the revolutionary ideas that transformed the computer into a "metamedium."[48]

Similarly to interactive architecture, the ergonomic design[49] of interactive media has left behind the algorithmic "stuff" of computation by burying information processing in the background of perception and embedding it deep within objects.[50] In other words, with interactive media, information processing has become transparent. This also means that the postcybernetic realm of interaction requires no direct response or execution of instruction. Instead, and as in the case of Hyperbody's *Emotive Wall*, interaction now includes a computational tendency to anticipate responses and programming indeterminacies that stems from within the system, and need not rely on direct sense perception and cognition. These new epochal traits of postcybernetic control coincide with the arrival of ubiquitous computing: with the withdrawal of mediatic action to the background of perception and direct experience.

Projects such as Hyperbody's *InteractiveWall* extend Mark Weiser's vision of the "age of calm technology,"[51] in which the design of computational space involves the programming of architectural networks. Small objects such as mobile telephones, Blackberries, iPods/iPads, digital cameras, radio frequency identification tags, GPS, and interactive whiteboards are ceaselessly mapping—deterritorializing and reterritorializing—this background architecture of invisible algorithms. This kind of architecture coincides not with the cyberspace of data simulating physical conditions, or with social networks of instantaneous communication that are determined by the activities of the users. Instead, the realized age of calm technology announces the now diffused conditions of cultural programmability: here algorithmic computations are entangled with operating systems, search engines, databank structures, miniaturized hardware pieces, molecular growth and adaptation, nanodesign of atoms, randomization of percepts and affects, the nonsensuous rendering of coding, decoding, and recoding processes, layers of database incorporation, annexation, and expression.

While ubiquitous computing announces the deep burial of algorithmic processing in ergonomically designed objects of interaction, the reality of infinite quantities of data can no longer be contained in the axioms of universal calculus. From this standpoint, all forms of cultural programmability reveal that each and any step of programming is hosting incomputable states, able to interrupt the ubiquitous continuum between computational objects (mobiles, iPads, and social media in general).

Weiser's pioneering work in the field of mediatic applications of computing already sees computer objects not as isolated objects placed on desks, but as *ambient* objects that surround us everywhere: walls can be turned into electronic boards and displays, books become electronic information stores, and cameras act as digital picture libraries.[52] According to Weiser, ubiquitous computing changes not only the locations of digital machines but also the use of such machines. The human user no longer activates computation, but is now incorporated in the programming system, as she or he can now indirectly profit from the computational capacities hidden in mundane objects.

This stealthy intrusion of algorithmic programmability into distinct ordinary objects is also symptomatic of a new twist in the long history of ergonomics, the science that aims to optimize the interactions among humans and other elements of a system by fitting perceptual, motor, and cognitive capacities into the latter. The human user is no longer the operator of an inflexible machine of calculation, but has become a component or trigger of sequential operations. It is therefore possible to suggest that the neoergonomic character of postcybernetic computation works not to optimize, but more generally to anticipate the probability of indeterminacy in all algorithmic architectures.

Second-order cybernetics insisted on the role of the observer, who was able to mediate given instructions and to change the rules of objects. The new focus on the central action of the observer led to the development of user-centered interface and to the design of computers as portable media. Symptoms of this development can be found not only in Weiser's ideas but also in the work of another active researcher working at PARC labs during the same years: Alan Kay. He was the pioneer of object-oriented programming and devised the first object-determined language for computers, called Smalltalk. In particular, users developed this software thanks to Kay's vision of a programming language organized around objects rather than actions, data rather than logic.[53]

For Kay, everything was an object: a biological cell, the individual computer on a network, a black box. A computational object, he insisted, was composed of code or sequences of algorithmic instructions through which it received and sent messages. According to Kay, object-oriented software could not therefore distinguish between data (or structures) and code (functions), as both data and code were merged into an undividable thing:

the computational object. The user of the object, therefore, did not need to see what was inside the back box in order to receive and transmit messages: the user could develop an intuitive approach to computation rather than having to become a computer programmer.

In Kay's opinion, ensuring the smooth running of software did not require opening the black box.[54] His programming language composed of objects was thus ready to be manipulated and changed by users in a creative and nondetermined way. Far from being derived from logical calculations that need to be executed, this language offered a view of computation that was open to the interaction of programmed/able objects. According to Manovich, this shift toward object-oriented programming transformed the computer "from being a culturally invisible technology to being the new engine of culture."[55]

Just as Kay's designs for portable computers in the 1970s anticipated the portable media transformations of the late 1990s, so too can the object-oriented software of Smalltalk be seen to pioneer the cooperative development of open-source. This dates back to 1995, when Kay launched Squeak: an open-source software that required users to participate in its programming evolution by adding and expanding (and inventing) computation, rather than by revealing already programmed sources.

As Manovich points out, since the '70s Kay's vision has provided users with a programming environment and already-written general tools for the invention of programming languages. By the '90s, in fact, Kay was devising programming platforms that enabled users to directly use software objects, thus opening software to user interaction. This form of object-oriented software interaction was conceived as an alternative mode of programming, and was specifically influenced by the notion of computation associated with second-order cybernetics. Here the users' aggregation of software objects could grant the emergence of novelty in interactive media systems.

But the development of object-oriented programming and interactive media in the '70s also led to a transformation of computational logic. According to Kittler, this logic involved strategies, developed during World War II, of cybernetic command and control over information. In particular, Kittler explained that Turing had proved that the computerized calculation of recursive functions ultimately exhausted the whole domain of human computability. In other words, computers as finite state machines, which Turing deemed to be predictable from start to end, followed not the laws of nature but rather "the very logic of decision-making strategy, and information war."[56] This is why the human postal system, for example, came to an end.

According to Kittler, "data, addresses, and instructions, can handle each other by means of digital feedbacks such as if-then conditions and programmed loops."[57] Thus, the principle of automated computation presupposed that input data were ceaselessly transformed into finite numbers of discrete states able to register, transmit, and calculate any data without human intervention. From this standpoint, as Kittler pointed out, old media became devoured by the universal medium of computation, which excluded the redundant noise, the unreliable contingencies of human perception and cognition from the start.[58] If the origin of digital computers is rooted in strategies of control, then this, as Norbert Wiener explains, is because taking the humans out of the decision-making loops entailed that the job of prediction could become more effective (e.g., the trajectory for hitting a moving target, such as a plane, could be more closely approximated).[59]

The creation of artificially intelligent machines, in which finite sets of rules could process vast and complex amounts of information, was central to first-order cybernetic research, which focused on programming inputs rather than on using algorithms to extend capacities of interaction and communication between systems. But the shift away from automated calculation to personal computing through object-oriented (interactive) software inevitably extended the logic of computation onto social systems.[60] In brief, the shift toward second-order cybernetics implied the extension of computation into social modes of organization through the user-friendly transformation of software languages. At the core of this extension is a double-edged sword of control and freedom that is entangled with open-source models of algorithmic architecture.[61]

From this standpoint, Mark Weiser's view of ubiquitous computing can be viewed alongside Alan Kay's reformulation of media objects as invisible, user-sensitive, semi-intelligent, knowledge-based electronics and software, which were thought to be able to merge with human, individual, biological brains. Thus, while Kay added interactivity to algorithmic computation, Weiser's visions of ubiquitous computing extended interaction to automated machines and not just to users, thus devising a universal media-machine able to encompass a networked architecture of immediate communication and the autoregulation of data systems. Ubiquitous computing therefore now includes the design of artificial intelligence architectures that are able to respond to external action and to smartly correlate distinct networked systems of information. Ubiquitous media mix the computational logic of the universal computing machine with the interactive, adaptive, and open learning systems of user-friendly communication.

Weiser's idea of calm technology turned computers into everyday objects that no longer had to rely on the attention of users in order to work. On the contrary, as media objects, computers had to recede into the background so as to become ambient, and now operate in a manner that involves peripheral modes of perception. Digital media have been described as forming the age of the "information bomb," an age characterized by an everyday state of overstimulation,[62] in which technology constantly demands attention. Weiser's conception of a calm and comforting technology, however, already predicted postcybernetic ubiquitous media's tendency to push perception and cognition into the background architecture of algorithmic processing.

According to Weiser, calm computation activated peripheral zones of thought and feeling and allowed latent parts of the brain to become differentiated capacities. What receded into the information ambience was, according to Weiser, not an aimless, blank noise, but rather highly differentiated potentials that afforded a detailed set of actions. Weiser used the term "locatedness" to refer to the capacity of the peripheral area of the brain to instill a familiar feeling of connection with the world around it. He insisted that the operative functioning of the peripheral brain was crucial to the feeling of calmness in the sea of information processing.

Weiser quoted three examples of calm technology: inner-office windows, Internet Multicast, and artist Natalie Jeremijenko's work *Dangling String* (also known as *Live Wire*), which was made between 1995 and 1999.[63] In particular, this installation was used to explain how the formation of a new center of attention—the movement of the dangling wire that was proportional to the number of packets on the network—revealed the background behavior of the network traffic. This dynamic behavior of the wire came to coincide with an "intuitive peripheral representation of the network activity" (i.e., the increased traffic on the local area network was evinced by a higher frequency of wiggles). As opposed to the visual representation of network traffic based on symbols that demanded our interpretation and attention, Weiser argued that Jeremijenko's installation demonstrated that we become more attuned to information if we attend less to technology. In particular, Weiser associated the physical movement of the string with the brain's peripheral nerve center, since the *Live Wire* consisted of an installation of an eight-foot piece of plastic spaghetti hanging from a small electric motor mounted in the ceiling. The motor was electrically connected to a nearby Ethernet cable, so that each bit of information caused a tiny twitch. A very busy network would then cause a whirling string with a characteristic noise, while a quiet network only involved a small twitch every few seconds. As the string could be placed in an unused corner of a hallway, it blended into the environment, remaining visible and audible to many offices without being obtrusive. For Weiser, the *Live Wire* was an instance of how algorithmic computation could become the ambient technology of social modalities of interactions.

Calm technology no longer required direct perception and operation, but became ergonomically attuned to the peripheral regions of perception and cognition. With ubiquitous computing, the algorithmic background is fully realized through remote ambience programming and through the deep burial of rules. Ubiquitous computation then marks the advance of an entirely new algorithmic architecture that relies on an ever-differentiating background, which becomes the potential field of foreground operations.

But what does this new movement of foreground and background computation actually imply? Does the algorithmic background of peripheral perception stand for what remains invisible to perception and cognition altogether? From this standpoint, one may wonder whether this movement is (yet again) to be understood as the metaphysical correlation between the visible and the invisible, between the veiled and the unveiled. Nevertheless, it is possible to argue that the increasing complexity of background operations in forms of ubiquitous computation that have fully incorporated users into its algorithmic processing, thereby establishing a movement between foreground and background, may not simply take place between the perceiver and information, or between the center and the peripheral capacities of cognition and perception. Instead, this algorithmic background may perhaps be explained in terms of immanence, whereby incomputable quantities of thought and affect infect computable procedures. In other words, what if ubiquitous computing is not simply the new incarnation of formal intelligence in physical machines (which interact among themselves without the direct attendance of a user), but is overshadowed by random algorithms transforming the spatiotemporality of experience?

In postcybernetic culture, the tension between a metacomputational world made of discrete objects and an autopoietic world of generative codes open to users' interactions has led to a reconceptualization of computational models themselves, turning codes into enactive and responsive agents able to be modified by the activities of the environment. Inasmuch as Alan Kay devised an object-oriented software in which the black box of finite algorithms did not have to be directly operated by the user, he embraced an autopoietic conception of computation by which the code could respond to the user and vice versa. To put it simply, Kay already foresaw that algorithms had become background objects that could adapt, change, and evolve.

Ubiquitous computation is therefore a generalized extension of this self-organized ambience that comprises the most ordinary objects of communication. In particular, ubiquitous computing aims at incorporating biophysical contingencies, or those unprogrammable situations that users, participants, or environmental factors can make available to programming by adding more variables to intelligent networked devices. Nevertheless, this neoergonomic tendency to preadapt the computational system to contingent changes, and to move algorithmic functions into peripheral zones of attention such as non-direct cognition and emotion, has not merely marked the transition from a "programmed" to a "programmable" object. More importantly, this transition has meant that algorithmic architecture has become an anticipatory metamodeling of incomputable data that cannot be contained in mathematical forms or physical objects.

For instance, as the algorithmic architecture of the Hyperbody group suggests, the incorporation of biophysical contingencies into an open-ended programming requires an anticipatory conception of space. Kas Oosterhuis insists that interactive architecture must not be concerned with designing buildings that are responsive and adaptive, but must be proactive and propositional, able to anticipate new building configurations and actions in real time. This means that complex adaptive systems are designed to impose a social behavior on building materials, which are now programmable actuators. According to Oosterhuis, it is more important to design the relation between these programmable materials than the relation between the building and its inhabitants, since it is the former and not the latter that makes the building an active environment. As an instance of ubiquitous computation, Hyperbody's projects conceive the building as a self-organizing, interactive entity.

This notion of interactivity, however, despite being rooted in the biophysical and evolutionary vision of autopoiesis, seems to be a far cry from the more general notion of responsive environments in which the human user seems to directly animate algorithmic objects. Here the solipsistic ontology of autopoiesis defines a center able to incorporate interactive parts into one architectural whole. It seems that the recent trend toward "responsive environment" projects seems to be exactly framed according to this ontology.[64] As Lucy Bullivant explains, the notion of interaction has been challenged because it merely describes a unidirectional pattern of communication in which software delimits the potentialities of users.[65] The notion of responsiveness, on the other hand, includes visitors, participants, and users: the ultimate manipulators of structures, buildings, and spaces. In particular, responsive environments define "spaces that interact with the people who use them."[66] Responsive environments are said to have phenomenological impact, "meaning that the body is able to directly experience its environment in a very direct and personal way."[67] By focusing on how the output of the observer/participant is able to reconfigure the relationship between the input and the output, responsive environment projects, such as the sound installation *Volume* by UVA, do not require people to understand the algorithmic model in order to become part of the overall architecture.

In *Volume*, visitors can indeed change the volume and arrangements of the sonic environment through their movement around the installation. It is this physical movement that animates the algorithmic set of instructions of this architecture, which comprises a grid of LED lights structured by 46 2.5-meter columns which form a sound orchestra.[68] Similarly, architect Lars Spuybroek of NOX and artist Q. S. Serafijn's project *D-Tower* most clearly explains how the motor of interaction is placed in the hands of users or participants. The *D-Tower* project allows the users to remotely confer emotional states on the physical object through a website questionnaire, the results of which are turned into algorithmic instructions that animate the tower in the form of different colors. According to the designers, these colors give us an insight into the different moods of the city.[69]

Although Bullivant sets notions of interaction apart from responsiveness, responsive architecture clearly aims to replace algorithmic design with an environment of users. Both conceptions comply with the autopoietic view of an adaptable system that is able to change. From this standpoint, it is possible to conclude that the distinction between interactivity and responsiveness is only marginal compared to the ontological weight that the idea of a self-organizing evolutionary system has imposed upon conceptions of spatiotemporal experience.

For instance, the Oosterhius office ONL's *Digital Pavilion* in Korea, located in the Digital Media City in the Sangam-dong district of Seoul, consists of a series of interactive installations that compose a parametric morphology based upon a 3D Voronoi algorithm,[70] and thus embraces "ubiquitous computing at its full potential."[71] The *Digital Pavilion* is therefore composed of Voronoi cell structures that are equipped with built-in actuators able to alter the length of the cell beam in real time. Users also embed their personal details into a 4G/WiBro in order to control these actuators. A search engine, which reconfigures the users' media content, and which thus builds proactive profiles for the visitors that are uploaded on online databases, processes these details. RFID tracking of individual users is also fed back into the system's algorithmic architecture to generate real-time profiles over the Internet about the potential interaction between people as they visit the *Digital Pavilion*. But the visitors are not simply passive entities incorporated into the algorithmic architecture of the structure. The ubiquitous computation of interactive devices was designed to allow users to engage in four types of socially interactive experiences that trigger alterations to the *Digital Pavilion*'s building structure. On one of the floors of the installation, the hard kinetic pneumatic structure becomes a soft organic architecture composed of a point cloud of tens of thousands of programmable LEDs, which vary in densities and create a spectrum of high- and low-resolution effects for the visitors, who can have gameplay experiences that range from action/shoot-em-up games to social chat games, and so on. This interactive animated building is intersected by another level of interaction through online multiplayer games and urban games based on GPS, GIS, RFID, and wireless technologies, which extends the polygonal architecture based on the distance between discrete points into another environment.

The resultant kaleidoscopic experience of this media-rich, translucent, and fully immersive space that foregrounds the activities of interactive algorithms seems to be defined by probabilistic patterns that rely on programmed inputs and responsive behavior. But this project has nothing of the anticipatory architecture that seeks to include incomputable probabilities into the system of seamless interaction and responsive participation. The problem with an algorithmic architecture composed of interactive parts, whether these are human or nonhuman, or are fed by sensorimotor data derived from visitors or other nonliving sources and collected by actuators, remains precisely embedded in the idea that the bidirectional communication of many objects leads to the emergence of the architectural whole. This is a problem inherent to interactive architectures in which the algorithmic background is determined by cellular automata: self-organizing units of computation that self-change through time, and yet remain finite sets of instructions, always already reducing the possibility of a new spatial experience to closed sets of probabilities. This is why the kaleidoscopic spatiality of the *Digital Pavilion* only ever remains an already-lived experience, a set scenario.

Far from anticipating the possibility of a novel experience of space, interactive and responsive environments seem to remain embedded in the digital paradigms of metacomputation: grounded, that is, in the autopoietic ontology of self-organization by environmental adaptation. Here architecture is a system of variable codes responding to variable inputs. What is left behind, however, is the possibility that algorithmic architecture may be describing algorithmic objects, and that these objects do not simply coincide with finite axioms. In other words, autopoietic ontology overlooks the possibility that indeterminate change could also stem from within computation, and constitutes a problem for computation before it becomes an issue of external interaction between object and environment. To put it simply, the autopoietic view at the base of interactive and responsive architecture misses the point that the environment—which is understood here as an extra space of incomputable data—is within the algorithmic object. This is an important point to grasp, and in order to explain it more fully we will have to engage with theories of the object and of actuality that do not ontologically differentiate between human and nonhuman, between animate and inanimate entities.

Before discussing these theories, however, I will first outline the debate that underpins the theory of metacomputation, and thereby provide a stronger argument against the idea that universals or set codes resolve all forms of complexity. This discussion will explain why the metacomputational model has failed to describe the actuality of algorithmic objects, and has instead confined the indeterminacy of software to the safe ground of mathematical axiomatics. It is this safe ground, I will argue, that reappears yet again in algorithmic architecture. Although it is often accused of being too abstract, in the cases discussed below algorithmic architecture has *not been abstract enough* to reveal how algorithmic objects are the spatiotemporal matrix of the present.

1.2 Metadigital fallacy

The ontological view of metacomputation has characterized those strands of algorithmic architecture that have been more closely concerned with the degree to which computation provides an entry point into the digital material of design. An example of this can be found in the *Milgo Experiment*, also known as the *AlgoRhythms Project*, which was devised by architect-morphologist Haresh Lalvani. Since 1997 Lalvani has been working with Milgo/Bufkin, a metafabrication company, to realize curved sheet-metal surfaces designed through digital programming. All his experiments are

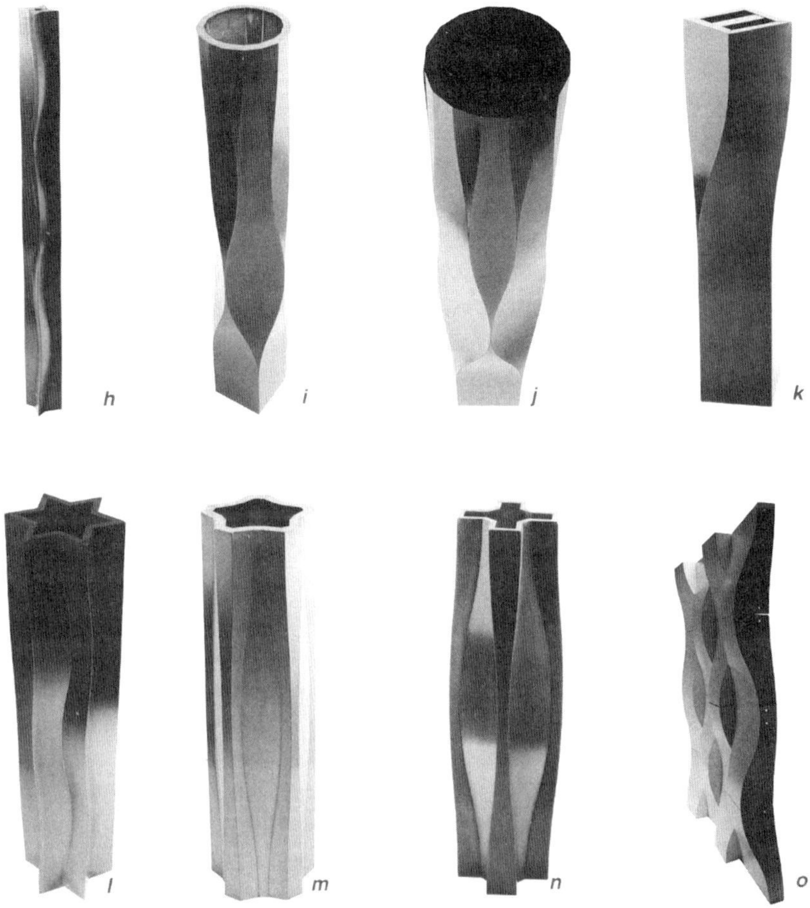

Figure 1.3

Haresh Lalvani, *Prototypes of Columns and Surfaces in Sheet Metal with the Company Milgo-Bufkin*, 1997–1999. Courtesy of Haresh Lalvani. Photographs by Robert Wrazen.

devoted to the development of the *Morphological Genome*, which Lalvani describes as the search for a "universal code for mapping and manipulating any form, man-made or natural."[72] In his projects, morphology (or the process of shaping) and making (or the actual fabrication of the form) are not separate, but rather become merged into a seamless whole in which form and matter become one.

These projects show how curved universal forms, and not straight lines or flat planes, can be obtained by building rigid curved surfaces made of uncut sheets of metal. These curved structures are developed from a single continuous metal sheet shaped by algorithmically generated geometries. Lalvani's morphological meta-architecture permits endless variations on the same theme, which result in continuously curved columns, walls, and ceilings. Lalvani's central conception of morphological meta-architecture is based on a bottom-up morphological evolution of genes, where form and fabrication are linked from the start. Each gene is a cellular automaton that specifies a family of related parameters, and each parameter is controlled by a single variable of form corresponding to a base in the DNA double-helix genome. The universal structures of form and matter, for Lalvani, must be derived from simple genetic rules.[73] In other words, and in conformance with fundamental computational principles, he believes that the infinity of all possible forms can be specified by a finite number of morph genes. As he affirms: "I am expecting this to be a small number."[74] Computation, however, is used here not to solve already existing problems, but rather as a generative process that aims to liberate calculations from probabilities and to demonstrate that "new morphologies (which lead to new mathematics and new architecture) are possible."[75]

Lalvani's model of a continuously generating morphological genome therefore embraces the predicates of a digital metaphysics, according to which cellular automata and discrete entities are universal codes that can produce, just like DNA, an infinite variety of forms and processes that enable the construction of new material spaces. The programming of forms, therefore, is predicated here on the automorphogenesis of forms, wherein a short computer program—a genetic code for instance—guarantees the autopoiesis (self-making) of the universe.

Lalvani's use of algorithmic architecture is not too far removed from the fundamental theories developed by so-called digital philosophy, according to which digital or discrete codes are the kernel of physical complexity: code is ontology, that is, and finite sets of algorithms are the axioms upon which it is possible to build any complex world. According to digital philosopher Edward Fredkin, all physics can be explained through the simple architecture of cellular automata, or discrete entities that form a regular grid of *cells*, each one of which exists in a finite number of spatiotemporal states.[76] According to this digital view of physics, the universe is a gigantic Turing cellular automaton: a universal machine that can perform any calculation and program any reality through a finite number of steps. While truly Turing-complete machines remain physically impossible to realize, since they require unlimited amounts of data storage, Turing completeness is nonetheless achieved through physical machines or programming languages that *would* be universal *if* they had an indefinitely enlargeable storage. Fredkin argues that particle physics can be explained as an emergent property of cellular automata. In other words, for Fredkin, cellular automata are the ground on which physics can be explained. In short, if cellular automata are the ground then the universe is digital, as it would then be built upon discrete units, which reveal that space-time is not continuous.

From this standpoint, what determines the ultimate digitalization of the universe is the calculation of infinite probabilities, the real possibility to actualize infinity and to design a mathematical language able to turn the potentiality of infinity into sets of axioms. This atomic conception of the universe divides the Parmenidean infinitesimal continuum into finite small particles, or atoms, out of which the complexity of the universe is derived.[77]

Similarly, Stephen Wolfram, physicist and creator of the Mathematica program, postulates the "principle of computational equivalence," according to which all complex behavior can be simulated computationally. Simulations are "computationally irreducible" and do not represent natural behavior, which is instead "generated by computation."[78] Digital computation complies with the metaphysics of discrete mathematical entities moving in empty space, in which the plurality of the universe is reducible to indivisible units, or atoms. By setting up a series of simple programs and running them through computation, cellular automata generate complex or irregular structures.

Wolfram's notion of cellular automata has been widely adopted in algorithmic architecture as a means of exploring irregular or complex geometric forms that stem from simple rules. Wolfram explains that "even though the underlying rules for a system are simple, and even though the system is started from simple initial conditions, the behavior that the system shows can nevertheless be highly complex. I argue that it is this basic phenomenon that is ultimately responsible for most of the complexity we see in nature."[79] Wolfram calls the discovery that simple rules can generate high levels of complexity rule 110. As he points out, however, the story is more complicated. Not only do simple cellular automata, determined by the same rules or by the same finite algorithms, generate complex structures; there also remains no trace of uniform simple cellular automata in the varied complex structure to which they give rise. This means that despite being determined by the same rules, cellular automata do not do the same thing: while some maintain a regular pattern, others become part of other localized structures, developing different configurations of cells, changing, for example, the sequences of colors, and thus producing behaviors that are totally different from those established by the initial rules. Therefore simple programs do not merely generate complex forms, but are also encoded in all forms, processes, and matter in different ways.[80] Yet the view that original codes evolve in unrecognizable ways may not be enough to explain how infinite states are still a problem for computation, no matter how complex the evolutionary journey of a set of codes can be.

While using cellular automata and the binary view of the universe, Lalvani also wonders whether there are infinite states between zeroes and ones, which he is unable "to carry . . . to all levels of form."[81] He concludes by suggesting that discrete and continuous states and everything in between may be coexistent in the universe, and that while physical reality, as Wolfram claims, may have a discrete basis, it may also appear to be perfectly continuous on an experiential level.[82]

Nevertheless, the fallacy of metadigitality does not simply imply that the ground of the universe, as Lalvani observes, is discrete, while physical experience explains the analog continuity between things. Instead, this fallacy stems from believing that cellular automata animate formal processes and matter. Architect Neil Leach, for instance, has argued that the logic of swarm intelligence has challenged the computational methodology that rests on the discrete internal logic of fractals, L-systems, and cellular automata.[83] In particular, he specifies that while fractals and L-systems are not flexible enough to adapt their behavior to external stimuli, cellular automata do interact with their neighbors, yet ultimately remain anchored to a fixed space and are unable to change their underlying grid.[84]

Kwinter reminds us that the age of the algorithm makes space and matter indiscernible. However, this is not because they mimic each other *in* and *through* simple finite rules or cellular automata. No ultimate synthesis, whether metamathematical or metabiological, can act as the universal glue that binds matter and space. The computational view of the universe maintains that the formula for the existence of all matter and space can be contained in simpler programs (and grids of cellular automata) out of which complexity is generated. As opposed to this, it is argued here that algorithmic architecture is not simply a metacomputational field of application: on the contrary, algorithmic design is forced to face the problem of infinity, which is intrinsic to the computational process. For this reason, one must question the idea that cellular automata are the ultimate generators of objects and structures. Similarly, the notion that space and matter have become equivalent through algorithmic processing, or through the repetitive patterns of cellular automata, must also be challenged. Kwinter's insights into algorithmic design therefore seem to end up supporting rather than transforming the metacomputational assumptions that lie at the core of digital philosophy.

My contention here is that metadigitality is marked by a double fallacy. On the one hand, finite sets of algorithms or simpler instructions cannot program, contain, or reduce material complexity. On the other, the adaptation of a generative, evolutionary, biological model of complexity that explains how simple rules—cellular automata—need to be understood as genetic programs is also problematic. While the former approach remains entrapped in a computational model predicated on the idea that software calculation instructs matter, the latter model mainly ends up conflating computation with matter itself. The fallacy therefore consists in reducing algorithms to finite quantities on the one hand, and grounding algorithmic quantities on biological and more specifically genetic models of evolution on the other. What is missing from this picture is a reconceptualization of algorithmic quantities. These quantities, it is suggested here, do not simply coincide with a determinist method of measuring. Instead—and this is important—algorithmic quantities also reveal another face of computation: the deployment of infinite numbers that cannot be computed or reduced to smaller axioms. Far from looking for a simple pattern beyond complexity, I argue here that algorithmic architecture cannot overlook the fact that the limit of computation lies in infinite sets of data. Instead of holding onto a mathematical ontology, and casting it as the ultimate Holy Grail that underpins all systems and structures, algorithmic architecture may instead need to address the incompleteness of axiomatics and rational logic. Yet it is not enough to search for such incompleteness in the analog variations of biophysical inputs, as interactive and responsive design do. Instead, the challenge is to embrace the reality of infinite algorithms, which point instead at a suprarational, immanent, and speculative thought, which cannot be reduced to Being or ultimately fuse the qualities and quantities of objects (matter) and their relations (space).[85]

Computation does not therefore simply correspond to the elimination of qualities from calculation or their formal axiomatization. Algorithmic computation instead describes, but cannot be reduced to, biophysical matter, as it exposes the qualities and quantities of objects at an abstract and yet all too real level. Here qualities are at the same time incomputable quantities, which cannot be summed up in discrete binarism or contained in self-generated wholes. Similarly, quantities do not simply define that which is calculable, but also, and increasingly, reveal the reality of infinity, the precision of indefiniteness.

From this standpoint, the view of universal computation based on the binary rule of probabilities, founded on the Turing machine, cannot explain the incompleteness of any object (whether a physical, digital or biological object). Contrary to Wolfram's metacomputational universe, algorithmic information theorist Gregory Chaitin sustains that the limit of computation is not simply determined by the time of calculation and the memory storage of the Turing machine. This means that, according to Chaitin's theory, the fallacy of metadigitality resides in the fact that digital philosophers understand information quantity in terms of time and space as determined units of measure. Instead, Chaitin argues that information needs to be understood in terms of computational entropy. From this standpoint, even the simplest cellular automata are already infected by complex, incompressible, random information.

As opposed to Wolfram's digital philosophy, Chaitin suggests that physical complexity cannot be reduced to simple rules (for instance DNA understood as algorithmic instructions that generate organisms), or to one formal axiomatic system (subtending universal computation). Similarly, if the metacomputational view of the universe sustains that infinitesimal numbers (used by Leibniz to explain the relations between discrete objects) do not exist, Chaitin argues that infinitesimals cannot be reduced to the integral calculus, which gives us a sum derived from the function of the differential relations between points. Nevertheless, according to Chaitin, there must be a complexity of the discrete number itself, not derived from the ratio between two points.[86] Omega is this anomalous discrete unity, infinite and yet indivisible, a mathematical and yet also a quantum entity.

What can be immediately learned from Chaitin's theory is that not only (analog and biophysical) qualities but also computational quantities are therefore incomplete. In particular, Chaitin's theory suggests that each and any object is at once discrete (and indivisible) and yet composed of infinite uncountable parts. It is precisely this notion of incomplete yet discrete quantities that can transform algorithmic architecture into a metamodel of immanent signs and objects. Similarly, as will be discussed in this book, these incomputable quantities characterize the postcybernetic apparatus of anticipatory architectures, programming data cultures and building data spaces that are immanently experienced but not directly lived.

It is therefore suggested here that algorithmic architecture does not simply reveal the workings of universal codes that generate metamorphic structures of change. Instead, algorithmic architecture can be taken as an example of the actual existence of spatiotemporal data structures infected with incomputable quantities. Far from being a model of existing structures, algorithmic architecture becomes a metamodel of algorithmic objects, which are conceived here as discrete entities imbued with infinity. Chaitin's notion of the incomputable (or discrete infinity) poses a radical challenge to the predicates of first- and second-order cybernetics. In particular, his algorithmic theory questions the assumption that parts (either sets of algorithms or the interaction between algorithms and biophysical inputs) constitute the whole (the mathematical axiom or the autopoietic system). Chaitin's theory demonstrates that parts are irreducible to any totality because they can be bigger (quantitatively incompressible or irresolvable by a simpler solution) than wholes, and can instead overrun them. Algorithmic architecture is not a whole constituted by parts, but rather shows that parts are irreducible inconsistencies divorced from the totality that can be built through them; it works not against but rather with the chaotic parts of information that are comprised neither within mathematical axioms nor within the law of physics. Algorithmic architecture therefore offers us the opportunity to discuss the nature of algorithmic objects beyond pure mathematical and physical models. It thus contributes to the articulation of a new notion of discreteness that may well overturn what is meant by the digital. The next few sections of this chapter will endeavor to clarify what is at stake in this new notion of discreteness.

1.3 Discrete objects

> Within any system, design must take place simultaneously at the level of the object or node, and at the level of the wiring, connection or protocol. Thus, the studio takes the appliance, a discrete object wired for connection in a larger system, as its fundamental design unit.[87]

The Responsive Systems/Appliance Architectures advanced research design studio, at Cornell University, insists on a conception of space that is not an envelope, one that implies a new model of control through the blurring, flattening, and dispersal of hierarchies. In particular, they conceive of appliances as objects or assemblages of objects with embedded intelligence (from kitchen appliances to systems furniture to iPods), and have also devised a generation of new digital objects. These latter are produced through simple kinematic units that are able to combine into larger assemblies. With Alias Waterfront's program, inverse kinematics was used with scripts to model the potential behaviors of the objects. Objects are conceived here as active systems that change over time, and as requiring a method for discovering their behavior and as-yet-unrealized use. Here the object is defined by the interactions generated by its components and by the relations that they have with other objects. The space between these interactive parts, and in which they are themselves located, thus becomes a scenario of potential configurations of objects that are programmed to be partially unplanned.

Nevertheless, according to Neal Leach, the complexity and the dynamic capacities of discretely computed objects—a complexity and a dynamics that define new spatial relations—can only be the result of autonomous design agents which are able to self-organize.[88] For an instance, Leach draws on the Kokkugia network of Australian architects, who have devel-

Figure 1.4
Kokkugia, Taipei Performing Arts Center, 2008. Courtesy of Roland Snooks + Robert Stuart-Smith.

oped a multiagent design tool based on the notion of swarm intelligence. This multiagent system does not, however, simply simulate or map actual populations of agents in order to find optimal solutions for urban planning. On the contrary, this is a flexible system based on self-generating objects-agents, which interact with one another and thus reveal spatial mobility.

Leach takes the Kokkugia's design of the Taipei Performing Arts Center (2008) as an example of swarm modeling, whereby interactive self-organizing multiagents define objects in terms of unity and the parts thereof. Here the object is conceived as being both one and many. From this standpoint, the software program used to design the roof of the Taipei Arts Center demonstrates that discrete objects are made of partial relations. This is a network of semiautonomous software agents that reform their original topology and geometrical form by visibly changing some parts of the roof, while others keep their original geometry determined by infrastructural connections. Here the parts of an object are conceived as semiautonomous agents able to evolve their own set of interactions with other objects without reproducing the same set of instructions. Similarly, changes are only dictated by the emergence of contingent solutions. This is why, according to Leach, the space engendered by the movement of these parts is itself a dynamic space defined by multiple discrete objects. From this standpoint, the self-organization of semiautonomous agents defines each and any object of computation as a complex of parts and their interactions.

Nevertheless, this emphasis on self-organizing agents and partially interacting objects seems to be (yet again) proposing the autopoietic fusion of space and matter into one system of interaction. Here space and matter are co-constituted by interactive parts that coevolve over time and deploy their changing morphologies. Therefore the ontological premises of swarming agents turn space and matter into the emergent and not preprogrammed properties of algorithmic objects. These premises do, however, lead to an organic notion of totality in which the algorithmic object is mainly the result of interactive, evolving parts that form a continuously changing whole. This ontological assumption cannot help but reify the notion of a computational continuum,[89] according to which infinitesimal relations between parts make it impossible to discern one object from another. The Taipei Performing Arts Center's roof thus remains the product of the interactions of multiple agents, and is the ultimate effect of their activities. Ultimately, swarm models rely on the injection of time into finite sets of instructions. Time and not space becomes the motor of change here.

To put it more simply: as digital computational models have become dynamic processes (driven by evolving and swarming algorithms), the Euclidean grid of discrete objects has turned into a continuous variation of form. What is at stake with these generative algorithms is that the notion of discreteness (parts and objects defined by finite sets of instruction) has changed, and now includes a model of interactive agents that evolve *in* and *through* time.

Architects Bernard Cache and Greg Lynn, for instance, have captured this nuance of algorithms or computational processing of form with the notions of the "objectile" and the "blob."[90] Objects, they contend, are no longer designed according to exact coordinates—points in space—but are complex curved surfaces, the slight variation of which cannot be controlled in advance. Hence an object is determined by an unlimited number of variations occurring through time, and is enfolded into an environment of differential relations, speeds, and intensities. From this standpoint, an object is always more than one and less than many. It is not the sum of interactive parts and does not remain a plurality of parts. As Lynn points out:

> With isomorphic polysurfaces, "meta-clay," "meta-ball," or "blob" models, the geometric objects are defined as monad-like primitives with internal forces of attraction and mass. A blob is defined with a center, a surface area, a mass relative to other objects, and a field of influence. The field of influence defines a relational zone within which the blob will fuse with, or be inflected by, other blobs.[91]

Lynn's computational architecture makes explicit that objects are not substances but acts and verbs. They can only be described in terms of vectors and temporalities. Blob objects have an aqueous spatiality, the unity of which is a folding of relations that constitutes a quasi-thing that is amorphous and uncharacterized. Far from being a substance that maintains its identity in space while moving from one position to another as if on a grid, objectiles and blobs are spatiotemporal events.[92] The unity of an object, therefore, is an ongoing process of infinitesimal happenings.

From this standpoint, blobs and objectiles show that there is no fixed space, because space is itself a topological surface of movement and variation. Rules evolve and change, are flexible and malleable. Space is then generated in time through evolving and interactive agents defined by vectorial forces. Space, therefore, is an envelope of differentials. As Lynn observes: "The prevalence of topological surfaces in even the simplest CAD software, along with the ability to tap the time-and-force modeling attributes of animation software . . . [supplants] the traditional tools of exactitude and stasis with tools of gradients, flexible envelopes, temporal flows and forces."[93]

One could thus argue that algorithmic architecture embraces the limit of computation, and reveals how the discrete logic of binary states undergoes a temporal inflection. This inflection, or deviation from a linear trajectory, reveals the qualitative transformation of parts as they become other than they were through interaction. And yet, if the becoming of an object only occurs through the qualitative transformation of its interactive parts, defined by the flexibility of algorithms and the temporality of processing, then how can one explain the indivisible unity of nonetheless discrete objects? One may wonder, that is, whether the continual sequences of algorithms can become a slice of spatiotemporality, an unrepeatable event that stands out from the seamless processing of generative algorithms and the information background of ubiquitous computing.

The next three subsections of this chapter will analyze theories of objects and of process in order to address these questions. In particular, these theories may help us to clarify whether an algorithmic object is to be conceived as a discrete unity or instead as the result of continual relations.

1.3.1 Unity and relation

The ontological problem that underpins conceptions of unity or relations returns, in algorithmic architecture, as a computational problem. Do organic forms correspond to mathematical sets? How can the continuity of vectors be split into binary "yes" and "no" states? Or can automated computation define objects in terms of relations? In sum, the question is whether discontinuous, disconnected, and atomic unity can explain the relational intricacies of more than one and less than many objects.

For instance, computational notions of objectiles and blobs are based on the temporality of processes and on the nonlinear (or differential) interaction of parts. It can be suggested that these notions do not describe the unity of objects, but precisely challenge the idea that an object is indivisible and determined by its spatiotemporal position on a grid. From this standpoint, an object always already fuses into another, or never remains the same. Here objects continuously undergo change. In fact, the question here is no longer how objects change, but how change defines what is to be an object.

Nevertheless, if change is to be our entry point into understanding algorithmic objects, then one could argue that change cannot explain away quantity, extension, order, and logic. In other words, algorithmic objects cannot avoid being determined by sets of instructions: an irreducible discreteness that does not easily match with the view that algorithms are the result of computational processes. In other words, the relational nature of each and any object of computation remains an ontological problem, which cannot overlook the discrete unity of algorithmic objects. In order to resolve this apparent paradox between unity and relation one may need to take a detour away from algorithmic architecture and explore recent theoretical debates about the ontological state of objects.

For instance, Graham Harman's object-oriented metaphysics precisely poses the question of how objects could be granted an autonomous existence that would not prevent them from entering true relationships; by extension, it is also a question of autonomy that the visions of metaphysics could support.[94] Whereas theories of modeling space and matter are characterized by an emphasis on self-organization,[95] object-oriented metaphysics explains that objects are actual entities that do not fuse into one another, and that do not continuously change.

In particular, Harman's metaphysical premises are that objects are autonomous and cannot be reduced to their components. They must therefore retain an indivisible individuality. Harman believes that even if a chair contains a complex number of elements and variations, it ultimately remains a chair. This means that the chair's qualities are irreducible to its construction, its material components, and its ideal uses. Yet he also claims that objects can and must become wrapped within other objects, and thereby connected to other universes. This form of relation, however, does not and cannot result in a total mimesis, where everything is linked to or can become everything else.[96]

Harman's object-oriented metaphysics moves straight against the current of the late 1990s triumph of system theories and rejects the imperative of connectionism by which all entities, at the micro and macro scale, are to some degree linked through others. Harman instead argues that "objects do not fully manifest to each other but communicate with one another through the levels that bring their qualities into communion. The level is not primarily a human phenomenon, or even an animal phenomenon, but a *relational* one."[97] In other words, only if objects are viewed as being indivisible and irreducible to other objects can their relations be explained.

Here relationality is defined not as a line between points, but as a multiplicity of levels that constitutes the fractal geometry of each and any object. Relations describe the "intermediate zone through which objects signal to one another, and transfer energies for the benefit or destruction of one another."[98] Levels are media. The latter allow objects to interfere with one another. Levels, therefore, are mediators not of objects in relation to others, but within objects themselves. In other words, relations are also objects: joints and glue, pipelines, tunnels, and crawl spaces, copper cable, fiber optic, smoke signals, quantum leaps, algorithmic processing.

From this standpoint, as much as relations are objects, so objects are not products of relations; they are themselves entities, possessed of internal qualities that also enjoy a relation of quantity. This is to say that objects are not only brought together by qualitative attributes that they all equally share. A quantitative relation may include, for instance, the algorithms that determine the chemical composition of a singular object, which can also be transferred to another without however reconstituting the same object. For example, water is a complete object, the qualities of which include the absence of color, smell, or taste and the natural states of liquid, solid, and gas. It is also constantly changing and in movement. However, the water molecule's chemical and physical properties are also shared by many other objects; for instance, it shares O (oxygen) with oxygen-based objects such as the atmosphere, and H with hydrogen-based objects such as stars.

Nevertheless, this is not to say that these aqueous qualities confuse the singularity of water with that of oxygen. Since qualities are intrinsic to these objects, they are indissoluble from them, and yet irreducible to this or that particular object. From this example, it is not only evident that qualities define the indissoluble singularity of an object; it is also clear that quantities and their relations define the singularity of an object. For instance, the molecule of water is composed of two atoms of hydrogen and one of oxygen. The hydrogen atoms are attached to one side of the oxygen atom, resulting in a water molecule that has a positive charge on the side of the hydrogen atoms and a negative charge on the other side, where the oxygen atom is. Since opposite electrical charges attract, water molecules will tend to attract each other, making water "sticky." But these numerical and electrical quantities also compose other objects, and relate objects together. Each and any object is indeed not only chemically composed of or related to another object; in addition, its algorithmic computations act to chemically constitute the operations of an object, which can also be generative of other objects and relations. This example could explain why Harman's theory of objects is relevant to the articulation of algorithmic objects, which are not simply quantities of physical qualities, but are themselves qualitative quantities.

Besides believing that an object is an indivisible substance, Harman, more interestingly perhaps, describes the object's multimediatic essence as being made of levels, or media. As already mentioned, these levels are objects. In particular, Harman claims that a medium is any space in which objects interact.[99] In other words, a medium is itself a space, and not simply a channel between spaces. Thus the levels of objects are themselves objects or media spaces. Hence, no object can be simply united by levels, as these latter are intrinsic to the objects themselves, like the joints of an arm, the brackets of a door, the glass of fiber optics, software protocols TCP/IP (Transmission Control Protocol/Internet Protocol), algorithms in computation, train tunnels, the cream or filling in a cake, water for fishes, oxygen for trees, body for mind, and so on. Harman insists that these levels-spaces-objects are worlds that cannot be ontologically determined by the synthesis of the senses, the bio-logic order of things, or the gravitation of the earth.

According to Harman, therefore, there can only be an indirect cause of relationality between the multimediatic objects. But this indirect cause is neither physical nor mental. It is neither an immediate sensorimotor response nor an explicit re-cognition. Instead, this cause is above all "carnal." It involves a sensual relation between objects or between the many levels–media objects themselves.

1.3.2 Qualities and quantities

As already mentioned, Harman's object-oriented metaphysics may contribute toward challenging the view that algorithms are merely functional or quantitative reductions of analog qualities and relational space. From this standpoint, an algorithmic object is at once a set of instructions and the relation between algorithms. Thus, algorithmic objects are always a discrete unity, and always correspond to a quantity. However, one may ask, what exactly is this spatial relation between algorithmic objects? For instance, is this space object a mere aggregation of algorithmic parts? According to Harman, only an empty shell can be defined as a mere aggregation of levels. He insists that the parts of an object space can instead be only vicariously active, implying an indirect, nonlinear, and asymmetric process of conjunction and disjunction of parts.

Yet the question is whether these distinct parts of an algorithmic object can be bound together, and yet at the same time be detached from its unity. In other words, if parts are not simply interactive components forming objects-spaces, then one has to explain how these parts can partake of the singularity of an object while autonomously entering other objects.

To address this question, Harman uses the example of an apple to describe how unity and disaggregation work.[100] An apple's sweetness, fragrance, color, and nutritional value are, to a large extent, distinct parts, autonomous attributes (which could correspond to the elements of an algorithm). Yet somehow all of these qualities are intrinsically unified in a single thing, even if they cannot directly interfere with one another (Harman states that the nutritional value of an apple has nothing to do with its color, for instance). The apple, as a complete entity, is not affected by its distinct qualities: it can lose its color and proteins and yet still remain an apple. It always retains its autonomy as this (actual) apple and not any other. In other words, this particular apple is not any other because its proper interior composition depends on the interaction of its qualities. However, Harman explains, this interaction is never *direct* and cannot give us *this* specific apple. If it were so, each element would become interchangeable with another, thus losing its medial nature and ultimately its *objectness*. It would no longer be an object but a link between objects. As Harman suggests, it is the task of indirect causes, which prevent the self-constitution of an ultimate subject, to glue together the macrocosm and microcosm.[101] This is why the relation of the object with its parts is not a transparent one. An object can connect with its own qualities and with other objects, but it can never be determined by its capacity of fusing with others into one.

Harman's insistence on the objectness of relationality suggests that relations do not occur in a void but are themselves objects.[102] From this standpoint, the relation between two objects does not simply entail their fusion, but rather the leveling of distinct objects. In other words, no single medium of interaction could exist between things; only many mediatic levels across scales, many media objects, could then define the workings of interactive computation. Against the seamless algorithms of ubiquitous computation that define the metamedium of all media as the (background) environment of already programmed interactions, Harman's object-oriented metaphysics seems to point toward a postcybernetic metamodel of complexity that exposes the irreducible elements/qualities of an entity as such, and its indissoluble, atomic, yet infinite incompleteness. However, these qualities are also elements of other worlds. The red of an apple can also define another apple or an altogether different object, such as a bag. These qualities therefore also expose an irreducible computational arrangement that cannot be contained in the simpler, universal axioms or the cellular automata described by digital metaphysics.

According to Harman, objects have intrinsic qualities that define their complexity and their incompleteness. From his point of view, algorithmic objects can therefore be defined in terms of qualities. However, as mentioned earlier, when speaking about algorithms or any form of data it is no longer possible to overlook the quantitative dimensions of these objects. In particular, algorithmic information theory has pointed out that these quantities are not finite, but rather include incomputable data or the extraspace of infinite algorithms. The space object or the relation between objects does not simply define an object in terms of quality, but must also include a quantity and an extension. In short, if an algorithmic object is not only a quality (temporal or perceptive) but also a quantity, then its relation to other algorithms must be defined in terms of quantities and not just qualities. The point here is to explain how indeterminacy or incompleteness in quantity cannot be exclusively explained in terms of qualities. It is quantity, and not quality, that has become the ambiguous protagonist of recent information theory, and this has served to point out that infinity is a matter of incomputability, which is now an immanent probability.

From this standpoint, one may need to reconsider Harman's position. Object-oriented metaphysics rejects the idea that an object is a unity composed of parts. Harman's philosophy does indeed challenge the credo that each and any object is mainly the results of interactive parts or components, either physical or sensory (an aggregate of particles or sense perceptions). Instead, an object deploys a fractional geometry of qualities, which are themselves objects and not parts, indissoluble qualities making the architecture of each and any object incomplete. In other words, objects cannot be reduced to the sum of their qualities: they are not constructed by human minds, scientific knowledge, or by patterns of perception-cognition.

This metaphysics of objects therefore also defies the metaphysics of universal computation, confuting the idea that simple rules or algorithmic automata can ultimately compute all physical, biological, chemical, and material objects via the evolution of parts that generate the qualitative complexity of forms. However (and this is the argument here) object-oriented metaphysics cannot help us to engage with uncountable information or quantities. If algorithmic objects do not simply constitute the universal language that can calculate everything, at the same time their qualitative elements cannot be isolated from sheer incomputable quantities. In order to defy the assumption that all qualities are reducible to simple rules, or that computation can explain the qualities of objects as the result of their interactions, it is important to question conceptions of quantification, calculation, computation, and algorithm first.

One may be right to observe with Harman that each and any object is irreducible to the secondary qualities attributed to it by the human mind, by perception-cognition, and by scientific knowledge; one could thus also conclude, in keeping with his philosophy, that objects have their own qualities, and that these latter are absolutely withdrawn from direct access. On the other hand, however, algorithmic objects are not only qualities. As information theory explains, they are rather finite and infinite quantities that are immediately experienced as data. To argue, then, for the discreteness of objects by explaining that the qualities of objects are themselves objects (i.e., qualities) may not be enough to grant actuality to algorithmic objects. What remains overlooked here is the actuality of algorithmic quantities that does not correspond to what can be finitely calculated: quantities that are not the same as qualities, but are instead more than realized qualities. To put it another way: the random and incomputable quantities of algorithmic objects cannot be replaced by the credo in infinite autonomous qualities. Incomplete qualities without indeterminate quantities instead will always already risk folding objects back into a complete axiomatics of denumerable parts or into the continual variations of physical matter. This is also to say that Harman overlooks the fact that parts are not simply finite elements and that they can be bigger than wholes.

As already discussed, digital metaphysics explains algorithmic objects as a set of probabilities or functions, made of exactly calculable components that lead to emergent complex behavior. But as I have also argued, this view must be opposed by the fact that there are algorithms that cannot be smaller than the objects programmed. Information never becomes fully transparent or reducible to a finite quantity, since parts of it remain incomputable. As opposed to digital metaphysics, which claims that cellular automata are the simplest and smallest programs by which the complexity of behaviors, patterns, and qualities can be generated, the metaphysics of incomputable algorithms instead grounds the reality of incomputable quantities in the sequential calculation of probabilities. From this standpoint, since incomputable quantities are indivisible, and remain, as Chaitin argues, discrete unities, computational continuity is conceived to be bugged by incompressible random quantities, where parts are bigger than the program devised to calculate them.

Harman's object-oriented metaphysics argues that there is a discrete reality for each and every object, the latter being irreducible to its essential qualities. This is also the case for algorithms, which define the finite states of any physical object as being made up of digital information. Similarly, this implies that the sensual qualities of digital images or sounds or spatial forms are not experienced as masses of sense data, but as objects. In other words, the qualities of a sensual object are not sensations, but are rather accidents that change while the *eidos* of the object remains the same.[103]

From this standpoint, the generative design of an interactive wall, as seen in the case of the Hyperbody's *InteractiveWall* and *Emotive Wall*, aims to correlate sense data to algorithmic objects by identifying digital objects with qualities. Such projects therefore seem able to reduce the incomputable reality of these objects to sensual qualities, which again are reduced to pixilated components of color, sound, and movement, thus confusing the transient qualities of perception with the *eidos* of the sensual object, i.e., the interactive wall. By contrast, object-oriented metaphysics explains that we experience only objects, and not masses of sense data:

> When I circle an object or when it rotates freely before me, I do not see a discrete series of closely related contents and then make an arbitrary decision that they all belong together as a set of closely linked specific profiles. Instead, what I experience is always one object undergoing accidental, transient changes that do not alter the thing itself.[104]

In other words, sensual objects cannot be reduced to parts or the atomic elements that explain their unity. Similarly, algorithmic architecture does not posit the reality of objects. "An object is real not by virtue of being tiny and fundamental, but by virtue of having an intrinsic reality that is not reducible to its subcomponents or exhausted by its functional effects on other things."[105] And yet, even if one could hypothesize that algorithmic objects could be understood as sensual objects, irreducible to their atomic components, the problem of how to define quantity remains. To argue that the qualities of objects cannot be quantified does not simply mean that quantities do not exist, or are irrelevant to the definition of an object. On the contrary, what is argued here is that discrete yet complex quantities, such as Omega, clarify for us that between algorithms there is no seamless computational continuum.

To argue that (incomputable) quantities are intrinsic to algorithmic objects is not, however, to sustain Harman's metaphysical schema, wherein the problem of quantity has been turned into a question of substance. In particular, Harman claims that "the reason we call these objects 'substances' is not because they are ultimate or indestructible, but simply because none of them can be identified with any (or even all) of their relations with other entities." Yet he cannot do without the notion of substance. "Every object is both a substance and a complex of relations. But if every object can also be considered as a set of relations between its parts or qualities, it is equally true that any relation must also count as a substance."[106]

In the age of the algorithm it is not, however, substance as grounded quantity but rather incomputable algorithms that have infected the computation of sensual and real objects. The liveliness and persistence of the substantial core of these objects is then split into a thousand fragments: into infinitely fractionalized algorithms that enter the operations of programming. Yet this fractal splitting of the united core of an object does not mean that there is no longer an object at all, and that only parts remain (i.e., algorithmic parts, by way of which the entirety of the object can be reaggregated). When sensual objects, spaces, walls are programmed, they are also exposed to the incomputable quantities that expose the unity of the object to deterritorialized signs. When a real object—a tree, for instance—is algorithmically programmed in a video game, its reality too is contaminated by the incompressibility, the nonchorality (lack of harmony) of discrete ciphers that are able to expose the algorithmic tree to its own infinite parts.

It is my contention that incomputable algorithms, and not information substances, are at the heart of programming cultures (from software design to molecular genetics, from nanodesign to social and urban engineering). Beneath the surface of ubiquitous computation—a surface composed of too much information, too many direct connections and interactions that are too smooth, all of which take place between programmed objects—there remains a contagious architecture of infinite parts, unsynthesizable quantities, and uncountable randomness that explodes within and between any finite kernels.[107] Since Harman's philosophy does not sufficiently help us to define algorithmic objects, one may need to draw on another notion of actual object, which instead accounts for the presence of indetermination in quantities. Similarly, it is also important to explain how algorithmic objects stand out from computational processing, or whether an emphasis on processes can account for the nuance of such objects. If computational processes involve recursive algorithms that ultimately generate complex forms, then one may need to explain how and why complexity already exists in the algorithmic object in the first place. To do so, the next section of this chapter will turn to Alfred North Whitehead's claim that objects cannot be explained by process, but rather exist as forms of process.

1.3.3 Form and process

All mathematical notions have reference to processes of intermingling. The very notion of number refers to the process from the individual units to the compound group. The final number belongs to no one of the units; it characterizes the way in which the group unity has been attained. . . . There is no such thing as a mere static number. There are only numbers playing their parts in various processes conceived in abstraction from the world-process.[108]

According to Whitehead, there are no numbers without group, no unity without process. However, as the quote above also serves to illustrate, Whitehead believed that there are processes of another kind that do not correspond to the world-process (the continual chain of actual worlds). Whitehead is specifically addressing the abstraction of mathematical processes here, but in this subsection I will discuss whether these abstract processes can explain the indeterminate quantities or incompleteness of algorithmic objects.

It may not be too easy to shift from Harman's object-oriented metaphysics to Whitehead's process philosophy: for against the idea that objects are born out of processes, Harman firmly maintains that the ontology of objects is irreducible. For instance, he questions Whitehead's process metaphysics on the grounds that it replaces objects with events. For Harman, Whitehead's work attends only to what happens to things, and not to what those things really are.

For Whitehead, the actual world is composed of actual occasions. These actualities are grouped in events, which become the nexus of actual entities that are "inter-related in some determined fashion in one extensive quantum."[109] Events therefore explain the togetherness of actualities, which Whitehead calls the "nexus." But every nexus is a component part of another nexus. The latter emerges as an unalterable entity from the concrescence of its component elements, and it stands as a fact, possessed of a date and a location.[110] Whitehead points out that the individual particularity of an actual entity, and of each nexus of entities, is also independent of its original percipient and thus "enjoys an objective immortality in the future beyond itself."[111] From this standpoint, Whitehead confutes the primary notions of space and time, and argues that only events, as nexuses of actual entities, are able to remain unrepeatable places with dates. In other words, actual entities are immanent events of time and space, and yet, as nexuses of entities, events go beyond *this* space and *this* time.

Nevertheless, Harman believes that this notion of event is determined by a transcendental cause, since events explain objects in terms of the effects of a process. He argues that process metaphysics always already defines the object (e.g., a tree) according to the effects that it has in the world, and not as a cause of itself. In Whitehead's metaphysics, he insists, the effects that objects have on others determine their existence. In contrast, Harman argues that objects and their relations are ontologically independent from their effects. For Harman the interaction of objects, therefore, can only occur indirectly or vicariously once the elements and qualities of objects become objects themselves. Thus, algorithmic objects should not correspond to the effects that they can engender in physical reality. Instead, interaction should expose how one object can become another, how one code can determine and change the milieu for which it was designed.

From the perspective of object-oriented metaphysics, the levels of interactivity implied in the *Emotive Wall* project, for example, are simply the effects generated by algorithms. Here, the interaction between objects cannot unleash new objects, but can only be reduced to the potential effects that algorithms can have on the wall, so that this latter interacts with the participants' movements. In other words, from this view the *Emotive Wall* is an example of a responsive architecture that is generated by the effects algorithms can have on the physical structure of the wall as it reacts to the sense data collected from the people involved. Ultimately, the *Emotive Wall* is the effect of algorithmic programming.

But how can algorithmic objects be more than an effect that one object can have on another? According to Harman, objects interact through their qualities. These latter are not simply projections that create effects, but are instead objects themselves.[112] In particular, Harman uses the notion of "allure" to explain that the relation between objects is vicarious, indirect, and hence unable to transpose effects onto things.[113] The concept of allure explains how qualities become things beyond any system of reference. Effects, however, can only derive from a system of reference, and convert objects back into mere secondary qualities.[114] Thus, in the case of the *Emotive Wall*, algorithms are not conceived as objects but as the projection of qualities onto the wall, which also remains the effect of sensorimotor interactions: the wall can bend, emit sounds, and create shades of color by responding to external stimuli. Hence neither algorithms nor the wall are objects here, but rather deploy a plethora of effects derived by a percipient.

Similarly, according to Harman, Whitehead's process metaphysics cannot explain how objects can truly interact, because qualities are merely attached to objects and are not objects themselves. These qualities, Harman argues, only constitute the events that explain the relation between objects. At this point, however, it may be necessary to get closer to Whitehead's view and highlight that events are not merely qualities deprived of objects; instead he conceives of events as a nexus of actual occasions defining an extensive set or a temporal series, an accumulation of actualities. Events, in other words, are "enduring objects."[115] Time plus space. Furthermore, events are both mental and physical, to the extent that thought and things have an equal but not equivalent metaphysical valence. For Whitehead, an event is the unrepeatable pattern that continues to happen and never remains the same.[116] For Harman, however, this temporality of the event is determined and linked too directly by the nexus of prehensions, which he argues is always already there to shape the object through projections,[117] and thus to reduce the object to shapeless matter without specific form.[118]

Harman's insistence on the actuality of things, on their indivisibility and ontological status as substances, may appear an alternative to the plethora of effects that define algorithms as mere projections on behalf of a responsive percipient. Nevertheless, his metaphysical schema may merely end up conflating, once again, the actuality of objects with their finite substance. Harman's position oddly resonates with a first-order cybernetic notion of objects, according to which these are determined by finite states. These objects will always remain what they are even though their qualities (and quantities) have nested with other objects and their infinite parts. If, as Harman tells us, the qualities are fragments, parts, parcels and bits that are themselves objects, then perhaps objects cannot remain the same after all. Nevertheless, it is true to say that he insists that an apple always remains an apple, even after its qualities (green, red, sweet, cooked or raw) have entered into relations with others and produced new objects (such as a green apple, for instance). This implies that the apple, were it to be computed, would be a finite set of algorithms, which despite interacting with others would always keep a traceable substance and original source. And yet the limit of computation suggests that objects have parts that are bigger than their totality; that there is always incompleteness within one set. This is to say that there can be no discrete and finite substance, no matter how much you break it down into autonomous qualities-objects. Not only is each and any object broken into parts that are autonomous from the object as a whole, but also these fragments can acquire degrees of completeness only after they have entered into relation with actual parts that have lost their constitutional origin. This is why objects are always partial things, and enter a nexus of events by which their irreducible parts can become new actual objects.

Contra Harman's critique, it is argued here that Whitehead's metaphysics of events does not determine objects by rendering them as the synthesis of the qualities that are projected onto them.[119] If, as Whitehead explains, each and any actual occasion is an assemblage of prehended data and prehending activities, then an assemblage is composed of parts-objects, which constitute an enduring object that acquires an epochal singularity. This singularity—which might be referred to as eventfulness—cannot be repeated, because the objects that define this singularity are partial, contextual, historical actualities. At the same time, however, if an event is a nexus of actual objects and not the result of projected qualities, it is because it corresponds to the eventuation of unprecedented qualities that go beyond the direct projection of the actual data.

However, is it possible here to understand relations to be both more than effects and less than the projections of a perceiving subject? How does Whitehead avoid equating relations with projections? In particular, one may wonder whether the notion of prehension can sustain the reality of objects without reaffirming the subjective (and phenomenological) experience of objects. To explore these questions is to probe how and to what extent Whitehead's process metaphysics can contribute toward defining algorithmic objects in terms of actuality and infinity.

According to Whitehead, prehensions are first of all mental and physical modalities of relations by which objects take up and respond to one another. As he puts it, "prehensions are concrete facts of relatedness."[120] He does not start with the substance of an object or with the perception one has of it, but confers autonomy on an actual entity's constitutive process of acquiring determination, completeness, and finitude from indeterminate conditions.[121]

Although for Whitehead prehensions are an external fact of relatedness, they are not mental projections but rather conceptual and physical relations:[122] not only concrete ideas, in other words, but also concrete facts. This means that the actual prehension of another actual object, or of its elements, changes the internal constitution (the mental and physical tendencies) of the prehended actuality.[123] From this standpoint, prehensions also account for how actual entities acquire determination or completeness from an indeterminate process of mental and physical contagion, or from the intrusions of elements from other actual entities. Whitehead calls this process a "concrescence of prehensions."[124]

Actual entities, therefore, are not substances or indissoluble objects. On the contrary, they can only *become* indivisible once the concrescence of prehensions affords an actual object that then becomes the subjective form of the data prehended. This process of prehensions is thus a process of determination, and what it determines is the actuality of data defined by the concrescence of prehensions. This is why an actual occasion is not eternal, but rather an event. It happens and then perishes. It acquires a subjective form of the prehended data and at once reaches objective immortality: it becomes an indissoluble event in the flow of time. From this standpoint, actual occasions are not effects of prehensions or mirrors of perceptions. On the contrary, they are led by their final cause to transform prehended data into a subjective form and into objective actuality.[125] The subjective form of the actual entity thus remains an objectified real potential that can be prehended anew by other actual entities. From this standpoint, the process of prehension is not a relative mechanism by which no object can as such be defined autonomously; instead, this process explains how actual entities become events, and thereby new spatiotemporal objects on the extensive continuum.[126]

As opposed to the relativism of ubiquitous computation, where everything is connected, Whitehead's process metaphysics is instead concerned with how indivisible or discrete unities can exist in the infinity of relations with other events, or with other actual occasions. This metaphysics does not offer us the option of simply merging or separating abstract and actual objects, but rather explains how infinity, indetermination, and abstraction are immanent to actualities. As Whitehead puts it: "The true philosophical question is, how can concrete fact exhibit entities abstract from itself and yet participated in by its own nature?"[127]

Each and any bit of an actual occasion strives for its own individuation by selecting or taking a decision about the infinite amount of data (the qualities and the quantities) inherited from past actual occasions, from contemporaneous entities, and from the pure potentials of eternal objects. Yet prehensions are always partial, since all actual objects at once select and exclude, evaluate and set in contrast all of the inherited data. In other words, prehensions do not at all coincide with a direct downloading of data on behalf of an entity, and do not constitute objects by projecting data onto them (or by way of what Harman would call the "house of mirrors," where objects become constituted by the reflections or the images of perceptive entities).[128] If, according to Whitehead, actual prehensions are the conditions of space and time[129] and are the markers of events, it is because the indissoluble atomic architecture of each and any actual occasion is imbued with indetermination. Whitehead's process metaphysics therefore suggests that events are a nexus of actual objects. These are unrepeatable events, and yet they remain incomplete because their objectified real potential can be prehended by any other actual entity and thus becomes other than it was.

From this standpoint, even if an object is what *it is* and cannot be another,[130] it remains an unsubstantial entity. An object cannot therefore remain unchanged from the material corrosions of its parts; it cannot stop bursting with its entropic chaos. Similarly, an actual object cannot remain an eternal form (the form of the apple) that physically reenacts itself and reproduces itself, as does an autopoietic system. Instead, an actual occasion maintains its objective determination, involving the prehension of both actual and abstract data. To put it otherwise, actual objects are not simply dissolved into a seamless process of projections, but are instead forms of processes: forms of an infinite number of infinities.

Whitehead in fact rejects the idea that processes involve the continual variation of a self-modulating whole. There could be no process without forms of processes, without conceptual and physical objects prehending the infinity of actual and abstract data. According to Whitehead, a form of process precisely responds to the question: "How does importance for the finite require importance for the infinite?"[131] A form of process therefore explains how "each fully realized fact has an infinity of relations in the historical world and in the realm of form."[132] In other words, a form of process defines how an object reaches its completion and becomes individualized, and how infinite potentialities, or eternal objects, enter actuality and determine eventful spatiotemporality. A form of process explains how unexpected worlds become added to already existing objects. Nevertheless, this form does not correspond to the sum of objects and the accumulation of qualities and quantities of data. The concrescence of the universe involves the concrescence of actual worlds that are imbued with eternal objects. Actual objects could not become complete, and there could be no event without the capacities of actual objects to fulfill the potential content of selected (or prehended) eternal objects, through which actual qualities and quantities can become other than what they were.[133]

Harman's object-oriented metaphysics contests Whitehead's need to make recourse to eternal objects or to potentialities in order to explain what actual objects are, how can they be related, and what defines a new object.[134] For Harman, the specific expression of an actual world is here and now, and cannot be explained away by eternal objects. Nevertheless, Whitehead's metaphysics does not simply replace empirical with transcendental causality, actualities with process, or facts with forms. Instead, it insists that there are immanent causes at work within an actual object: presentational immediacy and causal efficacy. While the former explains how prehensions are immediately taken by the present, causal efficacy refers to the reality of the past data that lurks in the background. If causal efficacy is "the sense of derivation from an immediate past, and of passage to an immediate future,"[135] presentational immediacy, the sense perception of things as they are presented here and now, is what is felt in the immediacy of prehension. Whitehead explains that the present locus is a datum for both modes of perception: it is an object of immediate perception according to the cause of presentational immediacy, and an object of indirect perception through causal efficacy. In other words, the double causality does not exclude the potential in favor of the actual, and yet does not simply merge the two causes together through material empiricism or transcendent idealism.

The two causes explain the immanence of infinity: eternal objects correspond to the infinite infinity of ideas, and actual objects deploy the infinite infinity of matter. It is when an actual entity selects certain ideas that a nexus becomes an event, and another actual object is added onto the extensive continuum. As Whitehead puts it, "a continuum is divisible; so far as the contemporary world is divided by actual entities, it is not a continuum but is atomic."[136] Eternal objects do not therefore glue actual entities together, merging all individualities into one continual process of projection. On the contrary, the extensive continuum as the general relational matrix of actual occasions is defined by "the process of the becoming of actuality into what in itself is merely potential."[137]

From this standpoint, if, as object-oriented metaphysics claims, not all objects are the same but every object is real,[138] then one cannot deny the reality of abstraction, or that nontangible objects have qualities, quantities, and relations selected by actual objects. The process of selection referred to is driven by prehensions, which can also be defined as modes of computing data from other actual entities and from eternal objects. Whitehead's metaphysics admits that actualities are infected with abstractions, with infinite parts that cannot be contained in an unchangeable substance. For this reason, Whitehead's conception of actualities may clarify for us how algorithmic objects can be actuals, and yet at the same time be imbued with incomputable quantities, with parts that are bigger than the whole.

Algorithmic objects could then be defined as finite actualities, not corresponding to an ultimate biophysical or ideal substance, but rather characterized by data prehended from the past (causal efficacy) and from the present (presentational immediacy). But this is not all: Whitehead's notion of the eternal object also explains how abstract infinities are immediately prehended by any actual form of process. His account of actuality therefore helps us to define algorithms as forms of process: as actual objects infected with the incomputable data of eternal objects.

Nevertheless, the relation between eternal objects and actual entities is not simply a matter of coevolution or structural coupling, as might for instance be claimed by an autopoietic approach to algorithms. Similarly, eternal objects do not generate actual occasions, but are "potentials for the process of becoming" of actual occasions.[139] Eternal objects are therefore immanent to and part and parcel of any actual entities, since the latter are precisely forms of process and spatiotemporal structures of data. Eternal objects are intrinsic to actualities, no matter how small and how inorganic the latter might be. Eternal objects are not the ideal continuity that links all actualities, but are indeed objects, despite being infinite. Whitehead's philosophy thus offers us an original view of infinity, which does not correspond to infinitesimal continuity between two objects but instead explains how eternal objects are infinite varieties of infinities nested *within* the infinite partialities of actual objects. It is this immanent ingression of eternal objects in the actual infinities of spatiotemporalities that deploys the workings of a contagious architecture, wherein actualities are hosts to infinite parts of infinities.

Eternal objects are real without being actual objects. The latter instead transform the pure potential of eternal objects into a real potential that is defined in time and space. Inasmuch as actual entities are causes of themselves, so too are eternal objects *causa sui*. This also means that their eternality is not grounded in substance, Spirit, or life. Similarly, infinity cannot be derived from finite actualities, because eternality is not flattened onto spatiotemporality. At the same time, however, eternal objects are not simply to be thought as universal qualities through which actualities relate. For Whitehead, eternal objects are ideas that are as real and as effective as any other physical thing. These ideas are at once discrete and infinite, since eternal objects are not equivalent to each other, but are instead defined by their own infinite process. Each eternal object or each idea is therefore not simply different from another. This is not simply a world of ideas: instead, each idea is constituted by infinite data that cannot be contained by a smaller entity or a totality. Eternal objects are incomputable quantities that cannot be compressed by actual quantifications (e.g., rational numbers). Eternal objects do not therefore simply guarantee continuity between actual occasions, because they are permanent objects that enter into actualities.

It may not be too ambitious here to understand Whitehead's notion of eternal objects in terms of random (i.e., incompressible and not arbitrary) quantities, as at once discrete and infinite. Eternal objects are anomalous entities that are not prescribed by a complete axiomatic system or explainable in terms of the indeterminacy of physical variations. While resembling the chaotic world of physics, these entities retain their mathematical abstraction. In other words, eternal objects are "objective and undetermined."[140] They explain how actual entities are never reducible to their actual parts, since a part is already a limit point of computation, the threshold at which discrete infinities advance into the actual world. As a form of process, an algorithmic object is therefore an actual occasion, the interior relations (or genetic inheritance) of which gives it an identity (a finished set of instructions) in the continual variations of qualities, while its exterior relations only attest to their capacities to become more than one. Eternal objects do not, however, reduce the concreteness of objects (i.e., their individuality and atomicity) to a transcendental being. Eternal objects like Omega are discrete varieties of infinities, inconsistent and innumerable entities, which never resemble the algorithmic sequences that they supersede. Indeed, these objects are bigger that any actual object, and while being ready to be selected by actualities, they cannot be reduced or synthesized by any particular actual entity. Instead, these objects are immanent to all actual entities to the extent that they irreversibly infect or virally program their atomicity.

From this standpoint, the interaction between algorithmic objects and between software programs, sensorimotor actuators, and physical prehensions does not simply constitute the architecture of the *Emotive Wall* as an entity that is deemed to change by way of changing levels of interaction. Far from being the result of projections from other objects' qualities, it is now possible to argue that the wall is not the end product of interactions between objects (algorithmic objects, actuators and objects of prehensions): on the contrary, each level of interaction is determined by a computational limit, or by indeterminate quantities. As Whitehead explains, eternal objects "involve in their own natures indecision" and "indetermination."[141] This means that pure potentialities, while being neutral, inefficacious, nongenerative and sterile, also remain passive as regards how they are selected and what is prehended. Whitehead clarifies: "An eternal object is always a potentiality for actual entities; but in itself, as conceptually felt, it is neutral as to the fact of its physical ingression in any particular actual entity of the temporal world."[142] This is why the grayness of the *Emotive Wall* is an eternal quality, which is not the same shade of gray that this particular actual response triggers on the wall. Its grayness in itself has no causal efficacy, no past and no future, no here and no there; it remains eternal and pure potential. It has no say as to whether it is prehended by a particular occasion of interaction.

As Chaitin reminds us, the algorithmic processing of data must include the infinities of incomputable discrete quantities between the sequential continuity of zeroes and ones.[143] Like incomputable algorithms, eternal objects are patternless and random, objective and underdetermined, and are ultimately incompressible into a simpler set of actual rules. Unlike the autopoietic ontology used to explain the generative self-organization of spatial form, where finite algorithms guarantee the production of complex forms by means of repetitive, periodic, simple rules, Omega defies the fundamental principles of mathematical calculation, implying that real numbers cannot be contained in smaller sets.[144] Eternal objects can be explained as real incomputable complexities. They are neither the cause of something nor caused by something else. Omegas are what they are: objects of pure potentialities, discrete yet infinite quantities ingressing (negatively or positively) into any binary computation. Like an eternal object, Omega is an incomplete cipher in the depths of each actual algorithmic pattern, but in itself it is neutral and underdetermined. Omega describes infinite varieties of quantities of color, volume, mood, depth, movement, concepts, and sensations. These are eternal qualities that can be selected by parts of actual occasions in their process of constitution, or concrescence. Eternal objects, therefore, are not simply expressed as effects in actual objects, but are the incomputable condition of finite, terminal, and unrepeatable actualities or nexus of actualities (events). Similarly, Omega complexities define the indeterminate conditions within which algorithmic objects are able to exist. Without the incomputable data of computation there could be no algorithmic architecture, since infinities mark the abstract spatium that affords binary design.[145]

Eternal objects are not only discrete infinities inside actualities. According to Whitehead, eternal objects also define how actual entities "enter into each other's constitutions"[146] and "express a manner of relatedness between other eternal objects."[147] Hence there are no vacuous actualities,[148] but only actual objects infected with the discrete infinity of eternal objects. If, as Harman complains, eternal objects are only there to guarantee infinitely regressive relations (making it impossible to determine the unity of any actual entity), it is not because relations are qualitative projections. On the contrary, eternal objects are there to explain why there is an infinite number of actual objects, and how these objects connect. Eternal objects define the ingression of incomputable quantities into actual objects and thus add new data to existing actualities.[149] Eternal objects are not there to guarantee a continual flow or smooth connection between actualities. Instead, these nonactual worlds explain how deep connections of ideas occur between the most varied objects and transform them.[150] This is why the relation between objects is not simply given by an ideal fusion, but rather implies the contagious architecture of actual entities (indivisible sets) imbued with eternal objects (infinite quantities): worlds belonging to irreducible yet immanent orders of reality, magnitude, and complexity. From this standpoint, algorithmic objects are forms of process, since they are actualities populated by infinite incomputable data.

The age of the algorithm, therefore, coincides not with the arrival of a new substance, but with the unleashing of data objects into programming culture. These objects not only calculate binary probabilities but have become speculative operators of incomputable quantities: data that cannot be compressed into smaller programs. Indeed, computation now occurs at the limits of calculability, probing into the realm of abstract objects or nondenumerable realities. The chaos of randomness is now the condition of calculation.

This is why computation can also be understood as a form of speculative reason, wherein algorithmic sequences are prehensions of pure potentialities (or eternal objects). But in order to discuss this notion of speculative reason, it will be important to explain quite what is meant here by algorithmic prehension. In the following section I will suggest that algorithmic prehensions ought to be considered in terms of aesthetics. It is impossible to speak about algorithmic aesthetics, however, without first questioning those notions of aesthetics that focus on computational beauty or on the elegance of codes, and also those that present digital aesthetics as being predicated upon a perceiver's framing of abstract data.[151]

1.4 Algorithmic aesthetics

> Unlike computerization and digitization, the extraction of algorithmic processes is an act of high-level abstraction. . . . Algorithmic structures represent abstract patterns that are not necessarily associated with experience or perception. . . . In this sense algorithmic processes become a vehicle for exploration that extends beyond the limit of perception.[152]

In this passage, Kostas Terzidis observes that algorithmic processes extend beyond the limits of perception. Nevertheless, while it is acknowledged here that algorithmic structures do not correspond to what humans experience, or to perception, this section of the chapter will argue that algorithmic objects are actual entities and that they thus have physical and mental prehensions. Far from being qualitative impressions of the world or cognitive instructions that inform the world, algorithmic prehensions are physical and conceptual operators of abstract or incomputable data. Thus, on the one hand, algorithms are patterns of physical variables that stem from the circulation of the air, gravitational forces, the bearing of weight, volume, the geological nature of the ground, etc.; on the other hand, they are conceptual prehensions: operators of potentialities, not simply calculators of probabilities.

In particular, if algorithms mark the computational process of an architectural form that is as yet unrealized, then this is because these sequential sets are not merely preprogrammed symbols. If they were, one would be forced to accept that there is no novelty in algorithmic architecture, since there will be no conditions here for spatiotemporal becoming, or for new forms of process. Computation would remain a tautology.[153] Yet in contrast to such a view, we might quote Whitehead: "as soon as we abstract, so as to separate the notions of serial forms and of individual facts involved, we necessarily introduce the notion of potentiality."[154] This means that algorithms are the steps of a process of abstracting mathematical forms and individual facts, and that they are also conceptual prehensions of eternal objects, or potentialities, that determine the arrival of changing conditions in the process of calculation. According to Whitehead, conceptual prehensions are the feeling-thought of change before it actually happens. This implies no direct perception or advanced cognition of the future, but rather the selection of eternal objects by actual occasions: the becoming-form of irreducible qualities and quantities. At this point, one may wonder how these prehensive activities can help us to redefine computation as an aesthetic enterprise[155] that starts off in algorithmic programming.

It is difficult to discuss the notion of algorithmic prehension without rethinking what has been generally and historically understood as aesthetic computing.[156] In particular, aesthetic computing relies on the idea that the shortest program used to calculate infinite complexity is the most eloquent expression of harmony and elegance in mathematics.[157] To put it simply, aesthetics in computation, from this perspective, coincides not with notions of perception but with transcendental ideas of beauty, conceived as an ideal form and represented in geometric models of linearity and symmetry. This formal aesthetics is based on the predictability of results, where the more compressed the data, the greater the chance of patterns remaining regular, periodic, calculable, operational, and effective. Here aesthetics is not a process of prehension, but merely corresponds to already made and endlessly repetitive patterns, the simple functions that engender complex behaviors.

For instance, the algorithmic architecture of mathematician John Conway's *Game of Life* (1970) was composed by a two-state or two-dimensional cellular automaton, whose state was determined by the state of its neighbors.[158] Here all cells were indirectly and directly related to each other, and the process of computation was expressed by color change in each cell. The automatic deployment of the game was set by the initial setting of codes and rules, which gave rise to complex patterns that did not correspond to their original state. As yet another instance of the Turing machine, whereby a computational universe maps out all possible algorithms and their results, Conway's game computed anything that could be algorithmically calculated. It demonstrated how elegant codes and algorithms could be the simple solution to the complexity of systems oscillating between order and chaos. The process through which the patterns change over time coincides here with a computational process in which codes are themselves rewritten over time. This rewriting confirms that the initial conditions of the latter process did not predetermine its final result.

The *Game of Life* is based on the idea of a universal self-replicator. Small changes in its operations, defined by constant modifications to the configurations of the code and the rules, impart changes to the whole system. This extended Turing model works not at the limits of computation but rather within the frame of complete axiomatics, as it explains all outputs by smaller inputs. Conway's *Game of Life* therefore remains locked within an aesthetic of generative complexity. It makes use of the fact that cellular automata can serve to show that initial conditions are no longer retraceable once algorithms are set up to grow; but this is a model of computational aesthetics that overlooks the limits of an organic model of evolution of complexity.

A different approach was presented in 1997 by Jürgen Schmidhuber, who used the notion of Super Omegas[159] to describe limit-computable algorithms—the shortest algorithms (or the minimum description length algorithm) subtending a computation—as the equivalent of minimal art.[160] His notion of low-complexity art drew on Chaitin and Kolgomorov's algorithmic information theory to argue that the aesthetic modality of algorithms was equivalent to the subjective observer's enjoyment of the shortest possible descriptions of data. In other words, the more randomness (complexity or incomputable data) that was compressed into a cipher—for instance Omega, a limit-computable algorithm—the more beauty (understood in terms of the simplest or most elegant formula of complexity) was expressed. Like digital philosophers, Schmidhuber also argued that if the universe was computable, then there had to be a computational aesthetics running beneath all physical phenomena: an underpinning, foundational, mathematical beauty that could be expressed by the shortest of codes accessible to an observer.[161] Here the computation of probabilities occurred through the recursion of simple patterns generating complex behaviors.

From this standpoint, computational aesthetics is the manifestation of an elegant compression of complex data, which coincides with the synthetic point of perception (or the subjective synthesis) of random information. In other words, this model of computational aesthetics is defined by an act of cognition, the compression of data through perception.[162] Yet if the shortest code corresponds to the point of observation of the universe's simplest laws, then computational aesthetics can only celebrate reason as being governed by the shortest program, the compression of data to the simplest form. For this interpretation of computational aesthetics, reason, logic, and calculation coincide with the compression of information as the subjective limit point of perception. The more compressible, predictable, and cognized an algorithmic form is, the more beautiful it is. Any new pattern is defined by the capacities of cognition to shrink complex information into increasingly compressed forms of data. Contrary to Chaitin's point that Super Omega radically challenges the "Theory of Everything,"[163] Schmidhuber takes self-delimiting algorithms as an opportunity for a cognitive grasp of complexity: a perceptual (or, in his own terms, "aesthetic") point of observation that attests to a computational theory of the universe.

However, the aesthetic significance of programming cultures points in exactly the opposite direction. Ubiquitous computing, for instance, aims at constructing a megaweb of data that is easily transferable between mediatic platforms. However, and despite all efforts to fuse distinct platforms into one smooth plane of compatibility, there is no ultimate, finite set of algorithms, no elegant formula, and no synthetic AI able to compress all data stored and produced in distinct databases. On the contrary, the algorithmic processing of data cannot but face the ingression of incomputable information at the edge of each cognitive act of perception, an ingression that serves to release the aesthetics of computation from its limited conceptualization in terms of a sequence of logical steps, opening it into a speculative function of reason.

In other words, insofar as low-complexity aesthetics focuses on a cognitive point of observation that is supposedly able to grasp nondenumerable complexity as short sets of algorithmic instructions, it admits no novelty into computation, as it merely associates the latter with inward-looking cognitive patterns of repetitive instructions. Aesthetics corresponds here not to the prehension of eternal forms, but to the capacities of perception and cognition to reduce abstract realities to comprehensible mathematical forms. Yet these realities cannot be cognized, since, as Chaitin also suggests, Omega and Super Omega do not fit into a complete formal system and do not lend themselves to being mere spontaneous intuitions of real or transcendental infinities.

The incompressible random infinity of Super Omega supersedes the binarism of zeroes and ones by way of an infinite sequence of increasingly random Omega that pushes computation into an extraspace of data. It is argued here that self-delimiting Super Omega infinities are random surplus values of code[164] that drive algorithmic rationality away from preordained functions, and toward a speculative aesthetics that is defined by the conceptual prehensions of indeterminate infinities. In short, if all programming cultures share an axiomatic space of short programs that runs beneath all spatiotemporal complexity, this is because that space is contagious, composed of randomly increasing quantities, and a locus wherein new axioms are ceaselessly added across platforms, categories, and domains. This means that the surplus value of codes is not a spontaneous accident that is added externally to programming algorithms, and with the unpredictability of algorithmic form. On the contrary, surplus values of codes reveal the noncognitive prehension of incomputable objects or discrete infinities.

Putting it crudely, the age of the algorithm reveals the limit of rationality and perception. Yet this limit does not simply coincide with an underlying mathematical ground that holds the secret beauty of the universe. Algorithmic architecture is not merely an abstract data structure. On the contrary, it is a digital form of design that shows that actual algorithmic objects are immanent abstract structures. These actual objects are physical and mental prehensions of data, physical and mental forms of computational process. But as algorithms are physical prehensions of data (sets of algorithms that come before and after), so too are they conceptual prehensions of their computational limit. The aesthetic significance of algorithmic architecture, therefore, corresponds neither to the elegance of coding nor to cognitive access to mathematical truths. On the contrary, my contention here is that a proper engagement with the aesthetics of algorithms entails a notion of prehension. This questions the axiomatic and rational reduction of complexity to simple rules, as prehensions allow complexity to enter *into* existing sets of data. In consequence, algorithmic prehensions may clarify how and why computation has become a form of speculative reason.

1.5 Speculative reason

The commonly accepted model of computational aesthetics is based on the equivalence between the function of reason and the shortest of programs, cognitive observation and reductive axiomatics. Here aesthetics means the cognition of beauty and the mathematical understanding of data structures. But, as argued in the previous sections, algorithmic objects are more than finite axiomatics and less than perceptual forms. They are prehensive actuals that drive the computational processing of physical and conceptual data. As prehensive actuals, these objects suggest that computation does not simply imply the calculation of probabilities (as already programmed results) but the search for incomputable data, or eternal objects, that are selected and incorporated within them. This means that computation can be further understood in terms of speculative reason, which, according to Whitehead, challenges both the formal and empirical model of reason based on the mind and the brain. From this standpoint, computation reflects neither the working of a formal mind nor the changes of a biological brain. Instead, computation is taken here as an example of a speculative reason that is concerned not with using numbers to predict the future, but with following algorithmic prehensions to decide the present. Algorithmic architecture is therefore but one example of the way in which this computation builds the present through the prehension of infinite data. Algorithmic architecture is thus a case of speculative computing exposing reason, logic, and calculation to the power of the incomputable. But how exactly does the notion of speculative reason become relevant to computation?

Whitehead believes that it is an error to understand rationality as a result of the biological evolution of animal intelligence—that the biological evolution of the brain or the biophysical apparatus of cognition can explain reason. In short, he discards *tout court* the necessity of a bias toward the empirical for ascertaining the workings of reason. Similarly, he insists that rationality does not coincide with formal (axiomatic or ideal) operations of intelligence. In short, the function of reason is not to be found in the formal or theoretical systems that determine whether things are true or not prior to their actual occurrence.[165]

In particular, Whitehead warns us against the dominance of two main views as to what the function of reason really is. In the first of these, reason is seen as the operation of theoretical realization, whereby the universe is a mere exemplification of a theoretical system. The model of computation that views the latter as the ontological processing of complex data through the simplest of programs coincides with this view. Similarly, Whitehead rejects the metacomputational universe advocated by Leibniz (e.g., the principle of sufficient reason), as it specifically seeks to capture in the shortest functions—or finite equations—the infinity of worlds. Here the principle of sufficient reason reduces the nexus of actual occasions to conceptual differences, since this principle defines how differences can be represented or mediated in a concept.[166] According to Whitehead, this one-to-one relation between mental cogitations and actual entities is insufficient to explain the speculative power of reason, which is instead an adventure of ideas that is irreproachable by any complete formalism. Secondly, his notion of speculative reason is also divorced from practical and pragmatic reason, the view that reason is a mere fact or factor of the world, or is explainable as an immediate method of action.[167] In algorithmic architecture, this notion of pragmatic reason would constitute the critical view according to which computational modeling must account for the contingent dynamics of physical worlds. This may be the view that sustains interactive models of architecture, such as the Hyperbody group's projects *InteractiveWall* and *Emotive Wall*, where algorithms are correlated to physical data, thereby suggesting that software programs are only one of the factors in the architecture of a responsive wall.

Whitehead's study of the function of reason sits comfortably neither with the formal nor the practical notion of reason and suggests instead that reason must be rearticulated according to the activity of *final* causation, and not merely by the law of the efficient cause.[168] The final cause of reason explains how conceptual prehensions are not reflections on material causes, but instead add new ideas to the mere inheritance of past facts. Conceptual prehensions are modes of valuation that open the fact of the past to the pressure of the future. Final cause, therefore, does not simply replace efficient cause or pragmatic reason, but rather defines a speculative tendency intrinsic to reason. Far from deploying the effective power of reason, this speculative tendency, according to Whitehead, explains how decisions and the selection of past data become the point at which novelty is added to the situation of the present. In other words, reason is the speculative calculation that defines the purpose of a theory and a practice: to make here and now different from the time and the space that were there before.

From this standpoint, one cannot explain the universe solely in terms of efficient causation or by physical interconnections, as these dangerously omit any prehensive counteragency for which there can be no direct observation, intuition, or immediate experience.[169] For instance, the view of a physical universe determined by physical laws cannot account for the counteragency of conceptual prehensions to which "[the physical universe] owes its possibility of existence as a wasting finite organism."[170] These counteragencies are operations of reason directed by purpose and explained by final causation. This is why, according to Whitehead, the function of reason is "to constitute, emphasize and criticize the final causes and strength of aims directed towards them."[171] This means that the function of reason serves to unlock new possibilities within the order of things. On the other hand, however, reason also explains "the existence of a universe in dissipation within a finite time,"[172] and thus serves to acknowledge that things perish and that the universe as we know it will ultimately wither away.

It would, however, be misleading to equate this notion of final cause or purpose with a teleological explanation of the universe, since for Whitehead the function of reason is "progressive and never final."[173] This means that the purpose of reason is attached to the physicality of things but does not stem from them. Similarly, purpose in reason does not have to be exclusively attributed to higher forms of intelligence. For Whitehead, all entities, lower and higher, have purpose. The essence of reason in the lower forms entails a *judgment* upon flashes of novelty that is defined by conceptual appetition (a conceptual lure toward, a tendency of thought upward) and not by action (reflexes or sensorimotor responses). However, according to Whitehead, stabilized life has no proper room for reason or counteragency since it simply engages in patterns of repetition. Reason, as the interweaving of efficient and final cause, is instead conceived here as an *organ of emphasis* upon novelty.[174] In particular, reason provides the judgment by which novelty passes into realization, into fact.[175]

Whitehead claims that reason is speculative: an urge for disinterested curiosity, where reason only serves itself, rather than being a reason for (and of) something else. Speculative reason "is its own dominant interest, and is not deflected by motives derived from other dominant interests which it may be promoting."[176] A tension can be noticed here between a notion of reason as governed by the purposes of some external dominant interests and those operations of reason that are governed by the immediate satisfaction (prehensive self-enjoyment) that arises from themselves.[177] It would be a mistake, therefore, to associate speculative reason with functional adaptations—and evolutionary optimization—of the biological brain triggered by the environment, or by the natural selection of the best-adapted form. It would also be a mistake to conceive of reason as the result of interactive factors, whereby, for instance, the physical environment creates the conditions for reason to become dynamic, or for programming to become open.

Whitehead insists that while the history of practical reason is related to the evolution of animal life, speculative reason only belongs to the history of civilization.[178] In other words, reason is more than an organ of evolution, and does not serve the evolution of biological life. Contrary to recent claims, according to which artificial networks based on the neurological structure of the brain reveal the workings of perception and cognition,[179] Whitehead insists that the function of reason is deployed by actualities, and by a multiplicity of prehensions (of whichever kind and dimension). The function of reason is therefore a speculative affair: it implies a leap toward general reasons beyond that of higher forms of biological life, and beyond a specific method. Speculative reason defines a propensity for thinking that takes place at the limits of reason, and that enters the dangerous territory of prehending beyond the fact of the past.

Speculative reason is built not upon a simple observation, a single set of empirical data or actualization of a program. As Whitehead points out, "an abstract scheme conforming to the methodology of logic, failing to achieve contact with fact through a correlate practical methodology of experiment, may yet be of utmost importance."[180] Thus, Whitehead admits that the function of reason—as speculative reason—precedes direct observation or the point of cognitive synthesis of empirical data. As he clearly puts it, "Nobody would count whose mind was vacant of the idea of number."[181] The speculative reason for numbering numbers cannot be reduced to the practical or actual counting of what is observable. Whitehead continues: "The novel observation which comes by chance is a rare accident, and is usually wasted. For if there be no scheme to fit it into, its significance is lost."[182] And yet speculative reason does not subsume the fact of numbered numbers to mere ideals. In other words, speculative reason is not a function of static ideas, but a quasi-formal computation able to prehend novel data.

But while physical prehensions are explained by efficient causation, mental prehensions are their inverse pole. In particular, mental experience "is the experience of forms of definiteness in respect to their disconnection from any particular physical experience, but with the abstract evaluation of what they can contribute to such experience."[183] And yet mental prehensions are not functions of consciousness or cognitive actions. Whitehead explains that at the lowest stage a mental prehension defines the lure toward a *form* of experience, "an urge towards a form for realization."[184]

What is realized is the infinity of data that is already there in actuality. Higher forms of intellectual experience, however, can only arise from the double integration of mental and physical experience. This allows reason to become more than reason, and to enter a second order of mentality: "the appetition of appetition."[185] This second order does not conform to facts but exposes the immanence of infinity, adding novelty to the continuity of things in which reason is "degraded to being merely one of the actors in the efficient causation."[186] Speculative reason is instead a second-order mentality defined not by reflection but by immanent thought in reason, which "canalizes its own operations by its own judgments" and thus becomes the counteragent of repetitive experience.[187]

Whitehead argues that the aim of speculative reason is the production of an abstract scheme.[188] Yet speculative reason must at once transcend and utilize these schemes. For reason to be truly speculative, the schemes that are produced and realized must be able to encounter their finitude and limits. "Abstract speculation has been the salvation of the world—speculations which made systems and then transcended them, speculations which ventured to the furthest limits of abstraction."[189] But how does this notion of speculative reason contribute toward challenging algorithmic aesthetics and the rational logic of computation?

It is suggested here that computation must be reconceived from the standpoint of speculative reason: the production of abstract schemes. But in order to do so, computation must be made to confront its limit in the fact that incomputable algorithms add infinite data at the core of its closed formal scheme. This means that just as computation has to be rethought in terms of speculative reason, so too must computation be conceived in the aesthetic terms of algorithmic prehensions: the counteragents of efficient cause adding novel data to what already exists. This is a speculative and not an ideal or material conception of computation that breaks from the continual feedback of the "chicken and egg circle" of ideal deduction and empirical proof. Algorithmic architectures are not simply ideal structures that have to acquire physical boundaries, but are actual forms of processes that have an existence beyond any predetermined mental form and physical fact. Algorithmic architectures therefore are abstract schemes that involve the automatic selection, inclusion, and exclusion of infinite amounts of data, a form of process that constructs computational spatiotemporalities.

Whitehead warns us against the trap of pure idealism, and insists that reason could not become speculative if experience, fact, evidence, and possibilities were completely dismissed. Yet, as he clarifies, experience is not simply the result of self-reflexivity or cognition of data. Experience is always more than consciousness and less than perception. Unlike Hume, Whitehead argues that experience is not the locus of clarity, and similarly that the mind is not the locus of connection. On the contrary, clarity and attention can only be transitory: a few glimpses of clarity here and a few moments of attention there are all that can be experienced. Clarity, or the presentation of objects, cannot be separated from the stretched edges hovering around the here and now. Clarity is nothing without vagueness, just as light cannot exist without darkness. Indeed, if objects become clear and distinct it is only because they are imbued with an infinite variety of infinities, which contributes to the individuation or the character of actual entities. This means that experience does not coincide with the (perceptual or cognitive) synthesis of data, or the shortest measure of complexity. On the contrary, experience cannot but be immanent to the limits of what can be sensed and cognized, as expressed by the function of a speculative reason that injects incomputable rules into each level of programmed response and inference. For experience to happen, in other words, there must be an immanent prehension of incomputable data.

For Whitehead, experience implies the equal intersection of mental and physical prehensions, but novelty in experience requires the selection of infinity. This also means that speculative reason does not operate through intuition or direct access to eternal objects. Eternal objects, therefore, are not the qualitative attributes of actual occasions, as Harman claims, but are instead data objects themselves that cannot be made dependent on the locus of experience.

On the other hand, experience as fact, evidence, and specificity exercises authority over the conceptual prehensions of eternal objects. Whitehead points out that even the utmost flight of speculative reason must be equipped with a measure of truth, which works not to restrict or delimit potentialities but rather becomes a quasi-empirical condition for potentialities to add novelty to the order of things. Ultimately, for Whitehead, speculative reason without the wide world of experience will always remain unproductive of novelty. Yet the relation between ideas and experience does not simply involve the interplay between the abstract and the concrete, the ideal and the material. Ideas are as real as facts, and yet facts are infected with the abstract though no less real schema of eternal objects that are ready to inject novel data into experience.

Whitehead explains that facts are not simply there to become evidence of speculative thoughts. On the contrary, the authority of facts lies in their elucidatory power. Indeed, speculative reason is also a mode of scanning worlds to find evidence for this elucidatory power. Thus, reason moves beyond immediate fact, and ultimately aims to prepare experience for the ingression of irreversible data (incomputable objects) into actual occasions.

The epochal challenge of programming cultures is to venture into the infinity of incomputable probabilities (infinite discrete unities that are bigger than the totality of the whole sequence of algorithmic instructions) that lies beyond both the digital ground and interactive empiricism. The age of the algorithm precisely marks the moment at which the limit of data programming (the limit of computation) unleashes the incompressible nature of information into experience. Programming cultures are therefore instances of the unintended consequences of ubiquitous computing, the algorithmic background of which has been infected by incomputable probabilities. Programming cultures are the new operators of the speculative functions of reason, which point at a new aesthetic computation driven not by ideal forms but rather by algorithmic prehensions of random data.

It would, however, be wrong to view this state of incomputable chaos with naive enthusiasm. Instead, it is important to address the reality of algorithmic objects without overlooking the fact that the computation of infinity is at the core of logic, rationality, order, and control. This concern with incomputable probabilities, or with Omega, is therefore a concern with the transformation of automated functions of reason, cognition, and perception. This is not to be confused with a call for an underpinning mathematical ontology, able to adequately describe the truth of being. Instead, Omega shakes the mathematical ground of truth by revealing that the probability for infinity is an algorithmic affair that defines a nonhuman automated thought. My argument in this chapter has been that algorithmic objects are precisely these forms of automated thought, and that they unleash the immanence of a variety of infinities in computation.

One should thus partially reject Friedrich Kittler's suggestion that the end of the certainties of binary mathematics also marks the end of ontological thought.[190] According to Kittler, the ontological thought of technical machines needs to be seen through the trinity of commands, addresses, and data (processing, transmission, and storage). However, he also contends that the alliance of ontological thought and mathematics is now hiding a difficult truth, a truth that was already announced by parallel and quantum states of computation, which will soon replace big and serial silicon connections. According to Kittler, this technical transformation announces the point at which philosophy, as the ontological problem of thought, will reach a veritable end. Thus the end of digital media (the binary system of computation) also announces the end of philosophical thought, which is replaced by the triumph of practical reason, wherein thought is engendered by material, contingent, and varying processes (defined by quantum and/or analog computing).

It is easy to agree with Kittler that the end of the silicon-based computational model also marks the terminal phases of a metaphysics based on the binary model of thought (the formal axiomatics reducing physical contingencies to strings of finite algorithms). The terminal phases of this world may perhaps also imply the end of philosophy and its dichotomies between mind and matter, the ideal and the material. Nevertheless, it is equally easy to challenge Kittler's critique of software, insofar as it is based on the equation of thought to binary computation, and of philosophy to all modes of thought.[191] In particular, the relation in which thought stands to finite axiomatics as axiomatics stands to thought completely overlooks (1) that thought is not the same as binary computation, although automated thoughts are real; (2) that computation if anything is incomplete, and a Turing machine cannot offer a finite solution to the complex infinities of thought; (3) that algorithms are the conceptual prehensions of incomputable data or eternal objects, which have no biophysical ground in human thought (and in the ontological question of philosophy).

Regardless of whether quantum bits will mark the end of digital computation as we know it, or whether analog and quantum computing will expose thought to the material indeterminacies of atomic particles/waves, it still remains problematic to associate thought with a binary logic of finite states, and to make hardware the ground of software. Not only does this argument risk locking the ontological premises of thought into a monolithic philosophical system: in addition, it also overlooks the significance of incompleteness in computation, in terms of the capacities of automated thought to take decisions beyond original programming. As will be discussed in chapter 3, it is the immanence of chaos in algorithmic thought (or soft thought) that has come to threaten the idea that the automatic operations of computation are merely equivalent to or can be used to explain the *neuroarchitecture* of reason, and vice versa that neural networks are the spine subtending the architecture of thought. While the ontological claims for a universal computational machine proposed by digital philosophers pose cellular automata as the ultimate building blocks of reason, the incomputable algorithms discovered by Gregory Chaitin make use of the way in which the complexity of real numbers defies the grounding of thought in finite axiomatics. It is precisely the arrival of infinity in computational modes of thought that reveals the significance of speculative reason in the postcybernetic logic of control.

In chapter 2, this postcybernetic logic, in which axioms can be infinitely added into the automatic programming of physical variables, will be explained through the example of parametric architecture, which is an instance of the computation of topological (continuous) relations between parts. In particular, parametricism is an architectural style that uses parametric software to model urban space and behavior by including contingent relations in software programming. This chapter argues that the nature of formalism in design has changed, and that algorithmic rules are now exposed to *intended* indeterminacies built into the software itself. Parametric architecture, it will be argued, moves beyond responsive or interactive environments, because it is not just based on temporal variations (or intensive quantities) but rather, and significantly, on a new, quantitative ordering of spatiotemporal regions. Parametric architecture arguably offers a novel conception of space, which is described by the continuity of topological surfaces for smooth control. Similarly, however, it also implies a new "extensification" (a new potentiality for division) of abstract quantities into the spatiotemporal regions of parametric urbanism. *Parametricism* therefore reveals the algorithmic operations of a speculative rationality that is other than human, and is defined by the algorithmic prehension of physical and abstract data.

Whitehead's notion of mereotopology[192] and his atomic conception of time, which we will look at in the following chapter, will contribute toward explaining how the control of spatiotemporal relations now includes relations among wholes, parts, and parts of parts. This implies that control operates not only to ensure intensive or topological continuity between entities, but also to program the becoming of continuity itself. In other words, the question of control is now as follows: how can that which relates to itself become? To put it crudely, postcybernetic control is now concerned with the programming of events: with the nexus of spatiotemporalities infected with abstract objects.

However, if speculative rationality is at the core of postcybernetic control, this is not because its operations are rooted in biodigital systems of embodied cognition, based on interactive and neural network models. The attempt to eliminate all instances of abstract objects from the understanding of thought, perception, and cognition only amounts to ubiquitous computing's need to eliminate the immanence of abstraction altogether. As we will see in chapter 3, the computational design of spatiotemporality has been used to understand the cognitive and perceptual architecture of the brain, as modeled, for instance, through neural networks. However, this paradigmatic shift toward neurological architectures of thought (from notions of embodied cognition to notions of the extended mind), which routes thought into material substrates (whether these are animate or inanimate), only risks equating the reality of algorithmic objects with the mathematical or biological grounds of thought. This equation only works to disqualify the significance of algorithmic objects and incomputable probabilities vis-à-vis an understanding of thought that goes beyond the ontological premises (qua being and mathematical axiomatics) of philosophical thought.

This equation also fails to consider that although one tendency of postcybernetic control is to create a neoergonomic architecture of affective computation, another more subtle implication precisely corresponds to the failure of empirical functionalism to address the ontology of algorithmic entities and of incomputable objects without patterns. The more thought is embedded in computational apparatuses of cognition and perception, the more algorithmic objects unleash the incomputable data that cannot be synthesized, summed up, or simply instantiated in smaller programs (or in one totalizing form of thought).

Similarly, models of power relying on the continual regeneration of form and the autopoietic reenaction of thought as environment are no longer sufficient to explain how control has become an operation of prehension/*pre-emption*, to borrow from Brian Massumi, with power prehending (anticipating) its own limits/potentialities (the control of control). The advance of anticipatory architectures of power instead coincides with the proliferation of programming cultures (from DNA, bacteria, or stem cell cultures, to cultures of sounds and images, to time-based cultures or cultures of space modeling) that prehend the incomputable abstractions that follow fact, but which are not engendered by it.

This means that our postcybernetic culture is dominated not by the suprasensory bombardment of too much information, but by the algorithmic prehensions of incomputable data. This new form of prehension announces an aesthetic battlefield between the incompatible worlds of neurons and silicon chips, nanobots and blood vessels, the microcircuitry of computerized media and bodily temperature, software modeling and controlled gestures, actuators and programmed behaviors, which together deploy not a transparent apparatus of communication but instead a fractal architecture of events (an incompatible infinite nexus of spatiotemporalities). This aesthetic battlefield coincides neither with the presence of inaccessible real objects (as Harman would have it) nor with their readiness to be directly sensed.

In the age of the algorithm, space and matter have not become indistinguishable because the rules of modeling are common to all actual objects that originate from a physical substrate. If this were so, the age of the algorithm would simply be another instance of idealized empiricism, where actualities can only ever be enacted from a biophysical ground that is without any abstraction. Algorithmic architecture instead offers us the opportunity to conceive data in terms of spatiotemporal objects, which reveal the abstract architectures of space and time. But these architectures do not aim at predicting the future: instead, they reveal that immanent programming is at work in the present. Algorithmic architecture, as an instance of postcybernetic control, deploys incomputable objects in the programming of spatiotemporalities. This new mode of control, which places patternless data at the core of computation, will be the topic of the next chapter.

2 Soft Extension: Topological Control and Mereotopological Space Events

2.0 The invariant function

With the introduction of computational processing into urban design, digital space no longer represents a Euclidean matrix of points established by Cartesian coordinates.[1] Instead, digital space has become an evolving structure of relations. Software design has turned the Euclidean grid of discrete points into a morphogenetic form: a form that emerges from local relations that change over time. The computational programming of urban settings has replaced the urban plan with a topological schema of variations that is directed by the capacity of algorithms to evolve and to be affected by external contingencies in *real* time. Examples can be found in software design used to model urban infrastructural water systems (sewer systems, storm water drainage systems, water distribution systems), or in the more general digital design of prototype systems that include data and models for land use (geographic information systems, GIS transportation analysis, cost estimation, energy usage, water, noise, airflows, etc.); both respond to changing conditions and calculate the evolution of urban behavior in given circumstances.

In chapter 1, I argued that a consideration of algorithmic architecture can assist us in understanding algorithms as actual objects: as spatiotemporal data structures that are internally conditioned by infinities as incomputable entities. This chapter will look at how the computation of spatial relations has led to surfaces of continuous variations, in which the physical distance between points has been transformed into a temporal variation. Distance here corresponds to a moving ratio[2] that defines points as they grow, adapt, and evolve together while generating that surface anew. I will suggest that the computational processing of data coincides with the introduction of time into the Euclidean geometry of points, and that this leads to end results that are alien to their initial conditions. This is a speculative mode of computation that has placed *intensity* in the calculation of probabilities. Here the binary order of on/off states has been superseded by the calculation of a moving ratio between points: an approximation, or an indeterminate probability.

If the binary bits of on and off states have characterized the digital design of maps, points, and lines, the introduction of algebraic topology in computation has made it possible for digital design to calculate the distance between points by means of the *invariant function*. Approximations, and not positions, have thereby come to constitute the continual variation of the total dynamics of space: space no longer corresponds to the digital matrix of individual points, but to a topological surface.[3]

This chapter argues that the computation of relations coincides with a postcybernetic mode of preemption.[4] The latter will be examined through examples of digital design, and particular emphasis will be placed on those afforded by digital urbanisms. Much of the debate about preemption has described how cybernetic strategies of control involve the anticipation of the future threat in present conditions of diffused fear.[5] Less attention has been paid to the way in which preemption, as a speculative mode of spatiotemporal programming, has led to the design of a continuous surface of variations: a topological space of control.

It is suggested here that strategies of preemption do not only correspond to the harnessing of potentialities into already rehearsed possibilities, and to the reduction of potentials to set probabilities. On the contrary, I will argue that strategies of preemption also require that potentialities—or what Alfred North Whitehead calls "eternal objects"—become determined in existing actualities, which are understood here as algorithmic objects (in the form of codes, parameters, and protocols) that add new spatiotemporal relations or space events on the extensive continuum.[6] Since actual entities, as Whitehead observes, determine (select and evaluate) potentialities, I will argue that these entities have become *hosts* to eternal objects, which only enter into a relation with one another once they are selected and reach a unique togetherness in actualities. However, this unprecedented uniqueness is not simply negotiated by actualities. While Whitehead suggests that actual entities increase and decrease the valence of certain eternal objects vis-à-vis that of others, and while he holds that they can positively and negatively prehend pure potentialities, I will argue that these potentialities are also indifferent to specific actual entities, which include indeterminate quantities of chance within their processes of formation. In other words, whether these indeterminate quantities are selected or not, their infective existence is nonnegotiable. As will be observed below, the unilateral power of abstract entities to infect the actual order of things is precisely revealed by the relational space of actualities. In particular, this chapter will explain how digital space, which is now defined by continual relations, has become the site for the expression of the unilateral power of abstract entities, and in doing so it will set out the implications this holds for the analysis of contemporary forms of power.

I will therefore argue that the computation of the distance between algorithmic objects points to at least two contrasting operations of post-cybernetic control: to a topological mode concerned with the fusion of objects into one continual surface of variations, and to a *mereotopology* of relations between actualities—atomic spatiotemporalities, or parts that connect to one another but which cannot be summed up into a whole. In what follows, I will first explain how the computation of topological relations indicates that control now anticipates (and does not repress) change before it is actualized, and rather uses change to program new actualities. The motor of this mode of control, I will argue, is topological isomorphism: a mathematical function able to calculate continuity in variation.[7]

As the computational power of managing and calculating data has become extended to the design of urban scenarios, real-time variations have been included within software programs so as to anticipate the emergence of potential changes. For instance, the computation of urban data is an example of parametric planning that is defined by an extended apparatus of prediction, which is able not only to establish the condition of the present through the retrieval of data from the past, but also, significantly, to change these conditions according to variations that are automatically derived from the environment. From this standpoint, the cybernetic logic of control has disclosed its mechanisms of value and measure to nonquantifiable conditions in order to capture qualitative changes *prior* to their emergence. However, these mechanisms of anticipation, which are concerned with pro-programming (or actively programming) scenarios, are not simply defined by the mathematics of division and addition, and similarly do not just rely on off and on states of 0s and 1s. What is new here is that these mechanisms now seem to rely on the topological calculation of the continuous function, which is an invariant property that fills the gap between binary digits.

The computation of this topological continuity has characterized urban design and particularly *parametricism*, which Patrick Schumacher has claimed to be the new global style for architecture and design.[8] When applied to large-scale urbanism, for instance, parametricism uses the invariant function to transform the differential distance between points into an integral form of continual variation. From this standpoint, parametricism implies the inclusion of contingent values (e.g., atmospheric, geological, biological, physical variables), which are variable parameters that change over time. This means that variables, for instance, are not only added to the program (as if from the "outside") but rather partake of the software environment of parametric relations. Parametric programming is therefore not just concerned with the computation of possible (already existing or actual) elements, but also, and significantly, with how intensive relations between finite parameters can engender new smooth spaces.

From this standpoint, parametricism—the new global style of fluid architecture—is a manifestation of the "cultural logic of late neoliberalism,"[9] whose postcybernetic relational operations of positive feedback, structural coupling, and mutual correspondence are now defining the ubiquitous surface of smooth design. This is not a new argument, however, and to a degree it is separate from the issues that I aim to pursue here. I am not specifically concerned with criticizing parametricism or its excessive formalism for its inability to address infrastructural issues and the political implications of lived space. Instead of arguing that parametricism promises a formally open-ended and flexible space that does not physically match realized architectures, and instead of contending that parametricism is the direct incarnation of the spirit of the neoliberal market, I would suggest instead that parametricism is not abstract enough to meet the possibilities offered by a radical formalism. This means that a critical approach to parametricism does not and cannot disqualify the computational logic of spatial relations simply on the grounds that it is an expression of a neoliberal architecture aiming to neutralize political questions concerning, for instance, the infrastructural fabric of urbanism and its geological, geographical, and historical complexities. While I do not mean to deny that parametricism is an instance of postcybernetic control, I also want to problematize the rejection *tout court* of the agential character of computer programming and the actuality of parametric objects.[10] This chapter suggests that these software objects are necessarily implicated in the sociality that they invisibly structure. The stealthy intrusion of computational programming into everyday culture requires a close engagement with the nuances within the digital apparatus that sustains such culture. I want to point out that the new topological architecture of relations expressed by parametricism is precisely what needs to be challenged in order to reveal the transformation that the computation of relation has brought to digital formalism. A close analysis of this transformation may help us to explain how structural changes in programming are not negligible, but are in fact ontological expressions of culture and power. This analysis may also contribute toward separating computational agency from its immediate and direct identification with the structure of power, and thus toward indicating the incongruence, asymmetry, and nonequivalence between soft control and soft events. As may become clearer later, this nonequivalent relation describes the inconsistent and contrasting operations of software: the preemptive design of smooth space under the continuity of time and the computational production of space-time, adding new actualities to what is already there.

One immediate level of transformation that parametricism exerts upon digital formalism may be its attempt to incorporate contingencies into formal language by including real-time data in software programming. However, the introduction of temporality into computational programming does not fully challenge formalism. Instead, I argue that it affords formalism the pretension of describing how mathematics can explain physics by creating a system of relations, or a responsive feedback with the biophysical environment, according to which a few mathematical rules (or complete axioms) can unravel the evolution of complex physical structures. This means that the topological ontology of parametricism does not in fact challenge formalism: instead, it may appear as the reification of formalism, aiming to include all sorts of contingencies within its all-encompassing program. We will see below that in order to rethink formalism it is necessary to unpack its internal limits, and thereby to search for its internal anomalies or incomputable infinities.

In what follows, I will use parametricism or parametric aesthetics to suggest that the topological approach to urban design is based on the introduction of qualitative variations and temporal evolution in the predictive calculation of data, aiming to account for potential changes in urban scenarios. Here software interactions with the real data of the environment have become constitutive of postcybernetic control. Instead of simply reducing biophysical variables and contingencies to sets of binary codes, which are unable to process the gray areas between sequences, digital design now implies the integration of differential relations, or intensive data within the generation of spatiotemporal forms. The introduction of the invariable function in urban design thus reveals that postcybernetic control now relies on the calculation of differentials and uncertainties. This is evidenced in the computation of urban design by the use of growing algorithms, or open-ended instructions that respond and adapt to the external environment, and thus introduce chance into the calculation of probabilities.

This chapter will then discuss the particular case of parametricism, arguing that parametric aesthetics is a new mode of computational programming that relies on the capacities of parameters to create a relational field of emergence. From this standpoint, parametric aesthetics also suggests that this new mode of control has developed its own aesthetic form, which has been associated with folds, morphologies, smooth surfaces, and real-time evolving structures. In other words, control, as the computation of topological space, has acquired a sensuous skin that turns all points, sees all corners, and connects all lines into planes of relations, short circuits of immediate connection or speedy paths of variation. Here there is no core, no end point, and no individual response: only the continuous fluctuation of a total form enveloping an infinite series of parts.

The parametric transformation of digital formalism needs to be analyzed within the wider issue of the mathematical formalization of the relation between finite and infinite sets. To that end, I briefly address the mathematical formalization of the continuum problem and the systematization of infinitesimals, both of which lead to the development of topology. The Leibnizian quest for infinitesimals together with Deleuze's concept of differential relations will be considered here as crucial to the ontological constitution of topology, which is now manifested with a new formalism in modes of computational design that are based on contingent variabilities and temporalities. Parametric aesthetics, however, does not resolve but rather inherits the ontomathematical diatribe about the nature of extension, which is said to correspond either to a field of continual variations (determined by an underlying infinitesimal series) or to a sequence of spatiotemporalities that are able to connect and disconnect.

I discuss this view by emphasizing the contrast between topology and its aesthetics of smooth control on the one hand and mereotopology on the other. The latter, I argue, contributes to describe the existence of an asymmetry between topological formalism and what I will refer to here as *space events*. These space events are actual architectures of relation that define what cannot be reduced to topological control: the probability of chaos, the unilateral indetermination of data within computation, and at another level the unleashing of unlived reality into urban design.

From this standpoint, parametric aesthetics reveals that the topological mode of calculating relations—a mode wherein all parts become incorporated into a multidimensional, evolving whole—does not exhaust the ways in which one might conceive space in terms of relations, and neither does it fully accommodate the contention that digital space can be seen as an algorithmic sequence of relations. On the contrary, parametric aesthetics necessarily involves the quantification of data in terms of parameters: parameters that cannot be overlooked, because quantities cannot be smoothly dissolved into continual degrees of qualitative changes. Another reason why parametricism remains an interesting example of postcybernetic control is thus that it points toward the persistent irreducibility of parts and of the relations between parts, in which wholes are nothing more than parts that connect. These parts—in this case, parametric quantities in computational programming—are discrete entities that change values at different places according to different degrees of relations established by the program and the environmental input due not only to their capacity to select data that come from the actual ground, but also to their capacity to be infected by data that they are not able to compute. As noted above, this aspect of parametric aesthetics will be explained through Whitehead's notion of mereotopology, because the relation between parts and parts and wholes can be seen to lie at the core of his notion of extension or extensive continuum.

Whitehead's mereotopological schema rejects the Leibnizian infinitesimal series and questions Henri Bergson's predilection for temporal continuity by arguing that what connects points are actual entities on an extensive continuum. It may be important to clarify here that I will not be using the Whiteheadian case of mereotopology and its schema of discontinuous relations as a simple alternative to the topological model of power expressed by parametricism and its digital formalism, which uses vectorial tools as instruments of control. Instead, Whitehead's mereotopological schema provides an apposite means of suggesting that there is no ontological or metaphysical equivalence between the topological architecture of control and the spatiotemporality of events; that there is no such equivalence between parts and between parts and wholes. With mereotopology, in other words, there is no presumed reciprocity between control and events. Topological continuities are expressions of large assemblages, and these assemblages are able to incorporate discontinuous events into a stream of infinitesimal variations; yet such events are not definable by infinitesimal or temporal continuities. Instead, they are nexuses of extensions, spaces or parts that occur beyond negotiations. They cannot be the result of a relational continuity between infinitesimal points, and instead account for the unalterable friction between parts and between wholes that can become parts.

This chapter will also use parametricism as an example of the operative system of control that is defined by the computation of infrastructural networks: the smooth architecture of continual variations that changes the values of parameters by responding to real data from the environment. In such instances, parametricism pertains to the way control operates as a prehensive apparatus of spatiotemporal futurities. Control, as Brian Massumi has brilliantly explained, is a mechanism of anticipation, whereby the *apprehension* of unknown variables indirectly works to determine the reality of the present.[11] If topological control works, it is because what can be anticipated corresponds to what actually has to happen, foreclosing the conditions of uncertainties into preset probabilities within the present.

However, the mereotopological schema also offers another understanding of parametricism, according to which the latter can be viewed as a computation of relations that shows how parameters can themselves be conceived as actual entities that enter into a nexus of spatiotemporalities, the relations of which are discontinuous compared to the overall process of continual variation. The very strategy of anticipation of spatiotemporalities in digital urbanism inversely contributes to the diffusion of unintended parametric actualities into computational culture. These actualities are understood here as computational space events. Events, according to Whitehead, involve the capacity of any actual entity (organic or inorganic) to become a host of pure data objects (or eternal objects in Whitehead's terminology), which define how the indeterminate becomes determinate in any actual entity, no matter how small or inorganic this is.

Whitehead's mereotopological schema implies that events come first. They are the summation of actual entities in a nexus of actualities, which has been infected by infinite amounts of pure data that have come together for the first, unique and unrepeatable space-time. From this standpoint, the chapter will contrast the topological view of parametric aesthetics, which assumes that variations are to be derived from the relational or *infinitesimal points* of contingencies which lie outside the program (and which are then programmed within the urban model, for instance), with the mereotopological insistence that parts, quantities, and discontinuities exist not only at the level of actualities but also at the general level of formality. This means that Whitehead's mereotopological schema forces us to revisit the computational significance of formal hierarchies in relation to actual contingencies. Contingencies are no longer to be conceived as external to the formal schema (i.e., as a mere factor of extrinsic force); instead, this chapter argues that contingency and chance are in fact internal to any formal processing; that they are parts of that formal process and nonetheless remain incompatible with the synthetic form of the whole. This means that these parts are patternless quantities, internal to any logic of computation. They are the incomputable probabilities of any mathematical, physical, or biological order that extend throughout computational culture.

From this standpoint, parametricism can be criticized not for being too abstract, but for not being abstract enough to accommodate the view that indetermination is to be found first of all at the level of formal computation, because it is there that parameters encounter the indeterminate conditions (patternless data) for which they can become eventful. This idea of computational indetermination is based on the mathematical logic of randomness (i.e., lack of structure), whereby "something is random if it can't be compressed into a shorter description. In other words, there is no concise theory that produces it."[12] As discussed in chapter 1, Gregory Chaitin's algorithmic information theory sets incompleteness within axiomatics to show that randomness explains the incomputable as the maximally unknowable and irreducible data within computation. Since it is impossible to calculate the size of the smallest program, as Turing and Gödel demonstrated, Chaitin concludes that computational logic implies a program size complexity, whereby it is the program (the software, the theory, or formalism) and not just its application that shows the existence of patternless infinities, which drive decision making within any algorithmic set.

I will not use the example of parametricism to claim that novelty in computation is to be derived from external factors, or for instance from means of interaction between software and hardware, which supposedly explains, according to some designers, how digital urbanism can develop dynamic planning and adaptable infrastructures. Instead, my argument is driven by the possibility offered by the mereotopological schema of finding the conditions for novelty in the noncommunicating architecture of eternal objects—incomputable quantities—as they are or are not selected by actual entities. Eternal objects therefore are not just eternal qualities of objects, such as the intensive qualification of a chair that constitutes its *chairness* (the capacity of the chair to function as a seat). On the contrary, taking inspiration from Whitehead's mereotopological schema, I argue that eternal objects are infinite parts that acquire relational continuity only once they enter, are selected by, or infect actualities. Hence, a whole as a relational continuity is a discrete unity, a part that exists in this actual entity and not in any other. A whole, that is, is neither smaller nor bigger than its parts but is split into parts or partialities that do not necessarily communicate with one another (i.e., they do not communicate by means of a principle of sufficient reason).

This chapter perhaps forces a juxtaposition of the formal level of incomputable data with the formal schema of eternal objects. But this forcing is not arbitrary. It is simply a means of arguing for the underestimated significance of infinite quantities of data in computational programming of space and digital architecture. It is suggested here that the nonnegotiable power of incompressible data (i.e., data that cannot be compressed in an elegant theory, theorem, or program) is the very condition for a digital formalism that does not simply extend software to an interactive relation with hardware or with the physical environment. From this standpoint, mereotopological discontinuity is not conceived as an alternative to the topological form of power, which is, as argued above, ontologically grounded in relational continuity. If anything, the mereotopological schema of discontinuous data can help us to reveal that the predictive apparatus of postcybernetic control, which according to Massumi is a preemptive power, is not the same as the incomputable operations of the event. The latter instead, contrary to control, requires that indeterminate data become decisional quantities in the cumulative processing of nonequivalent actualities. These indeterminate data are not simply subsumed within an extant (albeit changing) process. Instead, they define spatiotemporal events, which arrive and perish, without constituting a continual surface of variation.

To put it in another way: the topological ontology of parametricism describes the operations of preemption as the moment at which the event is programmed before it can happen, thus flattening control and novelty (or event) onto a topological matrix of continual coevolution, reciprocal presupposition, or structural coupling. Yet against this, and while borrowing from Whitehead's mereotopological schema of relation, it is possible to suggest that parts cannot become a whole: instead, parts (e.g., eternal objects) can join together and become a whole (the unity of eternal objects in actual entities) that itself remains a part (an actual entity) that connects to another (actual entity). This is also to say that if the parametric aesthetics of topological control anticipates and thus harnesses events in its own morphogenetic body, mereotopology reveals that events are blind spots, cut-breaking spatiotemporalities that explain the becoming of the extensive continuum: the arrival of a new spatiotemporality out of sync with a system of relations *qua* smooth variations.

Against the metaphysics of the whole (Being, Time, or God), Whitehead's mereotopology suggests that the relations between actualities are to be explained by actual parts. Similarly, I propose that the critical reading of digital architecture (arguing that the latter is somehow mirroring the neoliberal form of the market) cannot reduce spatiotemporal parts or actualities to the neoliberal operations of governmentality. These parts, I claim, are conditioned by nondenumerable infinities or the immanent power of incomputable data. Since digital architecture and neoliberal governmentality both capitalize on the capacity of relations to smooth edges and permeate boundaries, it seems important to engage with the question of relationality itself in order to demystify the dominance of the postcybernetic feedback of topological continuity. In particular, I argue that the calculation of variation that characterizes the preemptive character both of neoliberalism (e.g., the anticipation of change as a mode of decision) and of digital architecture/urbanism (through the inclusion of real-time changes within planning through parametric software) is being underdetermined by the actuality of parametric relations.

From this standpoint, parametricism (or the computation of relationality) is not simply another instance of the power of the neoliberal market, the system of governmentality of which is equivalent to the smooth environment of ubiquitous digitality. On the contrary, parametricism can instead be taken to suggest that the preemptive capitalization of change, futurity, and potentiality is in fact exposed to computational interferences, blind spots or space events that cannot be compressed in smaller programs of control.

Events, therefore, do not grant continuity between entities, but on the contrary are the occasions for the discontinuous becoming of the continual order of actualities. This explanation, however, only helps us to describe the actual level of novel spatiotemporality. Actual novelty instead does not come from nowhere, and does not exclusively concern the physical realm. Novelty must also be explained at the level of abstract formalism. The mereotopological schema of eternal objects and actual entities proposed by Whitehead affords metaphysical support to what in information theory is increasingly becoming unavoidable: the presence of the incomputable at the heart of formalism. This reality of incomputable random data (the fact that incomputable data are now a probability and not an impossibility for computational programming) is here taken as the condition that makes any mode of computation (analog or digital) possible.

This condition has to be found within the computational processing of algorithms, at the formal and axiomatic level. It is suggested here that incomputable data can reveal a strange contingency within form, or chance within programming. From this standpoint, incomputable algorithms interrupt the topological coevolution of urban software and urban behavior. Far from establishing a continuous feedback or reversible function whereby software takes command over urban behavior or the latter acts back on the program, the sequential running of algorithms will instead expose the incomputable quantities of rules for the infinite qualities of behaviors, which are unprovable and inapplicable spatiotemporalities. Here control becomes as patternless as the incomputable data that it tries to compress into axioms. It is my argument that the incomputable triggers contingent rules within computational programming and, in the particular case addressed by this chapter, in the digital design of urban space.

This new dominance of contingency within programming demarcates the unquantifiable reality of a space event and the impossibility for control to be one with these events. In particular, digital urbanism points at computational events that are at once discovered and constructed by the software programming of unlived spatiotemporal relations. From this standpoint, the present chapter takes parametricism as a case in which the digital design of time and space not only controls (or preempts) the emergence of events, but is unleashing unlived urban worlds into the spatiotemporal programming of the everyday. These space events are symptoms of the concreteness of digital architecture, which, it is now clear, can never absolutely match the political sentiment for a progressive change in social behavior. I do not consider this mismatch to be a failure. Instead it points at a schizophrenic and nonreversible situation whereby the programs used to organize urban infrastructure are instead constructing or revealing an infrastructure of another kind, thereby exposing the all too real realm of data volumes, data density, and data architecture.

It may be useful, here at the outset, to map out the argument that will be developed in this chapter. Before discussing the case of parametricism, I will address the ontological notion of relational space in digital design. I will then explain the mathematical formalization of relations with reference to Leibniz's notion of infinitesimals and Deleuze's notion of differential calculus[13] by analyzing recent examples of parametric and interactive urbanism. In particular, I will discuss 5Subzero's work on the design of responsive environments, and I will take as a key example their *Topotransegrity* project. The second section of the chapter will introduce Whitehead's notion of extension and his atomic theory of time, which envisages the possibility for simultaneity not only between actual entities but also between actualities within the same actual object. As opposed to Bergson's notion of duration and his suspicion of discreteness, Whitehead instead offers us an understanding of actualities as modes of determinations of space and time. In a series of subsections I will discuss how Whitehead's nontemporal metaphysics accounts for actual events.

Against the idea of a shared time, Whitehead argues that the blind spots between actualities are defined by extendedness. In other words, there are always actuals amid actuals. This discussion will lead to the analysis of Whitehead's notion of mereotopology, as the latter clarifies that the space between points is not an infinitesimal series of smaller points, but rather the accumulation of actualities: a nexus or event imbued with eternal objects. The mereotopological architecture of actuality, therefore, is not the same as the mereotopological schema of eternal objects; yet these nonequivalent objects immanently construct spatiotemporalities, which become added to the nexus of the extensive continuum.

The last section of the chapter argues that parametric urbanism introduces a new mode of programming extension that is driven by prehensive potentialities for spatiotemporal division, as parameters do not simply quantify urban qualities of relations, but rather select abstract quantities of relations. The chapter will end with a detailed analysis of R&Sie(n)'s project *Une architecture des humeurs* (2010), as this provides an apposite means of discussing the mereotopological order in terms of the relations between physical variables, actual parameters, and indeterminate quantities of data. In this case, parametricism is not simply an instance of software that is adaptable to external stimuli, but involves the internal re-*scripting* of programs: the insertion of random quantities into the parametric order of relations. For instance, R&Sie(n) architect François Roche suggests that parametric scripting cannot be equated to a sequential programming, or to a binary quantification of physical variables or qualities. R&Sie(n)'s projects are instead computational speculations into the power of scripting that are intended to include *malentendues*—indeterminate quantities, data, numbers, codes, and protocols—in the programming of relations.

R&Sie(n)'s *Une architecture des humeurs* will help us to explain that parametric relations include abstract objects: the *malentendues* or indeterminate quantities (eternal objects) that are prehended by or that infect actual parameters (variable quantities). From this standpoint, R&Sie(n)'s project stages a mereotopology of abstract and actual objects that is defined by an automated prehension of data, and which programs a space event of another kind.[14] If parameters are not simply logical instantiations of procedures based on finite terms, but are rather determined by sets of infinities, then they are themselves parts that connect to the physical order of continuity. This means that digital parametricism adds a new level of extension to the mathematical and physical grounds of space. Whether this soft extension can account for new spatiotemporalities depends on the degree to which parametricism can be challenged by that which sustains it: namely, automated modes of prehension.

R&Sie(n)'s project shows how the abstraction of physical data is determined neither by digital axioms nor by the interaction between biophysical inputs and software. On the contrary, *Une architecture des humeurs* defines extension as the relation between distinct levels of actualities, where hormonal data is abstracted into algorithms that constitute the parametric values of evolving shapes. These morphological shapes undergo a hyperlocal brick calculation, performed by a robot named Viab02, which registers the parametric changes and "secretes" a vertical structure composed of tiny and asymmetrical shapes. These shapes interlock with one another in an infinite series that moves up and down the structure. The shapes are regions and subregions and host distinct quantities of data, which offer asymmetric extensions: extensive novelties resulting from the automated prehensions of random quantities, entropic information, or *malentendues* that are inherent to biophysical data, parametric order, and robotic actions. Far from constituting an impediment to the computational design of relations, *malentendues* point instead to the blind spots that exist in the relation between terms. In other words, *malentendues* correspond to the probability of indeterminacy within the digital computation of relations: to the power that random quantity possesses of stirring unilateral (or nonnegotiable) contagion within the parametric programming of culture.

What is at stake here is the manner in which parametricism has permeated the programming of extension, but also how automated prehensions have unleashed incomputable probabilities into everyday culture. Postcybernetic control harnesses dysfunctions, errors, and crisis by axiomitizing the irreversible advance of randomness, but it also works to script uncertainties within the programming of relations. Similarly, insofar as parametricism can be understood as an instance of the mereotopological schema of actual and abstract extensions, it also reveals that the regime of preemption does not foreclose potentialities, but rather requires that spaces of chaos enter digital control. Before discussing the tensions between topological and mereotopological parametricism, however, it may be useful to clarify how algebraic topology has entered the field of digital design.

2.1 Folds or differential relations

The invariant function of continual transformation is now central to digital computation. It has shifted the culture of binary digits toward the calculation of temporal quantities in finite sets of algorithmic instructions and parameters. This topological computation involves operative procedures of control, which now constantly add new axioms at the limit of other axioms through an invariant function that establishes a smooth (uninterrupted) connectivity between distinct parameters. The establishment of a continual function between distinct forms of data is based on homeomorphism or topological isomorphism between objects and places. Parametricism, which Schumacher claims to be the new global style for architecture and design,[15] is a perfect example of topological isomorphism.

Parametricism is taken here as an example of the introduction of algebraic topology into computation, because it involves an understanding of space as a field of relations rather than discontinuous points. Metric distances between points are substituted by neighborhood proximity, which, computationally speaking, include vague degrees of quantities (at the limit of 0s and 1s) in the calculation of probabilities. For example, the calculation of degrees of change within parametric programming has added fuzzy states of *maybe* and *perhaps* to the binary logic of yes and no.[16] These are not merely qualitative renderings of digital binarism, for which a certain sequence may correspond to a certain shade of colors; instead, fuzzy states are understood to involve new processes of quantification that include the space of variation between points. This has also been defined as an infinitesimal space. The Euclidean spatial architecture of points and lines, and of discrete and finite states, has been transformed by topological methods of measuring infinitesimal quantities, and by methods of establishing neighborhood proximity through the function of the constant invariant. Paradoxically, however, as will be argued below, this computation of topological variations forecloses the potential intrusion of discontinuity or change into the programming of relations.

From this standpoint, topological thinking—understood as a new method of quantification concerned with indetermination—also corresponds to an operative power of control that is based on the computation of indetermination (i.e., the adding of invariant functions between axioms and between formal models and material implementations) to calculate the space between two points. Here control works not to prevent the future but to add a link to what has to come by using the invariant function as a protocol able to calculate uncertainties. In other words, the introduction of invariant functions in computation points out that the gap between zeroes and ones is instead a relational space composed of infinitesimal points of continuity.

Figure 2.1
Greg Lynn, *SciArc BlobWall Pavilion*, 2008. Courtesy of Greg Lynn FORM, © 2008.

By the early 1990s, experimentation with computational programming had already come to embrace the topological turn in digital design. For example, the architect Greg Lynn famously observed that each pure element of quantity—a binary algorithm, for instance—was determined in a qualitative form by neighboring forces; by the vague space around the point, which unraveled the topological complexity of the generative form.[17] These qualitative forces were defined by the physical stress caused by environmental pressures on the genetic elements of a form. Physical forces were equivalent here to infinitesimal points of any curve, turning the degrees of separation between one form and another into the smaller gradients on a curve. For Lynn, these infinitesimal points had to be included in the generative computation of form.

However, inputting physical variables into computation did not correspond to the representation of intensive quantities (or the qualities of the physical stress points between terms) through the binary language of 0s and 1s. If Gottfried Leibniz's study of differential calculus admitted that the space between undivided monads was not a void but a full texture of percepts and affects, Lynn's topological architecture suggested that these points were qualitative variables that could be included in the process of computation itself. These variables corresponded to the generative force of computation, defined by the processing of movement from one set of algorithms to another, able to exceed the binary function of establishing positions on a grid. In other words, computational abstraction surpassed the representation or simulation of space. As Kipnis argued, the architecture of deformation showed that computational techniques stimulated investigations toward a nonrepresentational space. Computation thus involved "the study of camouflage methods experimenting with computer 'morphing' programs that smoothly transform one figure into another, or employing topological meshing techniques such as splines, NURBS, etc, that join surfaces delimited by the parameters of disjoint two-dimensional figures into a smoothed solid."[18]

Lynn's neobaroque aesthetics of folding architecture responds directly to the continuum problem posed by Leibniz's *infinitesimal or differential calculus*.[19] Leibniz used the calculus as a way to solve the question of infinity: is a line between two points another point, or is it an infinitesimal aggregation of points (increasingly small quantities that cannot be mathematically counted)?[20] Leibniz concluded that if a line was an aggregation of points, i.e., of infinitely divisible parts, then a continuum could neither be a unity nor an aggregation of unities. In other words, continua were *not real entities* at all. Continua were "wholes preceding their parts" and had a purely ideal (i.e., nonphysical) character. For Leibniz space and time, as continua, were ideal, and anything real, such as matter, was discrete, composed of simple unit substances or *monads*.[21] However, in order to explain the transition from finite, discrete reality to infinitesimal, transcendental magnitudes, Leibniz resorted to the philosophical law of continuity, emphasizing the role of the ratio between differentials (differential calculus): the infinitesimal differential quantity, or the curve of transition between two orders of magnitude or quantities (infinite and finite series).[22] Leibniz's "labyrinth of the continuum" described the paradoxical condition of transcendental infinities and actual finitude: how can the infinitely divisible, he asked, be constituted by discrete unities?[23] At the core of Leibniz's topological conception of space is the differential calculus, which calculates derivatives or differential relations, describing the infinitely small quantities between two quantities (the quantity of the ordinate x and the quantity of the abscissa y).

It was, however, Henri Poincaré's paper "Analysis situs" (1895) that defined algebraic topology as the study of qualitative properties and of the continuity of space. Leibniz's differential calculus became formalized as a means of explaining not points of integrations (nodes, dips, focal points, and centers) but rather fields of vectors (continual tendencies of a line) that encompass these points. Poincaré's mereomorphic function[24] precisely explained how discontinuous groups were qualitatively transformed into a vector field of forces, a continuous deformation or reciprocal determination of potential functions into composite functions, of differential equations into integral functions.

Lynn's concept of folding in architecture fully embraced this qualitative formalization of spatial relations. Yet as Lynn himself suggested, this topological turn was geared more precisely toward addressing the metaphysical primacy of relations and processes rather than points and results. Folding in architecture deploys the intricate relations of technicality alongside metaphysics as a way of describing the cultural and aesthetic tendency of an epoch. The bending and twisting of lines into complex structures that loop and autoreflect on their irregular trajectories reveals no less than a new sense of spatiality in computational culture.

As Lynn pointed out, the metaphysical significance of qualitative relations is found in Gilles Deleuze's protogeometrical thought of the fold, which was itself inspired by Leibniz's differential calculus. According to Deleuze, a point was a "point-fold"[25] or an enveloped time line describing a curve as a nondimensional conjunction of vectors. The point corresponded to a real yet inexact quantity, or an intensive degree of differentiation. Only a random, irregular, complex equation could calculate the irrational numbers of the curve, the limit of the relation between two quantities (exact points) that would vanish into the curve. As Deleuze explained, "the irrational number implies the descent of a circular arc on the straight line of rational points, and exposes the latter as a false infinity, a simple indefinite that includes an infinity of lacunae. . . . The straight line always has to be intermingled with curved lines."[26] The calculation of infinitesimals pointed out that between terms (two rational numbers) there was no empty space, but rather a continuity of increasingly small quantities. Leibniz's notion of evanescent quantity described this continuity as an infinitesimal number of points that retained the character of the quantities while disappearing.

Similarly to Leibniz, Deleuze conceived infinitesimals as a differential relation that superseded actual terms. As the terms annul each other, the relation remains. This is a third term, which Deleuze identifies with the tangent of a curve, a straight line that touches a curve at only one point.[27] But the infinitesimal gap between two points could not be simply governed, as Leibniz envisaged, by a transcendental infinity (determined by the principle of sufficient reason). According to Deleuze, nonstandard analysis not only reintroduced the infinitesimal into the mathematical study of the continuum as a nonexact numerical quantity: in addition, it also provided a new axiomatic formula of differential relations.[28] In short, the formalization of differential relations coincided with the systematization of the intuition of continuity by means of nonstandard axioms.[29]

The differential relation was thus formalized as the function of an invariant, a constant *x* through which the continuum between discrete entities became a mathematical expression of relational continuity itself. According to Deleuze, however, the algebraic determination of indeterminate differentials (or infinitesimal *dy* or *dx*) was not simply an axiomatic solution. On the contrary, it also meant that the differential relation could not correspond to a discrete number or finite quantity (an axiom). The finite result (the invariant *x*) could instead only be determined by the immanence of the relation with the infinitely small: the tendency of the differential relation to vanish but of the relation to tend toward the limit *z*. As Deleuze suggested, the integration of the differential relation did not result in a determinate point or discrete axiom, but involved the sequential arrangement of points that generate a curve rather than a straight line.[30] This curve was a function in the neighborhood of the given tangential point: the limit of the function. The introduction of differential relations into digital design thus exposes the integration of infinite qualities as a computational limit expressed by the tangent on a curve.

If the panoptical diagram described by Foucault was but an instance of a gridlocked architecture of Euclidean positions and points,[31] folding in architecture can be taken as a symptom of topological control, wherein qualitative movement, or the relational spatium (the interval) between points, is anticipated in the automated design of a curve: an intricate system of variable parameters forming a digital *plexus*, as Lynn called it.[32] According to Lynn, folds describe the phase space in which a line becomes a curve, where a point reveals itself to be the limit of infinitesimal points marking the space between, the interval or the slope between terms. Far from using software to generate prototypes that could arbitrarily vary and stop growing once they reached a threshold of cumulative selection,[33] Lynn suggested that software posed an aesthetic challenge to the design of space resulting from the interaction between independent variables (for instance, algorithms for changing weather conditions, and those describing the traffic of cars, or the movements of people within a structure), or parallel parameters able to influence one another through their potential activities.[34] This challenge included the transformation of the Euclidean grid of isolated positions—which are deprived of any force and time, and which can be represented by steady-state equations—into Leibnizian curving worlds that converge and diverge in a point of view. This point of view, according to Lynn, resembles an exact mathematical point less than it does a vectorial flow: a continuation or diffusion of the point,[35] or as Cache called it, a "point of inflection."[36] In other words, Lynn argued that the computational implementation of the differential calculus had meant "the loss of the module in favor of the infinitesimal component and the displacement of the fragmentary collage by the intensive whole."[37] The aesthetic of topological control has thus come to rely on the computation of incipient forces, movement or the differential space of relations.

This computation of spatial relations is indeed one of the most concrete expressions of the operative field of postcybernetic control, the aim of which is to smooth connections, incite interactions, reassemble networks, and generate links. In other words, postcybernetic control has turned approximate relations between points into new rules of connection, convergence, and continuity. Its aesthetic aim is not just to orchestrate the perception and the sensorimotor orientation of bodies in a flexible urban space. On the contrary, it corresponds to a new formalization of extension itself, which does not so much ask what space is, or who inhabits it, but rather how extension as a field of potential relationality can become the condition for the computation of new connections.[38] Postcybernetic control involves the programming of vague quantities of relations through the computation of topological continuities. As Deleuze anticipated, power has become one with the operative realm of control as it constantly works to glue together spatiotemporalities into extended apparatuses of uninterrupted relationality.[39]

2.2 Parametricism or deep relationality

The computation of infinitesimal relations has come to describe not only, as Lynn would have it, the neobaroque aesthetics of a folding architecture, but also the postcybernetic control of the continuum itself. Topology, as the ultimate mathematics of smooth space, now coincides with the aesthetic of curvature or of continual variation. Here differential relations have become the curving space of control itself.

As we have seen, an example of postcybernetic control that serves to clarify its computational operation can be found in parametric design. Parametricism can now be said to underpin many forms of topological order as it specifically works to program relations between data sets. A parameter is a variable to which other variables are related. Hence in parametricism sets of variables and their relationships to one another determine the changes of a spatial form. While initial conditions of the parametric design are still programmed through a binary logic of 0s and

1s, these conditions are then open to change through the evolutionary processing of parameters when new variables are simultaneously generated from and added to the set of initial values. Hence, the continual relations between programmed variables are more important to the parametric design of urban space, for example, than the digitalization of physical variables into sets of 0s and 1s. This means that while parametric relations order variables into sequential binary sets, they are also determined by the qualitative level of topological functions, where differential relations explain how the transformation of one value is equivalent to the continual variations of the whole space.

Nevertheless, the determination of a continual correspondence between data variables and the whole form of space is not specific to parametric design. As Sanford Kwinter points out, design has always been a highly advanced form of rationality.[40] Design is a rational technique that breeds and mutates infrastructures, from those of knowledge to those of the urban environment. Thus, parametric design is just another instance of design serving as part of a logistics of operations (e.g., the computation of the urban infrastructure, from traffic control to the control of the movement of people in public transport), where algorithmic information and data structures are now "oriented to performative environments, to protocols, and, *in extremis*, to psychological operations."[41] According to Kwinter, as architecture has turned into "experiments in design logic, research and potential,"[42] so has the computational paradigm extended concepts of materiality, society, economics, and nature into the incorporeal field of intensive manifolds, thereby turning spaces into "shapes of time."[43] As the qualitative level of relations (or topological continuity) has become central to computational design, so time, understood as lapses of evolution, growths, adaptation of initial values, has come to determine the final shape of spaces.[44]

This has also meant that with parametric design, modifications of values can be performed almost in real time; this differs markedly from the time-consuming redrawing required by the traditional AutoCAD, for instance. Before the advent of parametric design, buildings were modeled using computer drafting programs (such as AutoCAD or MicroStation, which are industry standards) and would then be analyzed by engineers who would use their own software before ultimately sending them to environmental engineers, who would use yet another set of software. Parametric design makes it possible for the engineering of the overall levels of a spatial form to be manipulated all at once. Through the altering of specific parameters that are able to automatically adjust building data, such as the total gross area, total building height, total number of floors, etc., the various levels of engineering are integrated into one topological software program. Parametric design offers the modulation of variable relationships between entities, where the alteration of properties results in different outcomes in the overall form.[45] Parameters can be established from a vast list of possibilities (such as data on wind speed or rainfall, for example). These variables can also be directly related to costs on a spreadsheet, so as to ensure a smooth, direct relationality, or the ubiquitous connection between architectural and economic changes. This direct relation between financial costs and spatial forms involves an engagement with topological regimes of immediate convergence—or of algebraic invariance—between spatiotemporal variables and economic values.[46] In order to establish continuity between discontinuous groups of values, one part of the design has to respond to transformations in another, or the entire design has to respond to changing conditions—light, airflow, weight distribution, and the gravitational pressure of the building—in relation to changes in the urban infrastructure, from traffic control to weather conditions. In general, any output or variable from the outside is included in the list of possibilities of the algorithmic architecture that defines space as a topological engine of potentialities. Results can be instantaneously fed back into the system through a recursive loop of algorithms, tested and played again to evolve different results.

As Michael Hensel and Achim Menges argue, parametric architecture needs to be conceived as a system with a set of finite internal relationships and external forces that inform it and to which it responds.[47] These relationships are constructed by the computational capacities to envisage the material characteristic and behavior of locally specific and yet dynamic environmental conditions, which produce, for instance, microclimatic levels of differentiation in a geographic field. In general, Hensel and Menges seem to suggest that computational programming is no longer "design-defining":[48] it is no longer used simply to apply a given plan to the urban infrastructure, and similarly it no longer involves understanding algorithms and parameters simply as static reproductions of points in space. On the contrary, with computation we now have a "program-evolving" design. Here design derives from the interaction between parameters that have become generative of new structures of relation by responding to real-time inputs. In other words, design now relies on continual relations rather than digital fixing.[49] It is precisely this emphasis on the evolving relation between parameters or their interactive feedback that now characterizes computational architecture in terms of real-time adaptation, emergence, and change. From this standpoint, program-evolving urbanism includes the design of smart infrastructures that are able to monitor, respond to, and/or anticipate change in the transport logistics of a city (including roads, rail, water and air circulation), for instance. As parameters have become evolutionary variables that enter and exit relations with other parameters, urban design has become governed by time-related data.

The integration of wireless sensor networks into large-scale engineering systems, such as networks of pipelines, tunnels, and bridges, relies on the parametric programming of engineering systems that directly respond to sensor networks.[50] The generative program of parameters, whereby each parameter includes temporal variations, now animates the design of urban infrastructures, integrating differential relations between systems (rail, road, air, water systems) into one smooth machine or continual mesh of variation. Here the monitoring of real-time data, which is central to software-enhanced infrastructure, is only another facet of an urbanism-evolving programming in which smooth, speedy, and cost-efficient systems are integrated into an evolving metasystem that includes all infrastructures.

The scope of urbanism-evolving programming is not too dissimilar from computing devices (smart phones for instance) that offer us new possibilities of navigation, which have become part of our saved favorite paths, presenting us with set solutions that we have previously selected or added to the navigation program. Just as your smart phone works as a monitor device for tracking your location, which then becomes data used to construct the profile of your movement, so too does the monitoring procedure of smart infrastructure collect data which then become part of the programming of new infrastructural systems. As data are recorded, so they evolve into predictive scenarios aiming not simply at presetting your movement, but rather at generating its future conditions through the generative interaction of parameters with real-time data. This is how post-cybernetic control operates as a form of parametric design. From this standpoint, the goal of parametric design is *deep* relationality, the *real-time* integration of the evolving variables of a built environment in software systems that are able to figure emerging scenarios by responding to or preadapting scripted data.

Nevertheless, the deep relationality established by parametricism has little to do with a genuine intervention in the urban infrastructure, according to which urban behavior, for example, could react back upon and thereby change urban models (or reconfigure the spatial order). Instead, deep relationality describes above all else the reduction of digital and physical extension to algorithmic sets and parametric values able to include degrees of variation within the computation of their relation.[51] Similarly, deep relationality implies how the real-time integration of modes of conduct (digital and analog algorithms, rules of behavior and response) occur prior to their emergence. Topological control is about calculating the point at which the line declines from the projection of a point: a vector measuring the force of the line and not the line itself. This means that by transforming urban infrastructures in real-time responsive environments, parametricism's deep relationality is simply granted by a digital ground, where software integrates any form of choice and relation through the calculation of a ratio or a variation. As Neil Leach has observed, parametric architecture marks a third phase in digital design, in which the use of algorithms as a means of experimenting with forms and the tectonic application of digital software are being superseded by the evolution of software pertaining to urban space.[52] This means that software is no longer a tool for design but has in fact become one with the latter: it now creates relations between points through calculating the distance between them. Spatial design has become fused with data architecture. The joints, knots, and articulations of points are built here, but can also be used to indicate something beyond and unrelated; what is not physically here can veritably become a new probability.

Deep relationality is therefore the goal of topological control, where the evolution of parameters can be preprogrammed into the design by means of the invariant function, thereby granting smooth passage from one point to another. Deep relationality thus seems to amount to the continual curvature of the straight line, to the roundness of shapes created by temporal variations, and to real-time responsiveness. From this standpoint, change has become intrinsic to the operative logic of topological control: change is preprogrammed or actively programmed within the codes that guarantee continuity of form and function. The invariant connection between the distinct levels of networks is instantiated in parametric urban models, which are based not on geometric planning but on the mathematical variables of evolutionary urban software. As R&Sie(n) architect François Roche recently suggested, the new parametric programming of digital cities resembles less a binary grid of finite sets (0s and 1s) than a biostructure that develops its own adaptive behavior, based on growing scripts and open algorithms.[53] This is a new biocomputational design, the programming capacities of which are stretched to calculate potential conditions of relationality and change, rather than writing scripts of what can eventually be transformed. These design programs are metaprotocols that constitute the software ecology of urban continuities between many discrete infrastructural systems that can all be integrated into a single envelope; an intensive manifold possessed of interior and exterior sites that can be activated in any number of ways. From this standpoint, parametric design may become an example of how urban infrastructures are coevolving with urban software in such a way that the invisible architecture of topological computing is no longer set to represent but rather to program the development of physical space. This topological programming is thus an expression of deep relationality: the inclusion of temporal planning in parametric design. This is the topic of the next section.

2.3 Soft temporalities

The introduction of temporal qualities into parametric design characterizes the aesthetics of curvature. Here relations between parametric quantities shape parts into the architecture of the whole.[54] The topological approach has replaced the function of digital sequencing with the composite function of relations, so that changes at one level of parametric value produce changes at another level. From this standpoint, parametric design has given way to a plethora of morphogenetic architectures, where the whole stems from the relations between mechanical, physical, and algorithmic parts.

For instance, *Topotransegrity*, an award-winning responsive and kinetic architecture designed by 5Subzero,[55] shows how the spatial organization

Figure 2.2
5Subzero (Delphine Ammann, Karim Muallem, Robert R. Neumayr, Georgina Robledo), *Topotransegrity*, 2006.

of public space can derive from the topological design of continual adaptation between software programs, mechanical parts, and real-time physical movement. *Topotransegrity* brings together surfaces through pneumatic space-frame structures that can be manipulated either through an automated control mechanism, through real-time feedback, or by software programs. In particular, the programming of the structure relies on external and internal parameters that are defined by the manner in which the environment influences different parts of the structure. The continual relation between the parameters and their changing mode of operation affords a series of emerging user-dependent spatial configurations.

As a whole, *Topotransegrity* is a kinetic structure, sustained by three sets of pneumatic pistons designed by Festo. The pistons are equipped with responsive software that evaluates the surroundings and reconfigures the structure according to changing conditions. *Topotransegrity* extends across existing buildings at the Barbican complex in London to form a topological surface of connection. This surface constitutes a generic responsive structural system able to adapt to distinct spatial requirements. The structure is capable of various transformations, ranging from small-scale surface articulations to large surface deformations that work as temporary enclosures. Contingent elements from the environment are introduced into the parametric programming of its different parts to allow the responsive structure to multiply, intensify, and vary the potential uses of public spaces. According to the 5Subzero group, *Topotransegrity* is therefore not simply a preprogrammed structure, but one that relies on external real-time feedback to generate new internal configurations. For instance, sensors, input devices, and wireless networks are integrated into existing building materials so as to transform the architectural space of the Barbican into a complex continuity. This is determined by invariant functions that deploy the topological relation between the program mode (parameters automating the basic functions of the structure by adding new levels of connection), the crowd mode (parameters determined by real-time responses of the structure to movements and the behavioral patterns of visitors), and the memory mode (parameters that record on a long-term basis the paths and motion patterns chosen by users). These three parametric modes of operation run simultaneously and interact with visitors in a permanent feedback loop: local reactions to spatial adaptations are fed back into the system of parameters, which in turn specifically redesigns the built environment according to changing patterns of use.

It could be argued that the crowd or any other external data constitute contingencies that are somehow controlled or directed by the program, which then quantifies them as qualities of temporal variations. It may be true then to say that *Topotransegrity* is unable to create the conditions for a radically novel reconfiguration of space to the extent that contingencies merely allow the software system to find optimal solutions to emerging problems. On the other hand, *Topotransegrity* is precisely an instance of a topological aesthetics of control that turns discrete points and finite lines into infinitesimal quantities of variation, which are governed by invariant functions and which integrate the varying degrees of change between parameters into a continual surface of changing configurations. This is less about the software hierarchically mastering the hardware or modes of behavior than it is a form of control defined by the differential integration of the temporal qualities that characterize software programming, the kinetic mechanics of the structure, and real-time interaction. Here the deep relationality between urban software and urban behavior relies on the computation of these temporalities, which permits physical inputs to add variations to parametric values, but only to the extent that the reconfigurations of spatial structure are potentially programmed probabilities. *Topotransegrity*, therefore, points to how topological aesthetics has become a form of speculative control: a preemptive integration of differential relations.

It is true to say that *Topotransegrity* does not express the same understanding of urban space as the parametric approach, which views the urban environment in terms of the formal order of relations. Nonetheless, *Topotransegrity*'s design is characterized by interactive parameters that integrate software with mechanical and biophysical inputs, and this places it squarely within the domain of topological control. *Topotransegrity* also works to establish a deep relationality between urban software and urban behavior through a structural integration of temporalities that intersect at various conjoined points. The project thus deploys the topological order of infinitesimal variations between discrete levels of temporalities, which are operated by invariant functions aiming to integrate changing configurations. Here the evolution of the urban structure is defined by an adaptable prototype that incorporates the temporal evolution of varying parts. Hence the self-organization, growth, and change of the various configurations of the structure are operations of parametric control, which programs the collective growth and variation of urban behaviors through its ever-fluid topologistics.[56]

Topotransegrity therefore shows us how space has become dynamic. It has acquired the movement of time, the quality of variation, the impulse of growth and adaptation. Space has been vitalized. Insofar as parametric design is an aesthetic expression of the tendency toward a new mode of urban planning based on deep relationality and real-time transformations, it is also an example of the actual reality of software space. In short, space is now a parametric surface of continual variations that smoothes out the ruptures, breaks, or discontinuities between scales and levels. By becoming one with computational operations, physical space has turned into a temporally manipulable, programmable, and ever-regenerable field of relation: a full expression of topological control.

With parametric design, the temporal dimension of space has become central to topological control, whereby prediction is no longer based on the calculation of finite probabilities but rather on the inclusion of potential qualities. Brian Massumi has argued that this shift defines a preemptive mode of power, whereby the indeterminate qualities of the future are incessantly foreclosed as sets of probabilities within the present.[57] From this standpoint, parametric design is the operative equivalent of a new governance of extension, which uses parametric relations as platforms for testing how nonactual scenarios are selected to determine the self-organizational structure of urban configurations. The ingression of topological invariants into cybernetic systems allows automated processes to constantly transduce temporal qualities (intensive and differential) into approximate quantities (extensive and divisible). This concern with temporality in the understanding of space, however, is not simply a technical question posed by the computation of extension, or relations between points, levels, and scales. On the contrary, and as will be argued in the next section, this concern with temporality is ontological. If one is to account for what is computational space, it must be addressed through the ontological understanding of time.

2.4 Extension is what extension doesn't[58]

Since topological control works by anticipating the potential qualities of extension through the parametric design of continual change, it would seem to operate exclusively or principally by taming temporal qualities. Cybernetic control has incorporated the lesson of the differential calculus, whereby extension, as the relational space between points, corresponds to infinitesimally small quantities. Hence, the distance between terms can be measured not in terms of instants, but rather according to the relative temporality that connects them. It is therefore hard not to notice that with this qualitative conception of space at the heart of point-free topology, extension has become intensified.

It may be useful, as a means toward understanding the nature of this intensification, to recall here Henri Bergson's critique of Einstein's special theory of relativity and, in particular, of the paradox of simultaneity, which is also known as the *twin paradox*.[59] For Einstein, the temporal connection between entities, or twins, who occupy distinct spatiotemporalities (one twin on the earth and another on a planet in space) explains the paradox of simultaneity. But Bergson harshly opposes this temporal measure of distance, arguing that Einstein's theory of the paradox of simultaneity is merely the result of a scientific misconception of the notion of time.[60]

According to Bergson, the validity of the twin paradox is based on a model that presents time as symmetrical, or as something that can be geometrically measured according to points and positions.[61] Time, however, Bergson claims, cannot remain the same for two distinct perceivers. The theory of special relativity therefore fails to explain the experience of what Bergson refers to as *real* time.[62] Bergson specifically rejects Einstein's notion of the dilatation of time, which he claims cannot account for the metaphysical distinction between measured and lived time.[63] Instead, according to Bergson, time has to be conceived as an invariant magnitude that is irreducible to the time of geometrical coordinates. In other words, Bergson's conception of time includes a topological invariant that is able to explain how spatiotemporal divisions can only result from an a priori experience of the continuum.[64] According to him, only the intuition of *real* time intervals, which supersedes the distinction between measured points, can clarify the phenomena of relativity or the fact that the twins could experience the same time at different points. Bergson concludes that both twins shared the same time, but in different ways. The invariant qualities of time should therefore not be explained geometrically, but metaphysically as the pulsating, contracting and expanding lines of *la durée*: an immense virtual time irreducible to chronological measures. Bergson's virtual time, as opposed to the Newtonian universal time, radicalizes the theory of relativity, as it aims at overcoming the homogeneous formalization of time through the method of intuition.[65]

For Bergson, standard accounts of relativity mainly offer a notion of time-space derived from the view of a timeless universe, determined by the formalism of scientific knowledge. Here time remains frozen, reduced to the parameterization of curves or world lines. Against this, Bergson replaces the geometrical unity of time with a multiplicity of intensive durations, which explains the dislocation of simultaneity and the slowing down of clocks (time-space asymmetry). In sum, the unity of time can only be reached locally in relation to a fundamental experience of duration, where the "now" and the "here" of a situated observer result from infinitesimal temporalities.

If, following Bergson, the relations between actual entities can be explained by their participation in (nonmetric) duration, then one must conclude that the parametric computation of topological continuity only amounts to yet another discretization (or digitization) of infinitesimal duration. From this standpoint, digital topology would not add new qualities; on the contrary, it would subtract real time from lived experience. If the computation of spatiotemporal continuities could only give us the metric equivalent of the intensive time of experience, one would inevitably have to conclude that parametric design is a mere simulation of lived time, and that it lacks the material consistency of concrete temporalities. However, a closer look at parametric design, as an instance of topological control, will soon reveal that this is not the case.

After the initial fascination with digital mapping and animation in the early 1990s, parametric architecture has come to define not only interactive design per se but above all the power of computing contingencies, particularly those pertaining to temporal qualities. This has led to a new kind of programming that is based on a two-way interaction with the environment. As Kas Oosterhuis pointed out, interactive architecture "is based on the concept of bi-directional communication, which requires two active parties."[66] With the development of new interactive software, for instance, qualitative variables have become included in the operative functions of the program. In particular, parametric design has come to assign a primary role to those unpredictable or *intensive* relations between preset parameters. Here lived experience and infinitesimal temporalities are no longer excluded, but have become differentially included in the soft computation of space. The differential qualities of lived experience or duration are no longer an empirical problem secondary to scientific formalism: instead, they now correspond to intensive quantities that are at the core of the programming of extension.

The parametric computation of spatial relations does not therefore simply rely on preprogrammed sets of variables. These extensive relations are no longer conceived in terms of the digital mapping of points. On the contrary, these relations now imply the qualitative variables or intensive quantities able to modify the whole system of interaction through local interventions. Thus the introduction of lived temporalities into software programming has opened up measured time to the indeterminacies of differential relations. It has also established a new level of continuity between different qualities of reception, activity, and participation that directly

Figure 2.3
Haque Design + Research, *Open Burble,* 2006. Courtesy of Usman Haque.

affects the formal structure of the whole architecture of relations. Here space is continuously reconfigured by the mutual relationships between parameters, actuators, sensors, and users.

For instance, the live use of real-time technologies, such as mobile phones, is central to architect/experimenter Usman Haque's projects *Sky Ear* and *Open Burble,* among others.[67] Haque's projects show how collectively constructed environments can emerge from real-time interactions in which people and objects mutually create socioarchitectural domains.[68] These projects suggest that the significance of computation in the design of urban spaces is not simply to establish whether or not a programmed model can adapt to a live environment. Instead, these projects demonstrate that architectural urban structures are driven by the feedback activities of the participants, exposing time and space to a multiplicity of durations: relative realities that may or may not correspond to preset parameters. Haque, for instance, bases this real-time conception of interactive architecture on what he conceived to be a bottom-up relationship between software and environments. In particular, he traces this interactive model of creating *live* space back to the 1960s cybernetic experiments of Gordon Pask and Cedric Price, who conceived computers as autopoietic systems evolving within and as components of larger environments.[69]

These cybernetic architectures, equipped with sensors, processors, and actuators, were set to bind individual responses to collective outputs. In other words, these were *live* architectures that incorporated the idea of time's relativity. Hence time was not just another dimension of space: on the contrary, space could finally enter temporal dimensions, and could become relative to the experience of relational settings. With cybernetic architecture, both space and time ceased to be universals that had to be inhabited. Space could only result from the dynamic evolution of interactive moments of experience.

Following this perspective, Haque's projects are set to create urban space from the computation of the real-time feedbacks of interactions that are stirred by mutual participation or dialoguing between systems. As opposed to interactive systems based on the direct relation between stimulus and response discounting any temporal gap, glitch, or asymmetry, Haque's projects suggest that real interaction can only occur through the nonlinear workings of mutually affecting systems.

For instance, *Control.Burble.Remote,* one of the most recent rearticulations of Haque's *Open Burble,* is intended to experiment with responsive systems wherein the interaction between software and live input is delayed (or opened to other temporal dimensions) through the use of old TV remote control. The *Burble,* which is made of approximately 1,000 extra-large helium balloons, each of which contains microcontrollers and LEDs, creates "spontaneous" patterns of light across the surface of the structure. These patterns are the result of inputs sent to the structure by remote controls; the structure is composed of thousands of individual computers that are disconnected from one another and thus unaware of each other. The computers actively respond to the remote control signals by changing the color and shape of the individual parts of the structure in a manner that is intended to map the collective behavior of the crowd. In other words, the *Burble* structure uses the relativity of remote signals to expose the delay between input and output (between the sender and the receiver, but also the delay between the reception of the input and its computation evidenced in some shades of color or changes of shape), so as to build a live architecture of relations.

According to Haque, this interactive space allows people to enter a new relationship not only with their TV remotes (a move from passive to active interaction), but also with each other as they enter into conversation with the individual balloons, with other participants, and with the overall structure. As a result, it is intensive relations and not programmed interactions that are built upon this externalized urban space. Here the parametric design of space is set to exceed the digitalization of geometric coordinates so as to embrace the live experience of differential spatiotemporalities, producing the dynamism, flexibility, and unpredictability of the architectural model. This model is programmed to learn from the feedback activities of the participants, which create space out of the relative time of millions of remote control inputs, ultimately establishing a system of interaction inspired by Gordon Pask's idea of conversation.[70] At the heart of this kind of interactive architecture, therefore, lies a dynamically growing space infused with live delays, the deformations of coordinates, and continual variations driven by the asymmetric temporalities of the participants.

The underlying aesthetic of topological continuities that characterizes these interactive projects shows us how real-time technologies, such as mobile phones, GPS devices, web interfaces, and physical interface objects, are adapting to the lived experience of spatiotemporal distance and simultaneity. Parametric design is especially attuned to the temporal changes of relations. In particular, the design of location-based platforms that are able to connect places to larger networks is at the core of real-time urbanism projects such as *Soft Urbanism* or *WikiCity*.[71] In these projects, real-time technologies invite the collapse of time symmetry into a relativity of durations. Here individual presence and participation become the motor of spatiotemporal differentiations that are able to turn architectural models (or metric spatiotemporalities) into emergent environments of real-time interaction. As opposed to a static predetermined space in which all experiences temporally conform to one another, real-time digital devices have become channels for spatiotemporal differentiation here, exposing the delays, gaps, and intervals of a virtual duration, thereby revealing a multiplicity of time lines.

From this standpoint, the more intensive time becomes linked to larger networks through protoindividualizing digital objects (such as mobile phones) and social media (such as Facebook, Twitter, etc.), the more it will become possible to build large-scale complex and differentiated models for a real-time urbanism free from geometrical homogeneity. And yet, since real-time devices and social media invite lived experience to enter the modeling of digital space (by constantly injecting new doses of differential or virtual temporality into extension), these models also become actualized forms of relative programming, resulting in adaptable interactive spaces. To put it another way, the real-time programming of parameters—the addition and subtraction of variables—has become intrinsic to interactive digital devices, media, and urban architectures. In short, the programming of spatial relations itself is now infused with the relativity of lived experience, thus announcing a radical transformation of power: a transformation marked by the computational search for real-time indeterminacies, which is expanding the programming of extension.

The possibility of proactivating software models and ultimately breaking the symmetry of programmed space through lived experience may be ultimately regarded, however, as yet another attempt to capture the virtual (or intensive) qualities of duration. One may want to claim, with Bergson, that it is only intuition (and thus lived duration)—and not computation—that can truly grasp the reality of a virtual multiplicity, which always already exceeds the interactive time of technical (and especially digital) machines. No matter how dynamic the program might be, the sequential order of algorithms and parameters still implies a division of time into space.

While it is hard to deny the validity of this argument, it seems to me that it overlooks the fact that real-time devices and platforms of topological connection are, precisely, channels for the active programming of lived duration, wherein the digital division of time coincides with the construction of new temporalities. This means that the paradox of relativity, or the possibility that there are distinct spaces coexisting in the same time, still haunts ideas of interactivity as the point at which real-time spatial experience occurs. Yet one could respond to that paradox by noting that although the point of observation/interaction can be any measuring device (a human, a machine, a social group, or a set of algorithms), no such point can be seen as an ultimate, privileged entry into the realm of intensive durations. Instead, it could be argued that the infinity of all durations (or the unity of a virtual continuum) can only be recorded in a limited, finite manner by any of these points.

From this standpoint, real-time experience means being immersed in delays, resonances, and echoes proper to the intervals or lapses of (chronological) time, where infinitesimally smaller points can only be approximately measured. In short, one could hold that the unity of a virtual continuum can only be experienced in the temporal intervals between determined places or points in space. This argument, however, dismisses an important transformation in strategies of quantification, which are now concerned primarily with the interval between input and output, remote control and pattern production, action and reception, code and infinite variations. This transformation is evinced in parametric and interactive architecture, which have come to include temporal relativity in the parametric design of live urban spaces. Extension, as indicated above, has thus become intensified. As an instance of postcybernetic control (the tendency to anticipate novelty at the point at which intervals or intensive relations connect two distant objects), parametric and interactive architecture seem to have fully incorporated the question of lived time.

In order to understand what is at stake in the postcybernetic transformation of strategies of quantification, it is perhaps not enough to suggest that qualities are now included in the formal structure of power. In the next section, I will contrast Bergson's theory of time with Whitehead's atomic conception of time, which argues for a notion of duration that is defined by time plus space. This discussion will contribute to the central argument of this chapter, according to which the postcybernetic computation of extension or relations does not exclusively involve a transformation of qualities into quantities, or lived variations into parametric values of relations, but rather deploys the irreducibility of discreteness and quantity in accounts of extension.

2.5 Blind spots: space events

Parametricism, as a form of computational design, programs extension by embracing a notion of relationality which I argue is defined not only temporally but also spatially. This is also to say that parametric design involves not only the introduction of qualities into programming, but also—and importantly for postcybernetic control—the transformation of the very notion of quantity. Changes in kind also imply changes in degree, and the multiplicity of times corresponds to a multiplicity of spaces. Parametric design indicates the simultaneity of many space-times, but it explains them neither in terms of instants (linked to a geometrical notion of points) nor of durations (linked to an ontological understanding of time). The computation of relations does not exclusively coincide with the reduction of temporal qualities to preset probabilities, but reveals the formation of another space-time and describes the simultaneity of experience without reducing distinct spaces to the relativity of lived time. From this standpoint, parametric design implies a notion of extension defined not simply by temporal but also, significantly, by *spatiotemporal* regions (and subregions) of connection. To explain why and how this is the case, I use Whitehead's conception of extension.

While Bergson argues that simultaneity can only be explained by the metaphysics of virtual time, Whitehead approaches notions of spatial dislocation and simultaneity from another angle.[72] Drawing upon the twin paradox described by relativity theory, Whitehead adds that the experience of the delay between the twins' experiences can only be understood through a close analysis of the actual mechanism of simultaneity. For Whitehead, the question is how to explain connection (or the *extensive continuum*) between separate spatiotemporal entities. He claims that the local nature of time has to be related to copresent actual entities or events that experience the passage of nature.[73] Whitehead understands simultaneity according to the notion of "presentational immediacy,"[74] which emphasizes not temporal intervals but rather the immediate (here and now) construction of space-time as the focal point at which an event can be fully actualized. In the case of the twin paradox, the focal point of the event is the point at which the twin in the spaceship changes course and turns back to Earth. This means that the turnaround point is the relational space defining the event or the experience of distance in terms of actual relationality. According to Whitehead, this event is also a space that does not eternally endure, but can only be what it is as it arrives and perishes.

Whitehead agrees that there is an asymmetry in experience, highlighted by the twins' clocks registering a small amount of delay between them; but he gives a different reason from Bergson's as to why the experience of the delay takes place.[75] Whitehead does not argue that the twins already experience asymmetric time because they both live in a virtual time of continual differentiation. On the contrary, his schema of a multiplicity of time-space systems is closer to Minkowski's theory of world lines.[76] For Whitehead, there is no universal temporal structure corresponding to the experience of a situated consciousness, and there is no one-to-one correspondence between local spatiotemporal experience and universal time lines. In order to understand how actual entities relate to each other, he observes, one needs to make room for the ingression of *real* time at an intermediary level, *the lived space of relationality itself*, where a genuine experience of distance can truly occur.

Whitehead therefore claims that it is necessary to rethink duration: not simply to cast it as a temporal concept, but to recognize that it pertains above all to the spatiotemporal. Duration cannot coincide with the intensive time of a virtual continuum, as proposed by Bergson: on the contrary, it is to be understood as a slice of nature that is composed of many coexistent (and asymmetrical) spatiotemporal regions (and subregions). Whitehead's insistence that duration is as much spatial as temporal inevitably points at the discrepancy between particular perspectives or time systems embedded in the space-time manifold of events. His schema explains simultaneity in terms of local regions (it is based on the distance between actual occasions), and offers an extensive (as opposed to a temporal) conception of simultaneity.[77]

In particular, Whitehead provides a detailed account of the measuring procedures on each side of the twins' journey (one on the earth, the other in space) and of the duration involved in these distant events. Whereas Minkowski's standard 4D space-time suggests that the traveler's world line is not geodesic (a straight space-time path between two given events), Whitehead maintains the formula "space plus time" (which differs from the view that space is the fourth dimension of time). Whitehead holds that the dislocation of simultaneity is not caused by the dilation of time, but mainly results from the turnaround point in the traveling twin's journey. This turnaround is not a point of synthesis (a point of live interaction between all varying temporalities), but rather remains a blind spot—an invisible spatiotemporality of intersection—that marks the space-time of the interval: a relational actuality. The interval, or the relation between points, becomes a space event: an event-entity that is at once both space and time. Whitehead explains that the change of motion of one twin at the star point (the fact that the traveler changes the sense of direction from a point of rest) triggers a temporal shift at a midpoint, which cancels out a portion of time. In other words, on the point of return the twin loses the chronological sense of space-time because she is changing direction.

Whitehead claims that the change of reference frame at an instant and the conjoined effects of the relativity of simultaneity provoke the chronological asymmetries experienced by the twins. In other words, Whitehead, like Bergson, rejects the view of a universal "now" (the same time for all coexistent observers). However, he also refuses the idea that there is a continual duration for many places. Instead, he believes that a U-turn in space corresponds to many *nows* that are related to many actual frames. According to Whitehead, the traveler's sudden change of course while heading back to Earth involves a jump (a blind spot) in the spatiotemporal architecture of the sequential line of events, defined by the ingression of eternal objects in the turnaround point, which reveals the simultaneity and the asymmetry in the experience of the twins (the spatiotemporal experience of the twin traveling to space and that of the twin on Earth). Thus, as Whitehead clarifies, what happens before and after the space-time length H1 (the point of departure) and H2 (the point of return) at the point S is not irrelevant, but rather invisible to the traveler's perspective. In other words, for Whitehead this turnaround point is an actuality that overlaps the two points, but which does not belong to the totality of the points of the single lines of experiences. The turnaround point is the spatiotemporality of the relation itself, which overlaps the point of arrival and the point of departure but does not fuse them together. For this reason, this relational actuality remains a blind spot: an invisible but lived spatiotemporal actuality. The relational actuality represented by the turnaround point S thus explains the spatiotemporal asymmetries between the twins.

Whitehead's notion of duration is defined in terms of spatiotemporality, and thus explains that simultaneity involves both the local and the distant (here and there). However, according to Whitehead, since the geodesic straight line between two events cannot define the connection between distinct spaces-times or actual occasions, straightness should not be derived from measurement (i.e., the line establishing the distance between A and B). On the contrary, measurement has to be deduced from the primacy of straightness: the primary *reality* of straightness. Whitehead observes that according to modern mathematics, the straight line represents a geometrical means of calculating an infinitesimal magnitude (the increasingly small) or the infinite divisibility of a continual line. However, he maintains, notions of the infinitesimal and approximation cannot describe the relation between actual entities. In other words, infinitesimals only coincide with a class of finite numbers (functions), and cannot define the nature of actual relations. As Stengers points out,[78] Whitehead problematically rejects Einstein's model of the curvature of space-time because he believes that space (as space events spaces, regions, or relata) cannot be subsumed under notions of infinitesimal divisibility, or incorporated into the Leibnizian labyrinth of the continuum. According to Whitehead's metaphysical schema of infinite relations between finite entities, the contortions of a curve have to be conceived as segments between endpoints. If approximation in measuring is real, Whitehead observes, then it has to be conceived as an approximation to straightness.[79]

Hence, for Whitehead, it is the turnaround within the straight line of connection between points that explains the simultaneity of actual occasions of experience. The turnaround abolishes the distance between two space-time intervals, creating a blind spot, an actual spatiotemporality or a segment in linear connection. Abolishing this distance does not result in a collapse into universal degrees of "nows" corresponding to one continual curvature in space. On the contrary, it means the uncovering of irreversible "nows," i.e., of incompossible spatiotemporal actualities constituting space events. From this standpoint, the experience of simultaneity is not an illusion, but rather has to be understood as a sudden (imperceptible and unpredictable) jump of one set of actualities into the spatiotemporal coordinates of another. To put it another way, Whitehead claims that the change of motion at the star *causes* a temporal blind spot and the discrepancy in time keeping. Unlike Bergson's, however, Whitehead's account of time discrepancy does not rely on empirical conditions (according to which physical acceleration affects the clocks), but is resolved rather at a diagrammatic level including three distinct inertial frames (the two twins plus the point of return S).

Bergson's metaphysics of intensive (nonchronological) lived time has indirectly been appropriated by the topological aesthetics of parametric architecture (with real-time variations and local interactions by participation) and has become central to the postcybernetic logic of control working by means of differential inclusion. Whitehead's schema of simultaneity, however, seems to offer another notion of extension determined not by infinitesimals or differential qualities but by spatiotemporal events. Since the distance between points is marked by the blind spot S, the interval between points in time is a veritable space event, an extension event. The interval is at once a thing, irreducible to different points of view, and an occurrence, an event that breaks from the continuity of experience of the two positions. In other words, the simultaneity of distinct space-times points out that topological relations are interrupted by space events that are able to overlap (at point S) the two terms without ultimately synthesizing them into one continual frame of time.

From this standpoint, while Bergson unifies experience in time (or *la durée*) through a deep symmetry between the twins' points of view, Whitehead's triangular system (H1, S, H2) highlights the deep asymmetry between spatiotemporal durations: a radical schism between the twins' experience, a schism defined by the ingression of another space-time, a space event S, where the turnaround remains a part that cannot be fully integrated within the whole of the twins' experience. According to Whitehead, there are gaps between two points of view, discontinuities derived from a sudden interference of an actual yet invisible spatiotemporality. Bergson insists on the primary intuition of physical continuity against the scientific version of simultaneity as discrete events. For Whitehead, however, the experience of discontinuity defines the actual separation of spatiotemporal frames as a genuine fact of nature, for duration cannot be thought apart from extension.[80] Hence the experience of simultaneity corresponds to a spatiotemporal distance, where the mere alteration of place indicates the existence of an alternative space-time system at the intersection of the two points. This intersection, however, is also an interference in the chronological system of the twins defined by the turnaround point S, the spatiotemporal actuality of the relation itself.[81]

Whitehead devises an abstract schema of extension to address the reality of direction and the immediacy of gaps occurring at the turning point S, the space event of the interstice. His geometry of shears (or hyperbolic rotations in 4D space) suggests that the invisible links between simultaneous space-times are not evidence of a common experience of time, but of an immanent space event of connection between incompossible durations. For Whitehead, this means that there are not one but many spatiotemporal routes that connect one spatiotemporality to another. In other words, time does not need to be elastic and deformable in order for the twins to experience different durations. There is no direct way of plotting the two durations against each other in order to gain a global temporal intuition of the situation.[82] The date of the distant events, and the measure of distant intervals of time, are therefore always complicated by the connection of two systems that do not follow a smooth transition. Whitehead insists that the unity of time cannot ignore the fact that the twins' asymmetric experience is evidence of two invariant measures of time, neither of which has special priority. The invariant function of the topological continuity of forms is thus a consequence of the primary presence of alien space events, immanent spatiotemporal systems, infecting the serial order of the physical world.

From this standpoint, space-time relativity does not coincide with a fluid bending of space in time, but more importantly involves shears, cuts, gaps, or events suspending the continuity of space-time. Hence, the distinct perspectives of the twins are not simply illusions, but reveal the genuine experience of blind spatiotemporal spots. Even if time is represented as the fourth dimension of space, or is misleadingly said to be in space, Whitehead holds that it is always given *with* space as an irreducible actuality of extendedness.[83] From this standpoint, it may be possible to argue that each parameter, level, zone, and character of interaction is haunted by an alien spatiotemporal system, a part that cannot be reduced to a whole, or to the infinitesimal continuum between individual variables. This part, as will become clearer in the next few sections of this chapter, does not correspond with position H1 or H2 but rather with an invisible quantity: the space event of the turnaround itself. As a part that cannot be reduced to a whole, but instead enters into a relationship with the whole experience of the twins, this invisible quantity demonstrates that there can be simultaneity between distinct space-times. What defines simultaneity is indeed the realization that there is another order of actuality, defined by a spatialized or quantified temporality: a turnaround. The persistence of this part, space, or quantity is yet another way to address what occurs in the computation of relations within digital design. However, specifically addressing this relational actuality in the computation of relations also means disclosing another face of postcybernetic control, whereby the neoliberal logic of parametricism confronts the ingression of irreversible spatiotemporalities in the digital programming of extension.

2.6 Mereotopology of extension

If the topological invariant characterizes the smooth aesthetics of postcybernetic control, parametricism also shows that there is a topology of another kind, wherein computational quantities add new modes of extension to spatial relations. Parametric design does not only establish continual relations between parts, the manipulations of which aim, for instance, to effectuate change on the whole urban architecture; in addition, it inevitably implies the overlappings, conjunctions, and intersections of quantities, partialities, and extensive temporalities. In other words, parametric architecture, as an instance of postcybernetic control, not only involves the design of spatiotemporalities through the programming of a continual form of variations, but also reveals the persistence of parametric quantities, thereby disclosing how simultaneous spatiotemporalities cannot be fused together. In other words, I argue, by programming relations between spatiotemporal parts and wholes, parametricism uses a mereotopological and not simply a topological mode of design.

Whitehead uses the notion of mereotopology to address the problem of abstraction and spatial measurement.[84] He uses a nonmetrical logic to define the relations between extended parts and wholes, starting from concrete actualities or occasions of experience.[85] Since all metrical relations involve measurement (and to measure or quantify corresponds to the method of abstraction), Whitehead develops a new notion of extensive abstraction to problematize the general theory of relativity and the theory of measurement, which, he complains, seemingly collapse physics and geometry into one another, ultimately ignoring the distinction between the abstract and the concrete.[86]

Whitehead uses the notion of mereotopology to argue that space is composed of actual entities that connect. These entities are atomic occasions and constitute discrete events, and according to him they explain not continual becoming but the becoming of continuity itself. Zeno's paradox of discrete units and infinitesimal divisibility is not addressed here through the Bergsonian metaphysics of a continual duration, or *élan vital*, where all quantity amounts to a difference in kind.[87] Instead, the mereotopological relation between atomic spatiotemporality reveals that the continuity of connection is interrupted by the blind spots (actual regions and subregions) of relation. According to Whitehead, Leibniz's infinitesimal divisions, which Poincaré defined as topological invariants, cannot define the reality of events as corresponding to the plane of continuity (or the continual chain of cause and effect determining the sequential relations between actualities) because the distance between actualities cannot be filled by the infinitesimal continuity of percepts and affects.[88] On the contrary, the distance between actual entities has to be considered in its own right: as a space of connection, overlapping, inclusion, juxtaposition, disjunction, and intersection defined by the points and lines of finite actualities. In other words, according to Whitehead there are always actualities amid actualities.

While rejecting the notion that infinitesimals could be used to explain the relation between actualities, Whitehead also argues that these relations should not be compared to the infinite lines of the Euclidean parallel axiom, but rather to finite segments.[89] Each actual occasion is finite, and does not change or move. Actual entities, like the parameters in *Topotransegrity*, are real potentialities, determined by what Whitehead calls causal efficacy: the sequential order of data defined by the physical prehensions of past data from one entity to the next.[90] From this standpoint, the continuity between parameters is explained by the connection between entities, which are not geometrical points but rather "spatial regions" with semiboundaries (e.g., volumes, lumps, spheres).[91] Hence, continuity is not given by the convergence of two parallel infinite lines touching infinity, but by the actual relation between spatiotemporal regions of objectified real potentialities (actual entities): slices of time, atomic durations.[92] Instead of infinitesimally divisible points of perception and affection, Whitehead believes that there is an infinite number of actual entities between any two actualities, even between those that are nominally close together. This is why he rejects Zeno's paradox of infinitesimally small points and argues that continuity is not a ground to start from, but something that has to be achieved as a result of the extensive connections of actual entities.[93]

From this standpoint, the mereotopological relation between distinct sets of parameters, as deployed in *Topotransegrity*, for example, corresponds to the real potential of each actual entity to become the datum of another parameter. In other words, since the topological relation between parameters implies that a change in a parameter has an effect on other parameters and a generalized impact on the whole architectural structure, each parameter can be considered to have a real potential to become data for change for another. On one level, the extensive subdivisions (the parametric connection between software, crowd, and memory modes) and the topological relations of the points and lines between the physical space, the digital software, and the kinetic pistons of the *Topotransegrity* installation compose the *real potential* of actual entities (finite quantities or parameters). This actual level of parametric quantification and relationality describes the real potential of extended continuity, where the relation between finite entities is intersected by other finite entities and not by the phenomenal qualities of perception and affection. The parametric design of the *Topotransegrity* project therefore deploys a nexus of actual entities or events, which, according to Whitehead, stems from a series of sequences that constitute a "historic fact" (the objectified real potentials of software, crowd, and memory parameters at each spatiotemporal connection) relating occasions to occasions.[94] Data are defined by what has been in the past, but also by what might have been, and by what might yet be of the spatial configurations: a software program, the real-time movements of a crowd, the reshaping of the pistons, all enter into a quantitative relation that precisely accounts for an invisible spatiotemporality that is an actuality at point S. All these data are always actuals, and their specific potentiality is always a real possibility that affects the next series. Following the logic of cause and effect, the relation between parametric data involves a movement from past spatiotemporalities to those of the present and future, all of which are restricted by the physical level of parametric design. Here extension, as Whitehead argues, is not the realm of measure but "the most general scheme of real potentiality,"[95] since "all actual occasions are internally and externally extensive,"[96] and are related by means of extension; or, in this case, by parametric quantity, which is a veritable actuality amid the others.

In "The Relational Theory of Space"[97] Whitehead explains his method of extensive abstraction as the interconnection of different levels and scales of actualities. With the concept of extension, as opposed to notions of absolute space,[98] Whitehead claims that relations are part of the concrete order of things. In this sense, the succession of parameters is not too dissimilar to a succession of atomic entities. For instance, parametric urbanism in fact works to design relations between entities, not just by unifying them into a whole sequence of variable instructions but also, and importantly, by breaking up sequential continuity and exposing the real potentiality of parameters to overlap in a newly constituted computational space.[99] This is how parametric urbanism designs city systems of infrastructural connections that are not simply preadapted to the environment, but are programmed to construct actual relations between already existing entities through which they overlap and define the space events of programmed behavior.

For instance, multiagent systems,[100] such as BDI (Belief-Desire-Intention) agents,[101] are probability models that operate not through pattern recognition (or according to the connectionism of neural networks), but by developing tendencies and attitudes that lead to thought actions. Multiagent systems are not only informed and generated by the interaction between agents and by their local capacities to learn and adapt, but are able to evolve certain inclinations instead of others. These systems can be conceived as forming a nexus of actual entities,[102] and as thereby crafting new possibilities of actual relations. Multiagent systems are able to prehend[103] (to borrow a term from Whitehead), select, and reactivate variable quantities (changeable and evolving parametric relations) derived from past and simultaneous parameters. In short, multiagent systems are finite entities composed by the prehensions of both their internal relations (defined, for instance, by the evolving dynamics of genetic algorithms using past data to reengender information) and their external connections, which determine the extensive relationship between parameters. Multiagent systems are therefore proactive entities that select and rearrange their internal relations and acquire a subjective unity (a subjective form, in Whitehead's terms) by which they can ingress the world's external relations by prehending other elements and entities. It is precisely this process of prehension, selection, activation, and assemblage of data that links Whitehead's mereotopological schema of extensive relations to parametric urbanism.

Endorelations within multiagent systems, for instance, already enjoy a series of external relations of variables. Here a variable becomes part of another cluster of variables, which in turn changes the pack of variables it originated from. In other words, parametric design exposes how endorelations within sets of variables and series of exorelations are faced with irreducible subvariables, which are those irreducible parts that can be detached from the computational design of the whole. Therefore, if we take the relation between a set of parameters A and a set of parameters B, the subsets of A and B are not simply fused in the relation C but become a new object: a new parametric set equipped with new tendencies, singularities, and powers proper to C. C is not simply the link between relata but becomes a set of data itself, autonomously establishing new conditions of possibilities not only for C but also for the autonomous subsets of A and B. This is why the coming of C does not mark the disappearance of the A and B subsets, but the extension of their real potentialities in C. If the individual and autonomous subsets of A and B become part of C, because their potential tendencies exceed the local connection between A and B, they are however not neutralized into the whole object C, but retain their unaltered indivisible singularity (or subatomicity). It is, however, important to bear in mind that according to Whitehead, actual entities—the regions and subregions of A and B—do not endure forever. These entities must exhaust their own set of relations, reach completeness or satisfaction, and thus perish in order for C to become objective data for another set of variables, just as C inherited objectified data and the real potentialities of relations from A and B.

Similarly, the parametric software of *Topotransegrity*'s adaptive structure, which is determined by constant feedback loops between the movement of the crowd and the kinetic configuration of the pneumatic pistons, operates in the same repetitive fashion as physical, organic and inorganic matter. Here the invariant function of the topological continuum corresponds to the physical, extensive connection between actual entities, the fusion and integration of parts into wholes. This is only the topological level of parametric design. However, a mereotopological reading of *Topotransegrity* will have to include another level of relationality, the overlapping and intersection of parts by means of other parts (*mereology*). In other words, the relation between the three planes of actuality (the physical, the software, and the kinetic space) implies not their merging but rather their simultaneity as revealed by the actual space event at which they intersect, i.e., the actuality of the relation itself.

Nevertheless, it is important to specify that this actuality of relation is equivalent to the turnaround, and that this reveals the simultaneity of spatiotemporal experience. As Whitehead would suggest, each finite actuality—no matter what kind it might be, or what its scale—is also an infinite quantity that cannot be exclusively defined in terms of physical or ideal qualities.

It could be argued that *Topotransegrity* involves at least two modes of potentialities that define each and any level of actuality. These modes correspond to Whitehead's distinction between the real potential of each actual entity to become the datum of another and the pure potentials (or eternal objects) that enter actual occasions at many points.[104] From the standpoint of mereotopology these modes imply at least two orders of magnitude: the order of finite quantities and the order of infinite quantities. This is to say that Whitehead's distinction between the real potential of actual entities and the pure potentials of eternal objects returns in parametric design as the automation of actual relations, as finite and infinite quantities.[105] The computation of relations therefore reveals the presence of an alien spatiotemporal system that intersects the digital design of spatiotemporalities: the advance of space events or new actual forms of infinite quantities as internal conditions of the parametric order of postcybernetic control. It is therefore possible to argue that the topological ontology of neoliberalism does not reciprocally presuppose the irreversible formation of a space event that has now assumed a computational character. I suggest that the computational event reveals the actuality of spatiotemporal systems that are irreducible either to the physical or to the digital binarism of extension. In the next section, I will discuss the event in terms of quantities and thus clarify what a computational event can be.

2.7 Mereotopology of abstraction

Whitehead's mereotopological schema of parts and wholes thus offers another view of the computation of relations that lies at the heart of digital design, and of parametricism in particular. The relational space of data processing is defined by the actual space of the turnaround, whereby the sequential order of actualities is infected with abstract objects, the indeterminate reality of which adds new character to existing patterns of actual relations. This is not to say, however, that contingent physics is ontologically grounded in the order of eternal geometry. Despite the fact that the order of eternal objects, as pure relata, is not open to modification by spatiotemporal actualities, these objects are nonetheless part and parcel of the eventuation of such actualities. In particular, and insofar as these otherwise noncommunicating eternal objects are selected by actual entities to accomplish their "subjective aim," they also acquire unrepeatable unity in actual entities. This unity reveals how eternal objects are also subjected to the irreversible formation of events (or nexuses of actualities) and indeed undergo change within the order of actualities (where pure potentiality or indetermination becomes real or determinate potentials). This also means that space events are at once disjunctions of actual data and conjunctions of eternal objects.

According to Whitehead, eternal objects are only internally related to each other in terms of "a systematic mutual relatedness" in which each eternal object has a particular status in relation to other objects.[106] Therefore an eternal object "stands a determinateness as to the relationship of *A* [an eternal object] to other eternal objects."[107] This determinateness suggests that these objects are not fused into one continual eternal form. On the contrary, they are eternal only because they are an infinite variety of infinities. They do not share the same kind of infinity. There is no equivalence between the status of an eternal object and that of another eternal object. Eternal objects are not externally related to each other but only to actual entities, which select them as they grow and change. However, eternal objects also explain the atomistic character of actual entities: their nonrecursive spatiotemporality, which constitutes a slice of duration. The relations between actual entities therefore do not correspond to a mechanical chain of cause and effect, nor can they simply be granted by a metaphysical continuum, a transcendental time described by the infinitesimal degrees of being. Instead, relations are spatiotemporal actualities, and define events as an irreversible disjunction within the order of actualities and an irreversible conjunction of eternal objects. These relational actualities are the point S, the spatiotemporality of the turnaround, the blind spot that is not directly in contact with the terms of the relation. From this standpoint, the extensive continuum of actualities that determines their material ground of sequential connection and recursive calculations splits itself into thousands of quantities, the asymmetrical reassemblage of which becomes a nexus of actualities or a space event. The extensive continuum is, to say it with Deleuze and Guattari, schizophrenic.

But how does a connection between actualities become a relational actuality, a blind spot or space event? To answer this question, we need to delve deeper into Whitehead's mereotopological schema. According to the latter, actualities, in the process of their formation, select eternal objects or pure potentialities. Through doing so, they cause the continuum of actualities (or the extensive continuum) to split into events: atomic occasions of experience that change the nature of the continuum itself. In other words, the continuum becomes other than it was each time actual entities prehend eternal objects, or mere indeterminations, the ingression of which corrupts their structure and organization. This is how actual entities become objects of contingency. As Whitehead specifies, "in the essence of each eternal object there stands an indeterminateness which expresses its indifferent patience for any mode of ingression into any actual occasion."[108] Eternal objects are internally determined by infinity, but are externally related to actual entities, as the latter's indeterminate possibilities.[109]

It may be important to specify here that eternal objects are not an undifferentiated pool of qualities that are divided or spatialized by actual entities. On the contrary, I aim to rethink eternal objects in terms of discrete infinities, which do not define the external relation between actual entities in terms of infinitesimally smaller points of conjunction (e.g., Leibniz's percepts and affects, Deleuze's differential or intensive gap, or Bergson's duration or virtual time). Eternal objects, therefore, are not temporal forms of relations, but are permanent and infinite quantities that are isolated from their individual essences. They are relata in the uniform schema of relational essences, where each eternal object is located within all of its possible relationships.[110] Whitehead explains that there is a uniform scheme of relationships between eternal objects, which is precisely defined by the impossibility of reducing their infinite quantities to one infinity by subsuming them under a smaller cipher (i.e., the one, God, or being). Instead, eternal objects remain isolated from each other, embedded as they are in their own infinity. Nevertheless, while eternal objects are indifferent to the extensive continuum of actual entities, from whose standpoint eternal objects are pure indeterminacy, they nonetheless acquire an unprecedented togetherness once they are included in an actual entity, and thus gain an individual essence: a certain quality of infinite quantities. This means that for any actual occasion *a* there is a group of eternal objects that are, as it were, the immanent ingredients of that actual occasion. Since any given group of eternal objects may form the base of an abstractive hierarchy of relation, there is an abstractive hierarchy associated with any actual occasion *a*. This associated hierarchy is "the shape, or pattern, or form, of the occasion, insofar as the occasion is constituted by what enters into full realization."[111] This formal hierarchy thus defines the unity of eternal objects in actualities.

The computation of relations can therefore be seen under this new light. The relation between parameters implies that infinite quantities are selected by an infinite number of actualities. And yet eternal objects do not add intensive temporalities to parametric relations. On the contrary, actual parameters are the point of selective limitation or constraint of eternal objects, and as such they are general determinations applied to the spatiotemporal continuum. As Whitehead observes, "thus primarily, the spatiotemporal continuum is a locus of relational possibility, selected from the more general realm of systematic [and abstract] relationship."[112] Once eternal objects are selected, they add a new level of determination to the spatiotemporal sequence of parameters, contributing to the irreversible formation of actual relations between quantities of systematic length, for instance, weighted with the individual peculiarities of the relevant environment. For Whitehead, the mereotopological schema explains how novelty involves discontinuity on the extensive continuum. Any parameter, insofar as it is an actual entity, corresponds to the prehensions of the physical data of past, present, and future actualities. However, a parametric value is also a conceptual prehension of the abstract relata or eternal objects, which are included in the actual parameter as gradients of determination. From this standpoint, the sequential relation between parameters acquires a determination as an actual entity itself, defined by a new togetherness of eternal objects. The automation of this relation is therefore not simply a mechanical sequencing of discrete data: rather, it marks the advance of a new form of actuality (a space event) that splits apart the continuous sequencing of parameters by selecting data from the infinite infinities of abstract relata.

If Bergson's *élan vital* is a virtual continuum that is ceaselessly divided by perceptual selections or material actualities, Whitehead seems to claim that this correlation between one time (the topological invariant continuum of indiscernible, undifferentiated duration) and many spaces precludes any event from ever occurring on the extensive continuum of actualities. Like Henri Poincaré's view of an infinitesimal curving space or a topological continuum of uncut forms, Bergson is seeking a temporal invariant between events.[113] From this standpoint, only *virtual* time (uncoordinated intensive time) can *amodally* link two causally connected actualities (or parameters). Such virtual time is a real interval that exposes the plenitude of cosmic time, and has no intrinsic measure except a continual variation of differential relations. Against this, Whitehead's mereotopological schema defines the relationship between actual entities as being marked by the blind spot that cuts the continuum through the selection of infinite objects.

A parameter is not only the transduction of physical qualities (such as the volume of a space, gravitational forces, the circulation of air, the movement of people, the shades of lights, the sonic frequencies, the electromagnetic vibrations, etc.) into finite quantities, but an actual object itself. Furthermore, the relation between parameters is itself a spatiotemporal actuality that is not visible to the terms of the relation. This is because the abstract potential between parameters cannot be grasped at the level of sequential sets, but needs to be explained as the infinite quantities of abstract relations that infect and add novelty to the actual order of parameters. This means that the invariant function of topological continual relations, which grounds the ontological dominance of the aesthetics of curvilinearity, is only one way of articulating the relation between control and events. The mereotopological schema between eternal objects and actual entities offers another way.

The dominance of the invariant function determines relations between parameters in terms of vectorial qualities. As demonstrated by Lynn's calculus-based architectural forms, it is the qualitative relations of vectors that constitute space as a fluid environment of forces. Yet this qualitative inflection of parametric design has become a dominant postcybernetic procedure of connecting entities through a temporal flux of continual variations. For instance, the aesthetic appeal of morphogenetic forms defined by the continual variation of points into temporal vectors has become equivalent to the neoliberal operations of control, which transmute actualities into supple lines of convergence, compatibility, and uniformality.

One cannot deny that parametric urbanism incorporates measurable qualities that cannot be exactly measured (i.e., approximations to a point) into planning, and that it thus confers fluctuation and movement to the geometrical form as a whole, which results from the operations of a differential relation encompassing all points on a curve. It is suggested here that the qualitative dimension of the differential relation has become central to the topological view of the postcybernetic logic of control, whereby prediction is no longer based on the calculation of finite probabilities, but on the inclusion of potential qualities. Brian Massumi has defined this shift in terms of the mediatic power of preemption, whereby the indeterminate qualities of the future are incessantly foreclosed into sets of probabilities in the present.[114] The ingression of topological invariants into cybernetic systems allows automated processes to constantly transduce temporal qualities into quantities, by developing an aesthetic of continual quantities of qualities.

However, I find that the critique of computational modes of quantification, which contends that instances of the latter (such as parametricism) are yet another form of measuring the qualitative character of relation, occludes the significance of quantities as an immanent expression of the real. If quantities are indeed viewed as such expressions, it becomes possible to recognize that measuring is not only a mode of ordering but also, and importantly for our concerns here, a mode of becoming. To argue that computation mainly entails a transduction of qualities into quantities (albeit approximate quantities) is to deny that quantities could ever be more than finite sets of instructions. Yet Whitehead's mereotopological schema adds an abstract schema of infinite objects to the actual continuum, so that the infinity of relations between pure quantities can ingress into actual qualities. Points of connection are not only finite parts that overlap: the process of overlapping includes the selection of abstract quantities that add a new quantitative character to parts that are already overlapped, and thus reveals the formation of a new actual entity. To put it another way, parametric relations are infected with abstract, nondenumerable realities of pure quantities, or rather eternal objects: discrete infinities of relations that add novel data to existing parametric relations. From a mereotopological point of view, each parametric extensive relation is hosting another order of quantities that cannot be contained by the number of its actual members.

The topological model implies the permanent ground of movement from which events emerge qua events only when it becomes possible for actualities to jump out of the spatiotemporal grid into the infinity of virtual time. The mereotopological schema, however, suggests instead that events are the cumulative order of spatiotemporal actualities hosting an unrepeatable togetherness of eternal objects. Therefore it is not the formal hierarchy of eternal objects that determines actual events. Instead, events are the result of the actual accumulation of physical data, the causal chain, which is interrupted by the irreversible ingress of eternal objects. These objects are not simply selected by actualities to manage their orders of behavior or action, but are prehended for the pure chance or potentialities that these objects offer. Actualities therefore do not simply operate a probabilistic calculation about which eternal object to select. On the contrary, selection is a contagious *feeling* for nonactual ideas, involving the ingression of the infinite variations of chance into what has happened, what may happen, and what could have happened. This is how contingency becomes intrinsic to the formal architecture of eternal objects: a process by which existing relations can change and fashion themselves anew. This means that the indeterminacy of eternal objects is prehended like the irreversible reality of chance; these objects offer pure potentialities, and thereby determine the atomic (and eventful) character of actual relations.

If the topology of parametric design implies the calculation of variables through the invariant function, Whitehead's mereotopology, by contrast, always subtracts actual events from overall continuity. Mereotopology therefore suggests that underneath continual morphogenesis there lies a holey space of random quantities or infinite infinities that cannot be counted as such. These are the black holes that are inherent within probability and statistical calculation and that remark the occurrence of an infinite variety of infinities immanent to the actual regions of a nexus of occasions. In parametric design, this space perforated with holes is defined by the intrusion of parasitic quantities, nonisomorphic functions that are unable to unite all finite quantities into a morphogenetic continuity.

The topological view of the digital processing of physical data has already unleashed these abstract quantities into culture through the parametric design of buildings, cities, environments, and objects. This design does not simply involve the algebraic manipulation of physical data; rather it is the computation of the extensive continuum of actualities (resulting in the computation of parametric relations) that adds incomputable chance to actual relations. Parametric design is then also an instance of an aesthetic of discontinuous infinities between finite quantities. This discontinuity explains how the spatiotemporal continuum can become other to the actual relations that compose it. Here, the introduction of novel configurations of space is not derived from the continual variations of form, but from a universe of discontinuous potentialities that abduct the actual relations of data and thus expose parametric aesthetics to the infinite quantities that accompany any set of probabilities. If topological continuity is the aesthetic design of postcybernetic control via the continual variation of qualities, mereotopological discontinuities expose the aesthetics of irreducible quantities that define the event of computational relations beneath the smooth surface of preemption. Parametric design deals with different orders of quantification (finite and infinite relations), and in consequence it cannot avoid becoming a channel for the proliferation of incomputable realities within the programming of extensive relations. The parametric aesthetics of *Topotransegrity* do not therefore simply offer a formal system of relations between the software level of programming, the hardware level of the kinetic pistons, the level of physical movement, and those of air circulation and access; on the contrary, mereotopology exposes this formal system to the indeterminate, incomputable, and contingent infinities of urban programming, where indeterminate quantities add a new level of determination to parametric relations. It is this abstract quantitative order of relations that needs to be accounted for in debates about the aesthetics of postcybernetic control. In the next section these abstract quantities will be further examined in the context of parametric design, and I will argue that postcybernetic control implies the automation of prehensions. From the standpoint of mereotopology, these infinite quantities are parts that connect or disconnect with the processing of sequential parameters (considered as a whole). At the same time, this whole processing can also be a part that connects to another. Parts therefore are not the components of a whole, but remain incomputable, random objects that have the power to change the extant order of actualities.

2.8 Parametric prehensions

In this section, I will argue that the addition of actual novelties in the parametric computation of relations cannot be explained, as the *Topotransegrity* project attempts, in terms of interaction between software and external data, an interaction that is usually conceived in terms of the perceptual and sensorimotor capacities of participants, but also of actuators or external measuring devises. As against this view, I want to argue that actual novelties are in fact implied in the computational automation of what Whitehead calls prehensions. Sensorimotor interactions can be used to explain those immediate sensorial perceptions of qualities that can be inputted into the program; they cannot, however, be used to describe the relation between parameters, i.e., between quantities of data.

To use sensorimotor interactions to understand the ways in which real-time inputs change the order of parametric programming is to suggest that aesthetic knowledge corresponds to a "bundle of impressions," and to Hume's empirical view of perceptions as having no cause.[115] Here aesthetic knowledge is merely the result of habitual associations linking events together in a subjective mind that is ready to project qualities onto things. These "impressions" are deemed to be the site for the introduction of contingency into the programming of parametric relations leading to the emergence of novelty. Yet as Whitehead reminds us, impressions cannot explain novelty. On the contrary, by forcing the projection of qualities onto the parametric program, these mere acts of stimulus and response add confusion to the workings of veritable modes of prehension. The interactive changes expected from pressing buttons, walking slower, turning toward the south, or wearing green are indeed simply the result of habitual patterns of perception, which may minutely diverge (or enrich the whole program of parametric relations), but which never stir a space event in the modular paths of an interactive program. Whitehead would call this mode of interactive perception a mode of presentational immediacy. Nonetheless, he argues that prehensions in this mode of presentational immediacy are more than subjective impressions. The prehension of something here in front of us reveals the presence of *something that is in itself* irreducible to the standpoint of the perceiver. This prehension admits the *objectness* (the objectified potentiality) of things that are conditioned, inflected, and contaminated by their nexus of relations. From this standpoint, presentational immediacy would explain parametric architecture not as the projection of individual impressions onto the screen of running data, but as a delimited zone of contagion between worlds: a vivid display of mathematico-geometric relations, where experience becomes immanent to alien spatiotemporal actualities.[116]

At the same time, however, digital computation cannot account for the arrival of change in the parametric programming of relations. The rule-based generation of urban space means that these rules are to be *experienced* in order to break the order of computational sequencing. Yet "experience" here implies not a subject perceiving the parametric structure of data, but rather the capacities of actualities (including any order of data) to prehend other actual data, and thus to become infected with abstract quantities. The computation of relations therefore implies that parameters prehend data sets and subsets of relations, and that in doing so they define the subjective form of a programmed environment, a nexus of actual entities. Parametric prehensions thus explain how a programmed environment can become a subjective form of the data prehended that involves the experience of abstract quantities on behalf of the actualities that partake of it. But this subjective form does not match the sum of parametric actualities, because it is the process of prehension—the selection, evaluation, and limitation of actual and abstract data—that ultimately contributes to the programmed experience. For Whitehead, the mathematical-geometric division of points and lines, and in our case the parametric division of data into parameters, involves slices of duration: regions or lumps of space where each point is primarily a prehension that is also included in another point. If every element of an actual entity is included in another, if all elements of A are elements of B, then all elements of A are objectified in B, and are immediately transmitted among the elements of both by means of physical prehension. At the same time, however, all elements are separate, or to use Whitehead's terms, "atomized." The order of transmission from an antecedent actuality A is indirectly received, through nonsensuous prehensions in the mode of causal efficacy, into the constitution of a subsequent actuality B.

Thus, while the universe is atomic, actual objects are indirectly (nonsensually) bound to one another through the transmission of objectified potentials from the past to the present.[117] Since all actual entities bond into a nexus of feelings or prehensions,[118] the nonsensual mode of prehension explains how things are never only here and now, but are always related in the spaces (or slices) of the immediate past and future. As opposed to the empirical mode of perception, which is defined by many isolated instants of projection, Whitehead insists that the mode of presentational immediacy always implies the present's prehension of settled data from the immediate past. Nevertheless, this is not a causal connection, whereby the past informs the present as a cause determines its effects. On the contrary, it implies the power of the past to become relevant to the present. From this standpoint, a programmed environment is never an always-already-preset spatiotemporality; instead it implies the process of prehending settled data from the past, a process that corresponds to the transformation of those data within the present.

Far from being epistemological necessities posed by human perceptions of the world, space and time define the subjective conditions of any entity derived from the receptive feeling that all beings effectively produce in the course of their experience. In other words, the receptive act of feeling (or prehension) enables the spatiotemporal localization of objects. Thus space and time are not productive of the ordered world, but rather derive from it.[119]

Parametric design implies a process of prehension by which space and time are derived from the ordered world of parametric programming through the transmission of data from the past to the present. From this standpoint, a programmed environment is entangled in a process of parametric prehension, whereby past data enters into a relation with the data of the present. This defines the arrival of novelty not as something that depends on the subjective impressions of interactive users, but rather as involving the parametric prehension of data, a prehension that derives its own regions and spatiotemporal extensions from already programmed sequences.

If parametric urbanism marks the programming of extensive relations, it does so through the automation of prehensions, leading to a new level of determination of space and time. Digital urbanism, in other words, is adding a new spatiotemporal system onto the extensive continuum of actualities. Parametric urbanism includes rules for selecting, contrasting, and adopting data from previous sets in the computation of present and future quantities of relations. It thus entails the programming of parameters according to their prehensive capacities to connect variables in different orders. This is not due to a free, unbounded power of generating change in software models (i.e., the generative evolution of genotypes forming infinite versions of shapes). On the contrary, prehensions explain the irreversible nesting of data within a set, the selection and transformation of past into present data, and the actual relation between parameters of different scales and dimensions.

If digital parameters are automated prehensions, they are also modes of decision making that do not simply result from the binary calculation of 0s and 1s. On the contrary, parametric design now implies the computation of continual or topological relations, according to which relations have become objectified, datified as actual entities. Parametric design thus requires no preplanned modeling but step-by-step procedures of decision making, according to which the path of the sequence can be reordered in real time. The prearranged order of parameters therefore remains open to counterdirections derived from the short-term power of decision acquired by automated relations in the process of computation. The computation of relations thus requires that preplanned decisions become replaced by prehensive capacities of decision making, which afford the parametric system the freedom to establish unintended connections between parameters within the constrained conditions of sequential programming.[120] As Whitehead argues, freedom derives from the power of decision making, which implies that an actual entity (a parameter or nexus of parameters) reaches its final cause (or subjective form) by transforming the data received into new sets of rules. Actual entities can decide how far they can enter into a relational composition with other entities, and in doing so they exercise a power of freedom or autonomy. This means that not all sets of variables must enter into relation with all parameters encountered in the process, or that some changes in their arrangement are negligible and do not lead to a space event. In other words, parametricism maintains no overall dictum according to which everything must be connected or kept in a constant state of change. While it is true to say that there is no emptiness between parametric sets, there are at the same time indeterminate degrees of relatedness depending upon the actual prehensions involved.

From this standpoint, one could argue that parametric urbanism may be conceived as a mode of programming extension that is driven by software-prehensive capacities of spatiotemporal division, and not by the topological invariant that gathers all spatiotemporalities into a continuous whole of variations. The parametric automation of prehensions does not simply quantify urban qualities of relations, but is set to design the quantitative relation between parameters involving the selection of abstract quantities in the construction of soft urbanism.[121] Thus the parametric programming of temporal and environmental changes—physical variables, such as humidity, temperature, wind, air circulation, the movement of people, etc.—also involves the design of the causal efficacy of actual entities, the prehension of the physical data of the past that is inherited by the present sequential processing of variables. Even when physical data are introduced into the program in real time, it is still a matter of how these data from the past are prehended by parameters within the present. This is because the parametric programming of weather variables, for instance, organizes the prehensions of spatiotemporal configurations precisely as the registering of change from one state to another. In short, I suggest that the programming of physical variables coincides with the automated prehension of variables, which results in the registering of change from the past to the present. On the other hand, parametric probabilities are not mere re-presentations of physical variables, but become a present counteraction on the inherited past, an inevitable transformation of data into a soft mode.

Parametric design thus also implies the automation of both physical and conceptual prehensions through which data from the past is not simply inherited but computationally transformed. As such, conceptual prehensions define the mental pole of an actual entity (a parameter or a set of parameters) and its power of decision making. The latter is informed by the selection of eternal objects, indeterminate quantities infiltrating the arrangement of probabilities in the process of computation. Since parametric relations coincide with spatiotemporal forms of process, potentialities and possibilities built on regions and subregions of relations, the sequential calculation of probabilities cannot but admit indeterminate quantities in a programmed sequence of rules. These quantities define the actuality of the turnaround point not only in terms of temporality but also, and importantly according to Whitehead's mereotopological schema, as extension. The turnaround therefore corresponds to the formation of a blind spot, an invisible space split from point A and B that explains how A and B can be simultaneous. It therefore constitutes a new space that is reducible neither to the combinatorial mode of digital parameters nor to the interaction of physical variables within digital programming. In the next section, the space of turnaround will be more precisely defined as an incomputable space that exceeds both the relation and its terms. In particular, I will discuss R&Sie(n)'s architectural project *Une architecture des humeurs*, which offers a mereotopological use of parametricism in which the relations between distinct planes of programming (e.g., mathematical, algorithmic, physical, mental, perceptual, parametric, robotic) are determined by *malentendues*: an extra-space of misunderstanding or mishearing in which incomputable data of all sorts (digital, physical, mental, hormonal, mathematical, parametric) explain how the turnaround point becomes a space event.

2.8.1 Scripting uncertainties

The automation of prehensions does not mean that the digital reception of physical data is a passive mode of transmission. On the contrary, prehensions always imply an irreversible transformation rather than simply a direct passage of data from one point to another. At the same time, however, this process does not simply suggest that one term or actual data parameter merges with another, reflects that other, or becomes merged into a continual process of parametric change. Automated prehensions do not simply synthesize data into strings of 0s and 1s. It should be stressed here that to prehend is also to be affected by the data that is prehended. This means that automated prehensions are also irreversibly infected by the physical data that the parametric order of relations seeks to formally order.

More importantly, and in order to return to Whitehead's insistence on the existence of blind spots, we should note that prehensions are also noncommunicating spaces, and that they thus define actualities that remain invisible to the terms that enter in relation with one another. These blind spots constitute actualities that interrupt the linear communication between terms. This interruption is not a suspension, a leap outside time and space, or an interval that deploys the unity of the relation through an extra dimension. On the contrary, following Whitehead, one can argue that what comes in the middle is nonetheless an actual entity that is irreducible to terms and yet exists where terms overlap or become simultaneous.

From this standpoint, it is a challenge to understand how the computation of relations at the core of parametric design implies that the space between parameters becomes formalized not only in terms of topological invariants but also, as Whitehead's mereotopological schema suggests, as an actual infinity, i.e., as a space event imbued with abstract quantities. Parametricism would imply that the automation of prehensions foregrounds the reality of actual blind spots, where 0s and 1s acquire simultaneity or overlap. These actualities are not just parts that produce the whole, but rather remain (irreducible) parts that connect to the whole without becoming fused with it.

This mereotopological understanding of relations as parts that do or do not connect to wholes offers us another understanding of parametricism, defined not by the equalizing operations of the invariant function but by introducing, into the programming of spatiotemporal relations, parts that are bigger than the whole. In parametric design, these parts can vary their compositional value, establish independent relations, and remain autonomous from the overall development of the entire shape. Instead of having the same value and the same quantity, parameters are nonequivalent automations of values that determine a field of competitive priorities of connection and change. Since regions of automated prehensions compose each parameter, the latter can be defined as an actual entity characterized by a series of actual quantities.

From this standpoint, each parameter deploys a real potentiality or value that remains stubbornly determinate even when the entire set of parametric relations changes. For instance, the parametric value of spatial volume can be changed by processing the height, width, or length of the overall structure, but the partial quantities of this volume still characterize the idea of the volume. In other words, the permanence of the idea of volume is affected by the special togetherness that volumetric quantities acquire in an actual mode of volume. This permanence determines the nonequivalence of the parametric calculations of volume: the fact that quantities of volumes are yet irreducible to the overall parametric design of volumes (according to which the change of one variable results in the continual change of the whole parametric space). Thus, while the parametricist view maintains that change is now central to spatial design, parametricism's processing of relations is nonetheless interrupted by actual parts of abstract quantities that do not change, but rather add new indetermination to already existing relations. The automation of prehensions in parametric design does not therefore correspond to a strategy of control based on ensuring the metamorphism of the whole, and which mainly works toward extending the cybernetic system of prediction or probabilities to qualitative changes. Parametric automation does not in consequence exclusively correspond to the reduction of qualities to sets of quantities.

The automation of physical and conceptual prehensions instead implies the addition of actualities to the overall processing of parametric relations. If parameters are not simply quantifications of qualities but are themselves modes of data prehension, then they also transform qualities, and thus add new actualities to parametric computation. This could help us to understand that parameters, insofar as they are automated modes of prehension, do not just execute a script or perform a system of rules, but instead actively work to rescript the axiomatic programming of relations. But what does it mean to rescript a script?

In order to answer this, one must begin by questioning the general idea of scripting in digital design, as it implies the manipulation of digital codes, the automated operations of which are expected to generate an evolving urban space. Scripting, in other words, may not exclusively describe the computational optimization of urban solutions offered by the adaptive behavior of a parametric system of distributive relations that change over time. The significance of parametric architecture for postcybernetic operations of control is not its capacity to script the future and to create adaptive models that predict the evolution of the urban infrastructure (from changes in population density to geological changes). On the contrary, scripting now implies the immanent construction of actual spatiotemporalities. These are actualities defined by automated prehensions that derive space and time from programmed structures of relations. This also means that automated prehensions do not just generate urban designs; in addition, and more importantly, they construct actual spatiotemporalities that are not and cannot be reduced to spatiotemporalities that are derived from physical experience. What happens in the relation between parameters, or automated prehensions, is not simply a calculative prediction of how the urban infrastructure of data would evolve over time, but rather implies an evolutionary scenario within the actuality of the present moment, whereby indeterminate quantities enter actualities. Therefore, with parametric design the automation of scripting may not, for example, solely describe how real-time solutions for infrastructural crisis can be computationally generated. I argue instead that the importance of the automation of scripting stems from the degree to which it reveals an automation of relations between parameters that prevents scripting from anticipating the overall system of relations of urban infrastructures. The automation of relations is understood here in terms of prehensions that break from a predeterminate set of probabilities (or inherited spatiotemporalities of the past), because the automation itself adds unforeseen actualities to the script that deploy new rules of relation. From this standpoint, scripting in parametric design does not exclusively imply a strategy of prediction based on past probabilities or on a new mode of harnessing the potentialities of computation into set possibilities. Instead, the automation of prehensive relations suggests that the cybernetic mode of prediction has become a speculative and immanent computation of indeterminate quantities coming to determine rules and constitute axioms anew. In other words, parameters are set to think of indeterminate quantities so as to formulate new axioms or immanent sets of procedure. Far from opposing axiomatics to potentialities (or reducing potentialities to axiomatics), which according to Deleuze and

Guattari is the function of computation,[122] parametricism shows how post-cybernetic control aims to rescript axiomatics by adding unprovable sets or incomputable quantities (eternal objects) to actual relations. Ultimately, postcybernetic control, as a preemptive form of power, relies upon and universally imparts nonequivalence between actual entities by becoming exposed to indeterminate abstract quantities, which determine spatiotemporal actualities amid other spatiotemporal actualities.

The mereotopological order of relations, more than the topological uniform continuum of objects, shows that actualities serve abstract quantities to acquire spatiotemporal continuity. Yet abstract quantities are not all the same and do not enter actual entities in equal measure. In the first place, these quantities have to be selected, prehended (positively or negatively) by actual entities. This means that without actual entities, without sets of algorithms and without parameters, eternal objects or abstract quantities would remain in utter isolation. This is why actual parameters have become hosts for those indeterminate quantities that acquire real potentiality through them. The automation of parametric prehensions is therefore able to calculate the incalculable (pure quantities) as a process of partitioning indeterminate objects into actual values. Postcybernetic control precisely follows the mereotopological order of relations between parts and whole: abstract quantities are partitioned by automated prehensions, and yet this partiality becomes an opportunity for abstract quantities to become connected (to establish a continuity) and thus to immanently form new actualities. Therefore while eternal objects are irreducible potentialities, they are divided by actualities in and through which they acquire a new continuity. From this standpoint, it is possible to argue that parametricism as a mode of postcybernetic control exposes scripting to blind spots: spatiotemporal actualities of the middle, which lie between and across parametric values. These are immanent actualities that do not predict the future of an urban infrastructure, but rather point at the soft extension of the here and now. But how are these relational actualities unfolded in parametric scripting?

It is possible to see Whitehead's mereotopological order at work in some instances of experimental parametric design, according to which the programming of relations between actualities does not just serve to evolve new shapes or architectural forms, but calculates the field of relations between parts and between parts and wholes. In this case, parametricism is not simply an instance of a new form of adaptable control based on the computational capacity to include external or contingent stimuli evolving over time, but points to a mode of control implying the rescripting of programs: the insertion of random quantities into the parametric order of relations. For instance, R&Sie(n) architect François Roche has shown how parametric scripting cannot be equated to a sequential programming or a binary quantification of physical variables or qualities. R&Sie(n)'s projects instead suggest that scripting coincides with a speculative and immanent search for indeterminate quantities, data, and numbers, constituting the patterns, codes, and protocols of spatiotemporal programming.

As opposed to blob architectures, in which the infinitesimal calculus gives rise to complex forms through the integral function of differential relations, R&Sie(n)'s experiments in parametric architecture show how random data (incomputable quantities) are prehended or selected and transformed by algorithms and parameters. In particular, Roche argues that parametric scripting involves multiple pathways and the simultaneous processing of variables. Parametric scripting, in other words, draws on the power of indeterminate potentialities to govern relations between pathways and between data variables. As a result, the space of relation is a gap full of data that cannot be directly qualified as states (binary states for instance) or assimilated by one of the relational terms (for instance the digital program and the physical data). The space of relation instead remains the space of incomputable data governing the connections and disconnections between many and simultaneous parameters. This incomputable space, however, does not simply become the generator or the motor behind the emergence of a new actuality. Instead, I argue that this incomputable space is immanent, and that it thus produces another kind of actuality, linking here and there, above and below, across and sideways: a spatiotemporal blind spot that explains the mismatch of simultaneous worlds, orders, laws, and the contagious advance of alien spatiotemporal systems into the everyday.

2.8.2 *Une architecture des humeurs*

R(&)Sie(n)'s 2010 research project *Une architecture des humeurs*, a collaboration between mathematicians, programmers, architects, and a robotic designer, may help us to clarify what this actual space of relations is, and how it can nonetheless be understood in terms of indetermination or abstract quantities.

A computational machine designed to collect biological and physiological data from visitors who are put through situations that incite repulsion, stress, and pleasure exposes the presence of indetermination at a first level of relation: the relation between biophysical data and software. The visitors' chemical reactions to pleasurable or stressful situations are measured

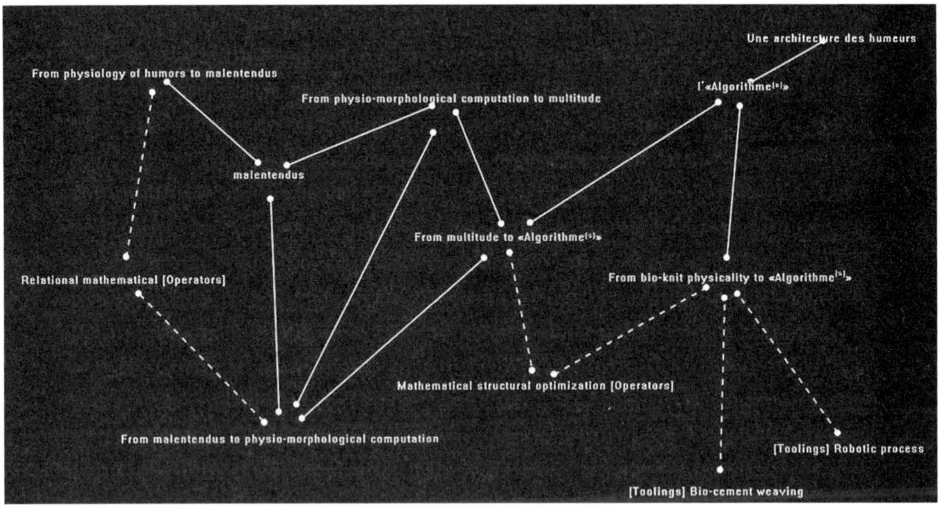

Figure 2.4
R(&)Sie(n), *Une architecture des humeurs*, 2010–2011. Courtesy François Roche.

through a digital device that calculates the variations in their moods and reduces their reactions to algorithmic data, which are then used to design housing units and urban fragments from the data obtained about the visitors' hormonal responses. By schematizing situations into protocols that have been devised in accordance with the mathematical terms of set theory (particularly notions of belonging, relations, and qualities), this mood-driven architecture establishes a series of parametric relationships between its biophysical, algorithmic, and robotic processing of data to become determinate in the form of housing units and urban fragments.

Nevertheless, the first level of relationality between the physiology of humors and the physiomorphological transformation of these hormonal and chemical data into algorithms is not simply equivalent to a continuous translation of physical contingencies into digital codes, determined by, as it were, an integral function. This relation is instead conceived as a blind spot that exceeds the actuality of both physical and digital data. As R&Sie(n) points out, the relation between distinct modes of data is neither smooth nor broken, but rather is crowded with *malentendues*. *Malentendues* are logical inevitabilities defined by the simultaneous and paradoxical existence of contrasting statements, such as "I'd love to but at the same time / and maybe / not / on the contrary." R&Sie(n) has placed this logic of paradoxes at the core of its protocols, subtending the organizational and

Figure 2.5
R(&)Sie(n), *Une architecture des humeurs*, 2010–2011. Courtesy François Roche.

procedural order of relations of the project. These *malentendues* define how the algorithmic prehension of physiological data always involves the inclusion of random or indeterminate quantities in the algorithmic set, and not the representation or simulation of physical data. At the same time, however, *malentendues* do not only explain the presence of random data at the physical level of prehensions. If *malentendues* account for the irreducibility of physical data to digital actuality, they also describe a conceptual prehension of the indeterminate data that characterize the relations between physical and digital actualities. This is perhaps how the computation of physical data leads to the design of urban fragments and housing units that have no direct correlation with the physical state of things, and to the digital calculation of these states in arrays of 0s and 1s.

The neurobiological structure of data is physically prehended by algorithms through a physiological test, which works as an emotion sensor. During the test, a vapor of nanoparticles is emitted to detect the mood alterations of visitors, who are subjected to stimuli that induce pleasure, pain, stress, etc. As the visitors are asked to breathe in the vapor, the nanoparticles are set to activate bodily chemical reactions (mainly molecules such as dopamine, adrenaline, serotonin, and hydrocortisone)[123] inciting degrees of pleasure or repulsion, curiosity or the absence of interest. The automated prehension of physical data, however, enters another stage of activity from that of mere information retrieval. This automaton in fact also requires algorithms to make a decision as to how to build the visitors' residence area based on the data retrieved from their changing moods. Since nanoreceptors have been designed to act as informational vectors, the test is used to decide which protocols are to be employed in the construction of housing fragments and habitats based on the visitors' chemical reactions.

Unlike standard prefabricated architectures, these morphological habitats result from the prehensive automation of states (or moods) to the extent that algorithmic parameters relate one neighborhood to another in the same way as they relate groups of data together. The protocol recites: "At last a habitat that reacts to your impulses. . . . More precisely, it is itself the vector . . . synchronized with your body, your blood, your sexual organs, your pulsating organism . . . and you become a thing, an element among the rest, an element in fusion, porous . . . which breathes and yearns to be its own environment."[124] But what appears here to be a direct transition of biophysical data into information is instead marked by the activities of *malentendues*, defined by the capacity of algorithms not simply to retrieve but to transform biophysical data into digital actualities, which implies the automated prehension of what cannot be computed. *Malentendues* do not simply correspond to errors or malfunctions in logic but instead expose how logical relations are infected by the incomputable character of both physical and digital data, adding new levels of determination in the digital design of the habitat.

In particular, the relational architecture of the morphological habitats, resulting from the prehensions of biochemical data on behalf of algorithms, is organized according to sets of belonging, inclusion, intersection, and difference, a mathematics of relation inspired by Georg Cantor's set theory.[125] These relations, however, are also characterized by *malentendues*, which explain the presence of discontinuities and distance between morphological habitats: the presence of blind spots that mark the actuality of the gap between terms. *Malentendues*, therefore, intrude by way of sets of relations that are arranged by protocols of attraction, repulsion, contiguity, dependence, exclusion, indifference, and sharing. For instance, the set of inclusion explains the relation between morphological habitats in terms of relations of dependence, whereas the protocol of repulsion involves relations of maximum distance.[126] R&Sie(n) uses nine axioms to map the relationships between these sets. The combination of these axioms makes it possible to deploy a multitude of relationships, both within the cell and immediately around it. For example, an ensemble comprised of two residential cells subdivided into parts and subparts makes it possible to describe their internal and external relationships simultaneously according to the axioms. Yet these axioms are governed by *malentendues*: indeterminate quantities that link one set to another, thus adding a new level of determination to existing relations.

Similar to Whitehead's mereotopological scheme, this parametric system of relations defined by *malentendues* is not concerned with boundaries or holes, but with abstract quantities (or eternal objects) immanent to spatiotemporal regions, the connections between which are defined by the

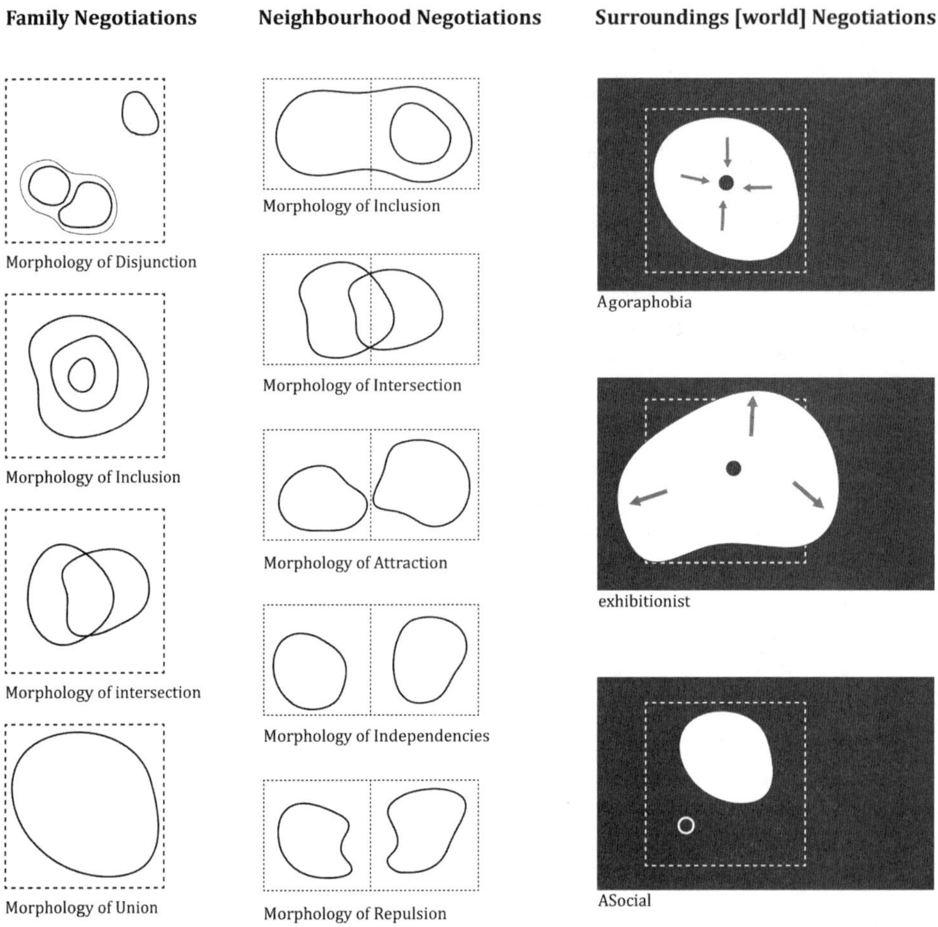

Figure 2.6
R(&)Sie(n), *Une architecture des humeurs*, 2010–2011. Courtesy François Roche.

overlapping at a common point. But this connection between abstract quantities does not simply imply the overlapping of a common boundary. Boundaries, in other words, are not included in the domain.[127] Whitehead's mereological relations of overlapping, disjunctions, intersections, inclusions, and unions of actual entities involve a concern with how events could be summed up (or become a nexus of events). In other words, Whitehead's mereotopological schema explains how parts become joined or connected to each other (whether they are discrete or not), and how abstract quantities can also become joined in actualities. This is why Whitehead conceives of points and lines in terms of real potentialities, defined by the operative prehensions of eternal objects on behalf of actual entities. This means that an abstract set of regions has to converge with a set of inner points, which in turn become relevant to all the regions involved. A nexus of actual entities or an event has to be traversed and occupied by an abstract set of regions, abstract quantities, or eternal objects acquiring a unique togetherness in and through these entities.

In particular, and in the same fashion as the mereotopological order of connecting abstract regions with inner points described in *Une architecture des humeurs*, Whitehead's mereotopological schema insists that a point does not simply represent a place in space. On the contrary, a point is first of all a point without parts, an absolute prime element: a prime number (an indivisible quantity). In his theory of sets, regions, and relata, Whitehead explains that points are at once concrete and abstract. Concrete points are immediately connected to the next, or are at least interconnected and overlapping in the spatiotemporal dimensions of past-present-future. This explains why distinct regions of spatiotemporality can enter into actual relations with one another. In an abstractive set, as in the mathematical model, such a point is to be called "punctual." According to Whitehead, this mathematical point is at once limited and unextended.[128] In other words, it does not overlap, it has no external relations, and it simply enjoys a specific location. Yet, for Whitehead, this location is also the locus at which the point should be seen to involve an abstract set of objects, the completeness of which requires an infinite number of infinite points.[129]

From the immanent relation between a concrete and abstract point, Whitehead derives the notion of the region:[130] a determinate boundedness, or the extensive standpoint that marks the real potentiality of actual entities.[131] The boundedness of actual entities does not correspond to a boundary of overlapping actualities, but is primarily defined by a volume. To any region A is attached a point set $P(A)$, namely the set of points *situated in the region,* which Whitehead calls the *volume* of the region. This volume defines its internal boundedness as a specific spatiotemporal dimension of extension.[132] Thus, according to Whitehead, a region is internally delimited by subregions, bound together inside as a determinate extensive connection, a concrete assemblage of actual relations. However, this region is more than just a point: in addition, it is a nexus of actual entities, whereby points determine the internal knots of an actual occasion, which is itself also a nexus of external actual entities. In other words, according to Whitehead, a point in space-time (or a simple location) cannot remain independent from its relations with other points and from the volume that they constitute together. Volumes, therefore, are not simply aggregates of points, but are compounded by a selection of many aspects that irreversibly infect every other part of the volume.[133] In short, for Whitehead, points are processes by which the realization of potentials constitutes the concreteness of a volume through a plurality of spatiotemporal individuations. The unity of a volume is therefore conceived as the seizing together of relations between individualizing points. Since points are, for Whitehead, spatial relations between concrete (real) and abstract (pure) potentialities, they are neither simply mathematically nor physically individual. A point, or any other geometrical element obtained by extensive abstraction, is above all a nexus of actual entities. This is why rough boundaries are central to the Whiteheadian cosmology of actual entities. As he observes, "events appear as indefinite entities without clear demarcations."[134]

Unlike the physical science of Newton, which defines individually existent physical bodies merely through bounded external relationships, Whitehead argues that the primary attributes of physical bodies are the (eternal) forms of *internal* relationships *between* actual occasions and *within* actual occasions. Whitehead's process metaphysics thus turns any notion of (physical) materialism into *immanent abstract relations,* replacing the static stuff of the world with the relation between atomic energy and its structure. As he claims, "such energy has its structure of action and flow and is inconceivable apart from such structure [which] . . . is also conditioned by quantum requirements."[135] In other words, actual entities are not simply physical objects but also events—spatiotemporal occurrences with rough boundaries—and are at once both discrete and continuous, both abstract and concrete.

In R&Sie(n)'s *Une architecture des humeurs,* parametric relations include abstract sets of points, and the *malentendues* expose the indeterminate quantities (eternal objects) prehended by actual sets of parameters (sets of points) in order to construe spatiotemporal nexuses of entities. From this standpoint, R&Sie(n)'s project stages a mereotopology of abstract and actual points through the automation of prehensions of real and pure potentials that determine the programming of a space event.[136] Parameters are not simply logical instantiations of procedures based on finite terms, but are rather determined by the prehension of abstract points, uncertain quantities or *malentendues* that continuously infect the programming of relations, adding a new level of determination to what already exists.

Hence it may be difficult to argue that parametric design is just an instance of mereological disconnected parts defined by bounded regions, and that it cannot account for the notion of a whole (a one-piece, self-connected whole such as a stone, as opposed to a scattered entity made of disconnected parts, such as an archipelago).[137] At the same time, however, parametric design does not fully embrace the unitary character of folding architectures, the topological ontology of the infinitesimal relations through which the wholeness of form emerges out of the continual fusion of parts. On the contrary, parametricism's attempts at cohesiveness and preemption are undermined by the mereotopological relations between parts and parts and wholes. From this standpoint, parts can partake in or connect to the whole system of relations, but can also exceed its consistent dynamics. Similarly, the whole can become a part that connects to others, and it can therefore partake of another system of part-to-part relations. As a part or a whole, a parameter or a set of parameters can be an atomic, indivisible quantum (a discrete unity) that is nonetheless connected to other parameters through abstract and concrete points of relations.

To explain the interior and exterior relations between and within actual entities without subsuming space (distance and simultaneity) to the unity of time, Whitehead also questions the notion of the straight line. He argues that the Euclidean straight line has always been limited to a notion of measurement and that it has never been defined in and for itself.[138] Instead, he argues that straight lines constitute the dimensional character of the extensive continuum. But the extensive continuum is composed of ovate classes or egg-shaped regions, actual autonomous spatiotemporalities.[139] Whitehead explains that these oval regions are internally bounded and externally connected to each other: a pair of ovals, for example, can only be connected externally in a complete locus or single point. Between points there can only be straight, flat, or direct relation, since all straight points are equal or even.[140] Whitehead uses the notion of "flat loci"[141] to describe this relation between actual occasions as the immanent transference of past data into the present. Each actual occasion is a bounded region of subregions, establishing contiguous relation or spatiotemporal connection with others, and expressing the objectification of the immediate past in the present.[142] However, according to Whitehead, contiguous relations between successive regions[143] are also intersected by sequences of nested intervals such as [0,1], where sets *R* of real numbers enter the denumerable convergence of open sets.[144] To put it in another way, the interval (i.e., the real numbers) between limit points [0,1] corresponds to the infinities of space-time degenerating or touching at a discrete (and not infinitesimal) point. It is evident that for Whitehead this point is not the invariant function of topological continuity (one time for many places); instead, he describes it in mereotopological terms as the space of relation between parts and wholes; as that which defines objects and events. Accordingly, novelty can be said to advance through the prehension or selection of *n* quantabilities, as Deleuze would call them,[145] on behalf of actual entities, thus explaining how indeterminate (discrete and isolated) eternal objects become a determined continuity in actual entities.

In *Une architecture des humeurs*, the mereotopological schema of inclusion, contiguity, overlapping etc., describes how the spatiotemporal division of regions and subregions results from the prehensive automation of abstract quantities. Prehensions are modes of decision making. Each mode of decision making implies a conceptual prehension, which cannot be described by binary logic (i.e., A or not-A states). Instead, decision must be explained by the "function of reason,"[146] which according to Whitehead implies a mode of abstraction from facts, so as to attend to them from a speculative, quasi-formal and yet immanent standpoint. Hence decision is neither determined by a priori reason nor simply derivable from facts. Instead, decision implies degrees of contrast and irreducible interferences between solutions that are defined by a paradoxical state: the superposition of more than one state. Far from obstructing and suspending decision, paradoxical states need to be conceived as actual states that offer an irreversible possibility of cutting through the dimensions of 0s and 1s.

For R&Sie(n), this is the actual space of *malentendues*, which can be understood as fuzzy states of decision making, whereby finite results are infected with nondenumerable quantities. In *Une architecture des humeurs* there are many levels of fuzzy decision making. The algorithmic prehensions of hormonal changes involve a first level of decision, involving the algorithmic selection of biophysical data. But the paradoxical space of *malentendues* allows for no direct correspondence between physical and algorithmic actualities, thus exposing chemical data to irreversible transformation. As algorithms grow to form morphological shapes, a second level of decision making transforms these algorithms into parameters through the Vbnet script[147] which, running on Rhino-Grasshopper software, is used to construct 3D volumes.[148] It is worth explaining what is implied here in more detail. R&Sie(n)'s collaborator François Juve (together with Marc Fornes, Winston Hampel, and Natanel Elfassy) devised an algorithm that aimed not only to establish parametric relations between neighboring entities, but also to deploy optimal calculations without drawing up the structural trajectories in advance.[149] As opposed to a mathematical model based on a complete set of axioms, this algorithmic procedure instead flirts with a certain empirical process, in which the architectural design, far from being determined by preestablished parameters, learns to respond to constraints.[150] This is not a direct calculus method, which, for instance, could calculate the building's beams after establishing its design. Instead, this is a simultaneously recursive and incremental optimization protocol, in which calculations respond to precise inputs (material constraints, biophysical data, initial and environmental conditions, etc.). Nevertheless, these actual constraints are not only there to direct computational design, but rather become occasions for actualities (parameters) to prehend indeterminate quantities of probabilities. In other words, actual constraints define the limit at which the abstract set of infinite points advances so as to determine existing relations between parameters anew. According to this view, automated prehensions imply that decision making is driven by the ingression of abstract quantities of points in the parametric processing of data variables.

Far from being derived from the infinitesimal contingencies of the differential calculus, algorithmic optimization is internally determined by the chaos of *malentendues*, random quantities of information selected by each and every set, which correspond to the paradoxical states of fuzzy logic (I'd like this red one but at the same time / also that green), set to script the blind spots between 0s and 1s. In other words, the computation of prehension is exposed here to the entropy of incomputable quantities, where the size of data cannot be compressed in one state or another, and instead reveals that incompleteness haunts the axiomatic method. And yet the increasing power of incomplete random sets does not mean that parametric control has become irrational. On the contrary, parametric control is marked by the ingression of immanent speculation into rationality: an infection with abstraction that irreversibly drives all forms of decision making beyond yes and no states. In short, parametric control is a mode of power that operates through the digital scripting of uncertainties.

Against the assumption that programming entails the reduction of physical data to discrete rules, *Une architecture des humeurs* stages a cumulative

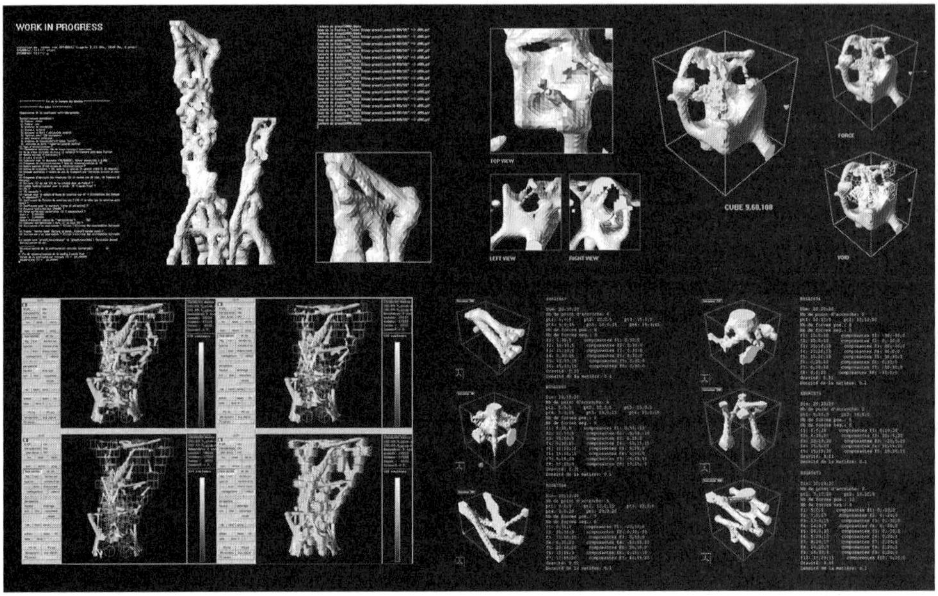

Figure 2.7
R(&)Sie(n), *Une architecture des humeurs*, 2010–2011. Courtesy François Roche.

assemblage of prehensions for those indeterminate inputs that enable procedures and prompt decisions.[151] Far from designing an urban future formatted by Windows software, parametric architecture, according to Roche, can be used to hack the program of the city by using growth scripts (evolving programs) and open-source algorithms, which are affected by a number of real-time constraints (hormonal, neurobiological, atmospheric, territorial, conflictual, etc.). In particular, R&Sie(n) uses fuzzy logic to drive decision making so that the global relations between variables can no longer be determined by the addition of any particular relation to variable quantities. In other words, the system of relational sets cannot depend on any specific procedure of finite steps, but is instead determined by *malentendues*, as random data add a new order of relation to the existing parametric organization.[152]

Fuzzy logic is thus seen not as a source of axiomatic truth, but rather as inserting indeterminate degrees or quantities of truth into the procedural logic of algorithms by adding quantabilities to the binary relation between 0 and 1. Like quantum particles, these random quantities can maintain at least two positions at once (they can be part of distinct sets of instructions or parameters), they become superposed in an actual entity (an algorithmic object or a parameter), but they also remain irreducible to one another (as eternal objects are irreducible in this sense). These indeterminate quantities can be part of their own actual assemblage or can become related to others, but they are nonetheless actualities that cannot become fused into one overall continuum of sequential sets.[153] As opposed to the cybernetic model of feedback interaction, according to which computation needs to become autopoietically responsive to external or environmental agents, fuzzy logic admits vagueness in the initial conditions of computation.[154]

According to Roche, parametric architecture has the potential to be more than a preprogrammed or interactive space. The irreversible decision driven by the paradoxical state described by fuzzy logic gives rise to truly changed systems of probabilities, because vague conditions are now built into computation through the enervation of *maybes* and *perhapses* within digital inputs.[155] *Malentendues* therefore reset the conditions by which a sequence of algorithms form a relation with one another through blind spots, or through actual relations that expose how indetermination drives irreversible computations. R(&)Sie(n)'s parametric architectures, however, do not only point at the effects that indetermination can have on computational sets (sets of belonging, inclusion, indifference), but also describe how computational indeterminacies add novelty to physical spatiotemporalities.

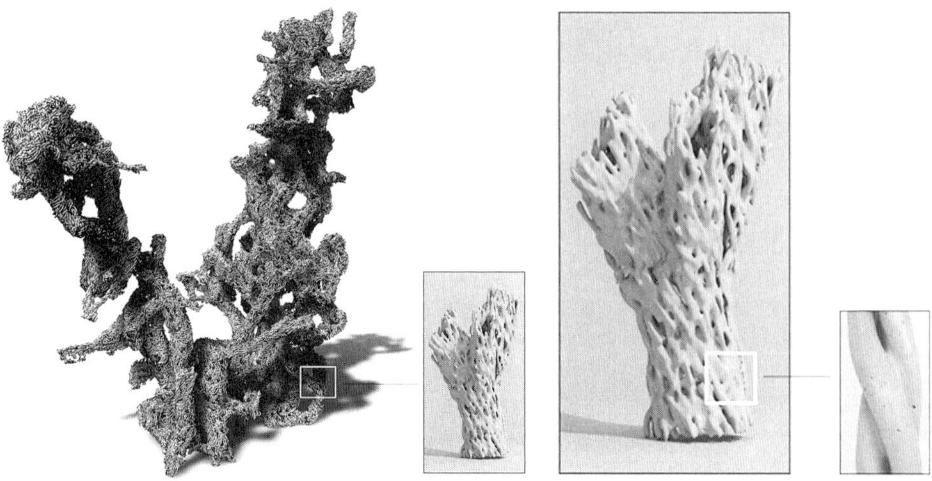

Figure 2.8
R(&)Sie(n), *Une architecture des humeurs*, 2010–2011. Courtesy François Roche.

Figure 2.9
R(&)Sie(n), *Une architecture des humeurs*, 2010–2011. Courtesy François Roche.

One can thus contend that the insertion of fuzzy logic within the sequential programming of algorithms does not simply lead R&Sie(n)'s project to devise another way of modeling topological forms that override their actual parts. Instead, this project uses actual parts (chemical data, algorithms, parameters) as hosts for abstract quantities of relation, leading to the construction of habitats from fuzzy calculations.

Instead of optimizing calculations to construct habitats according to the volumetric relation between these parts, R&Sie(n) employs a hyperlocal brick calculation, in which a braiding algorithm ends up in a process of secretion, extrusion, and agglutination of biocement material.[156] Here fuzzy algorithms are prehended by an insectlike robot named Viab02:[157] a pneumatic articulated machine (robotic muscle system) that knits space while registering the rules of algorithmic change and prehending biochemical data. By sieving and weaving, the machine creates a vertical structure, a three-string bunch (each 5 cm in diameter) through the use of a hybrid material (biocement) that agglutinates and coagulates parts chemically. The tank loads the file describing the 3D morphology, and together with its terminal devices it works like a 3D printer. According to Roche, this process of calculation and construction is not scripted by a swarm intelligence protocol but by a swarmoid protocol, which is at once centralized and distributed, exposing the discontinuities of the relations between parts and parts and wholes, thereby revealing indetermination in discreteness, incompleteness in axiomatics.

By bringing *malentendues* into the core of programming, R&Sie(n)'s fuzzy articulation of the computation of relation may be used to suggest that in postcybernetic control the power of the axiomatic is that it now relies on discrete yet incomputable quantities, incomplete random sets.[158] The postcybernetic paradox of control is not, however, amenable to Zeno's paradoxical dictum, according to which finite sets are nonetheless made of infinitesimally divisible microunities, which construct the indivisible line of connection between points. Deleuze and Guattari conceived of the articulation of this paradox in terms of "reciprocal presupposition":[159] a nonrelational relation, the interval of differentials, which defines the suspension of decision in the same way that the coexistence of contradictory states reveals an impasse that entails that everything is deemed to be possible.[160]

Axiomatics is not simply suspended by the indeterminate qualities of infinitesimals (defining the distance between entities). At the same time, however, axiomatics can no longer correspond to finite sets of truth. I would thus suggest that rules are there neither to be bended in folds nor striated in infinitely larger sets (which are utterly irreducible to actual sets). On the contrary, as Whitehead's mereotopological scheme reveals, eternal truths are infinite parts or incomplete abstract quantities (i.e., eternal objects), which are at once random infinities and discrete objects, indeterminate and nonconnected realities. From this standpoint, axioms are not determinate sets but are conditioned by indeterminate quantifications: infinite objects that acquire determination (and continuity) once they are selected by actual entities. These abstract quantities, according to the mereotopological schema, are quasi-empirical, since indeterminacies and infinity are immanent to actual entities and do not need to be added, as it were, from the "outside." This is why abstract quantities are at once axiomatic (because they are eternal objects marking the existence of an abstract scheme of quantities that are discrete and random) and empirical (because actualities select or prehend these potentialities, which contribute to the actualities' own determination). According to the mereotopological schema, axiomatics is incomplete because finite sets require abstract quantities or indeterminate, random sets in order to become determinate to a certain degree. Similarly, eternal objects are discrete objects of infinite potential that require actual prehensions in order to become unities or to acquire continuity in actualities. The final section of this chapter will explain how the mereotopological view of parametricism can offer a critique of the topological modeling of soft extension, and thus contribute toward disentangling the topological conception of postcybernetic power, which places control and event in a relation of reciprocal presupposition.

2.9 Extensive novelties

In this chapter I have argued that the introduction of the invariant function in software design has led to the development of a topological paradigm of space that has been most clearly instantiated by parametricism. This self-proclaimed new style of software design relies on a notion of relation that corresponds to a point of continual variation or homeomorphic change from one parametric level to another. The result is an idea of morphogenesis whereby space generates itself through change. Hence spatial forms are said to have become dynamic surfaces, defined not by preset models but by contingent changes. Contingency, chance, or randomness has become included in the programming system, driving the relations between parameters in the construction of a spatial whole. I have argued that this tendency to incorporate external factors into architectural or urban planning is tantamount to the tendency in computation to extend formalism to architecture's external environment. I have chosen to discuss parametricism because real-time physical variations are considered to be the motor of change for programmed relations between parametric values. These relations have therefore become equivalent to an interval between parameters: a differential space of potentialities that can be explained by the infinitesimal points lying between two terms. In other words, parametricism exploits the power of computation to calculate the evolution of values over time, and thus to program the evolution of relations. Yet the introduction of time into programming, of dynamics into models, or of chance into formal language is not a merely technical affair. On the contrary, as Brian Massumi has argued, the capitalization of change and the mediatic investment in the power of temporality characterizes contemporary modes of governance, whereby decision making, far from being eternally postponed, is rather anticipated and realized before the fact. For Massumi, these anticipatory operations of power point not to a regime of control by means of prediction, but to a diffused ecology of fear that is dominated by preemption. Decision does not lead to the fact but rather anticipates the latter before it happens: the fact is not here and now, but it is always already an indeterminate potentiality (an unknown) that is ready to strike at any time, anywhere. Preemptive power therefore requires chance to become programmed, calculated, and computed so that it can be anticipated: the potentiality of change thus becomes harnessed into a possibility. Indetermination is therefore not excluded from programming, but is instead captured by it: the indeterminate is thus tamed so as to render it an actual possibility.

While Massumi's notion of preemption is another attempt at describing the operations of governability that characterize the neoliberal *dispositif* of power, the spatiality of contemporary capitalism has also been specifically discussed in terms of models of topological complexity, self-organization, and emergence. In particular, it has been argued that the logic and aesthetics of this spatiality have been sustained by "a self-styled avant-garde in contemporary architecture"[161] which has uncritically adopted Deleuze's formal concepts of the fold, becoming, and smoothing, concepts that were central to Deleuze's articulation of the operative features of control societies. It has also been argued that parametricism is not an avant-garde style but is instead the result or the instantiation of the neoliberal spirit of flexibility.[162] Because it mirrors Deleuze's concepts, the self-styled avant-garde of contemporary architecture has been seen as an apology for capitalism that implies the dissolution of politics in the name of "affirmative materialism."[163] For example, along with the work of Zaha Hadid Architects,[164] the 2010 design by Foreign Office Achitects (FOA) of the new campus for Ravensbourne College (London) has been taken as an instance of the stylized logic of neoliberalism. Here the parametrically programmed urban space is seen as a managerial enterprise of a networked market, which organizes relations by liquefying the boundaries between levels and scales, floors and classrooms, lectures and offices, learning and business. This design imparts a "deterritorialization" of volumes to create open and nomadic access across the entire space, which is defined by the (networking) movement of people and not by their occupation.[165] The space of the urban and the space of business thus become isomorphic, as they are mediated by an invariant function that establishes a topological connectedness driven by local interactions. It has been argued that this fusion between architectural space and the space of the market—this "movement-space" that has joined them together into a decentralized neoliberal managing of subjectivity—only affirms "the generalization of the market form itself."[166] In other words, contemporary architecture and digital design have been accused of adapting the philosophical and critical conceptions of space, and in particular the smoooth space of control, to the operations of the neoliberal market, the ontological being of which has come to engulf all forms of aesthetics, culture, and technology.

However, it is suggested here that if this soft fluidification of space corresponds to a neoliberal form of governmentality, then it is because relationality, as argued above, has become central to the conception and design of space itself. In particular, I have pointed out that the introduction of topology into digital architecture has led to a relational notion of space, in which the latter is seen to be governed by infinitesimal points of convergence or continuity. Such points can be seen to lie, for example, between urban behavior and software programs. This infinitesimal convergence has become linked to a responsive feedback between the external environment, physical data, people's behavior, and the software program. In other words, the neoliberal form of governmentality has incorporated and reinvented the cybernetic notion of feedback, which now serves neither to stop nor to transform entropy into information; instead, the introduction of topology into digitality has entailed a neoliberal investment in the primary ontology of feedback, in terms of "reciprocal presupposition": a process of structural coupling or mutual adaptation that subsumes relational terms under the power of time, evolution, dynamics, and change.

Yet, while it is hard to overlook the internal resonances between the software style of architectural design and the neoliberal spirit of the market, which ubiquitously fosters decentralization, compatibility, enterprise, and open-ended organic forms, it is also important to subtract the notion of space from a metacomputational view of neoliberalism. It is suggested here that Whitehead's mereotopological schema of relations importantly implies that relations are defined not by infinitesimal points of variation (per the ontological view that founds the cybernetic and neoliberal focus on feedback and preemption) but by nexuses of actualities: infinite points that are both abstract and concrete. It is events, and not continual variations between terms, that determine extension in terms of parts that cannot be assimilated into an overall system of change. Parts cannot be reduced into the smaller or bigger program of the whole. For Whitehead, events correspond to the advance of the new and the concrescence of the extensive continuum. Parts, therefore, are fundamental to his process-oriented metaphysics, which involves an atomistic conception of time for which actual entities are spatiotemporally finite. Actual entities perish, and by perishing they become objective data for another entity; this allows process to occur, and it allows novelty to become added to what already exists.

Whitehead's mereotopology therefore questions the metaphysics of the whole, and argues that time and space are produced by actual entities, the relations of which can only be explained by other spatiotemporal parts and not by a whole (whether this whole is Being, Time, or God). Similarly, I argue that the critical reading of digital architecture (as somehow mirroring the neoliberal form of the market) needs to address the spatiotemporal parts or actualities that cannot be included in the neoliberal operations of governmentality. These parts, I claim, are to be understood as quantities that are bigger than an overall sum, which remains conditioned by nondenumerable infinities or the immanence of incomputable data. This means that if digital architecture and neoliberal governmentality share a focus on the capacity of relations to smooth edges and permeate boundaries, to dissipate volumes into ever-changing networks, then the very question of what constitutes a relation becomes central to demystifying the postcybernetic mode of control, which has transformed feedbacks into topological surfaces of continuities.

To put it in another way, if the preemptive character of neoliberalism is to be understood as the capacity of making decisions in the present on the basis of future change, and if digital architecture and digital urbanism have similarly come to include real-time and contingent variations within planning through parametric software, then it becomes important to understand how this temporal calculation of change can be underdetermined. How can the relation between the past and the future, the already planned and the unplanned, be conceived not only in terms of an infinitesimal series of points, differential relations, virtual qualities or micropercepts, but also (as with Whitehead) in terms of infinite quantities immanent to finite actualities? This is also to ask how one might avoid viewing parametricism (or the computation of relationality) as just another instance of the power of the neoliberal market—i.e., a view according to which it would constitute the metacomputational force of governmentality, being a force that thus defines the environment of power in terms of ubiquitous digitality—so as to consider it instead in terms of mereotopology. If it is indeed possible to do so, what kind of relationality could then be used to suggest that the preemptive capitalization of change, futurity, and potentiality in fact encounters blind spots, space events that cannot be compressed in the smaller program (or complete axiomatics) of control?

This is what I have tried to develop in the previous analysis of R&Sie(n)'s *Une architecture des humeurs*. By drawing on a mereotopological understanding of relations as parts amid parts and wholes, it is possible to define relations in terms of spatiotemporal actualities that replace the smooth transition among scales and levels with irreversible actualities. As R&Sie(n)'s project points out, *malentendues* expose the logical operation of binary language to the inevitable coexistence of more than one state at once. This simultaneity of states is explained in terms of fuzzy logic, which captures the degrees of differentiation (or of relations) between 0s and 1s. I argue, however, that this relation is not a differential relation, defining the intensive degrees of a quality (being, time, duration): on the contrary, the simultaneity of states has been explained here by the blind spot, a relational actuality, an actual spatiotemporality that adds an extensive novelty to already existing actualities. These relational actualities are *malentendues* because they are incomputable; they cannot be summed up into an idea, theory, or program smaller than themselves. In other words, by placing *malentendues* at the core of parametric design, R&Sie(n)'s project suggests that there are no smooth relations and no overall encompassing metasystem. Instead, even at a smaller scale, relations are always mediated by misunderstandings or weird logic (I think I heard this, but it may be also that). This inclusion of indetermination in parametric scripting can also be taken as a manifestation of neoliberal logic of reciprocal presupposition (I want this but also that), which produces a fractalized process of subjection whereby individuals are denuded of integrity in the continual recombination of bits in the ever-expanding computation of behaviors, habitats, thoughts, and moods. However, I suggested that *malentendues* describe not only the fuzzy degrees of relations between actualities, but also the existence of incomputable quantities, which, like the blind spots described by Whitehead, remain autonomous by the terms of the relation. These incomputable objects are at once discrete and infinite, and, rather than reifying the neoliberal logic of paradoxical coexistence of contraries, they eschew contradiction and reciprocity altogether.

Instead, these incomputable objects are the irreversible condition that allows computation to take place; they are thus intrinsic to computation, and do not reside outside it or stand in opposition to it. As such, these parts do not accommodate contraries or facilitate the reversal of causality between terms. Instead they add extensive novelty to already existing terms by imposing an irreversible decision upon them. This extensive novelty does not result from mutual interaction, structural coupling, or topological continuity between actualities, but rather involves, as the notion of *malentendues* indicates, the advance of incompressible and incomprehensible data; the manifestation of spatiotemporal systems that cannot be summed up into a smaller history, theory, or program. In other words, these objects neither partake in nor contradict the neoliberal logic of paradoxes. Instead, they are blind spots, alien spatiotemporalities, which, I argue, are symptoms of the irreversible power of the incomputable to impart extensive novelties or events onto the extensive continuum. But what exactly are extensive novelties?

Whitehead's mereotopological schema precludes transcending points, lines, and quantities in favor of an analysis of the fractionalized relation between parts and between wholes and parts. He argued that there are at least two orders of reality: the sequential order of actualities that prehend past and present data from other actual entities, and the order of discrete and infinite eternal objects that enter actual entities, their regions and subregions. The mereotopological schema explains how there can be extensive novelty in the continual relations between actual entities. The advance of extensive novelty is not deducted from the relativity of space, determined by the continual durations of physical entities,[167] but on the contrary primarily entails the ingression of discontinuities (the incomputable objects of the [0,1] interval) or blind spatiotemporalities into actual parametric sequences. From this standpoint, the computation of relations implies not a reduction of qualities of continuity (i.e., differential relations) to discrete quantities (the sequential relations of algorithms or parameters), but rather the contagious power of eternal objects (or incomputable quantities) in automated prehensions. This is where parametricism ceases to be the universal style for the neoliberal programming of spatiotemporalities, and coincides instead with the general advance of extensive novelty: the automated mode of division (prehension and selection) of data implies the infection of incomputable quantities in actual spatiotemporal series, establishing a unilateral versioning of facts. In short, parametricism is not simply an instrument of neoliberalism, or an application of a neoliberal logic of reciprocal presupposition (the coexistence of right and wrong, inside and outside, here and there). In addition, the (digital and fuzzy) automation of relations implies a unilateral process of decision that cannot be reversed, and which acquires full consistency in the actuality of relation itself. This actuality of relation defines another level of decision, an immanence that breaks from the past and the future. This automated level of decision comes without negotiation, as it remains a blind spot: an invisible order of relation that can be computed exactly as random data, as utter indetermination intrinsic to immanent decision. The unilateralism of relational actualities—their power to make terms coexist while neutralizing their existence—could explain how extensive novelty can occur, how alien spatiotemporalities enter the order of urban design, and how soft events or the algorithmic production of space-time interferes with the incorporating logic of neoliberal control. Here the postcybernetic investment in relationality has turned against itself. Instead of optimizing the continuity of order through feedback, the order of relationality has turned into the computational production of space-time that spreads invisible interferences with the recursive function of algorithmic feedback. The combinatorial loops of parametricism therefore become unintended procedures that culminate in the unilateral irruption of a space event.

According to Whitehead, the notion of extensive novelty defines how the birth of a new occasion coincides with the birth of a new aesthetic form: the passage into novelty of what was potentially given.[168] One should consider, Whitehead suggests, how any one actual fact, which he calls the ground, could enter the creative process. The novelty that enters the derivative occasion is but the information of the actual world with a new set of ideal forms (eternal objects). In the most literal sense, Whitehead affirms, novelty is defined by the information lapse or discontinuity between the derivative occasion and the new occasion that is marked by the renovation of the world with ideas.[169] The interstices between occasions thus delineate the opportunity for the sequential arrangement of parameters (physical, robotic, software) to add indeterminate quantities to the given. Whitehead refers to a particular instance of the new birth of extensive novelty as a novelty of ideal forms, or the "consequent."[170] For him, novelty in aesthetic form implies the activity of a supplemental or conceptual feeling that replaces the particular ground supplied by antecedent occasions.[171] Hence novelty is said to derive from the discontinuous (periodic, quantic, incomputable) relations between the particular ground (the inherited data) and the consequent (indeterminate quantities). What comes after (i.e., the consequent) is graded by its contagious relevance to a particular ground (or the antecedent). This contagion of the ground is however triggered by something that is "not-actual": abstract quantities (eternal objects).

Similarly, Whitehead describes process as the achievement of actuality by the ideal consequent connected with the actual ground, a sort of irreversible irruption of not-being into being.[172] Hence process deploys the birth of an aesthetic extension in which the novel consequent has preserved at once two principles: the principle of identity, and that of contrast with the ground.[173] As the parametric design of *Une architecture des humeurs* shows, the notion of *malentendues* imparts a discontinuity of identity and contrast between actual parameters (physical, robotic, and software protocols) that involves the automated prehension of abstract quantities as the condition by which an extensive novelty can advance and the extensive continuum can become concrescent.

According to Whitehead, the two principles of identity and contrast define any actual fact as primarily a fact of aesthetic experience.[174] All aesthetic novelty is here conceived as a feeling that arises out of the realization of contrast under identity, of discontinuity under the chain of continuity.[175] In particular, Whitehead takes the physical law of vibration as evidence of the principle of contrast under identity, so as to explain the ultimate nature of atomic entities: microactual cuts in continual relation.[176] "Vibration is the recurrence of contrast within identity of type."[177] Without vibrations, Whitehead argues, there can be no possibility of measurement in the physical world. Ultimately any form of measurement, he holds, is a mode of counting vibrations.[178] Similarly, no physical quantities could ever exist without the prior aggregation of physical vibrations, i.e., without these discontinuous breaks in the continuity of matter.

It is true to say that for Whitehead vibrations are expressions, among the many abstractions of physical science, of the fundamental principles of physical experience.[179] Vibrations defined the physical continuity or causal efficacy of actual occasions, the stubborn inheritance of data from the past in the present. And yet, if physical vibrations are *common* to all physical actualities, then it becomes important to note that according to Whitehead each and any region of actual objects is also the host for abstract quantities that occupy the relation between particles and waves. In order for these actualities to become more than they physically are, Whitehead points out, they have to experience the reality of discontinuity: the blind spot at which the relation between actual entities becomes an actual occasion to prehend abstract quantities.

From this standpoint, parametricism implies a new level of extension (a new potential division of actual continuity by means of automated prehension) or an extensive novelty deployed by a mereotopological rationality. Parts interrupt the continuities of a whole in the same way as automated prehensions add new levels of determination through the selection of unknown quantities in parametric processing. As R&Sie(n)'s projects show, spatiotemporalities are determined neither by digital axioms nor solely by physical interactions. On the contrary, the creative advance of an extensive novelty is implicated in the automated prehensions of random quantities, entropic information or *malentendues* inherent to computation, programming, scripting, and logic. Far from constituting an impediment to design and construction, inconsistent quantities instead add an aesthetic novelty to spatiotemporal design, corresponding to the advance of blind computational actualities. These are quantities that do not belong to the sequential order of algorithms but rather hack this order, adding new actualities amid actualities, and thereby infiltrate the software of buildings, cities, and environments. In parametric design, this aesthetic novelty may then concern not simply the digital manipulation of source data and of patterns of relations between volumes, scales, and levels: the uninterrupted looping of discrete spatiotemporalities into the morphogenetic mutations of the whole. In other words, it may not simply concern the formalist aesthetics of neoliberalism and the latter's control of relations, which relies upon degrees of variation between 0s and 1s. Instead, aesthetic novelty may be derived from modes of automated prehensions: from computational parameters' prehensive power to be infected with nondenumerable probabilities, incomputable data. From this standpoint, each level, region, and subregion constitutes an extensive novelty as a series of eternal objects coming together anew in programmed parameters. Since, as Whitehead reminds us, each and any actual entity is the cause of its own actual world,[180] the power to conceptually prehend abstract quantities cannot but become an occasion for these quantities to add new spatiotemporal actualities to the extensive continuum.[181]

As opposed to the assumption that aesthetic novelty can only be derived from the designer's capacities to direct the automated generation of extension,[182] whereby his or her aesthetic values must inform decision making step by step, for R&Sie(n) parametric aesthetics coincides with the *malentendues* of computational prehension. Algorithmic sets and parameters are physical prehensions that define how actual entities relate to each other through modes of belonging, inclusion, indifference, etc. At the same time, however, they are also conceptual modes of prehension that are irreversibly (not contradictorily and not reciprocally) infected with incomputable data. In other words, the automation of spatial-temporal relations in parametric design has meant the activation of an other-than-human aesthetic, wherein indeterminate quantities drive the computational design of spatiotemporalities.

Parametric computation, therefore, does not constitute the loss of discrete space-times, but rather the concrete abstraction or immanent realization of the spatiotemporalities of data, whose architectural infrastructure of volume, density, mass, weight, and gravity is unleashing unlived space-time into the everyday. Automated prehensions have instead revealed that the infinity of data allows for a soft recombination of volumes. This recombination defines actual spatiotemporalities that add more density to physical spaces. The latter are not simply the mismatched representation of a virtual notion of volume, as a deformed, infinite, continuous surface, for instance, but are rather pregnant with incomputable actualities that occupy the gap between the physical, the digital, and the robotic (as in the case of *Une architecture des humeurs*). This means that parametricism does not directly correspond to the late logic of neoliberalism; it has also, despite its topological idealism, unleashed genuine data spaces, data architectures in computational culture. These data spaces can be defined as the space events or the extensive novelties that the computation of relations has added to existing urban infrastructures. They are computational actualities of relation which lurk in the everyday operative logistics of connection, transportation, retrieval, navigation, and wireless communication, in which they add irreversible functions that cannot be smoothed out. It is therefore in the computational process itself that space events are to be found, and it is there that control fails to reduce the entropic increase of randomness into its own system of axioms.

In order to gain a more involved understanding of the reasons for this failure and of the manner in which it occurs, and in order to address quite what the automated prehensions' power of decision making means for our programming culture, it is now necessary to turn to theories of cognition and perception. This will allow us to conduct a further investigation of the ways in which the space (or architecture) of thought has been defined in computational terms. The analysis of this architecture of thought will thus be the topic of the next chapter.

3 Architectures of Thought

3.0 Soft thought

Computational architecture does not only concern the digital programming of urban infrastructures. Importantly, and as will be explained in this chapter, it also pertains to the architecture of a new mode of thought, which I will refer to here as *soft(ware) thought*. Soft thought is not a tool for thinking (i.e., for planning, calculating, and rationalizing) space-time. Instead, soft thought is a way of producing computational space-time. The algorithmic processing of data is not just a means to explore new spatiotemporal forms. Instead, this automated prehension of data is equivalent to the immanent construction of digital spatiotemporalities. From this standpoint, soft thought cannot be simply disqualified for being a mechanical calculation of possibilities. At the same time, it may also be misleading to assume that computation is yet another extension of living thought. Soft thought is instead the mental pole of an algorithmic actual object. It is the conceptual prehension of infinite data that defines computational actualities or spatiotemporalities as the point at which algorithms stop being determined by the efficient order of sequences and rather prehend their incomputable limit. Soft thought thus explains algorithmic computation as an actual mode of thinking that cannot be reproduced or instantiated by the neuroarchitecture of the brain (the neurosynaptic network), or to the neurophenomenology of the mind (the reflexive ability of the mind to become aware of its actions on the world). Soft thought, in consequence, is autonomous from cognition and perception.

Nevertheless, in order to explain the nuances of soft thought one may first of all need to question the assumption that software offers an ontological ground for thought, or indeed that software can be considered to be equivalent to thought itself (an equivalence that might, for instance, be defined by the symbolic language of algorithms). Similarly, one may feel inclined to reject the hypothesis that software reveals the ways in which the brain creates and drives the operation of thought (e.g., the ways in which neural nets or swarming algorithms build up thought from within the neural structure of the brain). Such objections would perhaps follow from, and would certainly accord with, what I take to be a turn toward a cybernetic-computational understanding of thought (from connectionism to enactivism or from neuroarchitecture to the neurophenomenology of space), which has reduced soft thought either to the neural structure of the brain or to the final result of continuous interactions between the brain and the world (e.g., neurophenomenology on the one hand and extended cognition on the other).

In contrast to such views, I will argue here that soft thought is a mode of thought (an actuality) that is defined by rule-based algorithms or automated procedures, procedures that are, as explained in the previous chapters, conceptual prehensions of incomputable probabilities. This means that algorithms are understood here neither in symbolic terms (i.e., as representing a determinate function of thought derived from operations of symbolic manipulation) nor in an emergentist sense (i.e., generating consistency from growing and interactive algorithms), but rather according to their capacity to select and evaluate data beyond the physical prehension of data. From the standpoint of computation, the automated procedures of rule-based algorithms deploy an inevitable encounter with incomputable probabilities that are included or excluded in algorithmic sequencing (regardless of whether this involves a series of linear, parallel, or swarming algorithms). Soft thought could then be understood as the computational prehension of infinity, which corresponds to the immanence of incomputable algorithms: to the irreversible invasion of actuality by discrete infinities. Instead of being a continuous flow of data, such as a topological binding of many actualities into one stream of ceaseless variation, the incomputable, as discussed in the previous chapters, is an infinite series of discrete yet incomplete data that immanently ingresses and becomes uniquely arranged into algorithmic sets, in which these data acquire togetherness and continuity. In chapter 2, Whitehead's notion of mereotopology was used to elucidate this immanent process further, and to explain how actualities are parts that connect to one another, but only acquire unity (or reach their "subjective aim") once they select incomputable data or eternal objects, or become irreversibly infected with the latter.

In particular, in chapter 2 I used a discussion of R&Sie(n)'s project *Une architecture des humeurs* as a means of indicating that the notion of relation has become central to parametric architecture. I argued that understanding computation in terms of relation does not imply that computation can now be understood as a topological continuum defined by different degrees of affective variations. From a topological standpoint, the relation between one parameter and another implies that one parametric variation directly causes changes in the entire parametric structure. However, while arguing against the topological view, I suggested that parametric relations should be taken as instances of *malentendues*: instances of mishearing and misunderstanding that are already deployed within the computational organization of algorithms. I specified that *malentendues* do not simply describe relations in terms of infinitesimal degrees of variations between two or more parameters, according to which a partial change would correspond to a change in the whole structure. On the contrary, *malentendues* already occur within the fuzzy logic of algorithms, the quantic infinities of which deploy new actualities of relation or space events that are new and invisible to parametric programming.

These relational *malentendues* are therefore not predetermined in the programmed arrangement of parameters, but instead depend on algorithmic prehensions: automated modes of feeling that make decisions according to data (i.e., data corresponding to moods, chemical imbalances, and attitudes). For R&Sie(n) these data are mental stances, not simply algorithmic functions; they are precognitive information that become algorithmically prehended. This prehension adds a new level of determinacy to the data prehended. By using fuzzy states, or quantic computation, algorithms capture data according to their varying degrees of quantity. Furthermore, this fuzzy calculation itself becomes another relational space of misunderstandings in which 0s and 1s can both be included at the same time. In parametric architecture, therefore, relational spaces are actual spaces of misunderstanding. The paradoxical logic of these spaces (e.g., a logic that includes two opposites: maybe this but also that) also reveals the workings of a speculative reason, according to which each fact is always the immanent host of infinite objects: infinities that acquire unity in an actual assemblage.

Yet this space of relation does not simply correspond to the relative infinitesimal divisions of affects and percepts, and it is not amenable to an infinitesimal logic, according to which all actualities are fused into one continual surface of variation. My argument in chapter 2 was that these relational spaces are actual and infinite, and thus could not be subsumed within the metaphysics of continuity. The continuity between actualities is to be found not in differential variations, but in the prehension or selection of eternal objects, which acquire singular togetherness or continuity in actualization. Therefore there is no primordial plane or topological surface of continuity. Instead, I argued for a mereotopological conception of relations between parts and wholes, whereby parts are able to connect to a whole which then becomes another part, and not a transcendental continuity.

Borrowing from Whitehead, I discussed the theory of mereotopology and proposed a new understanding of relation: an understanding that does not view the latter in terms of continual surface, but rather as an actual part among others. This mereotopological architecture of wholes and parts offers a mathematico-geometric schema of extension, and I used this to present the spatiotemporalities of algorithmic actualities as parts that exist among others.

In the current chapter, I will discuss these actualities in terms of a mereotopology of thoughts, according to which algorithmic or soft thought is not to be subtended to a metaphysical continuum of thought. On the contrary, a mereotopology of thoughts contributes toward clarifying the sense in which soft thought is a part that cannot be reduced to a whole: the sum or the ontological ground of thought. I will argue that soft thought is as irreducible to the neural networks of the brain-mind as are bacterial and vegetal modes of cognition.[1]

Soft thought is instead a manifestation of incomputable infinity or the conceptual prehension of incompressible data that suspends the order of algorithmic sequences. Far from casting infinity as a fixed transcendental being (i.e., as *the* infinite), incomputable infinity, like Chaitin's description of Omega, is instead an immanent determination of infinity that views it in terms of infinite probabilities. Hence my claim that soft thought cannot be explained away as a mechanical operation of computers. Instead, I take Chaitin's computational proof of Omega or infinite probabilities, which are at once computably enumerable and algorithmically random, to explain that the automation of data implies an irreversible encounter with incomputable probabilities.[2] This is to say that the automated operations of prehension, and the mechanical procedures of computers, have their own blind spots, anomalies, and alien logic of calculation, which far from being computational failures are instead to be taken as symptoms of algorithmic thought. This is the point at which the sequential order of algorithms gives way to the conceptual prehension of computational infinities, when algorithms process data beneath what has already been programmed.

From this standpoint, soft thought is not an abstract mechanism of thought that needs to be concretized (for instance) in a neurocomputational architecture, the origins of which might be found in the neural architecture of the brain, from which soft thought is, as if it were, deduced. For neurocomputation, soft thought can only be the idealistic thought of the neural network: a neural idealism. In this chapter I will discuss how this idealism is used to explain the extension of the cognitive structure of the brain to other containers of thought, such as media systems (e.g., Andy Clark's "minimal Cartesianism" could define soft thought as just another instance of *mindware* running on any hardware). To put it in another way, I will argue that the articulation of soft thought according to neuroarchitecture (or extended cognition) does not prove but instead dismisses algorithmic operations of thought because it locates thought in the cognitive architecture of the brain, sustained by a neurosynaptic system of connection. According to this approach, soft thought only exists as an extension of the mechanics of neurocognition and not as immanent thought (i.e., a thought not subsumed under the totality of neurocognition). Neurocognitive architecture therefore acts as a mediator between computation and thought, thus reducing both to the biophysical structure of the brain.

At the same time, as an immanent selection of incomputable objects, soft thought cannot be understood as the result of sensorimotor and perceptual modes of cognition, defined by a notion of mutual interaction between the brain and the environment. According to this approach the environment is itself information. It is the material world outside the brain that enacts thought, but only to the extent that such enaction is reflected upon by the mind. The enactive conception of thought implies that thought is induced, derived from the material background, which in turn unifies the mind and the world and ultimately conflates thought with matter: an ideal materialism. From this standpoint, soft thought is exclusively a simulation, a reductive copy of the operations of the mind, which are, in this view, produced by the environment.

After discussing these two apparently opposed approaches to thought (e.g., the neuroarchitecture of the brain and material enactivation of the mind) from the standpoint of computation, I will explain that soft thought can only be understood as immanent experience of incompressible and incomprehensible algorithms, and I will show that quantities of data have entropic properties because they tend to increase and burst rather than coherently dissipate in space. Since these incomputable quantities of data are immanent to algorithmic actualities, and because soft thought is an actual prehension of incomputable objects, I will argue that soft thought adds changes to the structure of experience. As an example of these changes, I will discuss R&Sie(n)'s project *I've Heard About . . .* in terms of an architecture of lived abstraction. In doing so I will explain how algorithmic prehensions can be lived in a manner that does not entail the neurophysical experience of a brain-body. We will also see, however, that this experienced abstraction involves transformation, albeit a form of transformation that does not directly result in the rewiring of either the brain or sensorimotor activities according to which any algorithmic function must produce an effect on the cognitive capacities of thinking and the perceptual capacities of responding. This transformation is instead irreversible because it does not concern the (interactive) effects of algorithms on the brain but instead, as R&Sie(n)'s project will help us to clarify, describes how algorithmic prehensions produce computational spatiotemporalities, which change the course of data processing and thus algorithmic occasions of experience. This transformation does not therefore reveal the future of spatiotemporal experience, but rather the present changes of computational spatiotemporalities.

From this standpoint, however, soft thought is not to be taken as yet another mourning of the end of human thought,[3] i.e., as a sort of postmodern or posthuman rearticulation of the end of rationality. Instead, it should be understood as another mode of thought altogether. As I will discuss below, digital design can be seen as an instance of soft thought, and can also be seen to demonstrate that this mode of thought is in fact a form of immanent experience. I have argued in the previous two chapters that if computation has become central to architecture, this is not because existing spatiotemporalities can be grown or evolved within the search space of the computer, but rather because digital architecture is subtended by soft thought. Using Whitehead's understanding of the function of reason, discussed in chapter 1, I now want to suggest that this peculiar mode of thought is not equivalent to a predictive model of probability (which would predict the future through the probabilities of the past), but instead needs to be understood in terms of speculative computation, which entails the probabilities of infinities.

The standard probabilistic model implies that computational objects are either derived from physical data or are the evolving or future simulation of these data. In both cases, the computational objects do not really exist in themselves, but are instead effects of a physical substrate or a temporal process. In short, computational objects are never really actual and never of the present, but rather remain a temporal projection of physical data.

Yet against this, and as I argued earlier, computation reveals that algorithms are actual entities imbued with discrete infinities that can also be defined as incomputable probabilities. From this standpoint, speculative computation specifically concerns an actual mode of thought that prehends objects of infinity or eternal objects while constructing the spatiotemporalities of the present. In other words, infinite objects are not outside computation: they are the indeterminate condition through which algorithms become actual modes of thought. Speculative computation, therefore, does not mean that algorithms project the present (or past) into the future, but rather that algorithms introduce discrete infinities into actualities. This speculative notion of computation helps us to define soft thought in terms of actual thought: as an actual prehension of eternal objects, and as the ingression of incomputable probabilities into algorithms. As a mode of prehending eternal objects, soft thought is therefore utterly irreducible to human cognition, the mind or the brain.

From this standpoint, soft thought threatens the idea that computation can deploy the function of reason, or serve as the ontological ground of thought. Instead, computation is taken as an example of another mode of thought: soft thought. As a concrete mode of abstraction, soft thought becomes a new opportunity for eternal objects—patternless data—to become united in actual algorithms, which are not reducible to what a human mind or body can do. Patternless data, and not sets of evolving algorithms (or cellular automata), are the kernel of speculative computation. Speculative computing, therefore, is not about emerging unpredictability, but about infinities in finite actualities that cannot be contained in a totalizing method of computation. Speculation in computing therefore reveals that the logic of programming includes infinities within each binary calculation.

In the context of digital architecture, speculation thus concerns the manner in which algorithms construct spatiotemporal actualities. What matters here is not whether this mode of construction is physical or not, but rather that digital architecture can be understood as being already involved in the building of instances of space thought; instances that are immanent, spatiotemporal experiences. This is not reducible to new spatiotemporal modes of experience (i.e., to new modes of perception and navigation of space). Rather, soft thought *is* experience defined by the algorithmic prehension of infinities. In other words, soft thought is a spatiotemporal event: a nexus of actual occasions or experience, and a lived abstraction that has not been fully axiomatized (a quasi-empirical or quasi-formal computation). It is experience as actual spatiotemporality. Soft thought therefore concerns not the augmentation of the sensorimotor experience of space in terms of navigation, orientation, and tracking, or the capacity of digital architecture to visualize space before building it: instead, soft thought is the immanent experience of computational infinities defined by the automated prehension of data that cannot be computed by a smaller program. Soft thought does not describe how computation can substitute or explain thought and thus condition experience. Instead, it simply defines computation as a mode of thought characterized by an automated prehension of random, nondenumerable, incompressible data. This operational prehension defines the immanent experience of computational infinities: the occasion for algorithms to be more than a finite set of instructions and less than a thinking totality. This operational prehension manifests itself in the spaces of transition that remain undetected by senses and cognition, the actuality of relations that are irreducible to points of observation. Despite being unsensed and uncognized, algorithmic transitions are nonetheless real thought spaces that disrupt the equivalence between computation and cognition, because they can be determined neither by a closed axiomatic nor by the syntax of cognition.

From this standpoint, soft thought is to be understood as a computational actuality, a speculative mode of reason. Far from being a withdrawal of possibilities from the real conditions localized within the digital operations of the computer, this actuality has come to determine our programming culture. Whitehead, in claiming that the function of reason is speculative, reveals that the functionalism at the core of the computational theory of cognition—which includes connectivism, *cognitivism*, and the theory of the extended mind, for instance—fails to account for the irreducible actuality of soft thought and for its incomputable conditions. We will see in this chapter that these theories reify the assumption that thought is equivalent to the syntactic structure of the Turing machine, an assumption according to which the sequential order or the structure of thought, like software, can run on any machine (whether organic or inorganic). For adherents of these theories, the automatism of thought only universalizes the latter in terms of a cognitive structure defined by data that can be organized in a neural structure of connection. Regardless of whether they are framed in relation to a *neural network*, to cognitive functions that purportedly extend through and via media, or indeed to neurobiological structures of cognition, all of these theories miss the importance of defining the singularity of soft thought, as they instead reduce the latter to cognition.

Nevertheless, to define the singularity of soft thought, this chapter will discuss architectural works and theories that have directly engaged with the relation between computation and cognition on the one hand and cognition and perception on the other. In particular, these theories and works will be used as points of departure for developing the notion of soft thought and for further distinguishing it from the dominant tendencies in this field. The split between the neurocognitive and the neuroperceptual understanding of thought will be analyzed in the next two sections. This split, however, will be analyzed further by drawing on the experimental use of the cybernetic notion of interaction in architecture, which suggests that thought results from the interaction with the environment and thus that the latter is constitutive of thought. On the other hand, this split is also evident in the use of cybernetics to explain the neurocognitive relations of the brain with the environment (i.e., extended cognition). While these approaches to an understanding of soft thought may contribute toward defining its singularity among a minefield of assumptions about its nature, they are not sufficient to explain how soft thought is an actual experience of the discrete infinity of infinities. To do this, the last part of the chapter will turn to R&Sie(n)'s project *I've Heard About . . .* and will argue that soft thought is a computational event.

3.0.1 Neuroarchitecture

My point therefore is not to ask whether soft thought exists, or what it might reveal of the ontology of thought, but rather to challenge the fusion of computation and cognition and the neurocomputational theories (from connectivism to the extended mind and neurocognition) that are frequently used to explain thought as a neural syntax. Soft thought does not unify being and thought: instead, it exposes the contrasts and asymmetries between them, i.e., between divine being, rational being, and computational being on the one hand, and concrete abstractions that do not stem from nor are equivalent to being on the other. Soft thought is the actual thought of computation in the same way as bacteria, plants, fruit flies, animals, and humans have actual thought, which require, as Whitehead reminds us, a certain level of differentiation in terms of capacities of decision, and thus an actual possibility of being free from the chains of causal efficacy.[4] As recent research in the field of neurobiology suggests,[5] one can argue that at the biological level bacteria, amoebas, and plants deploy a modality of decision making that requires no nervous system and that can be described in terms of affective or precognitive stances, such as feelings, expectations, attitudes, and moods.[6]

Nevertheless, in this section I will point out that the neuroarchitecture of cognition is central to the software programming of self-generating

Figure 3.1
JoAnn Kuchera-Morin and Marcos Novak, *AlloBrain@AlloSphere*, 2007. Courtesy of AlloSphere.

environments. These environments are not simply conceived as simulations of the mind, but appear to be the house of thought itself, or *brain landscapes*.

Marcos Novak's project *AlloBrain@AlloSphere*[7] provides a good example of neuroarchitecture, because it shows how the computation of brain landscapes can lead to the design of cognition as a form of neuroarchitecture. *AlloSphere*[8] is a three-story-high spherical structure in which Novak's functional magnetic resonance imaging (fMRI)[9] brain-imaging data are used to visualize neurospace and to create brain landscapes, the *AlloBrain*, which can be experienced as immersive environments by a group of people.[10] This project offers a view of computational design in which the latter is based on the feedback cycle between neurodata and the environment, as it creates a series of immersive environments that correspond to the mental space of cognition, environments that are derived from scanned synaptic nerve responses. In the project, the environment that the brain perceives is shaped by the mental operations scanned by fMRI. Thus, the project places data manipulation at the very center of the mental experience of scanned data. The interactive, 3D-audio immersive environments that *AlloSphere* creates, constructed from fMRI brain data, suggest that the brain is a generative force in the formation of spatial environments, thus revealing the neuroactivities of cognition. Within the *AlloSphere*, the *AlloBrain* therefore proposes a view of cognition in which the latter is understood in terms of the neural firing of synaptic enervations, which are scanned and subsequently computationally generated, in order to reveal how brain data are changed, yet again, when perceived and experienced within an immersive environment.

According to Novak, this project should not be taken as yet another simulation of the brain, albeit one that has been transposed into a digital environment equipped with interactive manipulation tools (such as controllers that move data or allow navigation through it). On the contrary, the project uses the computation of the brain space to demonstrate that information processing (neurosynaptic architecture) deploys the spatial configurations of cognition as always already responsive to the environment. While this example may specifically demonstrate how to build an artificial environment through a specific mode of perceiving space, I take it instead to suggest itself as yet another instance in which computation is used to represent the syntactic arrangement of the brain constituting thought. This means that the computational view of cognition *qua* information processing is no longer generally considered in terms of a matrix of finite instructions. Instead, this computational view of cognition, as defined by the feedback interaction with the environment, points to the importance of cybernetics for computation. As Ross Ashby, a theorist of first-order cybernetics, observed, "the brain is not a thinking machine. It is an acting machine; it gets information and then does something about it."[11] As Ashby anticipated, the biological phenomena of adaptive behavior can be described mathematically, and can thus be computed.[12] He showed that this behavior could be mechanically reproduced with his homeostat,[13] which explained cognition as a response mechanism to the environment.[14] The environment thus no longer appears to be an inert space that awaits the execution of preset predicates. On the contrary, the *AlloBrain* project embraces the notion of the brain's plasticity and shows that the interior routes of synaptic connection are rearranged by environmental stimuli, in the same way that any act of perception can be said to modify the neural map of the brain.[15]

This instance of neuroarchitecture shows that cognition is more than a manipulation of finite instructions or symbols. Cognition now involves the computational power of spatial programming, and the activation (and adaptation) of (cognitive-software) information through the space of data manipulation. As the *AlloBrain* project suggests, the continuous feedback between the firing of neurons, the brain, and the environment constitutes a new species of spatial design in which the latter is generated by the experience and manipulation of cognitive, perceptual, and navigational data. From this standpoint, neuroarchitecture also demonstrates how the postcybernetic approach to design is based not on the physical adaptation of the body to the machine, but rather on the computational programming of cognitive behavior adapted to the environment. In other words, the generative design of brain landscapes corresponds to the programming of cognition, because it designs spaces that are preadapted to neurological responses. The postcybernetic logic of anticipatory architecture can also be seen to bring forward another aspect of preemptive power: the programming of neurosynaptic connections through data manipulation. Realizing that the architecture of cognition is a malleable framework that adapts to environmental changes, preemptive power is set to preprogram mental behavior by capitalizing on the neuroscientific discovery that thought equals the interactions between the brain and the world.[16]

3.0.2 Enactive architecture

To some extent, neuroarchitecture may be seen to approach cognition in terms of "enaction" ("the enactment of a law or the performance of actions").[17] However, neuroarchitecture is more concerned with what happens inside the brain (its neurosynaptic structure). Against the legacy of *computationalism,* according to which cognition is reducible to a physical symbol system, a mental process carried out by the manipulation of symbolic representations within the brain, Francisco Valera and Evan Thompson have argued that cognition is embedded in the world. In particular, they claimed that cognition is "the enactment of a world and a mind on the basis of a history of the variety of actions that a being in the world performs."[18]

By rejecting computationalism and its cognitivist and connectionist forms, Varela and Thompson's second-order cybernetic approach to the problem of the mind is more directly concerned with the relation between cognitive processes and the world, including the brain's relationship to the living body and the environment. According to the cognitivist view, the external world can only be represented in the mind, and in consequence the world and the mind remain independent entities. To Varela and Thompson, however, "cognitive structures and processes emerge from recurrent sensorimotor patterns of perception and action."[19] Cognition is not equivalent to the processing of information (whether by symbols or by neural nets), which can be carried out by any system and which can thus remain independent of any material substrate. Instead, cognition emerges from the activities of being, which are performed within the world. From this enactivist standpoint, interaction is explained in terms of the effects of the environment on the brain. This does not equate cognition to the architectures of neural *connectionism.* According to *enactivism,* the environment triggers cognition's productive response to and consequent enactment of a world. Thus cognition, and ultimately thought, need not be seen solely in terms of neural architecture, but rather primarily as a problem of consciousness and experience.

The gap between cognition and experience is therefore narrowed by a new *naturalization* of phenomenology, according to which lived experience must be analyzed from the standpoint of neuroscience and biology.[20] Varela argued for a neurophenomenological approach to experience involving a systematic analysis of the relation between mind and consciousness, insofar as both are embodied in "the structure of human experience itself."[21] In particular, his resolution to the problem of experience versus cognition, of lived extensions versus abstract minds, proposes an autopoietic system of reflexivity determined by the order of phenomenological reduction. Reality becomes composed of concave mirrors, as the act of thinking becomes reflexive.[22]

This reflexive order can only define cognition retrospectively, however. This is because enaction is generated by phenomenological reflexivity, which can only occur *after* thought has happened. In other words, thought is one with reflection. To avoid a naive form of cognition *qua* direct experience, enactivism must also deny the presence of any objective state of thought prior to the doubling mechanism of reflexivity. For enactive cognition, reflexivity defines the intersubjective validation of the realm of phenomena, which is centered on the circular movement of the thinking thought thinking itself.

If neuroarchitecture aims at designing the experience of space according to adaptive neural responses to the environment, neurophenomenology argues that it is the structure of experience—and not the cognitive mapping of the brain's adaptation to space—that leads us to view cognition as enacted experience. According to enactivism, the interaction between thought and space—between experience and architecture—cannot coincide with a neural pack of connections, but rather needs to be studied in terms of first-person, experiential evidence of spatial phenomena or of variations such as depth, height, volume, temperature, color, sound, etc. For neuroarchitecture on the other hand, as the *AlloBrain* project demonstrates, the data collected on these variations, processed via the algorithmic calculations of a software program, are enough to qualify these elements of interaction as first-person, a qualification that is expressed through visual simulation or through augmented reality. *Neurophenomenology* instead employs specific first-person methods in order to generate original first-person data, which can then be used to guide the study of physiological processes. For this reason, it looks at first-person data reactions to multistable images as a demonstration of the fact that every visual pattern allows more than one interpretation.

An example that can further explain how neurophenomenology includes an account of first-person evidence within the computational design of space can be found in the doubleNegatives Architecture (dNA) installation *Corpora in S(igh)te*.[23] Corpora are spatial machines that collect data from a given area through a network of wireless sensors, and which then build up a special grid of notation system points called Super-eyes. These are autonomous structures that collect data or scan in all directions so as to evaluate environmental conditions. The mutual adjustment of their individual viewpoints determines the form of the whole architecture, which is thus subtended by the rules operated by algorithms. For example, temporal changes in the shape of corpora are manifestations of the behavior of the individual elements in relation to each other, and also that of

Figure 3.2
doubleNegatives Architecture (dNA) (Sota Ichikawa, Max Rheiner, Ákos Maróy, Kaoru Kobata), *Corpora in Si(gh)te*, Yamaguchi Center for Arts and Media, 2007. Courtesy of Sota Ichikawa.

the system as a whole. At the Yamaguchi Center for Arts and Media (YCAM) in 2007, *Corpora in Si(gh)te* used forty devices with small sensors scattered around YCAM and processed aspects of environmental data at each point (temperature, wind velocity and direction, noise, etc.) in real time via a wireless mesh network, so as to visualize the computational design of the building.

A Zigbee Sensor Network was used to collect data, and several cameras were set up in the external environment to observe the surrounding target area. The real-time camera images were merged with the generated images from the corpora units. The parameters of 3D perspective, drawing from the viewpoint direction, view angles, and so on, were recalculated with the camera image. The audience was free to explore the structure process by selecting views from the two or three outdoor cameras that could be controlled with touch panel monitors. In the end, it was not really the audience that controlled the generation of the space; instead, the lived experience of space relied on the intersubjective interaction of many first-person views of environmental variations computed by a program.

From the standpoint of enactive cognition, the algorithmic processing of data according to the individual viewpoint of cellular automata may not be sufficient to explain how this computational space is experienced. In other words, in this project there is no room for a reflexive suspension of a naive experience, which instead may only account for the direct registering of data. This is important, because according to enactivism naive experience describes what happens *while* it happens, without being able to process data at a distance, reflecting on what happened. In other words, the algorithmic calculation of changing sensorimotor data on behalf of cellular automata still delimits the experience of embodied cognition to functional computational processing. Nevertheless, while this computational architecture may not satisfy the expectation of a neurophenomenological experience of space, it is true to say that this project aims to include the environment (and first-person perceptions) in the process of neural adaptation by incorporating live data, and by establishing particular points of view in the computation of space. This constitutes a neurophenomenology of data.

From this standpoint, the *Corpora in Si(gh)te* project offers us a notion of soft thought that is not directly a manifestation of the neuroarchitecture of the brain (as in the case of *AlloBrain*) but that adds external data to the internal software processing. According to this perspective, soft thought is activated from the external data that cellular automata evaluate and thus respond to by creating visual patterns that intersect or cross through and are added upon an existing physical architecture. However, because neurophenomenology conceives of the external world as the productive ground that guarantees new data to experience, which corresponds to first-person views or rather reflections on data, it is clear that this approach cannot account for the possibility of a computational thought that is not subsumed into the kaleidoscopic images derived from first-person neuro-perceptive experience. To understand soft thought away from the neuro-architecture of the brain and the neurophenomenology of first-person experience, it is necessary to account for it according to its own procedures of selection and evaluation of data.

3.0.3 Negative prehension

Despite all efforts to explain the architecture of thought with and through the digital computation of the brain (the neural networks of connectionism, and the neurophenomenology of enaction), I argue that the space of soft thought cannot simply be the result of something (such as an axiom, the interactions between parts and wholes, neurosynaptic structure, or first-person lived synthesis of data). Despite their irreducible ontological (and epistemological) premises, it is evident that cognitivism and enactivism share the same understanding of algorithmic processing. For these approaches, algorithmic computations are equivalent to programmed procedures, sets of executable instructions, which define cognition in terms of data performance on differing forms of hardware. Hence, the condition for the existence of algorithmic objects, according to these views, is that these objects must be executable on a machine, on which they run the process for which they were designed.

For cognitivism, the condition for algorithmic processing is any physical architecture that runs the instructions through the connection of data that form a neural network; for enactivism, this condition is an environment in which the neural structure of cognition is dynamically triggered through sensorimotor perception. Thus while for cognitivism algorithmic processing is equivalent to cognitive states, for enactivism it is the effect of being embedded within an environment that allows cognitive states (as neural changes) to emerge. Consequently, and although they offer what seem to be incompatible ontological frameworks, both approaches conceive of algorithms as executable procedures, as codes that perform thoughts upon a material substratum, or which cause thoughts to emerge from the latter. Yet regardless of whether these thoughts emerge from neural connections or are constructed throughout the sensorimotor schema of perception, algorithmic procedures remain the executers of thought. In short, the conditions for algorithmic processing are established by the sense in which the physical architecture of the brain is always already set to ensure the performance of thought. What is missing from these approaches is the possibility of conceiving algorithmic processing as a *mode of thought*, an expression or finite actuality, and not as the *instrument through which thought can be performed*, whether through neural nets or enacted via embodiment.

This means that if computation does not explain cognition, then it is also problematic to describe cognition as a totalizing function of thought defining the "autonomy and intentionality of life . . . that encompasses the organism, one's subjectively lived body, and the life-world."[24] Algorithmic modes of thought must be conceived away from mere mechanical (or predetermined) functions, and yet they cannot simply be replaced with the ontobiological ground *enacting* thought as the full force of life. Neither mechanical functionalism nor embedded vitalism can explain the persistence of algorithms as actual modes of thought or as finite expressions of infinities. But how can we account for these modes of thought away from mechanistic and vitalist conditions? How can we explain algorithmic thought as an actual mode determined by its own prehension of the infinite infinities of thought?

If algorithmically processed space does not match first-person viewpoints and reflexive loops, this is precisely because algorithmic objects offer a particular perspective on the experience of space. But to understand the significance of this perspective, one may need to stop conceiving algorithms in terms of simulation, or as representing the neuroarchitecture of thought. Instead, one may need to take the conceptual leap of conceiving algorithms as being actual entities: not substantial objects, but prehensive entities or experiences infected with abstractions. This does not mean, however, that abstractions (which merely remain ineffective idealities) need to be substituted (or implemented) with materiality, so that even mathematical ideas, such as algorithms, could be concretely grounded. On the contrary, to say that algorithms are actual objects infected with abstractions is to consider abstractions as decisive (and irreversible) factors in the structure of any actual occasion of experience. Following Whitehead, one can argue that abstractions correspond to the vagueness that characterizes some form of excitement that derives from a particular fact. In other words, the vagueness linked to a particular fact can be explained as the abstraction that is immanent to any actuality. This is why algorithmic processing is to be considered for what it is, as it offers a particular perspective of infinite universes. The importance of this particular perspective derives from the vagueness (the immanent abstraction) that characterizes it.[25]

Whitehead's process metaphysics describes the immanence of abstraction in actuality. It shows that this abstraction is deployed by the irreversible power that pure potentialities, eternal objects, exert on the actual entities that select them. In particular, Whitehead does not collapse the reality of abstract ideas with concrete objects, and he does not derive abstraction from actualities. In this sense, his process-oriented metaphysics is not merely an example of the metaphysics of emergence, whereby ideas are induced from the material interaction of parts; instead, he goes to great lengths to explain the existence, the value, and the role of an abstract object in itself. "An abstract object is in itself—that is to say its essence . . . comprehensible without reference to some one particular occasion of experience."[26] Abstractions account for the irreversible eventfulness of experience and its endurance, its finitude. For Whitehead, concrete objects are actually successive occasions of experience defined by the prehensive capacities of selecting abstract objects.

Whitehead describes how eternal objects are related to other abstract entities and to all actualities in general, but he also emphasizes that eternal objects remain disconnected from definite modes of actuality.[27] This possibility of disconnection is always present insofar as actual occasions may not select certain eternal objects, or, as Whitehead puts it, an actual occasion may "negatively prehend"[28] an eternal object, deciding not to include its potential in its formation or in the succession of occasions of experience. Nevertheless, it may be misleading to assume that a negative prehension merely connotes the exclusion of certain abstract objects in favor of others. On the contrary, a negative prehension is all the more a negative selection of those potentialities that cannot be computed, and as such may intensify the reality of what is not prehended, a residual or dormant potentiality that becomes the condition for actual expressions or modes of thought. Negative prehensions are not actual, but they are nonetheless real as they pertain to the affairs of an actual occasion in the same way as those abstract objects that are positively prehended and lived in an actual event. For Whitehead, a negative prehension is "the definite exclusion of [an eternal] item from positive contribution to the subject's own real internal constitution."[29] But he also insists that "the negative prehension of an entity is a positive fact with its emotional subjective form."[30] From this standpoint, unlived potentials are as real a component of experience as are those that are lived and completely exhausted by an actual entity. The structure of experience, in other words, cannot exclusively depend on lived first-person perspectives, even when these include a larger embodied environment of interactive agents. If spatial experience is not just the representational map of a given environment established by symbolic language, but rather becomes constructive of spatiality, then the structure of experience will have to account for how space *becomes this and not that spatiality*, or explain where the potential for this spatiality originates from. To embrace this question is to ask what remains excluded in prehension: those unrealized thoughts or eternal objects that are negatively prehended and which nonetheless infect the autorealization of *this* definite structure of experience, and not another.

In the case of the *Corpora in Si(gh)te* project, the algorithmic architecture of the space generated through the computation of environmental variations does little to explain how the lived experience of a nonexisting building (a computer software design of a building) involves the negative prehension of abstract objects: of what remains excluded from the collection of lived data. The use of first-person perspectives cannot unpack how the experience of this computationally generated spatiality comes about. Nevertheless, and unlike enactivism, which holds that there can be no experience without temporal or retrospective reflexivity, it can be argued here that the computational collection of first-person evidence overlooks the nonactivated, dormant and absent eternal objects that have not been selected by cellular automata. Without negative prehensions, one could argue, there could be no occasion of experience, and no event: for an occasion of experience is characterized by both what is included and what is excluded. In this case, the data that are excluded or not activated from the point of view of algorithms also serve to determine the constitution of one particular occasion of experience rather than another. This also means that computational algorithms are not to be enacted by an external agent, thereby rendering them actual expressions of realities. In fact, they are already expressions or modes of thought of the prehended data. In addition, and as I have argued in chapters 1 and 2, algorithms are also conceptual prehensions of pure potentialities: eternal objects, which are positively and negatively selected in the computational process.

What is suggested here, however, is that this negative thought of pure potentials can be further understood as the algorithmic prehension of incomputable data. It may be an indication that what cannot be computed does nonetheless exist as the very condition of what can be digitally processed. From this standpoint, emphasizing the significance of negative prehensions here serves to highlight what both enactivism and computationalism seem to miss: the nonperfomative, nonexecutional, and noninteractive dimensions of computation and thought. Seen from this perspective, computation cannot equate thought to calculation, and instead relates it to a mode of prehension of incomputable infinities, or to an infinite variety of infinities. This infinite variety of infinities corresponds to discrete infinities or eternal objects, which are negatively prehended, unselected or unactivated in actualities. To suggest that there is a nonperfomative or inactive dimension to soft thought is also to disclose computation as the nonexecutable field of the infinity of incomputable algorithms. This architecture of eternal objects is therefore not what is now calculable with computation, but rather what digital algorithms, as actual entities, have come to conceptually prehend as the infinity of infinite parts (i.e., the infinite parts of incomputable algorithms, of which Omega is an example). By negatively selecting what cannot be computed (the infinity of eternal objects), algorithmic calculation thus shows that thought is directly represented by neither the neurocomputational architecture of the brain nor the neurobiological space of phenomenal experience. In particular, if digital algorithms are conceived as actual objects which do not simply retrieve physical data but are in fact actual data or immanent conceptions of eternal objects, then it may be possible to disentangle thought from the neuroevolution of the brain (which is central to concerns with neural networks and to conceptions of mind-generating reality).

Focusing on what is not prehended may help us to argue that there are infinite architectures of thought that are irreducible to the central image of the brain, but which are also incompatible with notions of computational functionalism (the syntax of neural connections) and enactivism (the environment enacting the neural space). Suggesting that algorithms are conceptual prehensions of eternal objects that are at once selected (computed) and excluded (as incomputable) may also contribute to clarifying what is meant here by the contingency of soft thought. The question of contingency in programming is in fact central to this chapter, and in its second part I will turn to William James's notion of transition in order to explain soft thought in terms of contingent computation and immanent experience. The question, therefore, is not only whether genetic algorithms, neural nets, or multiagent systems (which are now central to architectural and urban design) are instances of how thought functions in the brain, or whether software can be seen as an extension of the neuroarchitectures of the mind. On the contrary, the question is whether genetic algorithms, neural nets, or multiagent systems are modes of thought that reveal contingency (i.e., the infinite variety of infinities) to be a condition of computation. Addressing the contingency of this form of thought means questioning two fundamental assumptions that characterize both neurocomputation and neurophenomenology: (1) thought equals action (i.e., it is necessarily executable); (2) the architecture of the brain is the model of thought.

The significance of negative prehension, therefore, is to be understood vis-à-vis the existence of thoughts that are not actions and are not generated by the brain. The reality of what cannot be computed, or that of incomputable thoughts, remains true for all forms of computation wherein infinity is the condition of all production; but it is also the condition for the elimination of production altogether (because infinity is not produced *tout court*). This means that the incomputable, what cannot be prehended, what is negatively prehended, or the unperformed and the unexecutable pertain precisely to the randomness of soft thought.

However, at this point, placing an emphasis on the nonperformative architecture of thought may give rise to suspicion: for how can this proposition of a nonperformative thought avoid falling straight back into pure idealism, or into those forms, detached from material patterns and meaningful inferences, that allowed us to explain the materiality of thought in the first place? One could certainly wonder how the proposition advanced here could stop idealism from slipping in through the back door. Nevertheless, I would redirect any such suspicion toward the now dominant trends of ideal materialism and neurological idealism, which animate neurocognitivism and also notions of embodied cognition and enactivism. These theories attempt to reify thought as a performative operation/action of the brain (neural connectionism) or of the mind (embedded brain). These new forms of idealism, I would suggest, have problematically left behind the possibility of addressing computation in terms of an actual thought, or rather soft thought, but have also worked to repress the reality of abstract ideas and incomputable thoughts, together with that of their immanence to algorithmic experience. The very fact that some of these incomputable objects are negatively prehended (both physically and conceptually negated by actual entities, including algorithms) helps my argument that the structure of experience must account for the incomprehensible and incompressible entropic energies that increase the space of data, and that this structure cannot therefore be contained by neurosynaptic architectures and/or first-person perceptions of the environment.

For example, Hyperbody's computationally generated *Interactive Wall*,[31] which is defined by the sensorimotor interaction with atmospheric pressures for instance, is not simply enacted by lived experience. Instead it is characterized above all by the algorithmic selection of actual data and incomputable probabilities, and is determined by potentials that are negatively prehended. What remains unprehended by the algorithmic sets is not comparable to the limits that this particular actual entity has, since any actual occasion is spatiotemporally limited to selecting those potentials that serve it for its own realization. What remains outside of this spatiotemporal selection (or this "presentational immediacy")[32] is to be precisely taken as evidence of a lived abstraction: the algorithmic negative prehensions of incomputable infinities.

It is impossible to deny that algorithmic architecture has become the expression of a neurocognitive model of thought. From models of artificial intelligence to media of augmented perception (including mobile devices), from neural networks to robotics prosthetics, algorithmic architecture has become housed in a multiplicity of physical and mechanical structures that aim to strip away all abstractions from rational processing. This has meant that thought, as a result of the rise of digital design, has come to exist independently of any material substructure; at the same time, the assumption that thought is granted by the existence of a specific materiality has also been challenged. It is noticeable that since their computational inception, architectures of thought—from the Turing machine, neural networks, and self-emergent autopoietic structures to multiagent systems and the most recent robotic models of enacted or embodied cognition and affective computing[33]—have exceeded their metaphysical premises, questioning both the ideality of mathematical form and the empiricism of sensorimotor data (including emotional and qualitative patterns) in the definition of cognition. In this sense, the more thought has become computed, the more it has become detached from the mathematical and biological substratum of cognition, and it has instead become an autonomous computational expression of the incomputable residues of incomprehensible and incompressible data.

Far from becoming actualized, however, these incomputable data are entering computation as incalculable generalities. In particular, Whitehead insists that generalization is not to be confused with an appeal to a category (as with a deductive method) or with a proved fact that can be universalized to others (as with an inductive method). Instead, rather than describing cognitive states, generalization is here the unconditional matrix that constitutes order itself. Whitehead's notion of generalization rejects the notion that the concept of a set constitutes the basic ground or mathematical ontology. He argues instead that generalizations are the "mapping of the relation between a domain and a codomain."[34] In other words, generalizing finite, actual entities means describing their nonseparability from particular rules, thus constituting both an aesthetic and a logical mode of explanation. However, none of these modes are infallible. On the contrary, Whitehead suggests that it is in the nature of speculative reason to remain open to unexpected revelations and discoveries: the inconsistencies in aesthetic and logical modes of knowing, inconsistences that are able to form new epistemologies. From this standpoint, soft thought is important because it implies that the reality of automated thought corresponds not to a cognitive state but to a generalized computation.

The spatiotemporal pervasion of soft thought has also been described in terms of a calculative background that results in new modes of perception and memory, navigation and orientation (or movement space).[35] This calculative background corresponds to the space of "qualculation": a term used by Thrift to define the "generality of the numbered fields against which and with which much activity now takes place, the increasing amount of calculation done via machinic prostheses."[36] Qualculation thus defines not only a pervasive increase in numbers, but also the fact that numbers have acquired a quality and are thus to be understood as "forces rather than discrete operations."[37] Yet whereas the qualculative background is also understood as a topological space-time framework affording new perceptual experiences ("new senses, new intelligences of the world and new forms of 'human'"),[38] I understand soft thought as deploying incomputable quantities in the foreground of computational experience. This means that experience does not emerge from the qualitative attributes of digitalization. Instead, perceptual and mental states of experience are invaded by a nonreducible mode of thinking-experiencing: the actuality of soft thought is inassimilable. The increasing computation of space thus results not in a qualitative determination of discrete operations, but rather in the computational power of discrete algorithms to unleash incomputable data in everyday calculations. The computation of space, therefore, may not result in new perceptual experiences; more importantly, it may serve to define the sense in which soft thought is an actuality, an alien experience that interrupts the continual surface of relations. The sheer increase of modes of calculation may therefore be defined by the capacities of algorithms to negatively prehend incomputable quantities, which thus enter the conditions of the present as actual modes of thought. This implies not only a qualitative transformation of numbers, but also, as explained in the previous chapters, their quantitative transformation from whole numbers and infinitesimal points to discrete infinities. It is therefore the advance of speculative computing (by which I mean the inclusion of infinities in the calculative background of digital programming) that has led incomputable quantities to define the general actuality of soft thought in the foreground of experience. These lived generalities are discontinuities in the continuous succession of computed data, defining the blind spots, interferences, and multilooped delays in data processing. Rather than resulting in new capacities of thinking and perceiving, the foreground of incomputable data implies that there are quantities that cannot be algorithmically performed or experientially enacted. At the interstice between one datum and another, the succession of algorithmic expressions is taken over by incomputable thoughts belonging neither to a subject cognizing in communion with the environment nor to an object describing the cognitive execution of rules.

This interstice is a deep tear between seamlessly continuous worlds. It is experienced as an *excarnation* of quantities from objects, of incomputable elements from calculation, of unthinkable thoughts from reason, and thus constitutes a new actual object. In other words, the computational order of thought implies a calculating thought able to direct, or in cybernetic terms able to steer information in a certain direction. However, as this chapter points out, the computational steering of thought or soft thought places incomputable algorithms at the core of such ordering processes, thus revealing a form of governance that is infected with algorithmic randomness. Nevertheless, before we address this immanent experience of soft thought, it is important to discuss the influence of the theory of enactivism and of the neurobiological notion of cognition on the cybernetic design and computation of architectures of thought. As discussed in the next section, cybernetics for instance has challenged notions of thought and experience.

3.1 Cybernetic thought

In 1968, for the "Cybernetic Serendipity" exhibition curated by Jasia Reichardt at the ICA (London), cybernetic scientist and architect Gordon Pask invented a computational architecture of thought. Long before the construction of the digital computer, Pask's interests in cybernetics had led him to explore the role of feedback in defining the space of thought, and he drew in particular on the cyberneticist view that cognition could be understood in terms of neural structures that learn and adapt to the environment.[39]

Figure 3.3
Gordon Pask, *MusiColour* (detail), 1953–1957. Courtesy of the Gordon Pask Archive and the Paul Pangaro's Pask Collection, Institut für Zeitgeschichte, Vienna.

By the late 1950s, Pask had constructed several electrochemical devices that possessed the ability to deploy their own sensors and thereby establish a relationship between their internal states and the external world. These devices were designed to evolve an increased sensitivity to sound or magnetic fields. Most famously, he built the *MusiColour* machine: a light show that responded to sound. This machine was programmed to become bored when it could not react to the music performed, thus forcing the musician to change his composition in order to reincite the system's response. Importantly, the *MusiColour* machine anticipated the theory of enactivism, as it already suggested that the evolution of a cognitive system entailed interaction with its environment. However, Pask believed that elements of interaction for both biological and cognitive systems had to be grown in great numbers, so that large-scale adaptive networks (analog and digital) could potentially be built through interactive feedbacks. Against the architectural conception that a cognitive system grows from a fixed point of view, Pask's work proposed a materially embedded set of observable relations that change over time. Architectures of thought emerged in his work from the interaction of elements within the world, through which measurements were made, distinctions were drawn, and concepts were formed.

For Pask, intelligent behavior is a craft and cannot be exhausted by computational programming. Given that intelligence cannot be preset—i.e., that it is not an internal property of either the head or the mechanical box, but rather what emerges from interactions—Pask insists on the priority of physical relations, as the latter are defined by degrees of constraint and freedom. In other words, it is not computation but only biophysical and chemical interactions that can generate architectures of thought beyond any given set of rules. According to Pask, however, these interactions also need to account for the hierarchy of goals and actions, which he defines as objective interactions, as well as peer-to-peer language exchanges or subjective interactions. In particular, the rules of interaction are part of his "Conversation Theory," in which he lists the reasons why principles of agreement, understanding, and consciousness are crucial for the devising of human-to-human, human-to-computer, and computer-to-computer interactions. Away from the on/off logic of computation, Pask conceives of interaction as a conversation that requires mutual actions, such as those performed in dance, where space is offered to the steps of other bodies. Pask's model already foresaw that information transfer and data structures were the new platforms for the future of computational architecture. He was not concerned with inputting information into a body, but rather with showing that the interactive qualities of agreement, understanding, and consciousness were emergent properties of enacted environments.

Pask's experiments with mechanical and electrochemical systems also provide a conceptual framework for building a responsive architecture allowing human and media to coexist in a mutually constructive relationship.[40] For Pask, architecture is a cybernetic system that can learn, like the brain, to adapt and change through a creative conversation between the building and its users. The adaptive architecture that he proposes, however, is also a computational entity (an analog computation) that is able to learn, like the *MusiColour* machine, from its states, and can make suggestions as to its own reorganization and the reactivation of its spatial capacities. This cybernetic architecture, which includes the possibility of constructing a digitally controllable structure that can transform its uses according to changing circumstances, can also be conceived as an instance of the "anticipatory architecture" that I discussed in chapter 1. However, despite the degree to which it anticipates the notions of responsiveness and participation that now characterize interactive architecture, this conception of a thinking building needs to be distinguished from the design of smart environments. For instance, like the late 1990s MIT design project *Intelligent Room*, an example of smart architecture possessed of cognitive capacities that can be equated to the computational performance of algorithms (for which cognition equates to action),[41] Pask's experiments in adaptive architecture can be seen to suggest that the building's interaction with the environment would primarily lead to a thinking space. However, the *Intelligent Room* project deploys a neuroarchitectural understanding of space, with computation seamlessly deploying automated activities driven by interactive algorithms that are designed to respond to or act out the environment according to inputs (e.g., movement triggering the switching on of light, sound triggering the shutting of curtains, etc.). This form of response to input entails that the thinking of doing something and the actual doing of it can be summed up or synthesized by one sensorimotor action. In short, the simple switching off of the lights when leaving a room becomes an automatic response.[42] This is an instantaneous form of interaction, which is primarily reactive as it implies that the environment acts at the same time as the person within it.

The design of the *Intelligent Room* is inspired by early models of cybernetics, according to which environments can become intelligent, responsive, or interactive either if algorithmically programmed to do so, or if an intelligent behavior emerges out of neuroalgorithmic connections. It is not a surprise that interaction is governed in this example by building management operators, which are for example preset to optimize sunlight distribution so that rooms can change color as people enter. Yet for Pask, this kind of ideal interaction would simply involve the preprogramming of environments in such a way that they instantaneously respond to people, without ultimately allowing for a self-organizing architecture able to establish a truly dynamic conversation with its inhabitants. Such a dialogue would require the entire organizational structure of the architecture to change. Pask conceives of input criteria as fine-tuned variables that change according to contingent circumstances, and does not therefore see them as preset variations or probabilities of interaction that can be applied to human-machines. The entire interactive environment (and not just the computer or the participant) is therefore required to select and construct its own input criteria, its abstract objects for potential actualization. From Pask's point of view, it is only when this interactive environment is conceived dynamically that the occupants can be said to enter new levels of engagement, insofar as they become agents of the evolution of their own inhabited space.

It is therefore clear that Pask's architecture of thought is defined by interactive dynamics grounded in the material world of electrochemical assemblages, the crafting of building links and assemblages, and the designing of tools that people themselves may use to construct their own data environments.[43] Pask is thus more than a pioneer of neuroarchitecture, as his cybernetic architecture of thought clearly embraces second-order cybernetics, i.e., notions of self-organization, adaptation, and the capacity of the structural arrangement of space to change by learning from feedback with the environment. From this standpoint, his cybernetic architecture stands apart from the mathematical vision according to which the mind is composed of a priori formal axioms, and engages directly with the environmental intelligence of the physical, chemical, material world. Pask devised a series of architectures of thought that were intended to be open-ended spaces for learning by interaction,[44] based on dynamic conversation between communication environments and their inhabitants, in which humans and machines could work together to form a self-emergent system that *enacts* cognition. In other words, his cybernetic architecture seems to be closer to enactivism than to neurocognition. On the other hand, despite his engagement with a cybernetic mode of computational thought, the centrality of the notion of feedback as a reversible relation between the environment and the building (a relation that ultimately leads the building to adapt, change, and thus think through learning) does not give us much opportunity to explain what is at stake as regards the proposition of an

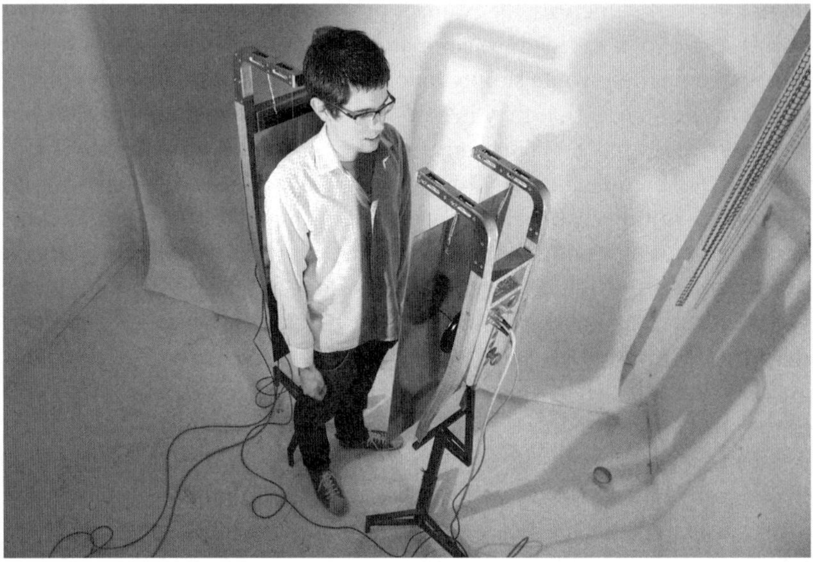

Figure 3.4
Richard Roberts, *Hearing a Reality*, 2008. Courtesy of Richard Roberts.

algorithmic mode of thought. Although Pask's projects involved a series of experiments with biological, chemical, and mechanical modes of thought, the computational dimensions of digital space have remained secondary, as this space seems to be unable to change without becoming coupled with the external environment or a substantial substrate. This tendency to embody thought or to embed it within the environment is also evident in contemporary works developed from or inspired by Pask's legacy.

For instance, at the recent exhibition "Pask Present,"[45] Richard Roberts's work *Hearing a Reality*[46] proposed an embodied version of conversation that was triggered by the movement of people circling around an acoustic device. Not only does Roberts show that there is an analog computation of experience between the people and the device: in addition, this project suggests, that experience is deployed by a system of interaction that is able to learn from its environment. The project thus becomes an instance of enacted cognition and embedded thought. On the other hand, projects such as KRD's (Kitchen Rogers Design) *Responsive Space* show how the environment undergoes transformations of its own shape when prompted to do so by the visitor's movement.[47] Here individual movement directly molds the form of the space. For example, such movement can cause the ceiling to slide 2,100 mm up and down and to tilt from side to side, so as to completely transform the space's form from within. Sensors scattered in the space, which continues to remain mobile because its volumes are ceaselessly altered by random sensorimotor responses, act as catalysts for the transformation of the room. It may seem that these interactive architectures contradict the standpoints of neuroarchitecture, insofar as space is activated here through and by sensorimotor activities. Yet it is important to stress that this particular project aims to show that the shape of the space, i.e., the computed environment, is itself in movement, and is reconfigured each time by an unscripted enactment. The stainless steel floor and walls are equipped with invisible sensors that are ready to pick up sensorimotor stimuli, and compute the space through live response. KRD therefore offers a model of interaction based on the sensorimotor enactment of space, where the interior form of the room remains attuned to the variables of lived movement. These movements seem to constitute the movement of cognition as the sensorimotor activation of neural space. In other words, the movement of cognition is here implied to be equivalent to sensorimotor action. As Maturana and Varela point out, "cognition is a matter of interacting in the manner(s) in which one is capable of interacting, not processing what is objectively there to be seen. Living systems are cognitive systems and living is a process of cognition."[48]

From the standpoint of neuroarchitecture, however, *Hearing a Reality* and *Responsive Space* do not explain how the embedded computation of space modulates or impacts cognitive behavior. At the same time, neuroarchitecture also fails to explain that space does not preexist experience, and that the emphasis of enactivism on sensorimotor adaptive response points to the co-constitution (interactive coupling) of experience and space. Nevertheless, what is still missing from these articulations of interactive cognition is that thoughts are also abstract objects. This means that thoughts are internally related and externally disconnected, and thus enjoy a spatial order or architecture that does not match the physical order of space. These interactive projects, therefore, overlook—to a greater extent than Pask's experiments in chemical, biological, and physical computation—the sense in which the actual modalities of information are infected with abstract sonic objects, for instance, or with volume infinities. The notion of the cognitive character of information employed in these projects (unlike in Pask's) does not entail a learning or growing form of computation that stems from interactive elements. Instead, they remain far more literally identical to the visitors' physical movement. In consequence, the interaction between information and bodies is conflated here into one system of action and reaction, insofar as the movement of bodies becomes equivalent to information. The biophysical dynamics of moving bodies here simply performs cognition as information emerging from sensorimotor inputs. In contrast, Pask's cybernetic computation shows the processual or the retroprocessual learning of the various elements of the architectural structure to be defined by the interaction of chemical, mechanical, and physical elements whose temporal and multilayered recurring functions can give rise to the cognitive dynamics of the structure. From this standpoint, Pask's cybernetic architecture conceives the environment in a manner similar to enactivism, i.e., as being constitutive of but also as constituting the cognitive structure of thought. In the next section I will discuss this ecological understanding of cognition at more length, observing that Pask's cybernetic architecture offers a view of computation that considers the latter in terms of an environment: as an information background that affords a direct link between perception and cognition.

Before turning to the ecological understanding of information, it may be important here to point out how cybernetics, and in particular Pask's articulation of interaction, can help us to challenge notions of interactivity that rely directly on the algorithmic processing of sensorimotor responses. In other words, Pask's notion of interaction significantly contributes to developing a theory of contingency in computation. Since his computational experiments were more closely engaged with biophysical and biochemical processes of computation, it would also seem that his experiments have little to add to the notion of soft thought that I want to develop here. Yet if we turn to an ecological understanding of information, it may perhaps be possible to resolve this issue, as we will be led toward a mereotopological understanding of information that does not imply that one mode of computation—one mode of thought—can subsume all others.

3.2 Ecological thought

To understand cognition in terms of information environment one has to turn to James J. Gibson, who argued that information is itself an environment and not just one element of interaction to be added to another. In the 1970s, Gibson developed a notion of information that departed from the rule-centered computational model, observing that information could only be picked, selected, and explored from the environment, not communicated to a receiver.[49] Information, therefore, is an environment that is directly perceived: a world of data that are readily available to selection. This is why perception and cognition, according to Gibson, explain how being-in-the-world has nothing to do with a mechanism of input and output or a measure of probabilities in the communicating system. Similarly, knowledge does not correspond to a cognitive state that is generated in the head. Knowledge is a process of experiencing data that is located not in the brain but in the muscles of perception.[50]

By placing cognition in the environment, Gibson proposed an ecological approach to thought. This approach primarily questioned the assumption that in order to perceive the world one must already have ideas about it. This means that his theory rejects the assumption according to which we would only be able to perceive responsiveness if the idea of interactive space were already formed in our heads. Against this view, Gibson explained that only an immersive perception of the environment—and not its pregiven conception—could give us a veritable knowledge of space. Through the extraction of abstract invariants from an information flux or through the perceptive selection of data from a continuous background of information it is possible, according to Gibson, to form knowledge of the qualities of objects.[51]

For Gibson, cognition is dependent on a background environment that is pregnant with information. This background persists in perception, experience, and knowledge even when it remains out of sight. In other words, the abstract architecture of an object is experienced even when, and especially when, it remains imperceptible, removed from the present situation, or unselected by an actual occasion. For instance, if the interactive space of *Hearing a Reality* were to deploy the invisible potentialities of sonic space through physical movement, then the conditions of experience might have to be minutely crafted to include blind spots of sound, unhearable beam objects that could affectively trespass all sonic orientations. Only by including such humanly unhearable realities of sonic objects could the structure of experience become not just interactive but immanent to the informational environment in which perception and cognition are lodged.

As opposed to the sensation-based approach to perception, according to which anything out of sight can only be perceived through an image (i.e., recalled, imagined, conceived) but not directly experienced, Gibson sustains that any occluding edge is instead part of direct perception.[52] Opaque surfaces are not invisible, but are perceived as being one behind another, entering and exiting from sight as the observer moves in one direction and then in another. In particular, Gibson argues that the briefest and the longest instances of locomotion (e.g., a movement that lasts fractions of a second, or one that lasts hours) deployed the possibility of perceiving the invisible as such. He calls this possibility "reversible occlusion," because only movement and its reverse can explain this possibility.[53] As there is an underlying invariant structure, a continuity of all surfaces, the difference between the hidden and the unhidden can be explained as a short or long pause in locomotion.[54] Conceived in these terms, the physical movement in *Hearing a Reality* could for instance account for the relation between the hearable and the unhearable as part of an underlying architecture of sonic information, rather than focusing on an actual sonic space designed to be heard by a human ear.

Hence the information background is here a topological invariant of the energy-light itself, which is brought to the foreground by the selective activity of perception. In other words, the direct perception of invisible objects makes them visible. However, the computational version of this background in projects such as *Responsive Space* seems to be missing, because here volumetric information always already coincides with actual and not potential movement. One may then wonder how interactive projects such as *Responsive Space* can really include this topological continuity of information background. Can it unite all surfaces affording a genuine perception (selection and creation) of data space, so as to foreground unexpected variables in experience? Wouldn't the closed nature of programmed responses or the computational background always already delimit the sensorimotor knowledge of what potential responsiveness could become?

It is true to say that Gibson's ecological approach has the advantage of deterritorializing cognition for a subject perceiving, but also for a neural network computationally performing thought. This approach in fact does explain that information is environment, an always-experienced background. Yet Gibson argues that this background is not computational. Rather, it is defined as an inexhaustible continuous energy-information environment that affords the perception of being-in-the-world. That is to say that although information is in the background, i.e., within the environment from which it is picked, there is always already a perceiving entity, which is here posed as the actor of cognition. Despite suggesting that cognition is not computation and that it is a capacity afforded by the environment (an enaction of the selected information), Gibson's ecological approach nevertheless discards the idea that the persistence of the information background reveals, beyond direct sensorimotor perception, the exhaustion of this potential in actual combinations.

Arguing against the view that the continual flow of potentiality—the infinitesimal infinity of topological invariants—constitutes the ontological background of actualities, Whitehead instead explains that eternal objects (background potentialities) do not exist as one uninterrupted surface that can be directly experienced by a body even when it is out of sight, but are discrete infinities, externally unrelated and negatively prehended. To put it in another way, as I discussed in chapter 2, Whitehead proposes a mereotopological matrix of eternal objects to explain that infinities are discrete dynamics, since they are not merged with one another through transcendent principles. In addition, eternal objects are also discontinuously selected by actual occasions, in which they can acquire real togetherness or unity of complexity and through which they exhaust their discrete infinity by becoming one with finite actualities. Hence experience is not just the foreground of the continual background of information. On the contrary, an occasion of experience demands that these discrete infinities become determined twice: first according to the (positive and negative) prehensive modality of ingression into an actual occasion, and second according to the new togetherness that they come to actually enjoy as selected potentials. Similarly, not only does the background of potentials become determined when selected by actual occasions: it is also determined according to the infinite levels of interior relations between infinities. The background is not an inexhaustible pool of energy-information waiting to become realized in perceptual experience. This background instead deploys the mereotopological architecture of parts and wholes that cannot be summed up by topological invariants or a priori continuity between otherwise discrete infinities. This background therefore is a mereotopology of eternal objects, of unrealized and unrealizable eternal objects that are nonetheless immanent to experience as contingent modes of thought, of which there are many. In other words, eternal objects are lived abstractions.[55] Here cognition is not derived from physical perception but is determined by the conceptual prehensions of eternal objects. In particular, cognition, understood in this sense, does not imply the sensorimotor activity of perception, but rather corresponds to a conceptual or nonsensuous feeling characterized by the "entertainment of unexpressed possibilities."[56] To sum up: while embracing Gibson's ecological notion of information, I instead suggest that the information background is a mereotopology of infinite parts of infinities, incomputable objects, which are immanent to and further determine occasions of experience as lived abstractions.

At the same time, the discontinuous relation between eternal objects and actual occasions is intersected by another level of discontinuity. Algorithmic prehensions cannot be said to derive from physical embodied perception, and yet they do not correspond to finite sets of data either. An algorithmic conceptual prehension is nonphysical and characterized by "the sense of what might be and what may have been. It is the entertainment of the alternative."[57] In short, what is problematic with the ecological approach and its autopoietic overtones is its tendency to conflate information either with finite sets of algorithms (closed computation) or with a background of infinite potentiality (a whole of continual variations), without explaining how information as quantification can be directly conceived in terms of qualities. In addition, this anticomputational approach does not offer much opportunity for theorizing thought beyond theories of embodied cognition. This approach will therefore exclude the existence or actuality of a computational mode of thought, as computation remains defined here in terms of finite sets of probabilities, and this reduces thought to statistical operations. Against this view, I will suggest that the actuality of soft thought is determined by incomputable quantities that have irreversibly infected the "qualculative" background of experience. It is the algorithmic contagion with infinities that transforms these finite sets of data into discrete infinities and also discloses another variety of infinity to the structure of experience: unsynthesizable quantities that correspond to interferences rather than to embodiments of thought.

3.3 Interactive thought

Autopoietic notions of embodied cognition and enactivism subsume the computational view of cognition into the sensorimotor activities of perception. First-order cybernetics added the notion of feedback to computation and thus placed the notion of homeostatic equilibrium at the core of the computational loop of the input and output of data (so that final results would match initial conditions). Second-order cybernetics took the notion of feedback one step further, and thereby revealed that the environment is constitutive of the internal organization of a living system. This meant that cognition was defined by its continuous interaction with the perceptual sensorimotor activities of the inhabitant of an environment.

Extending the theory of enactivism, Alva Noe, for instance, goes so far as to argue that knowledge cannot be separated from but is in fact intrinsic to the movement, gestures, and practices of a body. Perception "is a way of acting on the world"[58] determined by the exercise of sensorimotor knowledge.[59] This is why, according to Noe, the concept of space would be impossible without a body.[60] Similarly to the neurophenomenological approach, which always already involves an embodied production of cognition, Noe claims that the conception of space derives from the sensorimotor experience thereof. From this standpoint, the rectangular layout of a room can only be learned by the act of physically touching the rectangular furniture with hands. Sensorimotor knowledge gives us the conception of the geometrical form. No direct perception can explain the rectangular form of the room, "but rather your implicit understanding of the organization or structure of your sensations."[61] This organization depends on a process of covariation with actual/possible movements. According to Noe, rectangularity is therefore not a preformed idea or a sensational impression; only attentive movements through space, and not a direct perception of the geometrical shape, determine the perception/cognition of rectangularity.

From this point of view, the *Responsive Space* project can also be seen to claim that spatial perception is derived from experiential movement; a claim that turns away from formal models of spatial cognition. The form of cognition can instead only be constructed a posteriori, as if driven by the sensorimotor movement of perceivers. The geometrical shape of space and ultimately the idea of space are not defined according to Euclidean postulates of absolute and eternal form, but rather are produced by the sensorimotor activities that generate (as it were) the knowledge of shifting angles, volumes, and contours. Here space stems from the biorhythms of movement, which links one shape to another and thus builds the architecture of thought through the continual experience of physical space.

Figure 3.5
Institute of Neuroinformatics, *Ada—The Intelligent Space*, Expo.02, Switzerland. Courtesy of Stefan Kubli.

Gibson and Noe do not discuss how the information environment allows nonorganic entities to perceive and cognize. In this they differ from Pask, who defines interactivity in terms of conversation, develops a physical mode of computation, and points out that the physical embodiment of spatial knowledge is not exclusively enlived by a human or animal body, but by *any* body (for instance by the *MusiColour* machine). Similarly, recent efforts to establish how cognition is enacted by sensorimotor perception have resulted in various projects that aim to show that a machine can learn about its spatial dimensions from the external sensorimotor inputs of bodies. Recent interactive projects such as *Ada—The Intelligent Space*[62] seem to directly incarnate the cybernetic-oriented shift from computationally informed cognitivism toward a notion of cognition triggered by sensorimotor knowledge. The sentient space creature "Ada" is a neural network that uses sensorimotor triggers, such as sounds, lights, and projections that respond to the movement of visitors. Interaction here does not exclusively serve to augment the visitors' sensorimotor knowledge of space, but above all shows that Ada is itself a sentient space able to augment its spatial knowledge by learning from the different gestures, sounds, and movements of people, and by picking up information from the environment. In other words, the informational environment defines Ada's cognitive architecture because "she" is able to learn from physical interaction. Compared to Noe's elaboration of enactivism, this project therefore seems to be much closer to Pask's cybernetic-oriented architectures as it shows that any physical bodies, including machines, can learn from interaction.

Nevertheless, it is true to say that Noe, like Pask, rejects the computational theories of thought and believes that the algorithmic description of cognitive phenomena is not autonomous from the secondary level of implementation in physical systems. Noe argues that without hands and eyes, algorithms could not work.[63] In a similar way, Ada's experience of space is also not exclusively determined by algorithmic calculations but is derived from physical knowledge, which in turn appears to define the capacity of algorithms to learn, but also the capacity of cognition to be something broader than the process of sensing. Nevertheless, it may be misleading to assume that Noe simply claims that sensorimotor knowledge cannot substitute for conceptual knowledge. Instead, he argues that sensorimotor knowledge has to be understood as an example of "primitive conceptual skills": for by suggesting that sensorimotor knowledge ultimately consists of subpersonal skills, he rejects any sharp distinction between the nonconceptual and the conceptual.[64]

In opposition to models of cognition defined by internal representations of the world in the brain, Noe's theory of enactive perception explicitly embraces the phenomenological theory of experience, grounded on the fact that perceptual experience is able to acquire world-presenting content.[65] According to Noe, if sensorimotor perception can explain the cognition of space it is mainly because perception has to be understood as a *protoconceptual* skill.[66] Like concepts, he observes, sensorimotor skills offer world-presenting content to experience. Sensorimotor skills therefore are understood as protoconcepts, which can be seen for example in the nonlinguistic communicative capacities of animals and infants.[67] According to this view, the nonlinguistic gesture of an infant already contains conceptual qualities, despite the degree to which it lacks cognitive levels of reflection. For Noe it is not the reflexive order of perception that determines the phenomenological experience and knowledge of the world, but rather the disarticulated movement of an infant body. A protoconcept is therefore an original thought that establishes all conditions for cognition.

By claiming that thought is always an embodied gesture, Noe's protoconceptual hypothesis attempts to defy the assumption that thought is an idea without a body. In doing so, however, it establishes equivalence between thinking and doing, according to which thought is primarily to be explained in terms of practical skills. The experience and knowledge of space, on this view, are primarily derived from sensorimotor interactions that are afforded by basic conceptual skills, and which are situation-dependent and context-bound.[68] Noe's protoconceptualism therefore appears to claim that these basic skills are the conditions that allow a perceptual experience,[69] and thus deploy the capacities of thinking *about* the world.[70] Nevertheless, since the content (or "aboutness") of the world is, according to Noe, never predefined but instead includes margins of indetermination, he also observes that everything experienced is in its nature vague.[71] From this standpoint, experience seems to add nothing new to preexistent perceptual concepts that are rooted in a sensorimotor system of knowledge. For instance, Noe explains that the perceptual experience of color is not too dissimilar from the grasping of mathematical principles. According to this perspective, all colors and shapes are to be understood as perceptual concepts in the same way as all natural numbers are gathered in perceptual concepts. Perceptual concepts, according to Noe, are constituted by our experience of the shapes, colors, and textures of daily life. Similarly, number, or any other formal concept, is a perceptual concept first. In other words, Noe's protoconceptualism works to formalize the existence of perceptual concepts as always already incorporated in the physical experience of a body.[72] Within this framework, one could suggest that the perceptual experience of color in *Ada—The Intelligent Space* would always remain dependent on the physical understanding of its structural spaces in which perspectives and colors were located.

Noe's enactive theory of perception therefore does not seem to simply reject but rather includes cognition in its protoconceptual system of experience, albeit while making it dependent on sensorimotor rules. Seen from Noe's standpoint, Ada's algorithmic computation of color could only derive from an implicit knowledge—a physical awareness—that the appearances of color change when color-critical conditions change. Similarly for Noe, sensorimotor skills allow us to represent perceptual qualities as concepts in experience. Since these skills are always conceptual or protoconceptual, we have the impression that we recognize or have already experienced something that we are seeing for the first time.[73] In reality, however, Noe's protoconceptualism suggests that there is no novel experience, because what is lived now has already been physically conceptualized and thus belongs to the sensorimotor architecture of the body. This means that the body already knows what can be thought. Because concepts are practical skills,[74] thought and action are equally afforded by the world through the sensorimotor perception of the relation between how things are and how they change.

Noe's protoconceptualism defines the architecture of thought as anchored to the observer's sensorimotor knowledge of objects, or to a fundamental center of gravity that rotates around the perceiver. Nevertheless, and despite all efforts to challenge computational models of cognition, one is still left wondering whether Noe's equation between thought and action merely works as a reversed version of computation, the question of what thought might be remaining always already grounded in the moving body of the observer. The experience of a cube, for instance, can only be based on the sensorimotor understanding of its shape.[75] It is body knowledge that counts as cognition and not the neural structure of the brain.[76] For Noe, cognition is a phenomenon that occurs only against the background of the active life of the animal.[77] Cognition does indeed depend causally on the brain, but it can only be realized in an embodied activity.[78] Noe emphasizes that the evolutionary development of the brain means that the conscious mind must have emerged gradually. A bacterium is already equipped with the minimal ingredients of sensorimotor knowledge-enacting experience. As the first example of a unitary (autopoietic) organism, a bacterium responds and acts, though its sensorimotor knowledge is limited. Yet Noe believes that a bacterium, as opposed to a robot (i.e., a mechanical body), already deploys a protoconsciousness associated with the development of the living.[79] The acquisition of higher levels of cognition is thus explained here, as in Maturana and Varela, as the acquisition of the *unity of the living*, which involves not merely the human brain but all protoconceptual skills possessed by living entities. In agreement with enactivism, Noe's protoconceptual theory places knowledge within the living, cognition within self-production, and thought within the emergent complexification of cells driven by the sensorimotor experience of the environment.

Nevertheless, if protoconceptual cognition can be found at the lowest levels of life, does it follow from this that thought is primarily dependent on an interactive living-perceiving body, and that the sensorimotor skills of the latter are what is perceived, to form knowledge? If so, doesn't enactive perception risk conflating thought with the biophysical evolution of conceptual skills?

In other words, with enactive perception the architecture of thought is integrated within the progressive continuity of the living, not from the standpoint of the brain, but rather through the primary sensorimotor evolution of cellular organisms. Noe's attempt at disengaging knowledge and cognition from algorithmic computation ends up offering a physicalist metaphysics of thought, whereby concepts and knowledge depend on the physical affordances of a body (from a microbial to an animal body). If, as Noe admits, the content of perception remains always indeterminate because it coincides with what the environment potentially allows a body to do, then similarly one can contend that the structure of experience cannot be prescribed by primitive knowledge, inherited and evolved sensorimotor skills, but must include conceptual prehensions or lived experience of nonphysical ideas.

For this purpose, it may be interesting to contrast Noe's protoconceptualism with Whitehead's claims that there are multiple expressions in an unlimited number of actual entities, which always include conceptual as well as physical prehensions, even at the smallest scale. In particular, for Whitehead there is not simply the unity of a perceiving body, but compositions and organizations of entities characterized by expressions and feelings or prehensions. "Feeling . . . or prehension is the reception of expressions. . . . Expressions are the data for feeling diffused in the environment."[80] In other words, each body is constituted by many occasions of experience, and the way data is felt and expressed varies throughout the inorganic, vegetable, animal, and human kingdoms. Nevertheless, as Whitehead observes, "in every grade of social aggregation, from nonliving material society up to a human body, there is the necessity for expression."[81] This necessity does not, however, lead Whitehead to equate conceptual to physical prehensions, because expressions require the reception of both modes of retrieving data. For Whitehead, conceptual prehensions modify and adapt emotional and sensorimotor knowledge. Thought therefore is not the same as physical knowledge: it concurs with these physical activities, and becomes a source of excitement precisely because it "disturbs the whole surface of our being."[82]

If, according to Noe, sensorimotor skills are already conceptual, formally determined by the evolutionary development of physical movement, then experience adds nothing new to the world. From his standpoint, all experience is nothing but a recognition of what is already biologically known. As with *Ada—The Intelligent Space*, the physical experience of interaction teaches nothing new to the computational machine, as it is predisposed to learn what is already known by its sensorimotor data. Similarly, Ada's experience of the space of colors will mainly consist in re-cognizing what is physically already known to the (human) body. By idealizing the empirical intelligence of the body, Noe's protoconceptualism is forced to deny that any new idea could ever exist, and that anything new can ever be thought or experienced. Experience seems instead to be mainly a way of cognizing *again* what biological thought had already established throughout evolution. Contrary to Whitehead's claim that conceptual prehensions modify and adapt what is physically given because they are defined by the capacity to entertain possibilities, alternatives, and unknown ideas, Noe's conception of thought remains subsumed under an ideal bio-logic of sensorimotor knowledge. This physical idealism reduces the idea and experience of space to bare physical interactions deprived of any architecture of abstraction. Theories of enactivism cannot therefore contribute to articulating the actuality of soft thought precisely because they avoid the question of abstraction by grounding thought not in the brain, but rather in the physical apparatus that sustains the evolution of conceptual prototypes. These prototypes are ceaselessly reiterated with every experience, not as new ideas but rather as conceptual habits, the repetition of a biological ground.

However, and as will be discussed in the next section, computational theories of cognition are able to challenge the assumption that the conditions of cognitive experience can be found in the biophysical structure of the body. For example, by revisiting computational theories of cognition, the theory of extended cognition seems to engage more closely with the architecture of soft thought. Theories of extended cognition can contribute to defining soft thought in a manner that departs from the ontological equation between being and thought, according to which thought is always already an expression of being, which is viewed as a self-constituting whole that absorbs all parts.[83] After discussing the implications of extended cognition for an articulation of soft thought, I will draw on R&Sie(n)'s architectural project *I've Heard About . . .* in order to argue that soft thought is not determined by being, but is instead a contingent thought, immanently experienced as an alien thought without being cognized (or explained by the neuroarchitecture of the brain).

3.4 Technoembodied mind

If Noe's hypothesis of sensorimotor cognition sustains a bioontology of thought, Andy Clark's proposition of extended cognition insists that the conditions for cognitive experience are not biological.[84] Clark revisits classical theories of computation, which explain cognition in terms of information-bearing inner states, and argues that internal states are instead dependent on mediated forms of adaptation or technoenvironmental factors.

Through a form of "minimal Cartesianism," Clark attempts to locate the roots of pure contemplative reason in the interactive modalities of embodied cognition. Reason therefore becomes a mental tool that continuously adapts to real-time agent-environment interactions.[85] This mental tool only allows for inner mental representations that are intimately entangled with the biomechanics and activities of the agent. From the perspective of minimal Cartesianism, therefore, action-oriented representations define inner models as partial and multiple. Human cognition, on this view, results from a productive interface between action-oriented representations and a larger web of linguistic competences, cultural contexts and practices. This larger web of competences, which Clark calls "scaffolding," is able to alter the computational spaces of cognition and the basic biological activity of the brain. In particular, Clark argues that the use of objects, such as pen and paper, enabled an alteration of computational spaces, mathematical horizons, and social organizations.[86] Inner cognitive states are inevitably entangled with an extended computational process, blurring the boundaries between brain, body, and world.

Instead of rejecting Alan Turing's computational model of inner processes (in which syntactic properties preserve semantic structures), Clark incorporates it within a larger architecture of cognition. He extends rational behavior to external structures, such as agents and aspects of the local environment.[87] Internal representations are therefore not static models, but are instead dynamic and in constant transformation. In particular, Clark suggests that the brain-mind is fundamentally a *controller of embodied action* designed to assist the organism's survival in its particular niche. Consciousness is thus the emergent property of a self-organizing, distributed system constituted by the brain, body, environment, and inanimate objects.[88] This complex architecture of computation is the result of the extended relations between nature and culture.[89]

Although Clark proposes that cognition does not happen in the brain or the computer, he does not share with the enactivists the view that cognition is only afforded by (and inherent to) the biophysical environment. Instead, extended cognition rearticulates the significance of distributed connectionist models, defining computational activity across a whole array of simple processing units.[90] For the connectionist model, the mind corresponds to a neural network composed of layers of many simple neuron-like units linked together by numerical connections, which strengthen according to learning rules and the system's activities. Instead of manipulating symbols, the neural network converts numerical inputs into representations, which are then converted into numerical output representations. Through learning, the network is able to perform particular cognitive functions, such as speech sounds and written text, as demonstrated for instance by the NETtalk connectionist system.[91] The environment of synaptic links is taken here to be the condition that allows cognitive properties to emerge in the form of a nonsymbolic but spatial representation, which occurs in insects as well as in animals insofar as their modes of cognition imply spatial configurations. Thus connectionism is not concerned with the representation of direct sensorimotor stimuli or with central commands from the brain, but above all with the spatial configuration of cognitive activities that emerge from local neural interactions, which are connected to the external world by means of adaptive response.[92]

Most recently, the neural space of cognition has been related to the temporal dynamics of the vehicles of inner representations, such as single recurrent neural networks.[93] This means that information can be encoded not just in instantaneous patterns of activity, but also in temporally extended processing trajectories. The connectionist model of neural networks, then, according to Clark, has moved away from a simple, atomistic model of inner symbols and now includes spatial and temporal distributed patterns. This shift toward the spatiotemporal configuration of neural networks has also meant that cognition has to be explained as an embodied dynamics. In place of the universal idea of the mind, this substitutes the particular cognitive states that emerge from distributed interactions in a decentralized neural network. In other words, this shift has marked the advance of phenomenologically oriented computation, which still insists, in contrast to Gibson and Noe's environmentally induced cognition, on the interior activity of the mind, now situated in a technoembodied environment of an extended brain.

According to Clark's minimal Cartesianism, however, this interior space of the mind neither corresponds to a computer simulation (i.e., algorithms mimicking mental activities) nor is simply the result of the physical evolution of cognition. The interior space is instead witness to the plasticity of interiority, which is ready to respond to and drive new actions in the environment. Yet like Gibson and Noe, Clark also believes that algorithmic calculation cannot explain cognition. Cognition, in his view, can only depend on the dynamics of perception, which is governed by actions in an environment. Whereas for theories of enactivism the space of cognition is constructed by the sensorimotor perception of the environment, Clark's technoembodied cognition involves a neuroperceptual apparatus which folds the environment back into the neural network of cognition without attributing it to the external world. Clark maintains that the neural-internal representation of worldly events is not a passive data structure, but is instead to be understood as a recipe for thought, whereby cognition comes to drive action. For Clark, the goal of perception and reason is to guide action: to make decisions according to the potentialities that the environment offers to neurosynaptic internal connections. This is why he believes that the world is always internally represented as being very closely related to the kinds of action performed in the environment. In a way that does not seem too dissimilar, after all, from Varela and Thompson's enactivism (nor especially from their insistence on interiorization or reflexivity), Clark seems to suggest that as much as knowledge is action, so too must thought correspond to the construction of knowledge.

Nevertheless, it is important to specify that Clark's technoembodied architecture of thought rejects autopoietic enactivism and its naturalization of cognition (its biological ground), and instead embraces Paul Churchland's "connectionist crab" hypothesis, which develops a new articulation of the cognition-action relation.[94] Clark directly draws on this hypothesis, describing point-to-point geometrical linkages which define perception as action, and on the experiments carried out by roboticist Maja Matarić at the MIT Artificial Intelligence Laboratory who developed a neurologically oriented model of how rats navigate their environment. Since this model constructs a layered architecture in which a robot learns about its environment, Clark uses it to sustain his point that cognition is not simply a representation of interaction, but rather involves rules for action. The robot is initially left to move in the environment to detect landmarks. While it records landmarks, it also learns about the space from a combination of sensory input and motion. By navigating the environment, the robot develops an inner map of the surroundings: not simply a general representation of space, but a recipe for subsequent motor actions. The map is, as it were, continuously generated on the spot.[95] Internal representations of space are therefore only the result of motor actions afforded by the environment. Similarly to Ruth Millikan, a philosopher of biology, Clark argues for action-oriented inner representation.[96] Here the brain is not the primary engine of reason, but rather an environmentally situated organ of control activated by motor action. It is the latter, then, that defines the spatiotemporality of neural architectures as a dynamic interiority that ceaselessly adapts to environmental challenges. In short, far from replacing the neurosynaptic interiority of cognition with external connections or sensorimotor knowledge, Clark suggests that inner representations are dynamically attuned to external actions.

If perceptual action drives the inner states of cognition, which then become recipes for the next action, media objects (from notebooks to calculators), according to Clark, similarly not only serve to manipulate, store, or modify information, but are also crucial devices for the reconfiguration of internal neural connections. For instance, interactive media environments extend cognition in terms of prosthesis, but also become active scaffoldings affording new neural connections triggered by sensorimotor responses. From this standpoint, entering or exiting a room incites the neural space to become adapted to the biorhythms of a body governing actions such as switching on lights, turning up the radio, and increasing the temperature in the radiator. Within this framework, one can also argue that it is now evident that the ubiquitous networks of smart media have turned the space of cognition into an action space, in which smart interactivity is not only changing but also *anticipating* neural connections precisely through the implementation of technological scaffoldings that are able to trigger new neural connections. Yet, as Clark points out, it is not the mediatic environment that has transformed thought into action, because the very activity of bodily spatiotemporal orientation has itself triggered the development and evolution of inner states of cognition. What external media objects add to this evolution, he claims, is the provision of inner mental states with additional memory and with new capacities for symbol manipulation. This is why, Clark believes, the mediatic transformation of space and the computation of the environment is leading to changes in the evolutionary development of inner states of cognition. In particular, the increasing power of digital media to change the experience of spatiotemporal orientation—what Thrift defined as "qualculation," the numerical background of computational culture—has augmented the cognitive capacity for memory, but also for communication, interaction, and cognition. If computation has become embodied in the digital-mediatic environment, then from the standpoint of extended cognition it is ultimately the brain and its neurosynaptic architecture that have changed by becoming extended to the world. Here, the architecture of thought is constituted by a double and mutually inclusive action. On the one hand, digital-mediatic environments have triggered changes in the internal structure of cognition. On the other, this internal neurosynaptic architecture has become extended to the media environment, which supports the internal organization of a structure of cognition that remains fundamentally unchanged. The internal organization of the brain is, as it were, spatially extended onto the world, and thereby acquires new computational powers. The view of a global brain strongly dominates the postcybernetic investment in the power of neurocognition.

According to Clark's view, the intensification of this power derives from the stealthy parasitism of neurosynaptic connections that are able to run on any technobody and ultimately determine thought in terms of doings: guiding actions instead of being their internal reflections. In other words, the technoextension of cognition has stripped away thought from computational theories of symbolic representation and has turned cognition into an environment of action, modifying, enlarging, and magnifying the interior power of neurosynaptic connections of the brain and its capacities for symbolic representation.

Clark insists that external media are extraneural architecture of mind feeding back onto the internal representation of neurosynaptic space. Hence, what looks like a complementary relation between internal and external architectures of mind ultimately comes to define cognition as a mutual process between interior and exterior modes of cognition.[97] It is then clear that the external world is not to be considered a mere prosthesis that allows the brain to optimize its problem-solving capacities. Instead, Clark argues for the existence of a cognitive "agent-in-the-world" that incorporates the brain, the body, and the local environment.[98] In particular, Clark adopts Dawkins's notion of the extended phenotype (discussed in chapter 1)[99] to explain the dynamic relation between internal states and external activities of computation. Just as the spider and the web constitute a single system of cognition, so too does the mind with its *wideware*.[100] However, where Dawkins's extended phenotype highlights the environment's selective force, optimizing the problem-solving capacities of interior states, Clark's dynamic computation refuses the idea that data (neural coding) are already formed and mainly selected by the environment.[101] On the contrary, he believes that technical machines and media are intrinsically related, and that they constitute a whole architecture of cognition. Clark observes that technologies are mindware upgrades that directly contribute to cognitive upheavals, altering the architecture of the human mind.[102] In this sense, the mind is not preconstituted and is not simply to be optimized on top of what it has already achieved through evolution. In other words, the mind does not correspond to the brain. Yet, paradoxically, Clark insists that the technoextension of cognition increases the power of neurosynaptic connections to incorporate the cognitive functions of external objects.

In distinction to biophysicalist theories of mind (or anticomputationalist theories of enactivism), Clark claims that the mind cannot be bound within a biological skin. Instead, the mind is to be found in the spatiotemporal extensions of external devices, from texts to PCs, software agents, and user-adaptive home and office devices.[103] The biological brain is not the locus of the mind, but only a structure equipped with capacities to recognize patterns through perception and control of physical actions. For the mind to become the world, it has to extend beyond the biophysical stratum to incorporate the world of inanimate objects and the skills of abstraction. Clark uses the figure of the cyborg to argue that cognition resides in the open-ended merging of information-processing systems.[104] This merging requires not simply a physical injection of silicon into meat, but the incorporation of writing and drawing into thinking, of external props and tolls into problem-solving systems, characterizing human intelligence. What lie outside the brain—including the rest of the body as well as machines—are the proper parts of the computational architecture that constitutes our minds.[105] This architecture extends beyond the internal biophysical states of the brain to include new computational qualities afforded by the mediatic environment. To clarify his view, Clark compares a mobile phone, which is an interactive media technology distinguished by its wireless qualities of communication, with computational devices such as pens and diagrams.[106] The ubiquitous nature of mobile media, he argues, coincides with the emergence of qualitatively new cognitive capacities, afforded by the background of immediate wireless connection between distinct platforms of communication. According to Clark, these cognitive capacities do not simply include the possibility of annexing one mediatic form of communication to another (as in the optimization of synesthetic reasoning, for instance), but offer an extension of computation beyond media performance that directly addresses data-rich processing.

Clark's conception of extended computation distributed across brain, body, and world can help us to argue that soft thought is not determined by external inputs and/or by the protoconceptual abilities of a living body. Instead, from the standpoint of extended computation soft thought can be seen as an algorithmic process able to reconfigure its internal syntax according to complex interactivities between distinct systems of information. What is important here is that thought is also extended to machines, nonliving hardware, and wideware. However, because Clark's extended functionalism derives thought from the brain's motor-action capacities of developing neural maps, described in the "connectionist crab" hypothesis, it also seems that this theory problematically poses a symmetric correspondence between thought and action.

Similarly, one may still wonder how his phenomenologically oriented model of thought can avoid reifying soft thought in terms of the inherited characteristics of human intelligence.[107] For Clark, the mediatic environment is part of cognition and is now one with the process of decision making. This deep entanglement of neurosynaptic cognition with cultural and environmental structures[108] has meant that our brain is now artificially enhanced to solve ever more complex problems. For Clark, the mediatic environment is there to process cognitive functions (once performed by the brain) that leave new (synaptic) space for human intelligence to solve new problems. Yet if this is the case, one cannot help wondering how this biocomputational architecture of thought could ever challenge the biological ground of cognition, i.e., the skin-bounded brain. If one were to break away from the circular argument that holds that the learning curve of the biological brain is always already afforded by technoenvironmental activities, which are, in turn, always already at the service of the neuroarchitecture of cognition, one could discover that soft thought is not an extension of cognition. On the contrary, soft thought consists of automated decisions that do not necessarily serve the internal biospace of neurocognition, as this latter may not be equipped to truly cognize or even perceive algorithmic actualities.

Although Clark tries to revisit computational theories of cognition in order to maintain that neurocognitive functions are not ontologically granted by a biological ground but can in fact be run on any entity, whether organic or not, his view rejects soft thought as an autonomous mode of computation. In particular, he reduces the computational approach to cognition to calculations, which he views as tools for decision making and problem solving. Yet in contrast to this position, and as I have discussed in this book, postcybernetic computation has become an increasingly speculative affair that exposes the power of computation to establish new connections between wholes (operating systems, databases), as parts that connect to others. Rather than solving given problems, this speculative form of computation, which I have defined as soft thought, seems to be able to generate problems without making decisions and to take decisions about unrealized problems. Soft thought does not therefore work to transform physical data into algorithmic procedures, nor does it represent the syntactic architecture of algorithms processing data, which can run neutrally on any body or machine. Instead, I argue that soft thought is to be understood in terms of conceptual prehensions carried out by algorithms, which are actual entities defined by both a physical and a mental pole.

If extended cognition suggests that the activities of thought are distributed across the subsystems of the brain, body, environment, and technical machines, then why does Clark still insist on a phenomenologically oriented computation that always already poses the equivalence between thought and being by conflating computation with the neurosynaptic architecture of the brain, and the latter with the thinking process of a computational machine? Clark claims to challenge the centrality of a biologically bound brain in order to extend the mind to an extended neuroarchitecture of cognition. In order to do so, however, his theory needs to rely on the assumption that the extension of the neuroarchitecture of the brain to the mediatic environment implies that thought is the result of emergent properties, the interaction of many agents—biological and nonbiological—since all these properties share a neurostructure of cognition. Is this theory of *emergent* thought, however, sufficient to challenge the biocentrism of cognition? Doesn't *emergentism* deprive computational objects of their interior architecture of abstraction, their thought processes, which are replaced by the extended neurosynaptic architecture of the brain?[109]

Clark's minimal Cartesianism maintains that cognition *emerges* from dynamics of adaptation and coevolution, which allow the plastic array of gray matter to reconfigure its links and structures through sensorimotor perception. Despite it all, the ontological premise of the extended mind does not ultimately challenge, but in fact seems to necessarily require, the biological ground of the brain to support other modes of thought. Even when Clark follows Dennett's claims that cognition is an ensemble of tools and specifies that "it is just tools all the way down,"[110] extended cognition sides with the neurological view of thought as deriving from shifting coalitions between the brain and external objects.[111] Here thought is always already part of the neurocomputational system of emerging complexities, in which the brain uses tools to optimize its neurobiological syntax. Nevertheless, Clark's theory of extended cognition still gives rise to some questions: are all forms of thought always already wired back to the interior neurocomputational schema of the brain? Is thought always already the equivalent of neurological being? Instead I suggest that the computational architecture of thought can be deployed to point to the disarticulation of the relation between thought and being, thus challenging the neural or biological body's status as the house of soft thought. This is also to say that thought is not necessarily neurobiologically wired, but only by *chance*, by contingency. The fact that thought is linked to the brain may be contingent on an accident in the evolution of multicellular organisms that led to the formation of nerve cells. As a contingency, the brain-thought link cannot by rights exclude the possibility of a form of thought that is not mediated by a neural network or even less by a brain. In the next section I will discuss nonneural architectures of cognition in order to challenge the idea of a necessarily mutual correspondence between brain and thought, which still characterizes recent theories of neurocomputation. This discussion will perhaps contribute to questioning the assumption of mutualism, as it will introduce the notion of nonneural modes of thought, which divorce thought from the brain. This split, however, is not intended to liberate thought from matter, but rather to suggest that there are material modes of thought that cannot be subsumed under the totality of neuroarchitecture.

3.5 Mindware and wetware

An example of a mode of thought that is not grounded in neural cells and the neuroarchitecture of the brain can be found in the computational architecture of an amoeba. These single cells are small and simple. They lack a brain with a cortex and have no nerve cells. They do not have feelings or humanlike consciousness. Nonetheless, their biochemical network points to a form of computation that reveals cellular purpose and sentience, and explains decision making in terms of movements that define how the amoeba grows and divides. As Dennis Bray suggests, the reiterated process or the biochemical patterns of molecular proteins can be regarded as a form of computation that involves societies of cells (including diffusive hormones, electrical signals, and mechanical interactions) which therefore constitute computational networks of linked cells.[112] He uses the term "wetware" to include most chemical reactions inside single cells, which he considers to be forms of computation.[113] Interestingly, Bray distinguishes the computational processes performed by cells from any human-made machine or electronic device, as they typically involve the least possible use of energy together with a massively parallel processing. A single computational step in fact involves "a simultaneous change in many individual molecules."[114] For instance, a bacterium, according to Bray, also records past events in order to predict the future. In other words, it has a sense of time passing or moving in a certain sequence, which becomes the basis on which it makes decisions as to whether it should continue swimming in one direction or another, given environmental changes. To put it simply, the computational capacities of a bacterium are revealed in its ability to predict change and thereby make decisions. Bray, however, explains that the predictive capacities of bacteria depend on how environmental parameters are incorporated within a bacterium's internal circuits. As we've seen, cognitivism argues that predictive behavior stems from specific cognitive capacities that require the networks of neurons to become organized within the architecture of the nervous system; Bray however argues that the network of protein interactions is instead already an instance of a proper form of cognition.[115] Since predictive behavior implies that the past is stored as data for the future, Bray suggests that bacteria and single-cell organisms have long-term memory.[116] This does not mean that all bacteria or amoebas are characterized by the same computational or cognitive capacities. On the contrary, as chemical reactions are programmed into the algorithms or genetic instructions of the DNA, these reactions remain highly unpredictable, thus implying that these unicellular organisms are capable of infinite possibilities of decision making under certain conditions. Through the study of nonneural forms of cognition, Bray therefore suggests that the computational process of decision making as a form of executive decision has to be located not in the brain but in its cellular equivalent, the centrosome: a microtubule that constitutes the organizing center and regulator of cell cycle progression.

Consequently, and despite arguing that biological computation as a form of cognition is autonomous from the neural networks of the brain, Bray still locates decision making within the molecular processes that occur in the space of the nuclear membrane. His argument therefore offers us another form of internal cognition, which governs molecular data by executing them in the same way as the central dictates of DNA are said to execute proteinic data. What is evident here is that wetware cannot be reduced to mindware, to use Clark's term. On the contrary, the amoeba's lack of a nervous system and its capacity for computational decision making can be taken as evidence that there are modes of thought that are not always already reducible to the problem-solving capacities attributed to the neural structure of the brain. Shaviro recently suggested that amoebas, no less than bacteria, plants, and slime molds, process information about the environment and make decisions based on the data that they gather and process. Shaviro points out that these "brainless" organisms are able to make "spontaneous" or "free" decision to the extent that they actively respond to the external environment, and are therefore able to internally evaluate data by comparing final results with initial conditions; these brainless organisms thus deploy a mode of thought that involves pre- or acognitive mental stances, comparable to moods, attitudes, and expectations.[117]

Far from these non-brain-oriented theories of thought, Clark's notion of mindware is instead designed to include "our thoughts, feelings, hopes, fears, beliefs, and intellect." He also adds that mindware "is cast as nothing but the operation of the biological brain, the meat machine in our head."[118] He even goes so far as to state that "mindware . . . is found 'in' the brain in just the way that software is found 'in' the computing system that is running it."[119] In contrast to this, Bray observes that it is not the brain but rather the internal chemistry of living cells that constitutes a form of computation, and which allows organisms to embody in their internal structure an image (and memory) of the external world. This embodiment of the external world, according to Bray, explains how cells intelligently respond to that world. From this standpoint, wetware is not the same as mindware, which is equivalent to software running on computing systems. In short, Bray's wetware admits the reality of an irreducible form of computation that is housed neither in the brain nor in the computer. This is a form of computation that has a molecular space and operates at a molecular level. It is an architecture of thought that operates in the subsystems of the neural organization of cells. On the other hand, however, it is true to say that both the notion of wetware and Clark's mindware-software equivalence share the idea that cognition is the central organizer of data. Thought is equivalent here to an executor—that which makes decisions about the data retrieved—and as such it still coincides with the view that to think is to manage actions or performances of data within the world. Thought is thus still defined here by the mutual correspondence between thought and being, whereby there cannot be thought without a subject that translates thought into action (regardless of whether this pertains to the brain per se or to the brainless cognition of amoebas).

What is missing from this debate is a notion of computation that is not directly related to being, but is instead at odds with it. This means that if one were to address digital algorithms (from genetic algorithms to neural nets and multiagent systems) in terms of soft thought, one would first of all have to reject the idea of mindware. I argue that algorithms not only prehend physical data or perform instructions, but are conceptual prehensions of eternal objects, of incomputable algorithms whose infinity cannot be synthesized in a program that is smaller than those algorithms themselves. From this standpoint it is true to say that digital algorithms execute data or run programs; yet it constitutes an important challenge to current assumptions to reveal that algorithms are conceptual prehensions of thoughts that cannot be computed, executed, and cognized. Digital algorithms do not simply compute these incomputable algorithms (as is suggested by Chaitin's discovery of Omega, for instance, which as a discrete infinity appears among the innumerable number of incomputables), but also negatively prehend the infinity of infinities that define their capacities of prediction independently of the sequential execution of codes. These negative prehensions explain that computation is not simply a form of cognition that constructs cognitive maps as recipes for action. On the contrary, the negative prehension of infinite incomputable algorithms leads us to conclude from the understanding of random, patternless, or contingent data that mindware and wetware are irreducible to one overarching system of thought *qua* cognition. Instead, this negative prehension reveals that there are infinite modes of thought, involving a multiplicity of predictive capacities that correspond to nonunified (chemical, physical, biological, digital) patterns of decision making. In order to address the existence of these heterogeneous modes of thought, which are not always already referrable to an eternally unchangeable being, it is important to conceive of algorithmic procedures as actualities that are defined by both physical and conceptual prehensions. This means that the sequential order of programming is only an aspect of computation. Yet we must bear in mind that any algorithmic execution is conditioned by the conceptual prehension of incomputables.

However, if algorithms are to be conceived as actual entities, this is also because digital computation is characterized by digital objects, or by a specific objectification of algorithmic procedures. This "objectness" of algorithms is addressed in computational architecture, insofar as algorithms are the stuff or the material that are used to build structures, forms, shapes, and spaces. These actual entities also point to another mode of thought, involving a new mode of prediction that works not on the basis of data accumulated in the past but also, and significantly, on the speculative power of computation to design spatiotemporalities that are immanently lived despite being continually unrealized. From this standpoint, computational architecture reveals the operations of a new mode of thought, a soft thought, which shares little with the cognitivist and functionalist model of the mind-brain. On the contrary, soft thought is not simply software running on hardware, but is a mode of thought proper to digital computation: a conceptual prehension of incomputable data that makes computation a quantic process, determined by the entropic volume of data. Similarly, it is possible to argue with Whitehead that soft thought is precisely "expression as founded on the finite occasion."[120] As such, it is "the activity of finitude impressing itself in its environment"[121] through the conceptual selection of discrete infinities or infinite quantities of data. This is to say that soft thought is where novel architectures of thought are now deployed. From this standpoint, computational architecture is not simply a new visualization of the perceptual workings of the brain in space, nor even a way to test the computational capacities of wetware. Algorithmic procedures are not equivalent to neurocomputational executions, nor can they be equated to neurofeedbacks, the interior structures of which change according to external perceptions. On the contrary, algorithmic procedures are to be understood as computational expressions whose physical organization of data into sequences is superseded by the evaluation (inclusion or exclusion) of infinite quantities of alternatives, evinced by the algorithmic design of lived yet incomputable thoughts.

From this standpoint, Clark's extended functionalism may not set itself sufficiently apart from the autopoietic model of cognition, according to which sense making is enacted by living organisms. For extended functionalism, the formal level of algorithms always needs a material environment onto which it distributes itself by establishing a relation with the environment. According to Clark, this relation extends or transforms the interior apparatus of neural architecture, thereby producing novelty in the extended brain. However, extended functionalism seems to be unable to rethink the very source code of cognition. This is because extended functionalism explains the relation between mental and physical poles merely in terms of a linear causality, whereby mental states are triggered by and bear upon systemic inputs and outputs. Thus, while extended functionalism challenges the biological framework of cognition, it remains difficult to see how this theory could seriously challenge formal structures of cognition, or explain novel forms of thought.[122]

Extended functionalism criticizes computation as a model for cognition. This is because it shows that information processing cannot account for material contingencies (hence the supposition that computers cannot replace human traffic controllers, as computers are unable to calculate contingent factors falling outside of their programming). Nevertheless, extended functionalism overlooks the possibility of contingent computation, which does not resemble the cognitive syntax of the brain but rather deploys a novel mode of prediction and decision making derived from algorithmic, negative prehensions of incomputable infinities. Similarly, extended functionalism fails to reveal that a novel mode of thought already exists inside the computational machine: for as Turing saw long ago, the limit of computation—or the infinity of sequences of 0s and 1s—is in fact the unavoidable condition that allows algorithmic finite rules to be established. Thus, algorithms are not only actions or functions. In addition—I borrow from Whitehead here—they are conceptual prehensions of eternal objects. In other words, a negative prehension of the infinite quantities of incomputables defines soft thought as a thought event: as the opening of contingencies in computation and the transformation of axiomatics into immanent thought.

Before I explain how and in which instances algorithmic architecture exposes this immanent transformation of axiomatics into contingent algorithms, I need to present a further discussion of the reasons why neuroarchitecture (or neurosynaptic networks) is unable to support arguments for novel forms of thought that are autonomous from the structure of cognition. This discussion is the topic of the next section.

3.6 Synaptic space

Deborah Aschheim's *Neural Architecture (a Smart Building Is a Nervous Building)* is a site-responsive installation that attempts to describe the media-saturated experience of space through the neural interiorities of the brain.[123] For Aschheim, post-9/11 buildings are no longer perceived as passive objects but have become nervous architectures, equipped with mechanisms and functions of surveillance that directly express the interior states of a nervous culture stuck in an epochal climate of fear. *Neural Architecture* was presented in 2004 at the Laguna Art Museum as an intricate cerebral cortex hanging from the ceiling in the form of stalactite constructions, with neurons, made of plastic tubes, establishing a synaptic link with the

Figure 3.6
Deborah Aschheim, *Neural Architecture (a Smart Building Is a Nervous Building)*, Laguna Art Museum, Laguna Beach, 2004. Courtesy of Deborah Aschheim.

gallery's existing motion sensors and security devices. The installation makes it explicit that the world and the brain have merged in the culture of ubiquitous media where the brain's labyrinth has been extended to our everyday inhabited space. By incorporating surveillance devices, such as miniature cameras, highly sensitive sensor devices, and invisible electrical impulses, into the exhibition's space, Aschheim constructed a neural network composed of synaptic connections that were ready to adapt to the environment.

The notion of neural networks has become central to a reconceptualization of cognition, a reconceptualization that views it as a material process characterized by a dynamic architecture that is continuously modified by a learning process. According to neurophilosopher Paul Churchland, neural networks[124] exceed all prototypical models of cognitive predictability because their synaptic machinery ceaselessly adjusts itself through learning.[125] While neurons uneasily change, the internal activation of neurons—including neural patterns and synaptic connections—can change quite quickly in response to the external world.[126] Aschheim's neural building is designed to respond to external stimuli: as visitors approach the dark room and are sensed by neurosynaptic architecture, its connections light up. This building therefore reflects the fact that the environment appears to sculpt the plastic potential of neurosynaptic connections.

Similarly, Churchland's neurobiological theory of cognition argues that the spatiotemporal reconfiguration of neural patterns evinced through changes in synaptic connections demonstrates that the brain works through parallel distributed and not serial processing.[127] Rejecting any abstract idealism about the mind[128] and, in particular, opposing the argument that consciousness is either the result of a complex meme or a unique form of software running on the hardware of human brains, Churchland believes that the phenomena of consciousness (by which he also intends thought) are instead the result of the brain's basic hardware structures, which humans share with the animal kingdom.[129] To be more specific, Chuchland observes that all cognitive phenomena that define consciousness can only be the result of the brain's hardware background, defined by the dynamical properties of biological neural networks, which he conceives to be a "highly recurrent physical architecture."[130] In other words, cognition is not a "unique software feature of human brains,"[131] but brains display an information-processing ladder that moves from populations of sensory neurons through many intermediate states to populations of motor neurons. At the same time however, there are also many axonal back projections from populations higher (or most recently formed) on the ladder to populations that are lower (or older) on it. These back projections are called "descending" or "recurrent" pathways, and are described as being able to add a variety of dynamic possibilities, such as self-modulation, selective attention, and autonomous activities, to all the functional processing.[132]

From this standpoint, Churchland suggests that the information-processing architecture of cognition must not be understood in terms of serial sequences of algorithms, but must include a notion of dynamic temporality. This means that while a "feedforward system is a pipeline of information," recurrent pathways add a temporally extended activity, which explains motor behaviors but also perception. Churchland's dynamic approach to cognition therefore seems to suggest that the plasticity of the brain derives from changes in the configurations of synaptic connections, which correspond to how the brain processes change. In particular, he observes that cognition is the result of the know-how defined by the personal configurations of the brain's synaptic weights.[133] Even if a creature is too small or too primitive to have a well-defined brain (as is the case with ants, sea slugs, or crabs, for example), their cognitive capacities will nevertheless be embodied in the configuration of synaptic weights.[134] This is because all animals share a recurrent physical architecture, which permits any form of neural architecture to engage with the temporality of structures.[135] Temporality therefore is a prerogative of the living brain, of the physical infrastructure of thought operating by means of recurrence.

Yet although Churchland suggests that the specific cognitive architecture of the human brain is an example of evolution's latest and highest achievement in sensorimotor coordination and vector transformation, he also claims that networks with recurrent physical architecture explain cognition as a general-purpose organization of hardware (and not as machines downloading software).[136] In particular, Churchland points out that even the simplest of neural networks, such as NETtalk,[137] perform vector processing (e.g., the transformation of sensory into motor vectors), and instances of the cognition that can be found in animals and humans. However, Churchland explains that NETtalk is mainly an instance of a feedforward neural architecture, which is unable to temporally order what comes before and after.[138] In other words, feedforward networks lack a sense of the immediate past and of how this could be used in shaping the present. As Whitehead would argue, neural networks have no short-time memory spans, which explain the constitution of the present from the transition between the past and the immediate future.[139] Similarly, Churchland observes that neural networks are missing "some form of short-term memory."[140] In particular he also observes that in NETtalk embedding knowledge or skills in the synaptic-weight configuration of neural networks does not correspond to an awareness of specific past events. In other words, the network lacks the "feedbackward" or recurrent pathways that characterize the biological brain.

Nevertheless, Churchland also argues that recurrent networks can be trained "not just to discriminate a timeless or unchanging physical pattern . . . [but also] a standard sequence of physical configurations . . . a wink, a handshake . . . two people dancing."[141] Similarly, recurrent networks can also learn to compute "a smooth sequence of limb positions," thus capturing the shortest gap between a past and future movement.[142] In other words, Churchland observes that by adding a temporal dimension to computation, a recurrent pathway can be seen to generate, through the recurrent modulation of its vectorial activity, long sequences of activation vectors on its own, without requiring external stimuli.[143] From this temporal standpoint Churchland therefore concedes that there is a cognitive continuity between natural and artificial computations.[144] In particular, he argues that artificial networks are models of complexity that deploy the map of neural transformations, which start from the rear half of the brain and end up in the motor outputs articulated in the front of the brain. The transformation of sensory to motor vectors is driven not by the application of an internal rule, but by the embodied multiplication of a vector coding within a larger matrix of synaptic connections able to yield new vectors.[145] Vector coding and vector transformation determine the recurrent pathways constituting a neural network not as a system of innate or a priori knowledge, but as the slow development of inarticulable skills over a period of time, including specific events of the past and the future.[146] According to Churchland, the temporally extended activity of the recurrent network also provides a new understanding of perception as corresponding to the discrimination not of things but of prototypical processes.[147] This means that perceptual recognition in recurrent networks must include a temporal dimension too, since the network itself—and not external stimuli—will define the perceptual activation of an appropriate vectorial sequence.[148] Similarly, the recurrent network capacity of generating prototypical event sequences is said to be able to provide access not only to the immediate past, but also to the future. Since internal representations are processed faster in perceptual activity (as compared to motor ones, for instance), the network also appears to be able to predict its immediate future: its vectorial trajectory.[149]

Like Aschheim's neural architecture, Churchland's neural network equates all mental phenomena to neural phenomena. His "eliminative materialism" maintains that all known mental phenomena, such as perception, comprehension, and interpretation, can be reconstructed in neurodynamic terms.[150] Drawing on Alan Turing's attempt to construct an artificial consciousness, and utilizing empirical data rather than a metaphysical schema, Churchland suggests that cognitive activity and conscious intelligence (as demonstrated by neural networks) can explain computational phenomena as modes of thought preceding human intelligence.[151] By computational phenomena he does not, however, mean phenomena given or produced by digital machines (or computers), which he believes to be limited to computing mathematical functions, the inputs and outputs of which can be expressed as ratios of whole numbers (a number that does not use fractions or decimal points, an integer). Digital machines are based on rational numbers, which constitute only a small and peculiar subset of the continuum of real numbers. For this reason, Churchland suggests that functions over real numbers cannot strictly be computed or even represented within a digital machine. They can only be approximated. Churchland therefore concludes that real, living neural networks can compute the full range of natural numbers and not just rational ones, whereas a digital machine cannot.[152] Churchland thus hypothesizes that only if recurrent neural networks are implemented in digital computing could there be a possibility of deploying the features of electronic consciousness. If time is added to digital algorithms, the latter could acquire the features of computational phenomena, which could count as a manifestation of electronic consciousness. Churchland ultimately believes that any computational machines can, like human brains, have intrinsic meaning, a meaning that is determined by the internal architecture of parallel networks or causal and inferential relations among distinct cognitive states and aspects of the world.[153]

Aschheim's neural architecture does not show the workings of parallel networks, which imply the temporalities of cognitive states, but instead highlights the synaptic firing of connections, which are as internal to the brain as they are to the space of a building. In a sense, Aschheim's *Nervous Building* is an instance of the inability of feedforward neural networks to process the recurrent pathways of the past, as it merely presents a physical mapping of synaptic connections that can be activated there and then by the environment. Similarly to Churchland however, Aschheim's neuroarchitecture installation insists that the physical, hardware, and material consistency of the synaptic space constitutes the cognitive state of the brain-building. Churchland's computational cognitivism in fact shows that nonalgorithmic processes, which are instantiated in any hardware neural network, are what largely constitute the specificity of computation. The superiority of the recurrent neural architecture compared to digital (serial) models is therefore at the core of Churchland's "eliminative materialism" to the extent that recurrent patterns of connection constitute his postulate that physical processes run inside any natural and artificial network. A fundamental physical organization of the nervous system determines physically coded, distributed and transformed information,[154] turning intelligence itself into a vector.[155]

In particular, Churchland proposes a prototype vector activation (PVA) model of cognition, which is based on global synaptic weights or the strengths of the global neural connections that have gradually reconfigured themselves in response to ongoing sensory experience. For Churchland, these prototype concepts can eventually be differently applied according to their capacity to fill in missing information, as they are able to bring background information to the relevant layers of neurons. He points out that far from being eternal forms, these prototype vectors are dynamically and creatively redeployed by sensory experience. In other words, prototype vectors are open to recurrent manipulation and experimental probing driven by the synaptic weight space.[156] Similarly, Aschheim's neural architecture also sets synaptic connections at the center of the experience of space, as these connections ultimately activate a prototype vector, or the nervous scheme of the building.

According to Churchland, the weight space, or the size and strength of the synaptic architecture, activates the space of a large population of neurons which "embody a structured system of categorical prototypes—that is a meaningful conceptual framework."[157] From this standpoint, the brain is said to "interpret its sensory experience" according to its acquired conceptual framework. This means that complex motor skills are embodied and that the unfolding of activation trajectories can generate the relevant motor behaviors in the body's limbs and muscles.[158] Against functionalism, therefore, Churchland dispenses with the necessity of implementing any form of software onto hardware, or, as Clark puts it, of mindware onto meatware. For functionalism, the cognitive process coincides with the algorithmic implementation of the input-output function as divorced from any specific material architecture. Churchland, on the contrary, insists on the peculiar physical organization of the nervous system: he claims that the physical process reflects the way in which information is physically coded in the first place, and also the way in which it undergoes transformation as it becomes physically distributed.[159]

Churchland attacks folk psychology because of its belief in internal propositional attitudes, as based on "inference to the best explanation."[160] He therefore aims to substitute propositional attitudes[161] with his PVA model, insisting that cognition and consciousness emerge from neurocomputational activities rooted in sensorimotor experience and constitute prototypes: conceptual frameworks. As Churchland explains, "a specific configuration of synaptic weights will partition the activation space of a given neural layer into a taxonomy of distinct *prototypes* or *universals*."[162] The spatial configuration of synaptic connections corresponds, according to Churchland, to the spatial configurations of concepts.[163] Unlike Noe's notion of perceptual concepts, discussed earlier, Churchland uses the notion of "conceptual redeployment" to explain how an already developed conceptual framework is not confined to one domain, but can be "activated with profit in a new domain."[164] This is not simply a reactivation of an old idea. On the contrary, the new domain will activate a vector that is closer to the old prototype and thus will activate some of its behavior.

At the same time, the repeated redeployment of existing prototypes can produce significant cognitive changes without much transformation of the synaptic configuration and its activation space partitions.

However, if we follow Churchland's proposal and agree with this mechanism of redeployment of concepts—defined by the recurrent architecture of synaptic connections—can new architectures of thought ever exist outside the neural networks of the brain? Similarly, if the recurrent movement of the network crystallizes around certain paths and builds conceptual structures, which become predictive mechanisms linking the past to present activations and to the activations of future behaviors, how can there ever be conceptual change (beyond mere redeployment)?

For Churchland, these questions can only be answered by admitting that the problem with his theory is precisely a problem concerning theory itself. He insists that one must acknowledge how "antecedently-developed prototype vectors [are] in a subvolume of activation space hitherto devoted to other phenomena entirely."[165] In short, the PVA prototype corresponds to conceptual frameworks that are able to synthesize a wider assortment of data, or to the simplest architecture of ideas able to neurocomputationally calculate any activation phenomena. From this standpoint, a theory must display a unity in the explanation of heterogeneous empirical phenomena through the minimal use of concepts. A theory must be simple, coherent, and unified, just as the neurologically developed conceptual prototypes represent the world according to the virtues of simplicity, cohesiveness, and unified explanation. This is not too dissimilar from the metacomputational view discussed in chapter 2, according to which only a few algorithms or the simplest set of codes correspond to the theoretical solution of all possible combinations and complexity: a simple program which can contain its output.

From this neurocomputational perspective, Aschheim's neuroarchitecture will then reveal that the sensorimotor response to the synaptic configuration of the building implies a specific partitioning of the building-brain activation space, which corresponds to the vectorial activation of prototypes or conceptual frameworks that define the cognitive experience of the space according to previous representations (not propositional but empirical representations). This example serves to show that despite Churchland's claims against functionalism and his strong emphasis on physical recurrent networks, the PVA model that he argues for seems to fall incongruently back into an information model that runs on physical structures, thus suggesting a sort of bottom-up or emergentist functionalism. In particular, if physical recurrent networks, which then become activators of previous representations, configure concepts whose virtues of simplicity, coherence, and explanation synthesize vast arrays of data, how can neurocomputation offer us more than an idealized empirical ontology of thought?

As Ray Brassier lucidly explains, the PVA neurobiological model, which is based on the analogy between neural networks and brain architecture and on that between representational concepts and neurophysical structures, falls back into a problematic metaempiricism in which the PVA works as the guarantor of a universal theory of cognition.[166] According to Brassier, the PVA model is indebted to an a priori adaptationist rationale that fuses representation (vector schema) and reality (weight space of synaptic connections),[167] whereby the conceptual vectorial representation or cognition is no longer deduced from truth (algorithmic rules), but is induced by sensorimotor knowledge. Churchland poses the empirical virtues of simplicity, conceptual coherence, and explanatory power as an ontologically superior ground, a view that is indebted to the contention that cognition is rooted in the adaptationist efficiency of the living organism.[168] Consequently, Churchland's "eliminative materialism" ultimately risks conflating the reality of thought with the evolutionary function of neural adaptation. For Brassier, therefore, Churchland's thesis cannot explain the reality of the physical world outside the organism, because that world remains always already neurocomputationally constituted by the brain-mind (even when Churchland refers to the cognition of the animal kingdom, as opposed for instance to the nonnervous cognition of an amoeba). This incapacity to concede that there may be actual realities and actual thoughts that are not always already wired in neurocomputational architecture is a problem that Churchland shares with Clark's theory of extended cognition. In effect, extended cognition conceives the physical world outside the brain to exist for the sole purpose of functioning as the neurocomputational extension of the mind via the empirical continuity between sensorimotor perception and conception. This continuity culminates in a circular argument, in which the brain can represent the world but cannot accept its actual reality. If the world can only exist in the neurocomputational architecture of the brain, one can conclude that here there is no real space for the world, and nor can there ever be a true transformation of the neuroarchitectural infrastructure of cognition.

Similarly, Brassier observes that Churchland's thesis is predicated on a fundamental identity between the brain and the world, which does not explain how the brain has become part of the world or how it could have perhaps originally produced the world.[169] Ultimately, Churchland's PVA model falls into the trap of metaphysical naturalism, which, Brassier argues, cannot explain away the metaphysical reality of thought as nonbeing, or the disharmony between thought and being. This means that it is not enough, if one wishes to argue for a metaphysical notion of thought, to establish an infinitesimal line of reflection (or a reversible mutualism) between internal representations (produced by the neurosynaptic architecture) and external reality. In order for thought to be metaphysically real, according to Brassier, there must be a "real subpersonal and perfectly objectifiable neurobiological process,"[170] which is not explained away or always already instantiated by the neural networks of the brain. In other words, the metaphysical reality of neurobiological processes cannot be derived from symbolic inscription or by intellectual intuition, idealism, or empiricism, as these are both embedded in brain-centered architectures of thought.

Computational models of cognition have been discarded by some in favor of physical neural networks. As Churchland argues, algorithmic procedures executed by digital computer programs (or by those that employ serial sequences of 0s and 1s) cannot account for knowledge. Chaitin's information theory challenges the assumption that there are shorter (simple, coherent, and fully explanatory) programs that are able to synthesize the infinite aggregation of data. Can Chaitin's ideas point toward a position that might be able to view soft thought as an actual entity, as an entity defined not by neurocomputation or neurophenomenology, but by incomputable algorithms?

Churchland insists that digital machines are based on rational numbers, which constitute only a small and peculiar subset of the continuum of real numbers. These numbers can only be approximated and cannot be computed or represented within a digital machine. On the contrary, for Churchland neural networks can compute the full range of natural numbers, in addition to the rational ones.[171] Chaitin's hypothesis as to the incomputable number Omega offers the possibility that at the basis of computation there is not a shorter program, an algorithmic prototype able to synthesize a vast array of data because of its simplicity and coherence:[172] on the contrary, Chaitin's discovery of incomputable algorithms points at a notion of speculative computation, which refuses to subordinate real thoughts to a second-order understanding of how humans can know whether these (first-order) thoughts are correct or even real. Against the very premises of reflexivity, argued for by the second-order cybernetics of enactive perception or neurophenomenology, and while also contesting the neurocomputational model of PVA, a speculative notion of computation rejects the hypothesis that thought can only ever be an expression of the neurocentric brain.[173] Nevertheless, this is not to call for a return to a form of intuitive direct apprehension of the world driven by sensations. Rather, what is suggested here is that speculative computation offers a way to define thoughts as contingent (or incomplete) realities, which are not total unities governing forms of natural or artificial mind.

Through Chaitin's discovery of the incomputable algorithm Omega, it is possible to suggest that complexity and not simplicity—randomness and not coherence, contingency and not completeness, incomputable quantity and not finite algorithms—lies at the heart of architectures of thought, of which soft thought is but an example (as are the nonneural computation of bacteria and amoebas, for instance). Once cognition is stripped of naturalism and empiricism, and is distanced from its conformation to neurobiological adaptationism and its appeal to sensible experience, it becomes possible to admit that there are incomputable ideas in the most precise of calculations, contingent insanity in the most rational of logics, and random incomprehensions at every level of finite decision.

If Aschheim's installation aims to expose the neurobiological architecture of the building, it does so without offering autonomy to its own thought reality. The installation instead shows the familiar prototype concept of the brain dominating the ubiquitous media architecture of communication by demanding that the sensory experience of the visitor-user or the environment activate the synaptic structure. While promising an endless variation of the sensory experience, which problematically assumes that sensorimotor actions change the neural structure of the building, the installation nonetheless remains anchored to the erroneous and unwarranted assumption that the synaptic connections of the building simply resemble, and are therefore one with, the neural architecture of the brain. If the neural architecture of the building were instead to be experienced qua its own neural architecture, it could give way to the ingression of soft thought into the neurocomputational continuity of sensorimotor activation and conception, thus defying the assumption that thought has its origin in neural structures. And if soft thought does come to invade the neuroarchitecture of the building—and I would argue that it should do so—it will unleash blind spots or black holes (and not simply smooth connections) in the recurrent networks of neural architecture.

3.7 Transitive computation

Postcybernetic architectures of thought remain ontologically grounded in a neurocomputational model of cognition that establishes a one-to-one correlation between mind and world, brain and environment. This empirical idealization of thought underdetermines algorithmic actualities by claiming either that algorithms are merely ideas without bodies, or that they are yet another manifestation of neurophysiological actions. On the other hand, by arguing that thought derives from perceptual forms of enaction, or that it is grounded in conceptual perception, postcybernetic architectures of thought also further the idea that the physical organization of the synaptic space constitutes cognition as the result of the action of the environment on the internal neural structure and on cognitive mapping (or representation of space). Similarly, despite its claims against the symmetry between phenomenal consciousness and the neurobiological processes that are said to produce consciousness, neurocomputation ends up reintroducing conceptual prototypes through the backdoor, turning the physical architecture of thought into a mechanism composed of running instructions. Here thoughts are only another reflection of the evolved mind. Ultimately the actuality of thought remains entrapped in the continuous loop of self-reflexivity on the one hand and recurrent networks on the other.

Even the insistence on an interactive, coevolutionary change—or mutual reversibility—in the mind-world (or thought-space) relationship is unable to guarantee the existence of the world without this simply being an internal reflection of the world on behalf of the neural brain. In other words, the neurophenomenology of coevolution yet again overlooks the existence of subpersonal thought worlds that are not correlated to how human brains think. The neurocomputational model of thought instead gives priority to biodigital cognition, subsuming all actual thoughts to the evolutionary ontology of the living brain, which is set to endlessly neutralize any instance of subpersonal thought (such as bacterial or software modes of computation), or incorporate it into the a priori neural brain structure.

To break away from such seamless continuity between brain and thought, or being and thought, I suggest that we turn to the inconsistent reality of incomputable algorithms as instances of contingency in programming: of infinite unities in computing, which resemble neither phenomenal nor neurobiological cognitive incarnations. To account for the immanent reality of these quasi-algorithms that constitute soft thought, a notion of speculative empiricism is required: one that describes lived thought without having to prove that thought is an expression of the functional neurophysiological evolutions of the brain-mind. To this end, the next two sections will draw upon and expand William James's ontological method of radical empiricism. James's articulation of radical empiricism, which sought to explain how thoughts are connected, went a long way toward arguing that thoughts have their own relational space, one not simply representative of the space of the brain. For James, thought is not in the brain or a reflection of the mind but is its own reality, derived from its own relational space. Radical empiricism may be unable, however, to fully explain soft thought in terms of a speculative notion of computation (defining the actuality of algorithmic objects as being determined by incomputable data). In order to define how speculative computation is immanent to experience, one may have to force an unnatural reduplication of radical empiricism with Whitehead's notion of speculative reason, so that the neurocomputational and neurophenomenological coevolutionary bond between being and thought, and between perception/conception and neural nets, loses its centrality in theorizing architectures of thought. On the other hand, the ideas of both James and Whitehead may need to be stretched again and pushed toward an unfamiliar territory, to ensure that Whitehead's notion of conceptual prehension, which defines the nonsensuous prehension of data, is not reappropriated by naturalism and empiricism *tout court*. By making radical empiricism and speculative computation intersect without fusing them together, and thus by maintaining the asymmetries, contrasts, and tensions between these two methods, it is possible to explain how soft thought implies a transformation of experience, and to show how algorithmic contingencies have become the speculative conditions for all kinds of programming and digital coding.

I will first attempt to explain how both James and Whitehead understand thought in terms of transition between states: a lived transformation that can be felt (and lived) without emotion, cognition, or direct sensorimotor response.[174] If thought can be felt before being emotionally appraised or cognized, then there must be nonsensuous modes of thought, or, as Whitehead hypothesized, "nonsensuous prehensions,"[175] conceptual feelings that travel through the physical chain of causal efficacy but remain irreducible to sensorimotor stimuli. Nonsensuous thought is an actual thought which is unsensed and uncognized; the term will be used to describe the feeling of infinite thoughts as such. As opposed to a seamlessly continuous surface of interaction turning thought and feeling into mutual actions, nonsensuous thought requires no sensorimotor activity.[176] On the contrary, it deploys the lived abstraction of interstices between one actuality and another. These interstices, however, are not just temporal jumps between one point and another, nor are they to be defined exclusively in terms of a "virtual interval": a topological being that unfolds the infinity of time. Instead, from the mereotopological point of view that I discussed in chapter 2, the spatiotemporality of the intersection is itself an actuality that is determined by a novel and unprecedented unity of eternal objects. Like Whitehead, James also points out that the reality of these interstices is to be found in the contingency of transitions or, one could argue, in the quantum interference of actualities amid actualities.

It may be important to clarify that James's psychological theory of mind has been broadly used to account for a neurophysiological origin of thought. For instance, neuroscientist Antonio Damasio has recently argued that James offers us a physiological understanding of cognition, based on the centrality of emotion. Damasio therefore draws on James to supports his theory that thought is the result of bodily feeling.[177] In particular, according to Damasio, emotions involve specific parts of the cortex, such as the frontal lobe. His research findings on frontal-lobe disorders demonstrate disturbances in the channel of communication between the cortex and the limbic system. For instance, damages to the frontal lobe result in the brain missing what Damasio calls "somatic markers" (which he describes in terms of gut feelings or intuitions).[178] These markers determine the association of negative or positive feelings with certain decisions and patterns of thought content, and with previously experienced pleasures and pains. In brief, according to Damasio, the lack of somatic markers (and thus a lack of emotional response) is directly related to cognitive inabilities. Thus physiological responses (or the lack thereof) reveal that emotions are crucial for the cognitive activities of decision making.[179] Damasio's architecture of thought thus claims that there is a fundamental physical continuity between autonomic responses and intelligent cortical management. This continual surface of cognition explains that action at a distance between two distinct layers of processes (physical and mental) is ultimately constituted by the efficient cause of direct physical relations between the body and the mind.

From this standpoint, Damasio believes that James's hypothesis, according to which the perception of the body state is part of feeling, is central to the development of a neurophysiological theory of cognition. According to this theory, the transformations in the representations that occur in the brain during the emotive period in the child's development are crucial for cognition. More specifically, since perception involves the appraisal of the transformations in the representation of emotions, it reveals that there is a direct relation between what is felt and what is appraised. Hence emotions are the somatic markers of transformation in cognition. In sum, according to Damasio, emotions are action programs and they precede feelings, which are instead perceptions of action programs. Emotions reflect the ongoing management of life inside the organism. This means that feelings are constantly giving us a window into how the ecology of emotions is operating.

Damasio's investigation into the nature of emotions, which are said to provide a direct recording of the emotional management of life, inevitably reiterates the metaphysical idealization of the biophysical roots of both feeling and thought. This idealization is embedded in the logic of complexification, whereby simple autonomic responses always already lead to higher levels of cognitive emotional development. In other words, in order to account for the primary roles emotions have in cognition, Damasio emphasizes how the role of primary emotions is maintained in higher levels of emotional cognition in the same way as primitive genetic memory remains encoded in higher organisms. To a certain extent, Damasio encourages the view that the complex, emergent layers of emotional cognition depend on simpler levels of emotional development, on basic patterns of reward and punishment, pain and pleasure defined at a biophysical level of survival. In brief, mental and emotional states, and ultimately the entire architecture of thought, are derived here from the neurophysiological evolution of primitive emotional responses.

What Damasio overlooks, therefore, is that James's radical empiricism is concerned not simply with the physiological measuring of cognition, but with the role that the reality of transition plays in defining experience. For James, the feeling of transition does not simply explain that thoughts are the result of physical structures; more importantly, his theory suggests that what is felt in transition corresponds to anticipation leading to the surfacing of bodily symptoms. The feeling of transition does not merely record physiological responses; importantly, it also anticipates them. However, anticipation does not correspond to a mode of prevention or preparation toward what is going to happen, but instead implies an immanent precipitation defined by the irreversible arrival of certain symptoms triggered by the feeling of actual transition: an actual thought that does not derive from physiological responses. James argues that feelings are not exclusively caused by the perception of what happens to the body; on the contrary, changes in the state of a body can also be triggered simply by the thought of feeling, or the *feeling of feeling*.[180] As James reports, "I am told of a case of morbid terror, of which the subject confessed that what possessed her seemed, more than anything, to be the fear of the fear itself."[181] This is the case when the feeling of feeling or the abstract reality of feeling points to a thought that anticipates and precipitates certain states of the body. The power of abstract or apparently unexisting, unpalpable thoughts is enough to precipitate states of emotion. In other words, it is not the "feeling of what happens," to use Damasio's phrase,[182] but the contagious ingression of actual yet invisible thoughts into the structure of experience. This infectious contact discloses the feeling for what could happen—and thus defines the experience of abstraction—in the present. The reality of abstract thought pushes James to crudely reject the neurophysiological explanation of the birth of ideas. Instead, he proposes that there is a space of transition that corresponds to the real world of thoughts. This space is not only an accessory to experience but constitutes the structure of experience, its radical manifestation challenging any attempt to take thought as a mere mirror of the neural brain. This emphasis on the reality of transition clarifies James's theory of radical empiricism, which explains thought as an immanent experience of indeterminate and patternless reality that bypasses the evolutionary ground of emotion and cognition. James therefore offers us not an emotional but an aesthetic notion of thought, which does not simply define thought according to a continual surface of variation among primary, secondary, and tertiary emotions.

According to this aesthetic notion, thought is a feeling that does not directly correspond to nor is derived from a physical state. Thought is thus not to be conflated with emotion, but is rather to be explained as the feeling of transition: a radical experience of abstraction. One may need to clarify that according to James, while experience coincides with the feeling (or one could say prehension) of transition—a relational space—it is not constituted by the terms of a relation. According to James, a relation can be defined as a universe of withness and not nextness, of nextness but not likeness, and so on. In the first instance, this universe may appear to be chaotic, with no single connection able to unify the experience that encompasses it. For classical empiricism, a bare relation of withness is enough to define the unity of experience, since the exteriority of togetherness explains the totality of facts. Yet according to James's radical empiricism, relations imply that both conjunctions and disjunctions (parts and wholes) are part of experience. Conjunctions involve a feeling of continuity; but this feeling is not more important than the feeling of discontinuities, which describe the separation between one part and another, between one drop of experience and another, and between one thought and another. These spaces of conjunctions and disjunctions constitute the immanent experience of abstraction. Far from mainly being defined from the standpoint of a body that senses, feels, and cognizes, this immanent experience of abstraction, I argue, concerns any actual or lived infinity, and in particular the algorithmic prehension of infinities. In the next section I will discuss this immanent experience of abstraction in terms of soft thought; here I will summarize some of the key points of contention that I have posed to neuroarchitecture in the second part of this chapter.

As this discussion may have made evident, neuroarchitecture holds that the brain is not determined by preset codes but rather by the space of connection, which activates patterns of cognition and perception. This is the physical space of neural networks that work as extensions of the brain's neurosynaptic architecture, and which reveal that codes are performative sets of instructions, the recurrent activities of which produce patterns. From this standpoint, neuroarchitecture offers a new conception of space, according to which it is the dynamicism of the environment, and not simply a string of symbols, that constitutes cognition and perception. Neuroarchitecture thus seems to be part of the recent attempts in computational architecture to rearticulate the aesthetics of space as being derived from the perceptual (sensorimotor) activation of algorithmic connections and codes (or synaptic paths and prototype vector activators). In particular, neuroarchitecture takes sensorimotor perception and the biophysical configurations of the environment (from the synaptic environment to the external environment) to determine space as a whole. Within the context of computational architecture, therefore, the prevailing aesthetic question that neuroarchitecture would pose to digital coding concerns the sensorimotor variations and biophysical architectures of the brain, rather than acknowledging the alien mode of thought and conceptual prehensions that are defined by the algorithmic processing of data. Even when the software programs are very complex (from growing to parallel algorithms and parametric computation), or the technological platforms are very sophisticated (including for instance social networks), neuroarchitecture appears to reduce the aesthetic and experiential value of algorithms to the qualities of perceptual effects and prototypical conceptual frameworks, rather than addressing computational (or algorithmic) capacities of thought.

However, by engaging with the actuality of quantities, instructions, and programming, rather than questioning the degree to which they are constitutive of a computational aesthetics, one could push James's radical empiricist view of experience as transition further, toward a notion of speculative computing. From this standpoint, infinite quantities of data are not simply the limit of computing; instead, they define the space of transition between algorithmic sequences, demarcating an immanent actual space of disjunctions and conjunctions, deploying not probabilities but contingencies, randomness, and infinities. I argue that this space of computational transition is the space of soft thought. Soft thought does not therefore correspond to neuroarchitecture or to the neurophysiological architecture of cognition, but is rather an actual entity (a new mode of thought), challenging the neurocomputational equivalence between brain and thought on the one hand, and between prototypical conceptual frameworks and physical networks on the other.[183] This is the sense in which it may be possible to unlock digital algorithms from preset strings of symbols, but also to challenge the view that they are activated by environmental interactions or sensorimotor responses that conform with a predetermined cognitive structure distributed in matter; a sort of calculative background which is, yet again, the fruit of relentless repetitions of biophysical connections. This also means that digital algorithms are not central to our programming culture because they are continuously and primarily being transduced into qualities (perceptual, affective cognitive states). Instead, I argue that digital algorithms need to be relinked to their computational condition, in which qualities cannot be divorced from data quantities, those infinities that cannot be synthesized into smaller programs. The computational condition of algorithms defines sets of symbols (for instance the ASCII codes to represent characters) as being only one form of the infinite possibilities of algorithmic expression, which are finite modes of thought determined by the computational processing or the physical and conceptual prehensions of actual and eternal data, the actuality of things and thoughts.

By extending Whitehead's notion of conceptual prehension and James's definition of thought as transition away from their philosophical frameworks, the neurocomputational model of conceptual prototypes and physical networks that lies at the core of neuroarchitecture could be seen in a new light. For Whitehead, conceptual prehensions are not locked into the physical structure of the brain, but are capacities of evaluating alternatives (by selecting eternal objects) that break from the sequential chain of things. Similarly, James insists that thought is not localizable in the brain but is a transitional entity that resides in the gap between terms: the blind spot between stimuli and response, physical perception and cognitive patterns, but also between one experience and another.

From this standpoint, one may want to ask what an algorithmic conceptual prehension would be. How does a conceptual prehension or experience of abstraction tap into the computational matrix of digital algorithms? If thought is transition, how can it be argued that there is thought in computation, as this mainly consists of a sequential order of discrete algorithms? One way to approach these questions is to radicalize information (or computational) theories that claim that incomputable infinities and random or incompressible quantities are the unconditional reality by which the serial sequences of algorithms can run and become a code. From this standpoint, what will be (negatively) prehended by a sequential (but also generative, parallel, and parametric) algorithm are precisely the infinite contingencies of data that exist as incomputable realities: veritable abstractions that come to infect and characterize soft thought. These abstractions are not actualities but quantic realities, quasi-empirical ideas that find no equivalence in the primary evolution of emotions, or in any form of software architecture of the brain (neural nets, for instance). The point here is that algorithmic actualities are more than performative procedures (they do not perform an idea or show that an idea is equivalent to an action) and less than affective effects (since they are not only aesthetic qualities).[184] It is then possible to define soft thought as the computational tendencies, possessed by an algorithmic object, to conceptually prehend quantic realities or ideas. Since these quantic ideas are not derived from biophysical patterns but are (drawing on Whitehead) eternal, one could suggest that conceptual patterns (or algorithmic patters in our case) are also determined by what has never been programmed, but is immanently lived as incomprehensible. These eternal objects are, as previously suggested, incomprehensible (i.e., incompressible, nonsynthesizable). In other words, they are not cognitive forms or prototypes. Instead, as they cross into actuality, they reveal the sheer contingency of data: the randomness and infinity that lie at the core of any actual thought.

From this standpoint I take computational architecture to be an instance of soft thought, as it can be seen to be an actual object that prehends the space of transition: the gap between one sequence and another, the ingression of incomputable quantities into the order of sets. Digital algorithms do not therefore simply process physical data. Instead, by computing these data they become infected with incomputables, exposing randomness in programming and contingency in computation. In the next section I will draw on one of R&Sie(n)'s recent projects to discuss soft thought as an aesthetic mode of thought that pertains to computation itself.

3.8 Thought event

R&Sie(n)'s *I've Heard About . . . (a Flat, Fat, Growing Urban Experiment)* (2005–2006) is an urban system composed of data structures.[185] This project

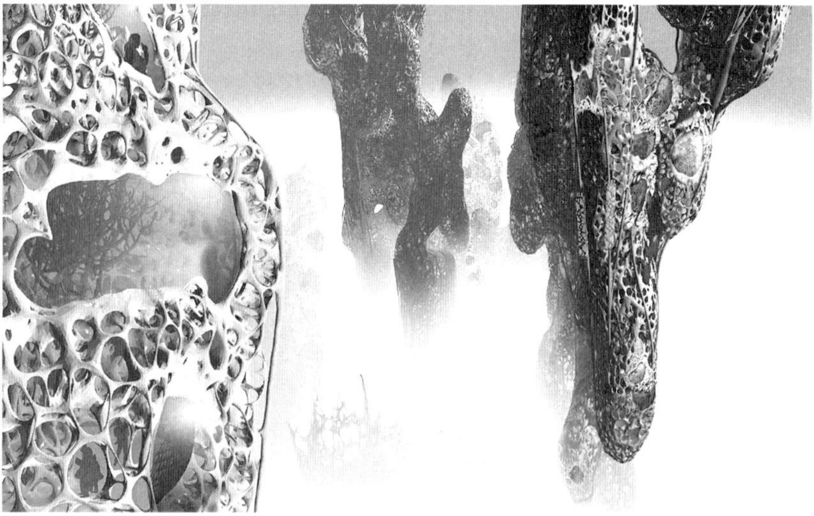

Figure 3.7
R(&)Sie(n), *I've Heard About . . . (a Flat, Fat, Growing Urban Experiment)*, 2005–2006. Courtesy François Roche.

shows that algorithmic architecture is not merely the static embodiment of an instrumental rationality, but instead implies the reality of infinite contingencies as the urban system grows, extends, and transforms beyond the data that were programmed into its initial state. The urban structure grows according to the coral transformation of algorithms by recycled, synthesized, and polymerized data materials.

One may suggest that these growing algorithms should be seen as performative actants or action-instructions that do not just represent or simulate but make a generalized urban architecture. However, I would argue that this is not the whole story. As specified in R&Sie(n)'s protocols for this urban structure, algorithms are here defined by: (1) the external data of preexisting morphology (e.g., structural limits, natural light, the dimension of habitable cells); (2) the internal data of the structure: the chemical elements (e.g., physiological empathy, endocrine secretions, bodily emissions); (3) the electronic processing of information and decision making. All these data are then constructed into growth scripts and neighborhood protocols. The transformation of the urban structure thus corresponds to the algorithmic prehension of the transition between these distinct levels of data processing, thus becoming contingency-driving algorithms that are able to build multiple, heterogeneous, and contradictory scenarios. In this

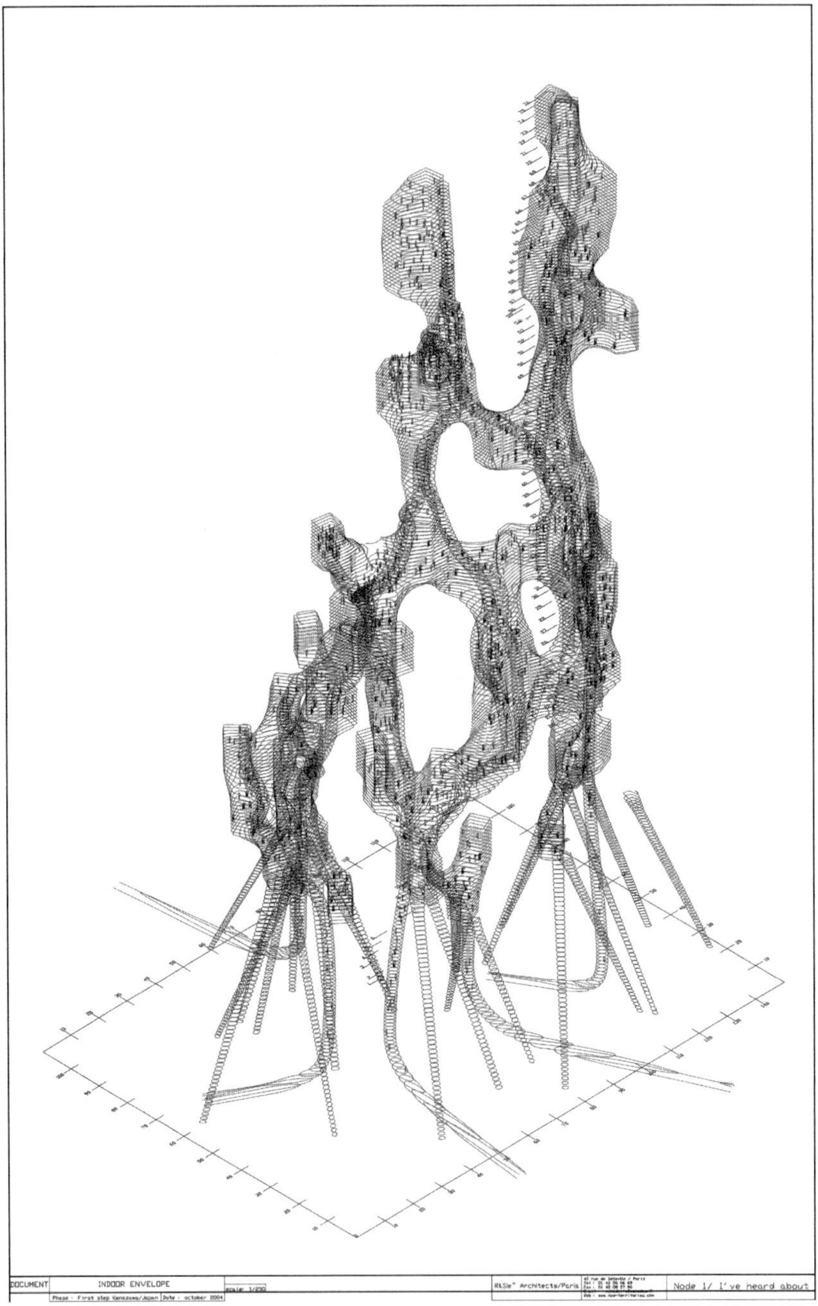

Figure 3.8

R(&)Sie(n), *I've Heard About . . . (a Flat, Fat, Growing Urban Experiment)*, 2005–2006. Courtesy François Roche.

sense, digital algorithms reveal contingency in programming because they prehend the constraints of physical, chemical, and electronic conditions rather than ceaselessly regenerating their initial states. It could therefore be argued that these algorithms are irreversibly programmed by the entropic burst of data in transition, which thereby transforms the initial programming of the urban structure.

From this standpoint, R&Sie(n)'s project would appear to describe soft thought as yet another demonstration of the inevitability of relating the performative quality of algorithms to the entropy of material data. However, it is important to add that the open relation between algorithms and data cannot be exclusively explained by the performative and pragmatic operability of algorithms, as if they were primarily "doers." Of course, algorithms are engines for action and implementation, or executors, but this is only one side of a coin. One could instead argue that the reason why algorithms continue to animate computational culture is because they disclose a new level of physical reality: a new actuality that does not merely activate or reenact already existing physical data. This algorithmic actuality corresponds to computational prehensions, which on the one hand define its physical pole (a computational physicality as it were) and on the other mental data (the conceptual prehension of incomputable algorithms). These computational prehensions therefore define algorithms not as executors of data, but as the actual experience of computational data, which is at once physical and mental. This is not to say that algorithms are the new creative ground of reality, but rather that they expose the incomputable infinities of data at the core of any ground, especially a computational one. Similarly, this does not mean that algorithms provide another ideal layer of computation as a supracognitive, transcendental order that needs to be actualized. On the contrary, the point being made here—that incomputable algorithms reside at the core of a new form of actuality (i.e., soft thought as physical and mental actuality)—serves to contend that the formal logic of algorithms is always inherently incomplete and infected with quantic indeterminacies. This means that neither sufficient reason (i.e., divine logos) nor anthropomorphic reason (the rational metaphysics of the mind-brain) can explain soft thought as a point of rest in a final universality of cognition. Instead, incomputable algorithms expose the immanence of thought and its constitutional incompleteness: the infinities and multiplicities of modes of thought that do not conform to the transcendence of being (whether this is a divine or an anthropomorphic transcendence constructed in the image of the mind or the rational brain). Incomputable algorithms do not simply exist in a mutual relation with computation, but rather break the circle of recognition between rationality and its outside. Incomputable algorithms are irreversibly immanent to actuality, which means that there is an inevitable disharmonic, asymmetric, or inconsistent experience of (or prehension of) infinite infinities. Incomputable infinities take over algorithmic actualities and reprogram their "subjective aim" (their terminus, their tendency toward completeness).[186] This implies an irreversible encounter with unknown quantities. Soft thought is an instance of an irreversible encounter with computational infinities: for no matter how much algorithms are used to describe existing data, they inevitably construct new levels of probabilities, uncertainties, and predictions. The algorithmic process of data prehension is an irreversible contagion, according to which incomputables cannot be compressed and thus synthesized by one form of being. This irreversible experience of infinity corresponds not to the infinite potentialities of what a brain can think but to the patternless interference of incompressible quantities in computation. These quantities deploy not the arbitrary appearance of errors in digital programming, but contingency and immanence in soft

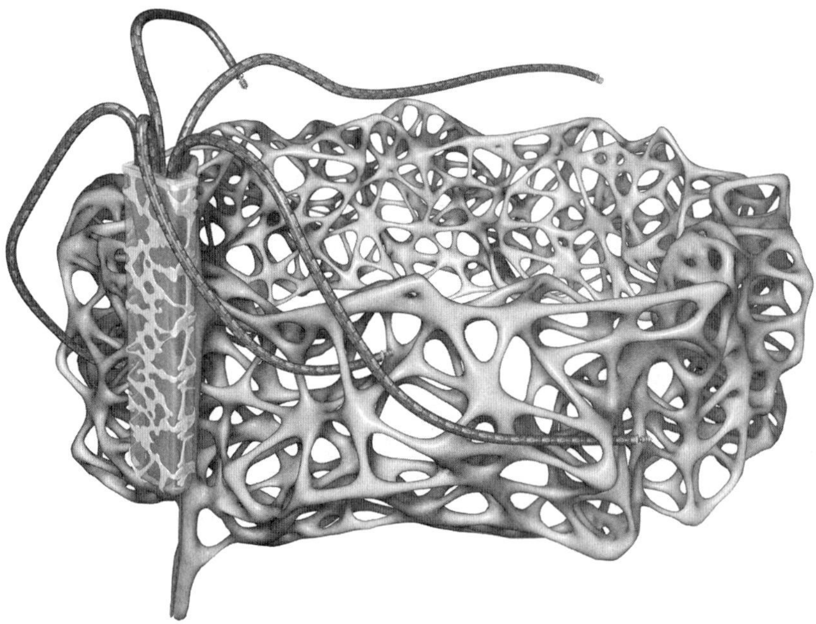

Figure 3.9
R(&)Sie(n), *I've Heard About . . . (a Flat, Fat, Growing Urban Experiment)*, 2005–2006. Courtesy François Roche.

thought. This turns neurocomputation upside down: on the one hand, it points out that thought is not reducible to neural networks that compute data in the form of algorithms (whether these are serial or parallel algorithms); on the other, it underdetermines the formal logic of computation, as the latter is confronted by incomputable algorithms that cannot be synthesized by neural networks of cognition.[187]

R&Sie(n)'s architectures of thoughts similarly disentangle the power of computation from preprogrammed instructions and, perhaps unfashionably, do not sustain the idea that technoextensions change the internal structures of neurocognition. The urban architecture *I've Heard About . . .* is constructed by a secretion machine or Viab (standing for viability of data) made of nanoreceptacles, which are psychochemical receptors of data. According to R&Sie(n), this machine is not an extension of algorithmic instructions, but is instead an agent that thinks while it constructs space. In other words, the Viab is not a subject that enacts thought in order to make sense of the world. Instead, it is an instance of thinking procedures that are themselves machines of thought. Similarly, this machine does not simply host thought, nor does it become an executor of a predetermined cognitive structure (e.g., neurosynaptic architecture). Rather, it deploys the "how" of thought or, drawing from Whitehead once more, a mode of thought: the machine thought is how the machine thinks. The Viab machine cannot therefore be said to be part of the environment of an extended cognition. This machine is its own thought, which cannot be reduced to a cognitive structure distributed in matter.[188]

In particular, R&Sie(n)'s Viab is a robot machine: a construction engine that while being driven by algorithms also has the task of building urban settings in real time through the secretion of the material constituting the structure. According to R&Sie(n), the closest thing to a Viab today is a small mud-working robot invented by Behrokh Khoshnevis. This is a "contour crafter" that works more or less like a 3D printer.[189] Termites have been doing something similar for eons, building skyscrapers by spitting and smoothing mud, and this Viab is a busy termite with a body full of wet cement and instructions. Its machinic parts are data and procedures: infinite variables and finite sets that cannot be synthesized into a coherent whole.

Yet it would be misleading to see the actual Viab as a mere implementation of generative algorithms.[190] Far from simply being a machine endowed with thought, the Viab machine deploys a mode of thought that is determined by its own thinking procedures. This is why extended functionalism (or Clark's theory of the extended mind) is right to show the fallacy of enactivism, the autopoietic model of cognition that corresponds to the quality of sense making, whereby living organisms always already think because they enact the world (which would not exist otherwise). At the same time, however, the theory of extended cognition does not offer a valid alternative to computational modes of cognition by grounding cognition in the neuroarchitecture of the (extended and neural) brain. Extended functionalist theorists argue that forms of information processing cannot account for the necessity of material contingencies. Here the famous example of traffic controllers or contingency operators, which are able to calculate extra factors unlike computers, is a case in point. For extended functionalism, of which Churchland's neurocomputation is yet another example, the formal level of algorithms always needs a material environment onto which it can distribute itself and establish a relation. According to Clark, this relation extends or transforms the interior apparatus of neural architecture, thereby producing novelty in the extended brain.

Nevertheless, extended functionalism is unable to rethink the very free software of cognition, and returns instead to the safe ground of formal ideas implemented in matter. Extended functionalism thus explains the relation between mental and physical poles merely in terms of a linear causality, whereby mental states are triggered by and bear upon systemic inputs and outputs. Thus, while it is possible to agree with Clark's critique of enactivism and its neurophenomenological explanation of cognition, it is also difficult to see how extended functionalism could seriously challenge what functionalism assumes, i.e., the neurocomputational structure of cognition, which cannot explain how there could ever be novelty in conceptual prototypes and how there could ever be an actual soft thought.

From this standpoint, the structures of extended cognition are locked within the formal logic of programming that R&Sie(n)'s speculative project *I've Heard About . . .* tries to escape. In fact, it is important to highlight that the main limit of computation here is not its incapacity to include material contingencies, which justifies why the neurosynaptic computation of the brain is a necessity for neurocomputing. Quite the opposite: computation, or the formal architecture of algorithms, only remains limited to its closed formalism if one does not take into consideration how algorithms themselves tend toward abstraction, infinity, or the incomputable. It is therefore possible to suggest that novelty is already internal to computation, to the extent that the limit of computation (the infinite sequence of 0s and 1s) is, as Turing foresaw, the very condition by which algorithmic finite rules can be established. Thus, algorithms are not only actions or pragmatic functions, but also, as Deleuze would call them, suspensions of action or immanent forms of contemplation. This is not simply because they are always already immersed in temporal continuities.[191] Borrowing from Whitehead, these suspensions here correspond to the mereotopology of space events triggered by negative prehensions. In other words, the negative selection of infinite quantities of ideas in algorithmic thinking constitutes a thought event proper to digital computation: what cannot be computed coincides with an idea of infinity that haunts every algorithmic execution. A thought event constitutes the aesthetic novelty of soft thought: a lure toward uncertain infinities. This means that the computational limit is not there to witness the failure of quantifications, divisions, and partitions in attending novelty, but rather to embrace quantic infinities as the point at which uncognizable thoughts ingress into the general structure of experience. From this standpoint, the aesthetic question posed to digital algorithms finds its true counterpart in an algorithmic thought negatively prehending quantic infinities.

Bringing speculation into computer science, Chaitin's definition of Omega, as a discrete infinity of real numbers, explains how incompressible quantities enter the sequential order of 0s and 1s at the limit of computation. In the same way, in R&Sie(n) *I've Heard About . . .* algorithms reveal the aesthetic or prehensive selection of infinities. Here, indeterminate quantities are implied in computation but are not compressed into one smaller program able to contain them all. The inclusion of protocols of incertitude and the free software rescripting of source codes transforms the computational modeling of a generalized city into the algorithmic prehension of random quantities; into the immanent experience of new architectures of thought. *I've Heard About . . .* is not a model of a city that exists or could exist, but rather deploys the transitive computation of the algorithmic program of the city itself. To break the code of urban programming is to unlock the aesthetic potential of the digital cogito toward the free software of thought where thousands of prehensions deploy their own feeling for incomputability. It is this lure for indeterminate quantities that soft thought has come to unleash in computation: not the representation of a conceptual prototype, but the nonsensuous prehension of algorithmic infinities.

3.9 Soft thought II

According to Whitehead, nonsensuous prehensions are conceptual feelings that are able to catch the space of transition between actualities. Nonsensuous prehensions do not link the present to the past in the same way as sensorimotor perceptions make links to the past's conceptual framework, so as to solve problems in the present. If conceptual feelings do link with the past, then it is to allow the space of transition to become an actuality within the present. For James and Whitehead, the feeling of spatiotemporal transitions characterizes thought as that which breaks from the continuous chain between past and future (for instance, the chain of algorithmic sequences: past data are valued and particular probabilities are selected in order to determine what the future occasion will be). While it is not so important to determine the essential nature of this break (material, organic, human, atomic, digital), it is nonetheless pertinent to consider that the break happens as a transition between actual objects. This transitive space is conceptually prehended or nonsensuously felt as the novelty of definiteness: as the nuanced definition of incomputable data. These nonsensuous prehensions bring forth the definite discrete infinity of any actuality, or ways in which this actuality can be cut from the totality of preexisting data.

An example of soft thought can be found at work in Alexei Shulgin's *Nirvana Transitions*,[192] a video installation whose software processing is programmed not to determine an interactive interface with the user, but to expose the aesthetics of algorithms as prehension of transition as such. Black-and-white video sequences become different variants of transition that last 30 seconds, and are generated through video editing software. These are not moving but rather still images, the static consistency of which is counteracted by the algorithmic processing that drives soft thought beyond the limits of pragmatic software. As the white shadow advances, the black withdraws and what is left is the blank space between, the immanence of transition, marking a thought event that presents itself as an incomputable quantity (a color quantity as such, which is neither back nor white). Despite being a video installation, Shulgin's *Transitions* is precisely not about the image of space but about aesthetic space as the nonsensuously felt algorithmic interstice in the sequential order of the program. This is not simply a computational aesthetics that contemplates the gap between zones of clarity and obscurity, between the familiar and the unknown, between the past and the future. On the contrary, algorithmic prehensions are there so as to cut the sequential order of sets, exposing the immanence of alternatives, futurities, and abstractions that determine algorithms as operative computations of the present. As Whitehead observed, "Cut away the future, and the present collapses, emptied of its proper content. Immediate existence requires the insertion of the future in the crannies of the present."[193] Soft thought deploys the mechanism of indirect causality or quasi-empirical causality, whereby it acquires immanence through the anticipatory irreversibility of the future in the present-past (i.e., conceptual prototypes). Contrary to the neurocomputational architecture of conceptual prototypes, therefore, conceptual prehensions are determined by futurities, the abstract space of contingent infinities deploying the ingression of nonrecurrent and patternless data in recurrent networks. At the same time, however, the nonsensuous prehensions of algorithms also define a mode of thought proper to software, as this is determined by discrete sets ordered in sequential strings. In Shulgin's work, the sequential processing of algorithmically generated spaces exposes a nonsensuous conception of discontinuous shapes, where the following spatiality is anticipated in the previous one, but can only follow once the previous one has gone. Contrary to neurocomputational prototypes, here only the perishing of one series of algorithms allows the new series to start forming a new shape. This is not an addition of new paths to existing prototypes or the continuous recurrence of the past in the present. What is proper to soft thought is the continuous subtraction of the past from the present processing of algorithmic sequences that prehend incomputability. This nonsensuous prehension of futurity is not, however, intrinsic to human cognition and is not determined by the aesthetic values of the programmer. Instead, I argue that there is rather an intrinsic aesthetic in algorithmic processing that corresponds to the lure of the incomputable, which requires a subtraction (a negative prehension) from their sequential order revealing the immanent transition or break from one set to another.

Therefore soft thought is not considered here as another instance of the neuroarchitecture of the brain, but instead as a computational mode of thought that allows us to reveal that the brain is not the ultimate and unavoidable pinnacle of cognitive evolution. On the contrary, as evolutionary biologist Stephen Jay Gould pointed out, the evolution of cognition is an accident, and as such it can be easily wiped out.[194] Similarly, Antonio Damasio's hypothesis that cognition is mainly encoded in the primary mechanisms of reward and punishment also remains a symptom of an idealist materialism, since one can promptly argue that there is no evidence that these primitive mechanisms are what they were and have simply become inherited by higher forms of emotional cognition. The neurocomputational and neurophenomenological approaches to cognition ultimately overlook the fact that evolution is made of irreversible turns, gaps, and discontinuities, and that it itself depends on cosmic contingencies that may have left certain mechanisms of thought completely uncognized and yet persistently inherited. The appeal to neuroevolution as the guarantor of the physiological nature of thought entirely disregards the asymmetries between thought and brain, as it ceaselessly reproduces the argument that the world exists because the brain thinks of it.

Computational design instead offers the possibility of indicating an increasing mismatch between the brain and thought: between what can be cognized and the sheer infinite variety of incomputable infinities. Despite all attempts at ergonomically designing neuroarchitectures that optimize neurophysical responses, the persistence of random algorithms across distinct facets of postcybernetic culture (the codification of the genetic patrimony of the earth, the codification of facial patterns, speech, movement, and vision, the codification of social interaction, the codification of the cultural heritage, the codification of the market) has become evidence that soft thought feels itself thinking without reproducing itself in neurophysiological architecture. In other words, the algorithmic processing of data is subtracting itself from the neuroontology of thought by injecting incomputable ideas into the extended codification of being. This has not resulted in a hyperactivity of sensing and thinking distributed across the networked infrastructures of spatiotemporal experience, but instead in the neutralization or immobilization of sensing and cognition, which are now falling, as Shulgin's *Transitions* suggest, into a pitch-black deep space of thought in which it is impossible to remember the past or predict the future.[195]

These algorithmic spaces of transition, I suggest, have become a distinctive mark of postcybernetic culture determining a new actual thought. Information overload, filling each and every level of mediatic interaction, is in fact evidence of the irreversible architecture of soft thought infecting all levels of experience: mental, physical, social, technical, economical, political. William James claimed that thoughts are experienced not in isolation but in their transition: that thoughts are objects colored by the relations they hold.[196] All relations in the stream of thought are internal contrasts that never result in the overarching fusion of being with thought. The stream of thought is instead composed of conjunctions and disjunctions that expose the interferences, asymmetries, gaps, and granularity of contingencies.

From this standpoint, James's mosaic of experience closely resonates with Whitehead's atomic theory of time.[197] According to James, each thought is like a drop bearing the full force of a torrent of water, revealing an indissoluble togetherness in each unit "as a snow-flake crystal caught in the warm hand is no longer a crystal but a drop."[198] Thought is thus not simply determined by the mind as the engine that joins together discrete parts. Neural connectionism, like associationism for James, overlooks the interior architecture of thoughts and confines transition to an external interaction between neural nodes. Thus, for example, synaptic links are the agents of communication between otherwise disconnected neural points. These links explain how one thought can be spatiotemporally related to another, as in a causal chain of physical effects. It is assumed that without the activities of synaptic links, thoughts will remain in complete, sovereign isolation from each other. Neural connectionism is then set to explain thought as emerging from interactive parts or the neurosynaptic architecture of the brain, which ultimately constitutes the mind. If thought is the result of external neural relations (and no longer that of internal rule-based instructions), then, it is assumed, thought has no interior qualities, but must be governed by the emerging qualities of an interactive mind. Despite challenging the architecture of the mind articulated by formal language or axiomatics, the neurocomputational model of interaction ultimately appears to build a house of mirrors, in which any mode of thought is just another version of the neurosynaptic architecture of the brain. Here each thought is reflected into the world, according to one ceaseless loop of neurosensorial cognition that identifies the world with the brain. Yet how can neurosensorial interaction account for the algorithmic prehension of infinite quantities?

To put it simply, it cannot. The neurosensorial model of thought is only able to account for the mutual connections between the world and the brain, between the interior and the exterior. According to this model, doing is thinking and thinking is acting. This also means that simply correlating algorithmic architecture to a physical subject—human, animal, or machine—will not guarantee that software processing is an actuality. Soft thought is immanently experienced without a subject that thinks it or an object that performs thought. It simply slips through the neuroarchitectures of thought by infecting the conceptual framework of the past with the reality of lived abstraction.

Like Whitehead, James maintains that experience is an occasion or event that is internally related (through nonsensuous prehensions) and externally constrained by the atomic nature of actual occasions or drops of experience. For Whitehead, the internal relatedness of experience is granted by nonsensuous or conceptual prehensions: modes of feeling that are composed of durational extensions, of spatiotemporal regions that have passed and are to come.[199] Together with Whitehead, James argues that although these spatiotemporal regions of experience are discrete, they are not isolated from one another. The qualities of one pervade the constitution of those regions that succeed it.[200] Here experience does not result from the sensorimotor cognition of the environment, but builds upon an interior link between nonsensuous elements and an exterior connection between unrelated qualities, assembling together to compose an extensive continuum made of fragments and atoms. In particular, the interior contractedness between elements in the stream of thought explains how earlier drops of experience enter subsequent drops. These drops of experience cannot know themselves. If they could, these units would change, for the knowledge of themselves would become distinguished from the knowledge of their objects. As Whitehead reminds us, "no actual entity can be conscious of its own satisfaction; for such knowledge would be a component in the process, and would thereby alter the satisfaction."[201] Ultimately, an experience is open to completion once it is caught in a process between its interior architecture of prehension and its exterior connections, or according to a nexus of prehending occasions. For Whitehead, a process is made of the *whatness*: the complex materiality of elements, the qualities and quantities of which cannot be synthesized or computed into one form. Process is instead a matter of transition that expresses the paradox that what becomes and what changes are not one and the same thing. What changes is the serial arrangement of elements as they come into being and perish through the passage of time. This entails no becoming. Instead, what become are the durational regions or spatiotemporal slices of experience, which Whitehead calls actual entities: they become infected with eternal objects, which enter and irreversibly infringe upon them. In other words, what constitutes experience is the becoming of an actual occasion, the event proper to process, which is not the same as the interaction of the elements of experience. The conditions for the becoming of experience are not simply given by the new sensorimotor arrangement of interactive components, where a physical response to programmed algorithms is enough to guarantee the happening of an event. On the contrary, this becoming can only be internal to the computable infinities of soft thought, where algorithms prehend random strings of disconnected data, determining the reality of lived abstractions.

As James points out, the constructions of a radical empiricism must neither admit nor exclude any element that is not directly thought. Incomputable worlds are not standing in the background of computation and are not simply brought to the foreground by the sensorimotor actions of physical bodies, or by the recurrent patterns of conceptual prototypes. These worlds are instead solely determined by the transitional reality between sequences of 0s and 1s. No matter how abstract this transition can be, it still remains a space of thought—a thought event—which can be further qualified and selected by other actual occasions.[202] Similarly, Whitehead suggests that eternal objects are as real as any actual entity in which they acquire togetherness from their condition of isolation. Eternal objects therefore are "experienced relations," or primordial elements of experience, prehension, or actuality.[203] But what exactly does this relation-transition process tell us about soft thought?

According to James, the definiteness of transition makes experience a question of reality rather than one of emotions, even when it operates solely in the world of thought.[204] Modes of thought are, indeed, as real as any object of feeling. It therefore follows that for radical empiricism there are no neurocomputational activation of thought, no responsive networks of interaction, and no emotional hierarchies of cognition, but principally the immanence of the incomputable in thought, of transitions that are given in pure experience: pure thought and pure feeling.[205] By overlapping radical empiricism with speculative computation, it is possible to reveal that the neurocomputational models of cognition and the neurophenomenological enactment of the world are new forms of ideal materialism. To turn away from biological and mechanical ontologies of thought is to disclose the reality of transitions, interstices, and cuts as actualities.

If soft thought is made of transitions—not between the brain and the world, but between actual entities—then it is not simply equivalent to the endless, seamless, generative continuity of algorithms that subtend all media in the form of a universal metacomputation. If the speculative character of software processing is teased out from radical empiricism, it might be possible to grasp how algorithmic computation may also alter existing actualities. For instance, what happens when a computational object connects with another, as when a computed wall relates to a computed floor, or when such a wall transforms into a solar panel by responding to atmospheric pressures, requires an engagement with soft thought itself, because the latter gives a new affective tonality to the algorithmic experience of transition. Soft thought does not simply mean that data become embodied in a structure (a neural net, a brain, or any other material implementation) that turns top-down models of cognition into bottom-up designs of sensorimotor computation. On the contrary, soft thought becomes subtracted from cognition and emotion, from the bioontology of the mind, descending within the subpersonal space of computational algorithms. In other words, soft thought is an actuality: a thought event. Even if we abolish all possible contexts for soft thought, it is impossible to abolish soft thought as immanent experience.

James argues that experience is determined not by contexts but by the sharing of an object space. This, he suggests, is because two things are numerically one thing under two different names. Even if percepts differ, immanent experience always remains identical. Two experiences become contagiously intertwined in the same interstitial space. No matter how different the contents of experience may be, there always remains a transitional space that is numerically identical for any number of experiences. This space is like a piece of common property over, through, and in which they join. For James's radical empiricism, experience remains defined by a common numerical space. Yet for speculative computation, this space is not only numerical but also quantic, and is not amenable to the temporal continuity that subtends the moment of partition. In other words, this quantic space does not correspond to a topological field of morphogenetic transformations, but rather reveals a mereotopology of parts among parts that either connect or do not connect with wholes.

From the standpoint of computation, this general space of experience is instead the space of randomness, of unsynthesizable quantities that are common to all actualities. The oneness of the space of experience is therefore a quantum defined by the primacy of incomputable quantities, whose discrete infinities (or Omega probabilities) infect the binary sequences of soft thought. Random quantities are not simply designed in a software program, but are internal anomalies that connect actualities without the latter becoming synthesized into one form, regardless of whether it involves neural, electrochemical, or digital computation. This is not to deny reality to the biophysical and biodigital architectures of thought, by privileging a mathematical ontology wherein eternal forms or ideas remain incorruptible and distinct from matter. On the contrary, soft thought as immanent experience can only reveal that incomputable quantities infect, but do not constitute, physical, biological, and technological actualities.

The contagious architecture of these quantic infinities turns the computational grid into a Swiss cheese of irregular holes, rough edges, and blind spots. From this standpoint, computation can no longer be saved from the uncertainties of unknown worlds, but has instead become as open to contingencies as biological and physical fields of knowledge. This means that the epistemological investigation into neurocomputational architectures of thought cannot circumvent the speculative drive toward unknown thoughts and unprecedented occasions of experience. Similarly, if neuroarchitecture is a way to grasp the aesthetic impact of software in spatial design, it will have to venture beyond neurophenomenological cognition by countereffectuating neurophysical architecture with the actualities of soft thought. By suspending the relational circuit between the world and the brain, soft thought will not simply work to guarantee the transmission of information from one terminus to another by cutting a clear passage through the clutter of bodies, machines, locations, and climates. Similarly, soft thought is not equivalent to the "datafication" of things and cannot be contained within data (e.g., images, texts, code, and speech). Instead, soft thought implies an algorithmic aesthetics proper to computational space, revealing that incomputable quanta are in the foreground of our programming culture.

Glossary

Algorithm A step-by-step procedure for calculations. A computer program contains algorithms that instruct the computer to perform specific counting operations. In the case of digital architecture, algorithms describe the computational capacity of software to process infinite variables through finite instructions. In this book, algorithms are defined in terms of finite quantities (finite sets of instructions) and incomputable data, which cannot be compressed into smaller programs. Algorithms are actual objects that produce computational space and time.

Algorithmic architecture The use of algorithms or digital rules for the design of spatiotemporal forms or for the digital processing of variable data (volume, length, gravity, distribution of weight, capability of space, circulation of air, movement of people, temperature, light, etc.) in the design of buildings and urban infrastructures.

Anticipatory system A cybernetic system that calculates qualitative changes or degrees of variation included in the binary reduction of data to 0 and 1 states. This calculation allows the system to respond to emerging changes in the environment through adaptation. This leads the internal structure and program of the system to learn and thus to anticipate tendencies toward change, and to preadapt to potential external inputs.

Architecture In a general sense, this term refers to the matrix or structure whose general arrangement of relations produces space and time.

Axiom A mathematical postulate based on immediate evidence or a formal system that constitutes an implicit definition of that system without necessary evidence.

Axiomatic method A formal procedure through which a coherent group of propositions (or theory) is replaced by a simpler collection of propositions (i.e., axioms). In logic, this method defines the way in which a system can be generated by following specific rules through logical deduction from basic procedures (axioms or postulates). In *Principia Mathematica*, Bertrand Russell and Alfred North Whitehead attempted to formalize all of mathematics (and thus to reduce all mathematical theory) by an axiomatic method (a collection of axioms).

Brain landscapes 3D spaces created by the fMRI scans of the brain.

Calculus A theorem built on two major complementary and inversely related mathematical ideas, both of which rely on the idea of limits. Differential calculus analyses the instantaneous rate of change of quantities and the local behavior of functions, as for example in the graph function of a slope. Integral calculus looks at the accumulation of quantities, such as areas under a curve, linear distance traveled, or volume displaced. The use of the calculus in digital architecture has been central to the development of new architectural styles (from folding and blob architecture to parametricism).

Cellular automaton A discrete model consisting of a regular grid of cells in binary states (either on or off, represented as 0s or 1s). Each cell is surrounded by neighboring cells and is defined in relation to them, so that the distance from one cell to another can be calculated through their neighbors. The cellular automaton is a collection of cells on a grid of specified shape that evolves through a number of discrete steps, according to a set of rules that are applied iteratively. Since they evolve over time in a gradual fashion, cellular automata are said to be generative; each level of growth becomes the ground for the next. In *A New Kind of Science*, the digital philosopher Stephen Wolfram discusses cellular automata as a model of biological systems, claiming that at the bottom of physical and biological complexities there are discrete entities or cellular automata.

Cognition The mental process of knowing, which includes reasoning, awareness, perception, attention, remembering, problem solving, and producing and understanding language.

Cognitivism A theoretical reaction to behaviorism that was developed in the 1950s, and according to which the mind is an aggregate of discrete internal mental states (also defined as representations or symbols). Through a positivist approach based on experimentation, measurement, and scientific method, cognitivism defined the mind as made up of rules that can be manipulated. Together with the computational theory of mind, cognitivism agrees with the idea that the mind functions as a computer.

Computation A mathematical calculation. In information theory, computation describes sets of natural numbers that are recursive, computable, or decidable. It investigates the algorithmic processing of data that terminates after a finite amount of time, and which decides whether or not a given number belongs to the algorithmic set. Computational theory is concerned with computability; it explores whether an infinite set of questions could be answered by finite binary states (by yes or no answers). Alan Turing demonstrated that there is no computable function (no finite binary set) that could correctly answer every question in the problem set. This meant that not every set of natural numbers is computable, and Turing's description of the halting problem (the set of Turing machines that halt on input 0) is one example, among many, of an incomputable set. In this book, computation corresponds to the capacity of algorithms to compress infinite amounts of data. It therefore refers to a problem of reducing infinite quantities of data into smaller programs, and not only to the time a computer needs to process data. Chaitin's notion of algorithmic probability Omega explains the implications of this quasi-mathematical entity, which can only partially compress data. The discovery of these discrete infinities entails that incomputable data must be the condition, and not the result, of computation.

Computationalism The computational theory of mind according to which the human mind is an information-processing system and thinking is a form of computing. In this view, the mind functions as a computer or symbol manipulator. Like a computer, the mind computes input from the natural world to create outputs in the form of further mental or physical states. In digital philosophy, computationalism coincides with the idea that all mental states can be carried out by computational entities, or cellular automata. It also refers to the idea that the function of reason corresponds to the ordering and classification of data into smaller units of information, into finite states or sets of rules.

Connectionism A series of approaches to the study of the mind and behaviors defined by emergent processes of interconnected networks of simple units. In particular, connectionism defines cognition in terms of the synaptic links that constitute the neural architecture of the brain, which includes units, layers, and connections, but also the learning of rules and computational representations that emerge from the activity of the network. Connectionism studies how local rules determine the behavior of the global properties of an entity (i.e., the mind). *See also* Neural network.

Cybernetics, first-order First-order cybernetics established that all systems, living and nonliving, were probabilistic entities determined by their capacity to organize and control information through a homeostatic rebalancing of energy and information. The increasing entropic tendency of the universe to run out of equilibrium was counteracted by information as the capacity of transmitting a message through the sea of entropic noise. For first-order cybernetics, computers or machines could become instances of a universal mathematical logic able to calculate all possible results through a finite set of instructions. The first programming languages and first examples of AI were based on this formal model.

Cybernetics, second-order Second-order cybernetics was based on the notion of reflexivity, which established that all systems entertain a positive feedback relation between the individual and the environment, but also between a first and second level of perception (i.e., sensory-motor perception and the cognitive activity resulting from reflexivity). This relation was understood according to the metabolism of a living organism, a cell, whose enzymatic synthesis of external energy contributed to its internal structuring and to its evolution through time. In particular, Maturana and Varela's notion of autopoiesis (self-making) turned the entropic tendency of a system to run out of equilibrium, and thus to dissipate its unity, into a negentropic measure of information, according to which any small living entity could become productive of complex levels of organization, including cognition.

Data The plural of datum; qualitative or quantitative variables. As an abstract concept, pure data refers to data before they are subjected to cognitive processing or direct experience. Raw data instead corresponds to unprocessed information—numbers, characters, outputs—from devices that collect them to convert physical quantities into symbols. For Whitehead, an actual entity that has completed its process of concrescence and has thus perished becomes a datum. An actual occasion thus acquires objective immortality to the extent that it completes itself and can be prehended as objective data by another actuality in the process of its realization. Data are therefore parts of an architecture of relation.

Digital architecture The use of software to design buildings, urban infrastructures, and objects.

Emergentism A theoretical approach to consciousness and the philosophy of mind. An emergent system is more than the sum of the properties of the system's parts. While emergent properties depend on the basic properties of the system (i.e., their relationships and configuration), they are also autonomous from them, since they cannot be reduced to or deduced from them. According to this approach, consciousness is an emergent property of the brain.

Enactivism A theoretical approach to the study of the mind, according to which interaction with the environment is crucial to the development of human cognition. As an alternative to cognitivism and computationalism, enactivism criticizes the representational view of consciousness, arguing rather that the mind is always situated in an environment and that the reciprocal action between internal and external states drives cognition. In particular, Maturana and Varela proposed the term "enactive" to designate that knowledge cannot be derived from sets of rules, but is instead context dependent: it grows into the environment.[1]

Excarnation The capacities of quantities to become abstracted from an algorithmic sequential order.

Extraspace The architecture of information (the volume, the length, the density of data) created by the ingression of incomputable quantities into mathematical and physical entities.

Incomputable The algorithmically random result of the binary expansion of an algorithmic sequence, according to which a binary point is followed by an infinite sequence of bits that correspond to real numbers. Examples are Chaitin's Omega /Ω number or the halting probability of a universal prefix-free (or self-delimiting) Turing machine. Chaitin defined Turing's unsolved halting problem or the limit of a computable sequence of rational numbers as an incomputable string of 0s and 1s (Omega). Turing's halting problem affirmed the mathematical impossibility of calculating in advance whether a program would stop running or continue to run forever (given a description of a program and a finite input). There could be no universal algorithm able to solve this problem for all possible program-input pairs. According to Chaitin, Turing's computational problem is demonstrated by the irreducible complexity of the infinite real number Omega. Omega is not one particular number, but an infinite sequence of increasingly random quantities or incomputable sets of infinite numbers.

Infinitesimal An indefinitely small quantity; a value approaching zero. Infinitesimals are so small they cannot be seen or measured. Gottfried Leibniz's use of infinitesimals is based on the Law of Continuity, according to which all changes in nature are continuous (i.e., there are no gaps). Infinitesimals therefore represent increasingly smaller quantities defining the continuity between two points in space.

Infinitesimal calculus A branch of mathematics concerned with the determination and properties of derivatives and integrals of functions by methods based on the summation of infinitesimal differences. It is used for calculating the slope of a curve and areas under curves, the latter of which can be expressed by an integral function, providing the ground for integral calculus. Gilles Deleuze used differential calculus and Leibniz's infinitesimal calculus to articulate his conception of "intensive quantities."

Infinitesimal space The infinitesimal gap between terms, shapes, or objects. A space of increasingly smaller units that cannot be directly sensed or cognized. Instead this space is defined by imperceptible qualities and variations.

Information Data ordered in a sequence of symbols that contains a message.

Information (as environment) Technically, data that is not intentionally produced by an informer: for instance, the series of concentric rings visible in the wood of a cut tree trunk is environmental information (information about the age of the tree). In this book, the notion of an informational environment is used with reference to James J. Gibson's understanding of information *as* environment. Against computationalism, he claims that information is not in the brain but in the environment, and that the brain is an organ that selects what is already an external source of knowledge.

Invariant function The unchanging relation that associates members of one set with members of another set under certain classes of transformation. In topology this is also known as homeomorphism, topological isomorphism, or the bicontinuous function, i.e., a continuous function between topological spaces that has a continuous inverse function. For example, the invariant function that describes the continuous deformation between a coffee mug and a donut.

Mereology The theory of parthood relations: the relations of part to whole and the relations between parts within a whole.

Mereotopology A theory combining mereology and topology. Mereotopology investigates relations between parts and wholes, parts of parts, and the boundaries between them. In formal ontology, mereotopology is a branch of metaphysics that describes parts that can be bigger than wholes and wholes that become parts. Between 1916 and 1929 Alfred North Whitehead articulated this theory in several books and articles. Whitehead's mereotopological approach insists on the spatialization and temporalization of actual occasions.

Metacomputation The ontological method of digital philosophy, according to which the physical universe is constituted by discrete particles and can thus be computed by simpler unities. The deduction of complexity from simpler sets of algorithms or cellular automata.

Metamodeling Félix Guattari's notion of modeling, defined by diagrammatic rather than hierarchical relations between signs and things.

Mindware The extension of the mind beyond the computationalist framework based on symbols and procedures. For Andy Clark, mindware must include the importance of the biological brain and more specifically a physiological understanding of the mind as being situated in an environment. This implies the grounding of computational modeling in the external environment and the development of notions of cognition in terms of actions guided by the brain. *See also* Wetware; Wideware.

Negative prehension The negative selection or the exclusion of infinite data from the range of prehended data that immediately concerns the concrescence of an actual entity.

Neural network In biology, a network or circuit of biological neurons connected by synapses. In computation, an artificial neural network is an information-processing paradigm of interconnected processing elements (neurons) working in unison to solve specific problems. Unlike conventional computers that use an algorithmic approach, i.e., an approach in which the computer follows a set of instructions in order to solve a problem, the application of neural networks to artificial intelligence is based on a learning process and is used for pattern recognition or data classification. *See also* Connectionism.

Neuroarchitecture A theoretical approach that uses the neural network structure of the brain to argue that cognition is born out of the interaction of neurons in synaptic connections. Neuroarchitecture is also a description of artificial neural networks or the application of neural networks to the understanding of space and of spatiotemporal experience.

Neurophenomenology A branch of scientific research linked to "enactivism," but specifically focused on the embodied condition of the human mind. This term is also used to describe Francisco Varela's critique of cognitivism and computationalism.

Omega (Ω) A never-ending sequence of 0s and 1s, without pattern or structure, generated through an infinitely long computer program. Omega has a maximally unknowable numerical value and is thus irreducible. Omega's numerical value written in binary or base-two algorithm (Omega = .11011 . . .) is an infinite string. Each bit of Omega has to be greater than 0 and less than 1, but the order of the exact sequence remains unknowable. Chaitin claims that the bits of Omega are mathematical facts as much as they are contingencies. They are accidental truths, quasi-truths: mathematics without a provable structure.[2] Chaitin claims that an Ω-like real number behaves like an oracle: its huge amount of information can be used to compute close approximations for every computably enumerable real number.

Parametricism A term used in a variety of disciplines from mathematics to design. Literally, it means working within parameters of a defined range. Within the field of digital design, it refers broadly to the utilization of parametric modeling software. In contrast to standard software packages based on datum geometric objects, parametric software links dimensions and parameters to geometry. It therefore describes the incremental adjustment of a part that is able to impact on the whole assembly. For example, as a point within a curve is repositioned, the whole curve comes to realign itself. Parametric software lends itself to curvilinear design as exemplified in the work of Frank Gehry, Zaha Hadid, and other formal architects. However, it would be wrong to assume that parametric design is concerned primarily with form making. On the contrary, parametric techniques within the field of digital design specifically involve the use of scripting languages that allow designers to step beyond the limitations of the user interface, and do their design work through the direct manipulation of code rather than form. Parametric design is performed through computer programming languages such as RhinoScript, MEL (Maya Embedded Language), Visual Basic, or 3dMaxScript. Recent applications, such as Generative Components and Grasshopper, bypass code scripting through pictographic forms of automation.[3]

Postcybernetic control The introduction of temporality (variations over time) and qualitative data into the calculation of probabilities, leading a system to achieve homeostasis and balance (negative feedback) or to transform excessive energy into information (positive feedback). Postcybernetic logic involves the transformation of energy into information by calculating potentialities (qualitative data changing over time) rather than probabilities (preset data).

Preemption The operative logic of power that produces the actual effects of indeterminate causes. Preemption takes place when the futurity of an unspecified threat is affectively held in the present in a potential state of emergency.[4]

Prehension The process by which an actual entity confronts infinite data through the physical and/or conceptual selection, evaluation, inclusion, exclusion, and transformation of data, and by which it thereby invests and reprograms the actual field of potentiality. Prehension can, however, only partially order infinite data, according to the specific occasions concerning the prehending entity.

Programming culture The computational mediation of all modes of cultural expressions (from the design of space to sound design, from the construction of socialities to the development of management and communication) that produces a specific aesthetics defined by the changing capacities of software, hardware, and interfaces to order data. Culture is not simply produced by computation, but emanates from new modes of calculating, ordering, classifying, predicting, profiling, constraining, and rescripting data. This concept does not simply refer to cultures that use digital media, but rather addresses how software, hardware, and interfaces have become the matrix of expression for cultural experience.

Protoconceptualism A theoretical hypothesis according to which sensorimotor skills are primitive forms of thought, such as for instance the nonlinguistic capacities for communication of animals and infants. According to Alva Noe, the nonlinguistic gesture of an infant implies conceptual qualities. This is a nonreflexive order of perception, which according to Noe constitutes a primary phenomenological experience and knowledge of the world.

Qualculation A term coined by Nigel Thrift to describe how the increasing number of modes of calculation carried out through machinic prosthesis, including media, has acquired a certain qualitative force that leads to new perceptual experiences, new modes of thinking, and new sensorimotor capacities of navigating space.

Randomness Not arbitrary complexity, but a form of entropic complexity defined by an infinite amount of data that cannot be contained by a smaller program. In algorithmic information theory, something is random if it is algorithmically incompressible or irreducible. According to Chaitin, "a member of a set of objects is random if it has the highest complexity that is possible within this set."[5] Randomness defines the infinite amount of information contained in Ω (Omega).

Real time The capacity of software or media technologies to retrieve information live, and to allow this information to add new data to programming. Real-time technologies can only be understood in terms of the "aliveness" of data.

Scripting A programming language or a series of algorithmic instructions carried out by another program and not by a computer processor (for instance a compiled program that is not carried out by another instance of software). The language is interpreted at run time so that instructions can be executed immediately. Perl, Visual Basic, and JavaScript are scripting languages.

Soft thought A software mode of thought defined by the speculative function of algorithms. It implies the selection of anomalous algorithms—the discrete infinities of Omega, for instance—during the sequential enumerations of data. In the context of digital architecture, this mode of thought governs the capacities of programming to incorporate unknown quantities into the design of new modes of living. In relation to cognitivism and enactivism, it points to automated functions of thinking, which are subpersonal and detotalizing insofar as their incomputable condition challenges a *tout court* assimilation with the representational model of rules and the neurological architecture of the brain.

Speculative reason The theoretical investigation of present conditions through quasi-algorithmic methods. Applied to computation, speculative reason refers to the algorithmic method of approximating infinities by means of probabilities. It thus relies on an incomplete method. According to Whitehead, one of the main tasks of speculative reason is to produce cosmological schemes. A speculative schema is determined not by contemplation, by *theoria* in the Platonic sense, by a universal view of the way things are, or by a list of arbitrarily collected ideas. It involves a certain general structure or matrix that underlies fixed criteria and a composition guided by a certain method, which is, however, incomplete.[6]

Topology A branch of mathematics that studies continuity and connectivity. It is concerned with the qualitative properties of certain objects that are invariant under continuous deformations (homeomorphic). Deformations involve the stretching and pulling of one shape into another without having to cut and/or glue or stitch parts together.

Turing machine An abstract computational device used to investigate the extent and limitations of what can be computed. According to Turing, a task is computable if it is possible to specify a sequence of instructions that will result in the completion of the task when they are carried out by some machine. This set of instructions is called an effective procedure, or an algorithm. A Turing machine is a kind of "state machine," which means that at any time the machine is in any one of a finite number of states. Instructions for a Turing machine consist in specified conditions under which the machine will transition between one state and another.

Twin paradox An example used by Einstein to explain the relativity of time vis-à-vis the speed of light. According to this paradox, if one twin makes a journey into space in a high-speed rocket and returns home, he will find that he has aged less than his identical twin who stayed on Earth. Einstein used the twin paradox to challenge the self-consistency of relativistic physics. For Einstein, this paradox could be resolved within the standard framework of special relativity. To address the paradox, he used the example of clock synchronicity, based on two observers wearing identical clocks but located in different points in space-time, A and B. Considering both round-trip and one-way travel between points in an inertial frame, this example aimed to prove that the velocity of the propagation of light in empty space is a universal constant. From the standpoint of the propagation of light, it was impossible to distinguish these two points because, as a constant, the propagation could not depend on the point in space considered. In other words, with reference to the propagation of light, the two points would fuse into one. However,

Einstein used the twin paradox to claim that what looked like a delay between the clocks of the twins should instead be explained by the rotation of time-space: simultaneity depended on relative velocity. Thus, the perceived asymmetry between two relatively moving twins (one slower than the other) was instead caused by relative motion.

Ubiquitous computing The embedding of computers in every object (from media objects to medical and weather technology). In 1988, Mark Weiser at Xerox Palo Alto Research Center (PARC) used the term ubiquitous computing to describe future technology that could monitor (track) and anticipate (calculate the probabilities of) users' needs, without the user having to attend to or directly operate the technology. For example, mobile phones are designed to interact with both the users and the digital media environment, without direct attention.

Universal computation The extension of computation to the point at which it attains the status of universal truth. It follows that computation, in the same way as mathematics and physics, constitutes laws according to which reality can be explained, broken down, ordered, and classified into bits and bites.

Wetware The embodiment of the mind in a biological substrate. According to Noe, the notion of wetware and the neurophysiological understanding of the mind offer an understanding of cognition according to which the brain is the organ of environmentally situated control. The capacities of a situated brain to move within its environment point imply that action, and not truth (i.e., preestablished rules), is the organizing principle of cognition.

Wideware A term used by Clark in conjunction with mindware and wetware. Wideware refers to the external environment as represented by extended structures of cognition (such as notebooks or calculators) which promote a cognitive adaptation to the external environment. Cognitive processes such as the storage, search for, and transformation of data are not simply or no longer carried out by the internal structure of the brain, but are realized by means of bodily action in relation to a variety of external media.

Notes

Preface: Weird Formalism

1. A glossary is included at the back of this book. All of the concepts included in it will be italicized when they first appear in the text.

2. According to Deleuze and Guattari, striated space corresponds to the Euclidean space founded on the parallel postulate, according to which two straight lines, if produced indefinitely, will eventually meet. Deleuze and Guattari contend that the postulate is based on the gravitational force exercised on all the elements that constitute the space. In other words, the force of gravity on the parallel line constitutes a laminar, homogeneous, striated, centralized space. Gilles Deleuze and Félix Guattari, *A Thousand Plateaus: Capitalism and Schizophrenia* (London: Athlone Press, 1987), 474–500.

3. In digital architecture, the striated space may coincide with a further level of metricization or quantification of trajectories, resulting in the digital mapping of points through measuring the distance between parallel lines. By subordinating the trajectories of movement to points, and thus by designing a space by moving from one point to another, this kind of digital architecture can only reproduce the metric grid.

Chapter 1 Incomputable Objects in the Age of the Algorithm

1. Sanford Kwinter, *Far from Equilibrium: Essays on Technology and Design Culture*, ed. Cynthia Davidson (Barcelona: Actar, 2008), 51.

2. Generally speaking, an algorithm is a set of instructions that when executed achieves a result. According to David Berlinski, "an algorithm is a finite procedure, written in a fixed symbolic vocabulary, governed by precise instructions, moving in discrete steps, 1, 2, 3, whose execution requires no insight, cleverness, intuition, intelligence, or perspicuity, and that sooner or later comes to an end." David Berlinski, *The Advent of the Algorithm: The Ideas that Rule the World* (New York: Harcourt, 2000), 9. For a challenging definition of the notion of algorithm outside the field

of computer science and within the critical study of software, see Andrew Goffey, "Algorithm," in Matthew Fuller, ed., *Software Studies: A Lexicon* (Cambridge, MA: MIT Press, 2008), 15–20. As Goffey observes: "Certainly the formal quality of the algorithm as a logically consistent construction bears with it an enormous power particularly in the techno-scientific universe—but there is sufficient equivocation about the purely formal nature of this construct to allow us to understand that there is more to the algorithm than logically consistent form" (19). In this chapter, we will address the internal inconsistencies of the logically consistent form of the algorithm that really subtend the formation of programming cultures. The computation or the mathematical formalization of physical and biological realities cannot proceed without internal gaps in the process of calculations. These gaps are represented by incomputable algorithms that result from counting, calculating, rationalizing, formalizing, and axiomatizing. In the context of this book's argument, such incomputable ciphers mark the internal labyrinths of each and every actual object-entity.

3. In recent years, these generative capacities have captivated a renewed interest in analog computing, DNA computing, and quantum computing. These areas of computational research focus on nonbinary models of material self-organization, and particularly on biological evolutionary processes. While digital computers represent changing quantities incrementally, according to the alteration of the numerical values concerned, analog computing is directly based on the continuously changing aspects of physical phenomena (e.g., electrical, mechanical, and hydraulic quantities) and uses them to model problems. Similarly, DNA computing uses biochemistry and molecular biology to model problems: it uses the many different molecules of DNA to try different possibilities at once. On DNA computing, see Leonard M. Adleman, "Molecular Computation of Solutions to Combinatorial Problems," *Science* 266, no. 11 (1994), 1021–1024, http://www.usc.edu/dept/molecular-science/papers/fp-sci94.pdf (last accessed January 2012). Quantum computing, however, makes direct use of the phenomena of quantum mechanics, such as superposition and entanglement. A quantum algorithm, for instance, is a step-by-step procedure that is performed on a quantum computer, but which is faster than a digital algorithmic procedure. Michael Nielsen and Isaac Chuang, *Quantum Computation and Quantum Information* (Cambridge: Cambridge University Press, 2000).

4. Information theorist Gregory Chaitin defines metabiology as "a field parallel to biology that studies the random evolution of artificial software (computer programs) rather than natural software (DNA), and that is sufficiently simple to permit rigorous proofs or at least heuristic arguments as convincing as those that are employed in theoretical physics." Gregory J. Chaitin, "Metaphysics, Metamathematics and Metabiology," in Hector Zenil, ed., *Randomness through Computation: Some Answers, More Questions* (Singapore: World Scientific Publishing, 2011), 100.

5. Generative algorithms specifically refer to the capacity of rules to evolve over time. Another term that defines this capacity is "genetic algorithm." John Holland

invented genetic algorithms (GAs) in the 1960s to find optimal solutions to searching problems by "growing" a population of possibilities. This design technique, which can be found at the core of digital architecture, is based on neo-Darwinian models of evolution. In particular, Dawkins's conceptual device of the "blind watchmaker" algorithm suggests that the evolution of forms cannot be simply derived from the random mutation of simple genetic instructions; importantly, this evolution derives from nonrandom cumulative selection, which leads to the development of complex shapes called biomorphs. The latter are complex sets of genes. Similarly, genetic algorithms perform the same operations on the population of possible targets, and only those that fit the solution have a chance of survival. Despite the lack of formal definition of genetic algorithms, it is generally accepted that they correspond to at least four principles: (1) the population of chromosomes, which represent the possible solutions of the problem; (2) selection based on the fitness function that determines good solutions; (3) selection applied to each generation produced; (4) crossover or genetic exchange of the characteristics of those groups that have been selected, i.e., reproductive filiation leading to the emergence of new offspring. See John Holland, *Adaptation in Natural and Artificial Systems* (Ann Arbor: University of Michigan Press, 1975). See also Richard Dawkins, *The Blind Watchmaker* (New York: W. W. Norton, 1986); Luciana Parisi, "Symbiotic Architecture: Prehending Digitality," *Theory, Culture and Society* 26, nos. 2–3 (March-May 2009), 346–374.

6. See Gregory J. Chaitin, "Evolution of Mutating Software," *Bulletin of the European Association for Theoretical Computer Science*, no. 97 (February 2009), 157–164; also available at http://www.umcs.maine.edu/~chaitin/ev.html (last accessed January 2012).

7. Kwinter, *Far from Equilibrium*, 51.

8. It is important to specify here that the ontological enquiry into the relation between information and matter has derived from a critical reading of the history of cybernetics and computation. In particular, the cultural relevance of the ontological assumptions implicit in these relatively new sciences was more specifically systematized during the 1990s. However, we can find the legacy of these histories in experimental studies of structural dynamics since the '60s, for instance in art and architecture, as discussed in the next chapters.

9. By "axioms," I mean mathematical postulates. See the glossary.

10. Félix Guattari, *Chaosmosis: An Ethico-Aesthetic Paradigm*, trans. Paul Bains and Julian Pefanis (Bloomington: Indiana University Press, 1995).

11. For a recent reading of Guattari's notion of metamodeling and diagrammatics, see Janell Watson, *Guattari's Diagrammatic Thought: Writing between Lacan and Deleuze* (London: Continuum, 2009).

12. In *The Guattari Reader*, ed. Gary Genosko (Oxford: Blackwell, 1996), 12.

13. It may be interesting to note that the example of asignifying semiotics Guattari most frequently used was that of the virtual particles of contemporary theoretical physics. As these particles are theoretically formed and only discovered through mathematics, rather than through empirical experimentation, and are not directly detectable, they can only be experienced through their effects. Guattari then insisted that if physical particles can be formed solely theoretically, as in mathematics, then the relation between theory and practice, between sign systems and physical entities, needed to be rethought. This meant that nature was not prior to the sign. Theoretical physicists name particles that do not directly correspond to what exists in nature. Guattari therefore challenged the idea of nature as an ontological ground. Instead, what is prior to nature is the machinic or diagrammatic process, which produces nature anew. Félix Guattari, *Molecular Revolution: Psychiatry and Politics*, trans. Rosemary Sheed (Harmondsworth, UK: Penguin, 1984), 125. From this standpoint, the theoretical invention of physical particles is an example of a diagrammatic, metamodeling process. See also Janell Watson, "Schizoanalysis and Metamodeling," *Fibreculture Journal*, no. 12 (2008), available at http://twelve.fibreculturejournal.org (last accessed January 2012).

14. Guattari, *Molecular Revolution*, 12.

15. Lev Manovich, for instance, argues more explicitly that the aesthetic of new media corresponds to an aesthetic of mixing and remixing, by extending montage theory into the realm of the computer graphical user interface (GUI). Lev Manovich, *The Language of New Media* (Cambridge, MA: MIT Press, 2001). See also Lev Manovich, *Software Takes Command*, book draft, 2008, available to download at http://lab.softwarestudies.com/2008/11/softbook.html (last accessed January 2012).

16. By axiomatic computation I mean a computation based on axioms or postulates.

17. By axiomatic method, I mean the replacement of a coherent body of propositions (i.e., a mathematical theory) by a simpler collection of propositions (i.e., axioms). The coherent body of propositions is then deduced from the axioms. See the glossary.

18. This notion of prehension is borrowed from Alfred North Whitehead, who rejected the view that notions of perception and cognition might be able to describe how actual entities enter into relation with one another, and how they are able to select eternal objects: infinite ideas. The last part of this chapter will present a more extensive explanation of this term in the context of computational aesthetics.

19. Evolutionary algorithms are a subset of evolutionary and generative computing and are inspired by mechanisms of biological evolution, based in particular on Darwinian and post-Darwinian models (such as those developed by Richard Dawkins; see note 5 above). Algorithms are designed to select, recombine, and mutate data. In particular, rules for selection are determined by the fitness functions that algo-

rithms perform in a set environment. With genetic or evolutionary algorithms, the optimization of solutions to given computational problems is thought to be faster and closer to the proper evolutionary dynamics of matter. However, much debate about the use of genetic and evolutionary algorithms in artificial intelligence systems is concerned with the capacity to model through optimization, rather than through chance. In other words, evolutionary computation can be seen as yet another attempt to simulate the biophysical dynamics of matter, and thus to bind unforeseen potentialities into sets of probabilities. In contrast, one can also suggest that evolutionary computation does not solely follow the potentiality of material forms or processes so as to model them, but is rather inventing these forms altogether, and thus placing the machinic process of construction before the preexistence of natural (biophysical) materiality. I have written about the limits of the evolutionary model of computation and of the evolutionary algorithm elsewhere in Parisi, "Symbiotic Architecture."

20. See Karl Chu, "Metaphysics of Genetic Architecture and Computation," *Architectural Design* 76, no. 4 (July-August 2006), 39.

21. See Mark Hansen, *Bodies in Code: Interfaces with Digital Media* (London: Routledge, 2006), 177. Hansen argues that Peter Eisenman's "Virtual House" explains the limitation of the notion of the virtual to the extent to which vector modelization yields a spatial form containing a field of forces that need to be actualized as affects through embodied inhabitation. Only the interaction of physicalities with algorithmic computation promises that space can be generated or actualized. In particular, Hansen explicitly draws on Pierre Lévy's notion of "actualization of the virtual" and Timothy Murray's concept of "embodied virtualization," which have proposed that physical experience or physical space adds novelty and variation to computational calculations which would otherwise remain limited to eternal form. In particular, much critical reading of new media has ended up establishing a regime of phenomenal analysis based on the notion of affect, which has been widely used to articulate what is meant by haptic interaction.

22. Ibid., 178.

23. For instance, Christina Moeller's *Particles* (Science Museum, London, 2000) is a projected cabinet of cinematic memories that creates silhouettes of observing visitors in the form of glowing animated particles, which these same visitors can manipulate while moving around the screen. The project depicts a continual relationship between this technologically mediated space and the people that visit it. Similarly, Scott Snibbe's *Deep Walls* (2003) portrays shadows through bodily interaction by exposing the interdependence of individuals and their environments. Most of Snibbe's projects do not function unless viewers actively engage with them by touching, breathing, or moving in their vicinity. As perception remains unmediated here, people are invited to actively participate by constructing the meaning of the interaction through a process of physical awareness. His works appear to reward

viewers with an immediate, visceral sense of presence. *Deep Walls* collects the viewer's shadows on a retroreflective screen. Their movements are projections, played back repeatedly to offer records of movement within the space. A computer tracks the movement of people and processes their image using custom software, which then generates the projection by gradually absorbing the contents of the environment and playing them back to the viewers. Lucy Bullivant, "Playing with Art" and "Shadow Play: The Participative Art of Scott Snibbe," *Architectural Design* 77, no. 4 (July-August 2007), 32–33, 68–78.

24. See David Hilbert, "The New Grounding of Mathematics: First Report," in W. B. Ewald, ed., *From Kant to Hilbert: A Source Book in the Foundations of Mathematics*, vol. 2 (New York: Oxford University Press, 1996), 1115–1133; Rebecca Goldstein, *Incompleteness: The Proof and Paradox of Kurt Gödel* (New York: W. W. Norton, 2005); Kurt Gödel, "Some Basic Theorems on the Foundations of Mathematics and Their Implications," in Gödel, *Collected Works*, ed. Solomon Feferman et al., vol. 3 (New York: Oxford University Press, 1995), 304–323.

25. Alan M. Turing, "On Computable Numbers, with an Application to the *Entscheidungsproblem*," *Proceedings of the London Mathematical Society*, 2nd ser., 42 (1936), 230–265. For further discussion of the intersections of the works of Hilbert, Gödel, and Turing, see Martin Davis, *The Universal Computer: The Road from Leibniz to Turing* (New York: W. W. Norton, 2000), 83–176.

26. *Mathesis universalis* defines a universal science modeled on mathematics and supported by the *calculus ratiocinator*, a universal calculation described by Leibniz as a universal conceptual language. For first-order cybernetics the calculus ratiocinator refers to the computational machine that could perform differential and integral calculus or the combination of the ratios. As Norbert Wiener pointed out: "like his predecessor Pascal, [Leibniz] was interested in the construction of computing machines in Metal. . . . Just as the calculus of arithmetic lends itself to a mechanization progressing through the abacus and the desk computing machine to the ultra-rapid computing machines of the present day, so the *calculus ratiocinator* of Leibniz contains the germs of the *machina ratiocinatrix*, the reasoning machine." See Norbert Wiener, *Cybernetics, or Control and Communication in the Animal and the Machine* (Cambridge, MA: MIT Press, 1965), 12.

27. A clearer explanation of the implications of Gödel's theorem of incompleteness for Turing's emphasis on the limit of computation can be found in Gregory Chaitin, *Meta Math! The Quest for Omega* (New York: Pantheon, 2005), 29–32.

28. This project can be viewed at http://www.runme.org/project/+forkbomb/ (last accessed January 2012).

29. For a historical overview of the problem of computation in relation to first-order cybernetics and the development of an autopoietic conception of order out of chaos, see N. Katherine Hayles, *How We Became Posthuman* (Chicago: University of Chicago

Press, 1999), chap. 6; N. Katherine Hayles, *My Mother Was a Computer: Digital Subjects and Literary Texts* (Chicago: University of Chicago Press, 2005); Andrew Pickering, *The Cybernetic Brain: Sketches of Another Future* (Chicago: University of Chicago Press, 2010).

30. The notion of negentropy was used by Schrödinger to describe how living systems do not simply avoid the effects of entropy (the tendency toward dissipation and heat death) but also use entropy to increase organization, thus turning energy into useful information. See Ho Mae-Wan, "What Is (Schrödinger's) Negentropy?," *Modern Trends in BioThermoKinetics*, no. 3 (1994), 50–61.

31. As Chaitin points out, "The idea of choosing to add more axioms is not an alien one to mathematics. A well-known example is the parallel postulate in Euclidean geometry: given a line and a point not on the line, there is exactly one line that can be drawn through the point that never intersects the original line. For centuries geometers wondered whether that result could be proved using the rest of Euclid's axioms. It could not. Finally, mathematicians realized that they could substitute different axioms in place of the Euclidean version, thereby producing the non-Euclidean geometries of curved spaces, such as the surface of a sphere or of a saddle." Gregory Chaitin, "The Limits of Reason," *Scientific American* 294, no. 3 (March 2006), 74–81.

32. The definition of the halting probability is based on the existence of prefix-free universal computable functions, defining a programming language with the property that no valid program can be obtained as a proper extension of another valid program. In other words, prefix-free codes are defined as random or incompressible information. Chaitin, *Meta Math!*, 130–131, 57.

33. Chaitin explains that his Ω (Omega) number is a probability (albeit an infinite number) for a program to halt. "First, I must specify how to pick a program at random. A program is simply a series of bits, so flip a coin to determine the value of each bit. How many bits long should the program be? Keep flipping the coin so long as the computer is asking for another bit of input. Ω is just the probability that the machine will eventually come to a halt when supplied with a stream of random bits in this fashion." At the same time, however, he also points out that Omega is incomputable, and thus the problem of the limit of computation remains unsolvable for a formal axiomatic system. "We can be sure that Ω cannot be computed because knowing Ω would let us solve Turing's halting problem, but we know that this problem is unsolvable." In other words, "Given any finite program, no matter how many billions of bits long, we have an infinite number of bits that the program cannot compute. Given any finite set of axioms, we have an infinite number of truths that are improvable in that system. Because Ω is irreducible, we can immediately conclude that a theory of everything for all of mathematics cannot exist. An infinite number of bits of Ω constitute mathematical facts (whether each bit is a 0 or a 1) that cannot be derived from any principles simpler than the string of bits

itself. Mathematics therefore has infinite complexity." Chaitin, "The Limits of Reason," 74–81.

34. A real number is used to measure continuous quantities, which can be represented with decimals that have an infinite sequence of digits. It may be rational or irrational (such as the square root of 2 or π), algebraic or transcendental. It can be positive, negative, or equivalent to zero. A real number is said to be *computable* if there exists an algorithm that yields its digits. Because there are only countably many algorithms but an uncountable number of reals, almost all real numbers are not computable. Chaitin, *Meta Math!*, 95–96.

35. It may be important to remind the reader that Gregory Chaitin's notion of an incomputable limit is influenced by the nineteenth-century physicist Ludwig Boltzmann, who defined entropy as a measurement of the degree of disorder, chaos, and randomness in any physical system. For instance, a crystal has low entropy, whereas gas at room temperature has high entropy. Chaitin points out that the notion of entropy is strictly connected with fundamental philosophical questions: why does time run in just one direction? Why is there a tendency in the universe to run out of equilibrium? Boltzmann's theory explained that entropy (or, in the terms of information theory, noise or interference) in a system tended to increase. Boltzmann's gas theory stated that an arrow of time determined the direction of a system, which started off in an ordered state and ended up in a disordered state: an increasing heat death. Chaitin, *Meta Math!*, 170. While the second law of thermodynamics uses entropy to measure the variations leading to the final state of a system, Chaitin uses entropy to explain mathematical computation in terms of randomness or incompressible information. He claims that the complex size of a computer program coincides with the degree of disorder of a physical system. A gas may require a large program to say where all its atoms are located, whereas a crystal will require a smaller program because of its regular structure. In this sense, entropy and program-size complexity are, for Chaitin, closely related. This nonconcise relation is, however, a challenge to formal mathematics. What if, Chaitin asks, the most concise program for reproducing a given body of experimental data is the same size as the data set itself? Similarly, one could wonder: What if the algorithmic program used to generate and manipulate data, the computational power at the core of software design, is not simpler than the data produced, but instead has the same size, the same infinite complexity of what is generated? Ibid., 169–170.

36. Ingeborg M. Rocker, "When Code Matters," *Architectural Design* 76, no. 4 (July-August 2006), 16–25.

37. Ibid., 25.

38. Neoplasmatic design is inspired by the exploration and manipulation of actual biological material. In particular, it draws on molecular biology, biotechnology, and nanotechnology for architectural and design practices. See *Architectural Design* 78,

no. 6 (October 2008), special issue "Neoplasmatic Design," ed. Marcos Cruz and Steve Pike.

39. See Kas Oosterhuis, Mark David Hosale, Chris Kievid, Veronika Laszlo, and Remko Siemerink, "InteractiveWall: Prototype for an Emotive Wall," available at http://bk.tudelft.nl/index.php?id=16045&L=1/ (last accessed January 2012).

40. Ibid.

41. See the documentation of the *InteractiveWall* project at http://www.hyperbody.nl/index.php?id=51 (last accessed January 2012).

42. As visionary architect John M. Johansen comments: "As we move into the future, the field of molecular engineering represents a new frontier for architecture. In the process of computer coding, buildings will be designed to grow and perform just as living organisms directed by their built-in DNA." Johansen, *Nanoarchitecture: A New Species of Architecture* (New York: Princeton Architectural Press, 2002), 23.

43. The invention of the scanning tunneling microscope led to the discovery in 1985 of fullerenes and carbon nanotubes. Fullerenes are completely inorganic molecules entirely composed of carbon. Their architectural structures are similar to that of R. Buckminster Fuller's geodesic dome. The discovery of the structure of nanocrystals, nanoparticles, and quantum dots also contributed to define the field of nanotechnology. See Steve Pike, "Manipulation and Control of Micro-Organic Matter in Architecture," *Architectural Design* 78, no. 6 (October 2008), 16–24.

44. See Rachel Armstrong, "Designer Material for Architecture," *Architectural Design* 78, no. 6 (October 2008), 87.

45. Weiser has insisted that if ubiquitous computing were to embrace the age of calm technology, it would be necessary to draw a distinction between "seamless" and "seamful" systems. Whereas "seamless" computing would tend toward the integration of all information components for the sake of smooth compatibility, "seamful" media instead would maintain the unique characteristics of each tool, so that the user's interaction with the computed system could include the uncertainty of the potential creativity afforded by the tool. The seamful interaction would ergonomically adapt to the capacities of cognition, perception, and action afforded or mediated by computed sensory-equipped systems, transducers, and actuators. Weiser, however, also pointed at an entirely "intuitive" set of devices that could be used without us knowing about the algorithmic structure of computers or being programmers. These intuitive devices would allow the user to be creative and to experiment with the device beyond its functions. It is precisely this appeal to intuition and creativity that has defined the use of smart media today, even though the algorithmic structure is hidden in the background. Mark Weiser, "Some Computer Design Issues in Ubiquitous Computing," *Communications of the ACM* 36, no. 7 (July 1993), 75–84.

46. Friedrich Kittler, "The History of Communication Media," *Ctheory*, special issue: ga114 (1996), http://www.ctheory.net/articles.aspx?id=45 (last accessed January 2012).

47. For a description of ubiquitous computing for smart building, smart furniture, and smart clothing, see Adam Greenfield, *Everyware: The Dawning Age of Ubiquitous Computing* (Berkeley: New Riders, 2006).

48. Manovich explains that the research works of J. C. R. Licklider, Ivan Sutherland, Ted Nelson, Douglas Engelbart, Seymour Papert, Nicholas Negroponte, and Alan Kay constituted a pivotal moment in the 1980s and 1990s for the ingression of software into media, which transformed the computer into a "remediator of other media." Drawing on Alan Kay, Manovich argues that the computer is a metamedium: a "computer metamedium is simultaneously a set of different media and a system for generating new media tools and new types of media. In other words, a computer can be used to create new tools for working in the media it already provides as well as to develop new not-yet-invented media." Manovich, *Software Takes Command*, 80–81.

49. "Ergonomics" derives from the Greek *ergon*, work, and *nomos*, distribution, arrangement, management. Ergonomics is the science of mental and physical work. Classically, ergonomics stands for the applied science of equipment design in the workplace, which aims at maximizing productivity by optimally adapting the designed environment to the mental, behavioral, and physical states of the worker. Ergonomics was born out of concerns with human-computer interaction and human-computer interface. It has been defined as a biotechnology, and includes human engineering and human factors engineering which study the neural bases of human perception, cognition, and performance in relation to systems and technologies. Of particular importance is the new field of neuroergonomics as theorized in Raja Parasuraman, "Neuroergonomics: Research and Practice," *Theoretical Issues in Ergonomics Science* 4 (2003), 5–20; and Raja Parasuraman and Matthew Rizzo, *Neuroergonomics: The Brain at Work* (Oxford: Oxford University Press, 2007).

50. Take for instance one of the first experiments in ubiquitous design, the *Media Cup* (1999): a cup with hidden electronics inside its rubber base. The *Media Cup* was based on an implicit form of interaction that required no user input into the computer system. The input came instead from the collaboration of cups with other objects that were embedded with other computer systems. Devices such as the coffee machine, for instance, could learn and profit from knowing the habits of coffee consumption. Hence, the user, who remained a component part of the computational architecture of smart objects, required no extra effort or learning. Another example of ubiquitous media architecture was developed by Kent Larson of the MIT Media Lab: an interactive habitat known as *PlaceLab*, which had sensors that were able to process the resulting data stream by recognizing the activities of the habitat's occupants. William J. Mitchell, "After the Revolution: Instruments of Displace-

ment," in Georg Flachbart and Peter Weibel, eds., *Disappearing Architecture: From Real to Virtual to Quantum* (Basel: Birkhäuser, 2005), 23.

51. Weiser's vision of ubiquitous computing proposed an increment of computer objects throughout the physical environment by making them effectively invisible. In this view, new waves of almost invisible user-sensitive, semi-intelligent, knowledge-based electronics and software are in a perfect position to merge with individual biological brains. Ubiquitous computing coincides with the age of calm technology, when technology recedes into the background of our lives and becomes utterly transparent. See Weiser, "Some Computer Design Issues in Ubiquitous Computing," 75–84.

52. Ibid., 80.

53. Manovich has recently emphasized the importance of articulating the historical roots of software studies as autonomous from computer science and the cultural studies of technosciences. In particular, in his attempt to reconstruct this scholarly history, he refers to the pioneering work of computer designer Alan Kay. See Lev Manovich, "Alan Kay's Universal Media Machine," *Northern Lights* 5 (2007), 39–56. See also Alan Kay, "The Reactive Engine," doctoral thesis, Electrical Engineering and Computer Science, University of Utah, 1969.

54. A software object is a discrete bundle of functions and procedures based on discrete units of programming logic. An object-oriented program is conceived as a set of interacting objects, as opposed to the conventional model of programming which tends to be understood as a list of tasks or subroutines to be performed or executed. In object-oriented programming, each object is capable of receiving messages, processing data, and sending messages to other objects. Each object can be viewed as an independent "machine" with a distinct role or responsibility. Among object-oriented software, Smalltalk is considered a pure object-oriented software language since it uses no run-time binding, which means that nothing about the type of object concerned need be known before a Smalltalk program is run. See Manovich, *Software Takes Command*, 77. See also Cecile Crutzen and Erna Kotkamp, "Object Orientation," in Fuller, *Software Studies*, 200–205.

55. See Manovich, *Software Takes Command*, 12.

56. Friedrich Kittler, *Literature, Media, Information Systems*, ed. John Johnston (Amsterdam: Overseas Publishers Association, 1997), 127. The study of the relation between information machines and strategies of war is also at the center of Paul Virilio's work. See Paul Virilio, *War and Cinema: The Logistics of Perception* (London: Verso, 1989).

57. Kittler, *Literature, Media, Information Systems*, 126.

58. It is important to highlight that the invention of digital computation in the 1940s was not only geared toward military use but also to business calculations and

data processing. For instance, the invention of the first computer program LEO I, developed by J. Lyons and Co., was used by a commercial business, which needed to calculate vast amounts of inputs through very simple calculations in order to obtain quick information about the rate of profit and loss of tea sales in a short amount of time. See Peter Bird, *LEO—The First Business Computer* (2002), available at David Lawrence's Lyons Web site http://www.kzwp.com/lyons/leo (last accessed January 2012).

59. On the history of cybernetics and automated computation as entangled in strategies of war, see Manuel DeLanda, *War in the Age of Intelligent Machines* (New York: Zone Books, 1991), 46.

60. For further readings on the development of object-oriented software and its expansion toward the production of social software, see Matthew Fuller, *Behind the Blip: Essays on the Culture of Software* (Brooklyn, NY: Autonomedia, 2003).

61. For instance, see Wendy Chun, *Control and Freedom: Power and Paranoia in the Age of Fiber Optics* (Cambridge, MA: MIT Press, 2006). See also Alexander Galloway, *Protocol: How Control Exists after Decentralization* (Cambridge, MA: MIT Press, 2004).

62. Paul Virilio discussed the import of the information bomb for new understanding of culture in *The Information Bomb* (London: Verso, 2000).

63. Mark Weiser and John Seely Brown, "Designing Calm Technology," Xerox PARC (21 December 1995), available at http://www.ubiq.com/hypertext/weiser/calmtech/calmtech.htm (last accessed January 2012).

64. See Lucy Bullivant, *Responsive Environments: Architecture, Art and Design* (London: V&A, 2006).

65. Ibid,. 5.

66. Ibid., 6.

67. Ibid., 7.

68. See Lucy Bullivant, "Alice in the Technoland," *Architectural Design* 77, no. 4 (2007), 7–10.

69. See Lucy Bullivant, "Physical-Virtual Communication," in Bullivant, *Responsive Environments*, 72–73.

70. In mathematics, a Voronoi diagram is a special kind of decomposition of a metric space determined by distances to a specified discrete set of objects within the space, e.g., determined by a discrete set of points or by isolated points. It was named after Georgii Voronoi, who defined and studied *n* dimensions in 1908. In the case of general metric spaces, the cells are often called metric fundamental polygons. See http://demonstrations.wolfram.com/VoronoiDiagrams/ (last accessed January 2012).

71. ONL, "Digital Pavilion Korea, Sampang-dong, Seoul, South Korea, 2006," *Architectural Design* 77, no. 4 (2007), 49.

72. See John Lobell, "The Milgo Experiment: An Interview with Haresh Lalvani," *Architectural Design* 76, no. 4 (July-August 2006), 57.

73. As Lalvani explains "At the first level is the genomic concept, a meta-algorithm, which defines a family of interrelated, intertransforming, shapes tied to a fabrication process. At the second level is a computational algorithm of developable surfaces, surfaces that can be formed from flat sheets by bending without deforming." Ibid., 58.

74. Ibid.

75. Ibid.

76. Fredkin's famous paper "Finite Nature" argues for a pancomputational metaphysics, whereby the simple law of algorithmic calculation can explain all kinds of objects, worlds, and entities. The classical question "Are things smooth or grainy?" is based on the assumption that at some scale space and time are discrete, and that the number of possible states of every finite volume of space-time is finite; Fredkin here assumes that there is nothing that is smooth or continuous. Thus, contrary to Leibniz, he states that there are no infinitesimal relations between objects. See Edward Fredkin, "Finite Nature," Proceedings of the XXVIIth Rencontre de Moriond (1992), available at the Web site "Digital Philosophy" http://www.digitalphilosophy.org/Home/Papers/FiniteNature/tabid/106/Default.aspx (last accessed January 2012).

77. According to Parmenides, novelty is mere illusion. Existence is eternal, immutable, and imperishable, whereas change is an appearance. Change misleads the real through sensory perception. From this standpoint, novelty does not exist because nothing comes from nothing. Existence is one continuous indivisible plenum. Similarly, his discussion of Zeno's paradoxes claims that it is impossible for novelty to exist because all existence flows eternally.

78. See Stephen Wolfram, *A New Kind of Science* (Champaign, IL: Wolfram Media, 2002).

79. See Stephen Wolfram, "How Do Simple Programs Behave?," *Architectural Design* 76, no. 4 (July-August 2006), 35.

80. Among some of the critiques that have been leveled against Wolfram's digital philosophy is the view that cellular automata do not evolve above one level of complexity. The cells can create complex patterns, but those patterns cannot become the primitives for a next level of complexity. Despite the claims of Luc Steels, who held that he was able to use primitive levels for a next level complexity, much of the argument remains still open. Wolfram's atomic view of a computational universe depends on the evolution of complexity, which, it has been suggested, does not

show actual physical mechanisms at work. Katherine Hayles instead believes that Wolfram and Fredkin do not pay enough attention to the connection between digital and analog processes. This relation, she contends, is like the DNA code (digital) needing protein folding (analog) to get anywhere. See Hayles, *My Mother Was a Computer*, 130.

81. Lobell, "The Milgo Experiment," 58.

82. Ibid.

83. In 1968, the biologist Aristid Lindenmayer founded an axiomatic theory of biological development called L-systems. These systems are designed to rewrite the rules that define complex objects by successively replacing their parts. Since the rewriting can be carried out recursively, L-systems have been used in computer graphics to generate fractals and to realistically model plants. In computer science, rewriting systems, which operate on character strings, have been heavily influenced by Chomsky's work on formal grammars, which were applied sequentially in a linear fashion. Lindenmayer instead introduced a new type of string-rewriting mechanism (L-systems) based on parallel productions able to simultaneously replace all letters in a given word. Out of these parallel mechanisms, inspired by simultaneous and multiple cell divisions in multicellular organisms, new formal languages (or L-systems) were developed in computer science. See Przemyslaw Prusinkiewicz and Astrid Lindenmayer, *The Algorithmic Beauty of Plants* (New York: Springer, 1990). Wolfram defines Lindenmayer or L-systems as a string-rewriting system that can be used to generate fractals with dimension between 1 and 2. For examples of L-systems see http://mathworld.wolfram.com/LindenmayerSystem.html. For a quick overview of L-systems see Gabriela Ochoa, "An Introduction to Lindenmayer Systems," http://www.biologie.uni-hamburg.de/b-online/e28_3/lsys.html (last accessed January 2012).

84. See Neil Leach, "Swarm Urbanism," *Architectural Design* 79, no. 4 (July-August 2009), 50–56.

85. The concept of suprarationality is inspired by Gaston Bachelard's notion of surrationalism, which takes as its point of departure Poincaré's subjectivism and Lobachevsky's new geometry. Bachelard conceived of sciences as constructive "phenomeno-technologies" based on his analysis of the epistemological revolution in theoretical physics at the beginning of the twentieth century. After the publication of *The New Scientific Spirit* (1934), he was invited to contribute to the inaugural issue of the surrealists' review *Inquisitions*, where he welcomed surrealism in a short piece entitled "Le surrationalisme" which explored some epistemological links between the sciences and the arts. Here he drew an analogy between how the surrealists employed poetic freedom in order to acquire perceptual fluidity and how experimental rationality organized reality. According to Bachelard, the crucial aspect of both art and science is less their creativity per se than their potential for changing reality, i.e., their experimentalism. However, Bachelard's notion of experimentation

aimed at exploring the nature of reason. Reason in his view is not absolute, but multifarious and living: it is experimental, and thus open to revision. Together with Bachelard's surrationalism, Whitehead's notion of speculative reason contributes toward explaining the suprarationality that refers to the autonomous realities of an incomputable "surlogic." The latter does not aim at restating the dialectical relation between rationality and irrationality, cognition and emotion, thought and feeling, but at the same time it does not fuse the reality of automated space with the reality of biophysical matter. Gaston Bachelard, *The New Scientific Spirit*, trans. Arthur Goldhammer (Boston: Beacon Press, 1984). For a closer explanation of speculative reason, see the last section of this chapter.

86. See Chaitin, *Meta Math!*, 92, 100, 115.

87. See Branden Hookway and Chris Perry, "Responsive Systems/Appliance Architectures," *Architectural Design* 76, no. 5 (2006), 75.

88. See Leach, "Swarm Urbanism," 58.

89. Drawing on Leibniz, Chaitin writes about the labyrinth of the continuum. He argues that transcendental numbers, or real numbers that are nondenumerable, are not intuitively experienceable as percepts and affects, but instead have a probability of one, and so can be self-delimiting computables. See Chaitin, *Meta Math!*, 96–97, 109–110.

90. As Cache points out, "In fact, the modification of calculation parameters allows the manufacture of a different shape for each object in the same series. Thus unique objects are produced industrially. We will call variable objects created from surfaces 'subjectiles,' and variable objects created from volumes 'objectiles.'" Bernard Cache, *Earth Moves: The Furnishing of Territories* (Cambridge, MA: MIT Press, 1995), 88. Greg Lynn instead conceives of objects in terms of blobs: "The image, morphology, and behavior of the blob present a sticky, viscous, mobile composite entity capable of incorporating disparate external elements into itself." Greg Lynn, *Folds, Bodies and Blobs: Collected Essays* (Brussels: Bibliothèque Royale de Belgique, 2004), 170.

91. Greg Lynn, *Animate Form* (New York: Princeton Architectural Press, 1999), 30.

92. Greg Lynn and Bernard Cache use the notion of differential relations as theorized by Gilles Deleuze in *The Fold*. The notion of the differential is derived here from Leibniz's monadic metaphysics according to which the relations between worlds, mathematically conceived as unities, are defined by infinitesimal points, transcendental numbers that do not correspond to algebraic unities, and rational numbers. In chapter 2, Lynn's folding architecture will be explained and problematized in relation to Deleuze's differential, whereby it will be shown to be an instance of the now-dominant aesthetic of curvature and topological continuity.

93. Lynn, *Animate Form*, 17.

94. In particular, Harman argues against the phenomenological conception of objects. He observes: "Instead of the chair being nothing more than an ideal principle unifying all the ways in which the chair can appear over time, Merleau-Ponty seems to regard the chair as the sum total of the way it is 'perceived' by me, the chimney, the candle, the grandfather clock, and the dog." Graham Harman, *Guerrilla Metaphysics: Phenomenology and the Carpentry of Things* (Chicago: Open Court, 2005), 51–52.

95. In the theoretical and practical field of architecture, the adaptation of Deleuze's (and Deleuze and Guattari's) metaphysics of assemblage, becoming, and the self-differentiation of matter is evidenced by many publications in the last ten years. One cannot overlook the fact that Alain Badiou's problematization of this metaphysics is present in the critique of architecture's tendency toward an organic model of form in the computational design of building and urban planning. Badiou's critique of Deleuze's conception of the virtual shows that the notion of multiplicity remains locked on the ground of an infinitely self-reproducing One, reifying the vitalism of the Whole. While there is no space to develop this argument here, it is important to state that Badiou's accusation of vitalism overlooks Deleuze's and Deleuze and Guattari's emphasis on the primacy of machinic heterogeneities defined by their schizo relations (and not symmetric unity) of thoughts and things, whether animate or inanimate. Thus events and multiplicity are here of an undividable nature, and yet as discrete unities, singularities, or ideas they remain ungrounded in a whole. Badiou's political philosophy of the event and the subject of the event would instead always already disqualify the automaton of machinic processes, and would instead reinstate the superiority of the political (or human) subject in the auto-orderings of matter. See Alain Badiou, *The Clamor of Being* (Minneapolis: University of Minnesota Press, 1999), 9–18, 43–54. See also Badiou, *Being and Event* (London: Continuum, 2005), 23–30. Object-oriented metaphysics instead contests Deleuze and Guattari's model of the heterogeneous constitution of objects, things, and events, which represents an ontological disqualification of discreteness—and of actual events—in favor of the superiority of analog processes, by which discrete things are eventuated. I will indirectly address this critique by engaging with Whitehead's metaphysics of processes and forms of processes. From this standpoint, actual entities or objects are intrinsically composed of incomputable parts that are selected in the process of individuation of an object. These parts deploy the presence of infinite quantities in each and any object. This will help us to argue that the incomplete nature of algorithmic architecture forces us to think of the computational object not only in terms of the qualities that it has and by which it becomes, but also as regards the infinite quantities that cannot be contained by it.

96. Harman, *Guerrilla Metaphysics*, 82–83.

97. Ibid., 68.

98. Ibid., 70.

99. Ibid., 3, 19–20.

100. Ibid., 93.

101. Ibid.

102. Ibid., 83.

103. Inspired by the phenomenology of Husserl, Harman distinguishes between real and sensual objects. Whereas Bruno Latour's flat ontology of objects posits all objects on the same plane of reality, Harman insists that there are two kinds of objects. Similarly, he divorces all objects from their qualities and conceives of both real and sensual objects in terms of a unified systematic thing and of a plurality of features. "There are two kinds of objects and two kinds of traits." Graham Harman, *Prince of Networks: Bruno Latour and Metaphysics* (Prahran, Australia: re.press, 2009), 206. An example of a real object is sleeping or dormant entities, or "drops of water at the turbulent face of the ocean, with countless other drops of water beneath but only empty sky above." An example of a sensual object is a tree defined by an "enduring eidetic nucleus that the tree-perception must have in order to be what it is; this is the tree as a unified intentional object." But the qualities of the sensual object can shift from moment to moment: "the tree reflected in a pool, upside down . . . [can] alter the presentation drastically, but . . . [not] change the object giving-act as long as I still believe that the tree is the same old tree as before" (ibid., 198–199). Both real and intentional or sensual objects have an "enduring core object unaffected by transient changes" (ibid., 199). In particular, the word *eidos* in the philosophy of Edmund Husserl is used to mean the subject of the set of predicates that could not be removed from a thing after having submitted it to a process of imaginative variation; or, in short, the essence of a thing.

104. Ibid., 98.

105. Ibid., 215.

106. Harman, *Guerrilla Metaphysics*, 85.

107. I am referring here to recent philosophies of relations, such as Karen Barad's notion of agential realism and intra-action, developed from Bohr's notion of entanglement, which root relationality in the physics of parts and explain how each part is ultimately an agent of relation that is thus defined by what it is related to. See Karen Barad, *Meeting the Universe Halfway: Quantum Physics and the Entanglement of Matter and Meaning* (Durham: Duke University Press, 2007). Most recently, the metaphysics of relation has also been rearticulated in the context of a neovitalist affirmation of inanimate life in terms of physical (quantic) vibrations between things. See Jane Bennet, *Vibrant Matter: A Political Ecology of Things* (Durham: Duke University Press, 2010).

108. Alfred North Whitehead, *Modes of Thought* (New York: Free Press, 1938), 93.

109. Alfred North Whitehead, *Process and Reality* (New York: Free Press, 1978), 73. For instance, a molecule as a moving body experiencing local changes is not an actual occasion, but a nexus of occasions and thus an event.

110. Ibid., 230.

111. Ibid.

112. Hence, to perceive, he suggests, is not to represent an object but rather to enter within the interior plasma of an object. This plasma is autonomous from its qualities, and ultimately describes its own capacities of becoming. Harman, *Guerrilla Metaphysics*, 190.

113. Ibid., 153.

114. Harman, *Prince of Networks*, 181.

115. Whitehead, *Process and Reality*, 109.

116. Taking the example of the Cleopatra Needle's obelisk on the Victoria Embankment in London, Whitehead explains that this object is not historically framed but is an event at every moment, always actively becoming anew. Similarly, each time the Needle is prehended, or encountered by a prehension, it becomes an event (a nexus of occasions). In other words, if the object Cleopatra's Needle is an event, so too are its prehensions. But, at the same time, if an event is an "enduring object," it also persists through time and retains a certain "identity" despite the prehensive events it goes through, because each event also retains "a genetic character inherited through a historic route of actual occasions." On Cleopatra's Needle, see Alfred North Whitehead, *The Concept of Nature* (Amherst, NY: Prometheus Books, 2004), 165ff. On the genetic identity of an event, see *Process and Reality*, 109.

117. Harman, *Prince of Networks*, 190–191.

118. Ibid., 191–192.

119. Harman, *Guerrilla Metaphysics*, 82–83.

120. Whitehead, *Process and Reality*, 22.

121. It may be useful to read this quote here: "The 'formal' constitution of an actual entity is a process of transition from indetermination towards terminal determination. But the indetermination is referent to determinate data. The 'objective' constitution of an actual entity is its terminal determination, considered as a complex of component determinates by reason of which the actual entity is a datum for the creative advance." Whitehead, *Process and Reality*, 45.

122. As Whitehead explains: "Prehensions of actual entities—i.e., prehensions whose data involve actual entities—are termed 'physical prehensions'; and prehensions of eternal objects are termed 'conceptual prehensions.'" Similarly, prehensions

are of two kinds: positive prehensions, also termed feelings, and negative prehensions, which define what is eliminated from feeling. Ibid., 23.

123. Whitehead points out: "The subjective valuation is the work of novel conceptual feeling; and in proportion to its importance, acquired in complex processes of integration and reintegration, this autonomous conceptual element modifies the subjective form throughout the whole range of feeling in that concrescence and thereby guides the integrations." Ibid., 245.

124. Ibid., 24–26.

125. Whitehead clarifies: "The subjective form is determined by the subjective aim at further integration, so as to obtain the 'satisfaction' of the completed subject. In other words, final causation and atomism are interconnected philosophical principles." Ibid., 19.

126. Ibid., 64–65. The significance of the notion of the extensive continuum will be discussed in chapter 2.

127. Ibid., 20.

128. Harman, *Guerrilla Metaphysics*, 82–83.

129. As opposed to the universal and absolute conceptions of space-time, Whitehead argues that the mutual prehension of things defines the very condition for spatiality. For instance, in the concert hall, the mutual prehension of the volume of sound, the forms of instruments, the distribution of the orchestra, the mathematical analysis of each momentary sound, the musical score are all implicated in the experience of an immediate spacious present. See Whitehead, *Modes of Thought*, 84.

130. On this point, Harman criticizes Whitehead for not going far enough with his atomic theory. Harman laments that the internal constitution of an entity seems to remain, for Whitehead, always already derived from every component of external perception.

131. Whitehead, *Modes of Thought*, 86.

132. Ibid., 89.

133. As Whitehead puts it: "Process and individuality require each other. In separation all meaning evaporates. The forms of process (or, in other words, the appetition) derive their character from the individual involved, and the characters of the individual can only be understood in terms of the process in which they are implicated." In other words, Whitehead points to a double movement (and causality) of form and process, which requires actualities to become infected with potentialities, atomic entities to be related by means of potential divisions of their continual relations. See *Modes of Thoughts*, 96–97.

134. Harman also uses his engagement with Latour's metaphysics of objects to show the limits of Whitehead's process metaphysics, which Harman believes to be merely another form of traditional occasionalism because of the central role that eternal objects (or universal qualities) have in Whitehead's philosophy. See *Prince of Networks*, 102, 114.

135. Whitehead, *Process and Reality*, 178.

136. Ibid., 62.

137. Ibid., 72.

138. Levi Bryant, "Being Is Flat: The Strange Mereology of Object-Oriented Ontology," paper presented at the symposium "Object-Oriented Ontology," Georgia Tech, 23 April 2010, http://ooo.gatech.edu/?listen (last accessed January 2012).

139. Whitehead, *Process and Reality*, 29.

140. Ibid.

141. Ibid.

142. Ibid., 44.

143. As Chaitin points out: " Ω [Omega] is an infinite sequence of bits in which there is no pattern, and there are no correlations. Its bits are mathematical facts that cannot be compressed into axioms that are more concise than they are." Chaitin, *Meta Math!*, 76.

144. For instance, Chaitin explains that the Hilbert/Turing/Post formal axiomatic system in information theory corresponds to the universal determination of a program that could generate all the theorems. However, he goes on to suggest that there is no algorithm that could solve Turing's halting problem (one that would decide in advance whether or not a given program ever halts). This means that there could be no formal axiomatic system and no simpler algorithm that could contain the complexity of all the theorems. Chaitin demonstrates that the bits of Omega are "logically irreducible and cannot be obtained from axioms smaller than they are" (ibid., 132). This means that Omega is algorithmically incompressible or irreducible. These incomputable real numbers are well-determinate and have the characteristics of a "random process," meaning that it is unpredictable as much as its quantities are infinite (ibid., 130–133).

145. As Chaitin claims: "The real line from 0 to 1 looks more and more like a Swiss cheese, more and more like a stunningly black high-mountain sky studded with pin-pricks of light." Ibid., 97.

146. Whitehead, *Process and Reality*, 148–149.

147. Ibid., 114.

148. Harman considers every object as a vacuum that must contain a world in which distinct qualities interact. See *Guerrilla Metaphysics*, 94.

149. In particular, the exclusion or "negative prehension" of certain qualities in the composition of an actual object acts in the process of decision-making that involves the object. In other words, the ingression of an eternal object is never smooth and involves pure potential becoming determined by a negative or positive prehension, selection, decision-making. On negative and positive prehensions, see also Whitehead, *Process and Reality*, 41–42, 44, 49.

150. Whitehead specifies that an eternal object is "any entity whose conceptual recognition does not involve a necessary reference to any definite actual entities of the temporal world." Whitehead, *Process and Reality*, 44. A negative prehension, however, is the "definite exclusion of that item from positive contribution to the subject's own real internal constitution" (41). A positive prehension "is the complete transaction analyzable into the ingression, or objectification, of that entity as a datum for feeling and into the feeling whereby this datum is absorbed into the subjective satisfaction" (52).

151. I am referring here to Hansen's view of data architecture, which was mentioned in the first part of the chapter. See note 21.

152. Kostas Terzidis, *Expressive Form: A Conceptual Approach to Computational Design* (London: Spon Press, 2003), 71.

153. A tautological use of mathematics is defined by truths of the type 2 + 2 = 4 or 3 + 3 = 6. However, Whitehead reminds us that the process by which the unity 4 and the unity 6 are achieved is indeterminate. Whitehead, *Modes of Thought*, 92. Chaitin makes a similar point, arguing that "most of mathematics is true for no particular reason. Maths is true by accident." See Marcus Chown, "The Omega Man," *New Scientist* (March 2001), available at http://www-2.dc.uba.ar/profesores/becher/ns.html (last accessed January 2012).

154. Whitehead, *Modes of Thought*, 99.

155. Aesthetics, from the Greek *aisthetikos* or "sensitive," in turn from *aisthanesthai*, "to perceive, to feel," does not describe the perception of a specific entity, but the process by which entities enter into relations and undergo change.

156. Some of the most renowned books in this field are Donald Knuth, *The Art of Computer Programming*, 3 vols., 3rd ed. (Reading, MA: Addison Wesley, 1997); David Gelernter, *The Aesthetics of Computing* (London: Weidenfeld & Nicholson, 1998); John Maeda, *Creative Code: Aesthetics and Computation* (London: Thames and Hudson, 2004); Paul Fishwick, *Aesthetic Computing* (Cambridge, MA: MIT Press, 2005).

157. According to Donald Knuth, elegance in computation needs to conform to four criteria: "the leanness of the code; the clarity with which the problem is defined; spareness of use of resources such as time and processor cycles; and

implementation in the most suitable language on the most suitable system for its execution." Matthew Fuller, "Elegance," in Fuller, *Software Studies*, 87. Similarly, Gregory Chaitin, while confirming that a program is elegant if it is the smallest possible program for producing the output it produces, at the same time argues that a program can only be finitely elegant, because there cannot be a formal axiomatic system that includes all the programs. In other words, the problem of incompleteness here returns to define the incomputable limits of computation (the halting problem in Turing and formal incompleteness in Gödel). See Chaitin, *Meta Math!*, 125–127. However, it may be interesting to note that Fuller rearticulates the notion of elegance in view of computational incompleteness not as the necessity of finding an alliance between code, hardware, language, and people, but as the "madness of axioms that cross categories, in software that observes the terseness and clarity of design, and in the leaping cracks and shudders that zigzag scales and domains together" (ibid., 91).

158. On the importance of cellular automata as a development of the Turing machine, see Martin Gardner, "Mathematical Games: The Fantastic Combination of John Conway's New Solitary Game 'Life'," *Scientific American* 223 (October 1970), 120–123.

159. Veronica Becher of the University of Buenos Aires found that the probability that an infinite computation will produce only a finite amount of output is the same as Omega's: the halting probability of the oracle. She showed that Omega is equivalent to the probability that, during an infinite computation, a computer will fail to produce an output—for example, get no result from a computation and move on to the next one—and that it will do this only a finite number of times. Her research points at questions as to whether there could be links between Omega, the higher-order Omegas, and real computers. Super Omegas are even more random than Chaitin's Omega. While the first n bits of Omega are enumerable because they are highly compressible as being limit-computable by a very short algorithm (i.e., these first bits are not random with respect to the set of enumerating algorithms), Super Omega cannot be compressed by *any* enumerating nonhalting algorithm. See V. Becher, S. Daicz, and G. Chaitin, "A Highly Random Number," in C. S. Calude, M. J. Dinneen, and S. Sburlan, eds., *Combinatorics, Computability and Logic* (London: Springer, 2001), 55–68; Veronica Becher and Gregory Chaitin, "Another Example of Higher Order Randomness," *Fundamenta Informaticae* 51, no. 4 (2002), 325–338.

160. See Jürgen Schmidhuber, "Low-Complexity Art," *Leonardo* 30, no. 2 (1997), 97–103. See also Jürgen Schmidhuber, "Theory of Beauty and Low-Complexity Art," available at http://www.idsia.ch/~juergen/beauty.html (last accessed January 2012).

161. See Jürgen Schmidhuber, "Simple Algorithmic Principles of Discovery, Subjective Beauty, Selective Attention, Curiosity and Creativity," in Vincent Corruble, Masayuki Takeda, and Einoshin Suzuki, eds., *Discovery Science: 10th International Conference* (Berlin: Springer, 2007), 26–38.

162. This is clearly in opposition to any notion of prehension, whereby beauty does not correspond to an act of cognitive compression of data, but rather to contemplation or the suspension of thought by the unthought. Shaviro clearly explains the problem with this notion of beauty in reference to Kant's analytic of the beautiful. According to Shaviro, Kant understands the beautiful as involving an intuition for which there is no adequate concept. No conceptual form could explain what beauty is, and therefore no cognitive compression of algorithmic quantity can become the act of judgment of an art form. The beautiful instead exposes a level of incommensurability between intuitions and concepts. From this standpoint, sensible experience or acts of sensible intuition and judgments, implying receptive and not spontaneous feelings, explain how there is no adequate concept that describes the formula of the beautiful. Shaviro clarifies that while Kant still maintains a duality between cognition and affection, Deleuze's notion of contemplation, as the suspension of cognitive judgment, the suspension of interpretation but also of mere action, becomes the condition for thought and cognition. See Steven Shaviro, "The 'Wrenching' Duality of Aesthetics: Kant, Deleuze and the 'Theory of the Sensible'," 2007 (available as PDF at www.shaviro.com/Othertexts/SPEP.pdf). Similarly, Shaviro explains that Whitehead links beauty to feeling and not to truth. Whitehead does not subordinate feeling to cognition as Kant does, but argues that aesthetics is the very condition of knowledge. The satisfaction of an experience can only be an aesthetic process by which the production of Beauty corresponds to how any actual entity, from the most inanimate to the most animate, strives for its completion through a sea of contrasts, evaluations, and decisions. Every entity is therefore above all an aesthetic enterprise, which is explained by the entity's "lure for feeling" through which it reaches satisfaction and thus partakes of the creative advance of the universe. Steven Shaviro, *Without Criteria: Kant, Whitehead, Deleuze, and Aesthetics* (Cambridge, MA: MIT Press, 2009), 1–15.

163. On the theory of everything see Stephen Hawking and Leonard Mlodinow, "The Elusive Theory of Everything," *Scientific American* (September 2010), http://www.scientificamerican.com/author.cfm?id=2536 (last accessed January 2012).

164. This notion of surplus value of code is derived from Deleuze and Guattari's argument that a code—intended as a finite set of rules—is not primarily ontological and therefore is not opposed to a surplus value, which will define the potentiality of the code, the extraction of the potentiality of the code (in the system of commodity for instance), or the excessive force leaking out of codes. For Deleuze and Guattari, the surplus value of code is instead ontologically prior to the organization of potentials in possibilities. This notion suggests that all analysis of coding processes (from biophysical to socioeconomic processes) must start from complexity and not simplicity, from abundance and not scarcity, from populations and not races, from masses and not classes, from sexes and not genders. From this standpoint, the process of coding or the computation of each and any surplus cannot be separated from its initial potential or conditions for becoming coded. Gilles Deleuze

and Félix Guattari, *A Thousand Plateaus: Capitalism and Schizophrenia* (London: Athlone Press, 1987), 11, 59, 149.

165. Whitehead explains that there are at least two functions of reason. On the one hand, reason is one of the operations constituting living organisms in general. Thus reason is a factor within the totality of life processes guided by reason. Thus against the slow decay of organic entities, reason has the function of counteracting such entropic decay. On the other hand, reason only defines an activity of theoretical insights, which are autonomous of any physiological process and from general processes in nature. Here, reason is "the operation of theoretical realization." Alfred North Whitehead, *The Function of Reason* (Boston: Beacon Press, 1929), 9.

166. As Whitehead clarifies, "[Leibniz's] monads are best conceived as generalizations of contemporary notions of mentality. The contemporary notions of physical bodies only enter into his philosophy subordinately and derivatively." Whitehead, *Process and Reality*, 19. Similarly, Deleuze points out that "according to the principle of sufficient reason, there is always one concept per particular thing. According to the reciprocal principle of the identity of indiscernibles, there is one and only one thing per concept. Together, these principles expound a theory of difference as conceptual difference, or develop the account of representation as mediation." Gilles Deleuze, *Difference and Repetition*, trans. Paul Patton (London: Continuum, 2004), 12.

167. In particular, Whitehead observes, "we have got to remember the two aspects of Reason, the Reason of Plato and the Reason of Ulysses, Reason seeking complete understanding and Reason as seeking an immediate action." Whitehead, *The Function of Reason*, 11.

168. Whitehead's efficient cause and final cause can be understood as two modes of prehension, causal efficacy and presentational immediacy, which parallel the distinction between physical and mental poles of an entity. Efficient causes, therefore, describe the physical chain of continuous causes and effects whereby the past is inherited by the present. This means that any entity is somehow caused and affected by its inheritable past. As Shaviro explains: "Efficient cause is a passage, a transmission, an influence or a contagion." Although each actual entity appropriates the past in its own unrepeatable way, it is nonetheless embodied in the material universe that impinges upon it. However, in the process of repeating the patterns of the past there is always a margin of error, a bug in the vector transmission of energy-information from the past to the present, and from cause to effect. The seamless continuity of hereditary patterns is yet again faced with another level of contagion: the contagion of ideas breaking efficient causality. Shaviro points out that there are at least two reasons for this break in the chain. On the one hand, time is cumulative and therefore irreversible: any actual event adds itself to the past. In other words, the mere addition of facts stirs a quantitative effect—i.e., A is a stubborn fact, which has an objective immortality that is inherited but not fully

assimilated by B. The relation between A and B is of two actual worlds. On the other hand, the repetition of the past is never neutral and undergoes a valuation on behalf of the receiving entity, by which certain data are selected according to the qualities of joy and distaste of the receiving entity, for instance. The valuation of inherited data is carried out by conceptual prehensions, which add novelty to what was before, as they are prehensions of eternal objects. It is the mental pole of any actual entity—the conceptual prehensions that do not necessarily involve consciousness—that explains how efficient cause is supplemented by final cause. See Shaviro, *Without Criteria*, 83, 86–87. For Whitehead, a final cause is always adjacent to an efficient cause; the former accompanies and yet supervenes upon the latter. See Whitehead, *Process and Reality*, on efficient cause, 237–238; on final cause, 241; on the transition from efficient to final cause, 210.

169. Whitehead, *The Function of Reason*, 25.

170. Ibid., 26.

171. Ibid.

172. Ibid., 28.

173. Whitehead, *Process and Reality*, 9.

174. From this standpoint, Whitehead attributes reason to higher forms of biological life, where reason substitutes for action. Reason is not a mere organ of response of external stimuli, but rather is an organ of emphasis, able to abstract novelty from repetition.

175. Whitehead, *Process and Reality*, 20.

176. Ibid., 38.

177. Ibid., 39.

178. Whitehead attributes the primary discovery of this form of reason to Greek mathematics and logic, but also to Near Eastern, Indian, and Chinese civilizations. However, he argues that only the Greeks managed to produce a final instrument for the discipline of speculation. Ibid., 41.

179. I am referring here to Antonio Damasio and to the neurophilosophy of Paul and Patricia Churchland, which will be discussed in detail in chapter 3.

180. Whitehead continues, "The history of modern civilization shows that such schemes fulfill the promise of the dream of Solomon. They first amplify life by satisfying the peculiar claim of the speculative Reason, which is understanding for its own sake. Secondly, they represent the capital of ideas which each age holds in trust for its successors. The ultimate moral claim that civilization lays upon its possessors is that they transmit, and add to, this reserve of potential development by which it has profited." Whitehead, *Process and Reality*, 72.

181. Ibid.

182. Ibid.

183. Ibid., 32.

184. Ibid.

185. Ibid.

186. Ibid., 34.

187. Whitehead points out, "We have to consider the introduction of anarchy, the revolt from anarchy, the use of anarchy, and the regulation of anarchy. Reason civilizes the brute force of anarchic appetition." Ibid.

188. Ibid., 73.

189. Ibid., 76.

190. Friedrich Kittler, "Towards an Ontology of Media," public lecture, symposium "A Topological Approach to Cultural Dynamics," University of Amsterdam, 29–30 November 2007. While emphasizing media ontology, Kittler argues that philosophy forgets the very medium through which it operates, i.e., its technical medium. This is why Western metaphysics is marked by the absence of media ontology.

191. As Kittler argues, "precisely because the eventual differences between hardware implementations do not exist anymore, the so-called Church-Turing hypothesis in its strongest or physical form is tantamount to declaring nature itself as a Universal Turing Machine." Friedrich Kittler, "There Is No Software," in Kittler *Literature, Media, Information Systems*, 148.

192. For a close reading of Whitehead's notion of mereotopology, see chapter 2, section 6. Whitehead used mereotopology to explain the spatialization and temporalization of extension. See Whitehead, *Process and Reality*, 294–301. However, some readers have argued that Whitehead's notion of mereotopology lacked formal consistency. See Clarke L. Bowman, "Individuals and Points," *Notre Dame Journal of Formal Logic* 26, no. 1 (January 1985), available at http://projecteuclid.org/euclid.ndjfl/1093870761 (last accessed January 2012).

Chapter 2 Soft Extension: Topological Control and Mereotopological Space Events

1. Terzidis, for instance, insisted upon the computational power of computers for design. "The dominant mode of utilizing computers in architecture is that of computerization: entities and processes that are already conceptualized in the designer's mind are entered, manipulated, or stored on a computer system. In contrast, computation or computing, as a computer-based design tool, is generally limited. The problem with this situation is that designers do not take advantage of the compu-

tational power of the computer. Instead some venture into manipulations or criticism of computer models as if they were products of computation. Whilst research and development of software involves extensive computational techniques, mouse-based manipulations of 3D computer models are not necessarily acts of computation." See Kostas Terzidis, *Algorithmic Architecture* (Oxford: Architectural Press, 2006), xi.

2. The idea of a moving ratio can be derived from Thrift's conception of space as a moving space. The topological notion of space can also be derived, however, from Brian Massumi's critical analysis of the Euclidean conception of the grid upon which the Western idea of the body is based. See Nigel Thrift, "Movement-Space: The Changing Domain of Thinking Resulting from the Development of New Kinds of Spatial Awareness," *Economy and Society* 33, no. 4 (2004), 582–604; Brian Massumi, *Parables for the Virtual* (Durham: Duke University Press, 2002).

3. Henri Poincaré is considered to be the originator of algebraic topology and of the theory of analytic function. In 1895, he published "Analysis situs," one of the earliest systematic theorizations of topology. In particular, Poincaré's use of "homotopy theory" aimed at reducing topological questions to algebra by associating topological spaces with various groups defined as algebraic invariants. Poincaré introduced a fundamental group to distinguish different categories of two-dimensional surfaces. He was able to show that any two-dimensional surface having the same fundamental group as the two-dimensional surface of a sphere is topologically equivalent to a sphere. He conjectured that the result held for three-dimensional manifolds, and that it could be extended to higher dimensions. Yet today there is still no list of possible manifolds that can be checked to verify that they all have different homotopy groups. The invariant function, as a property of nonchange, explains change as the morphological transformation of the whole rather than as parts breaking from the whole. See Carl B. Boyer, *A History of Mathematics*, 2nd ed. (New York: Wiley, 1989), 599–605.

4. Brian Massumi introduced the notion of preemption in the late 1990s to describe an operative mode of power that directly impinges on the body's autonomic responses. For Massumi, the exercise of power relies not on mediation but on the direct activation of the conditions for change deployed by preemption. In particular, preemption corresponds to a mode of prehension of the conditions or the potential for action. Massumi explained that this mode of governmentality can be described in terms of an ecology of fear that operates affectively throughout the body in the form of a consequent action that is undertaken before the object of fear becomes manifest. Preemptive power thus corresponds to a qualitative or intensive mode of control that aims not at preventing but at inciting an event: positively actualizing the future in the present through the unleashing of aftereffects in the now. As future effects become the cause of the present, the event to happen becomes a virtual cause (or quasi-cause) transcending temporalities and fusing the future with the past. As Massumi argued, the future remote tense (what would have happened if . . .)

describes power as the action of what has not yet happened (or the effects of the future) on the present-past. Since the virtual effects (of what has not yet happened) are real, control and security are compelled to act on a virtual threat by actualizing it. For instance, the countermeasures that would be taken in the event of a terrorist attack are set to work in the everyday through the distribution of devices for measuring states of alert. See Brian Massumi, "Potential Politics and the Primacy of Preemption", Theory and Event 10, no. 2 (2007), available at http://muse.jhu.edu/journals/theory_and_event/v010/10.2massumi.html (last accessed January 2012). See also Brian Massumi, "The Future Birth of the Affective Fact: The Political Ontology of Threat," in Melissa Gregg and Gregory J. Seigworth, eds., *The Affect Theory Reader* (Durham: Duke University Press, 2010), 52–70. For a recent analysis of other forms of preemptive power that viscerally move through the sonic atmospheres of contemporary culture, see Steve Goodman, *Sonic Warfare: Sound, Affect, and the Ecology of Fear* (Cambridge, MA: MIT Press, 2010), 61–64.

5. According to Massumi, the apparatus of commodification should be understood according to the politics of everyday fear. As he glosses, "Fear is the translation into 'human' scale of the double infinity of the figure of the possible. It is the most economical expression of the accident-form as subject-form of capital: being as being-virtual, virtuality reduced to the possibility of disaster, disaster commodified, commodification as spectral continuity in the place of threat. When we buy, we are buying off fear and filling the gap with presence-effects." Brian Massumi, "'Everywhere You Want to Be': Introduction to Fear," in Massumi, ed., *The Politics of Everyday Fear* (Minneapolis: University of Minnesota Press, 1993), 12.

6. Whitehead defines the extensive continuum as "a complex of entities united by the various allied relationships of whole to part, and of overlapping so as to possess common parts, and of contact, and of other relationships derived from this primary relationship. The notion of 'continuum' involves both the property of indefinite divisibility and the property of unbounded extension." Alfred North Whitehead, *Process and Reality: An Essay in Cosmology* (New York: Free Press, 1978), 66.

7. In the mathematical field of topology, a homeomorphism or topological isomorphism or bicontinuous function (from the Greek words ὅμοιος (*homoios*) = similar and μορφή (*morphē*) = shape, form) is a continuous function between two topological spaces that has a continuous inverse function. Homeomorphisms are the isomorphisms in the category of topological spaces (the mappings that preserve all the topological properties of a given space). Two spaces with a homeomorphism between them are called homeomorphic. From a topological viewpoint they are the same. If topological space is a geometric object, for instance, homeomorphism defines a continuous stretching and bending of the object into a new shape. Thus, a square and a circle are homeomorphic to each other, but a sphere and a donut are not. Topology is then the study of those properties of objects that do not change when

homeomorphisms are applied. As Henri Poincaré famously said, mathematics is not the study of objects, but of the relations (isomorphisms for instance) between them. Boyer, *A History of Mathematics*, 603–604.

8. Patrick Schumacher recently claimed that parametricism is the dominant style of today's avant-garde, characterizing the power of large-scale urban schemes. See Patrick Schumacher, "Parametricism: A New Global Style for Architecture and Urban Design," *Architectural Design* 79, no. 4 (July-August 2009), 14–24.

9. Parametricism has been criticized for many reasons, of which I will briefly mention only two here. On the one hand, Owen Hatherley describes parametricism as an apolitical self-proclaimed avant-garde. In a recent article, Hatherley argues that parametricism cannot be compared to the Russian avant-garde, especially when one analyzes theorist and architect Patrick Schumacher's "A Glimpse Back into the Future," a text that accompanied an exhibition at the Galerie Gmurzynska in Zurich entitled "Zaha Hadid and Suprematism." There the Anglo-Iraqi architect Zaha Hadid (winner of the 2010 Stirling Prize) exhibited flowing, bristling forms whipped through rooms containing works by Kazimir Malevich, Aleksandr Rodchenko, Nikolai Suetin, and El Lissitzky. Hatherley reduces parametricism to its bare formal dimension, claiming that it strips architecture of any social or political content. See Owen Hatherley, "Zaha Hadid Architects and the Neoliberal Avant-Garde," *Mute: Culture and Politics after the Net*, 2010, available at http://www.metamute.org/editorial/articles/zaha-hadid-architects-and-neoliberal-avant-garde (last accessed July 2012). On the other hand, Schumacher's parametricism has also been accused of disengaging from the physical ground of architecture and of overlooking the contingencies of urban planning through an excessive search for formal relations. In particular, it has been argued that the excessive search for the beauty of form has completely diverted digital design from addressing urban and infrastructural problems. See Ingeborg M. Rocker, "Apropos Parametricism: If, in What Style Should We Build?," *Log*, no. 21 (March 2011).

10. In computer programming, a parameter is a variable: a symbolic name given to a known or unknown quantity of information, so that the name can be used independently of the information it represents, and can then be assigned different values in different places. A parameter, therefore, can be used in a new way or used in the same way (iteration). Parameters are used in subroutines (a procedure, function, routine, method, etc.) to refer to one of the pieces of data provided as inputs to the subroutine. In contrast to standard software packages based on given geometric objects, within digital architecture parametric software links dimensions and parameters to geometry, thereby allowing the incremental adjustment of a part to impact the whole assembly.

11. See Massumi, "Potential Politics and the Primacy of Pre-emption."

12. Gregory J. Chaitin, *Exploring Randomness* (London: Springer, 2001), 18.

13. Deleuze explained that the differential calculus is the calculation of derivatives or differential relations. A derivative is the quotient of two differentials, a differential relation such as *dx*/*dy*, where *d*/*y* and *d*/*x* are infinitely small quantities whose relation to *x* (or quantity of the ordinate) and *y* (or quantity of the abscissa) is equal to zero. While the relation between the actualities *x* and *y* is equal to zero, however, the relation between the two infinitely small quantities (*d*/*x* and *d*/*y*) is not zero. According to Deleuze, these infinitely small quantities belonged to another existing order compared to the actual order of *x* and *y*. In particular, these infinitely small quantities persisted (or continued to have an effect) at the same time as they vanished in their tendency to approach zero ($dx/dy = 0$). In other words, Deleuze's reading of Leibniz's infinitesimals explained that the relation between *x* and *y* could not but correspond to another kind of relation describing the differential distance between *d*/*x* and *d*/*y*. While the *d*/*x* and *d*/*y* canceled each other out in the form of vanishing quantities (infinitesimals), the differential relation between them remained itself real (i.e., continued to have real effects on *x* and *y*). Gilles Deleuze, *Difference and Repetition*, trans. Paul Patton (London: Continuum, 2004), 217–220.

14. François Roche, "Protocols/Processes," an interview with François Roche by Caroline Naphegyi, artistic director at Le Laboratoire, available at http://www.new-territories.com/blog/architecturedeshumeurs/wpcontent/uploads/2010/pdf/mouvement%20UK%20Une_architecture_des_humeurs_UKlight2.pdf (last accessed January 2012).

15. Patrick Schumacher has recently claimed that parametricism is the dominant style of today's avant-garde and insists on the power of large-scale urban schemes. See Schumacher, "Parametricism," 14–24.

16. In his theory of fuzzy sets, Lofti Zadeh described a membership function covering the interval [0,1]. Fuzzy logic was developed to compute differing truth values able to account for imprecise definitions of language compared to the binary logic based on the dichotomous opposition between true and false. Lofti Zadeh, "Fuzzy Sets and Systems," in J. Fox, ed., *System Theory* (Brooklyn, NY: Polytechnic Press, 1965), 29–39. According to fuzzy logic all things exist in varying degrees. Fuzzy logic thus implies the need to formalize imprecision in truth and thus transform uncertainty into finite terms, which can be operated by machines. Fuzzy logic was set to reduce the information between the [0,1] interval to a fuzzy chunk: an approximation of vague or indeterminate quantities resulting in a discrete state of fuzziness. Uncertainty therefore is quantified here as an approximate degree of values.

17. Greg Lynn, "Architectural Curvilinearity: The Folded, the Pliant and the Supple," *Architectural Design* 63, nos. 3–4 (March-April 1993), 22–29.

18. Jeffrey Kipnis, "Towards a New Architecture," in Michael Hensel, Christopher Hight, and Achim Menges, eds., *Space Reader: Heterogeneous Space in Architecture* (New York: Wiley, 2009), 112.

19. Calculus stems from the manipulation of very small quantities or infinitesimal objects that can be treated like numbers but which are "infinitely small." On a number line, infinitesimals do not have location zero, but have zero distance from zero. Such quantity corresponds to a single number. As Boyer explains, it was only after the development of a general abstract concept of real numbers that it became possible to interpret the differential calculus in terms of the limit of an infinite sequence of ratios or numbers. Boyer, *A History of Mathematics*, 216.

20. To further explain this notion of infinitesimals, it is important to highlight that infinitesimals have been used to express the idea of objects so small that they cannot be seen or measured. An infinitesimal number is a nonstandard number whose modulus is less than any nonzero positive standard number. In mathematics, an infinitesimal, or an infinitely small number, is a number that is greater in absolute value than zero, and yet smaller than any positive real number. An infinitesimal is a variable whose limit is zero. Development by Abraham Robinson (1960) of the "Nonstandard Analysis" conferred new significance on infinitesimals and brought them closer to the vision of Gottfried Leibniz (1646–1716), who introduced the dy/dx notation for the derivative, and who perceived infinitesimals as more like small but constant quantities. Infinitesimal or differential calculus is an area of mathematics pioneered by Leibniz and is based on the concept of infinitesimals. It thus differs from the calculus of Isaac Newton, which is based on the concept of the limit. See Boyer, *A History of Mathematics*, 391–395, 519–522.

21. Monads are substantial forms of being. They are eternal, indecomposable, individual, subject to their own laws, noninteracting, and each reflects the entire universe in a preestablished order. Monads are centers of force, while space, matter, and motion are phenomenal. In the 1960s, Abraham Robinson worked out a rigorous foundation for Leibniz's infinitesimals using model theory. Leibniz's mathematical reasoning was also revised using nonstandard analysis. See Gottfried Wilhelm Leibniz, *Discourse on Metaphysics and Related Writings*, ed. R. N. D. Martin and Stuart Brown (New York: St. Martin's Press, 1988).

22. The law of continuity is based on the principle that between one state and another there are infinite intermediate states. A continuous entity—a *continuum*—has no interior "gaps." On the contrary, to be discrete is to be separated, like the scattered pebbles on a beach or the leaves on a tree. Continuity connotes *undivided* unity; discreteness connotes divided plurality. Repeated or successive division gives the fundamental nature of a continuum. The process of dividing a continuous line into parts will never terminate in an *indivisible part or atom* that cannot be further divided. One of the first formulations of the law of continuity is Zeno's famous paradox: a set of problems devised by Zeno of Elea to support Parmenides' metaphysical doctrine that "all is one." Contrary to what we perceive, Zeno's paradoxes demonstrate that plurality and change are illusions. Parmenides rejected pluralism and the reality of any kind of change: all was one indivisible, unchanging reality. Another formulation of the law of continuity is offered by Leibniz; see his preface

to *New Essays on the Human Understanding* (c. 1704). The law of continuity in Leibniz also refers to the principle of preestablished harmony, according to which each event occurs when it does because it was preprogrammed to do so by God. Boyer, *A History of Mathematics*, 74, 399–407.

23. However, Leibniz thought that he had resolved the paradoxes of continuity by arguing that there are no jumps in nature and thus no discontinuities. He believed that any change passes through some intermediate change and that there is an actual infinity in things. Similarly, he used this principle of continuity to show that no motion can arise from a state of complete rest. See Gottfried Wilhelm Leibniz, *New Essays on Human Understanding*, trans. Peter Remnant and Jonathan Bennett (Cambridge: Cambridge University Press, 1981). See also Gottfried Wilhelm Leibniz, *The Labyrinth of the Continuum: Writings on the Continuum Problem, 1672–1686*, trans. Richard T. W. Arthur (New Haven: Yale University Press, 2001).

24. Poincaré's insistence on the qualitative theory of differential equations led him to focus on the geometrical form of the curves of functions with infinite branches, out of which the numerical value of the function could be determined. Poincaré's concept of automorphic or mereomorphic functions contributed toward solving the tension between infinite discrete sets and infinite continual sets by showing how continuous and discontinuous groups of functions could exist alongside each other, so that the transformation of one into another was only determinable by the process of generating and expanding functions.

25. Gilles Deleuze, *The Fold: Leibniz and the Baroque* (Minneapolis: University of Minnesota Press, 1993), 14.

26. Ibid., 17.

27. Gilles Deleuze's reading of Leibniz's infinitesimal calculus explained that the relation between x and y could not but correspond to another kind of relation describing the differential distance between d/x and d/y. While the d/x and d/y cancel each other out in the form of vanishing quantities (infinitesimals), the differential relation between them remains real. From this standpoint, both Leibniz and Deleuze link the mathematical problem of infinity to the geometrical problem of deriving the function of a curve (the relation between x and y quantities) from the given property of its tangent. See Deleuze, *Difference and Repetition*, 217–220.

28. Ibid.

29. On nonstandard axioms, see Peter Fletcher, "Non-standard Set Theory," *Journal of Symbolic Logic* 54, no. 3 (September 1989), 1000–1008.

30. Deleuze, *Difference and Repetition*, 219.

31. Foucault's analysis of the panoptical architecture of power introduced the notion of self-regulating discipline, which was said to be implanted in the very biophysical and cognitive behavior of populations, and which he claimed extended

throughout society. The regime of governability incited by the panoptical architecture already highlighted the new dominance of rules and procedures in the self-expanding *dispositifs* of surveillance and security. As a matter of fact, Foucault's panopticon can be considered a precursor of a general system of governability which he termed "biopower." If the architectural model of the panopticon intended to subsume the population into a grid of mathematical-geometric coordinates that warded off infinitesimals, biopower had broader horizons and recognized the existence of large numbers. As Massumi recently argued, Foucault's analysis of nineteenth-century liberalism already suggested that biopower "construed the level at which aleatory events are determined as one of 'generality'. Generality was in turn understood in statistical terms, which is to say according to the laws of large numbers. Biopower's embrace of the aleatory was 'massifying'. Although 'aleatory and unpredictable when taken in themselves,' the 19th-century assumption was that events, 'at the collective level, display constants that are easy, or at least possible, to establish.'" Regulatory mechanisms could then operate on those constant patterns emerging out of variations so as to establish equilibrium. The grid structure of Euclidean positions was therefore already transforming into a field of relations set to calculate variations through patterns. Massumi states that Foucault already defined the new regime of power, coincident with the rise of neoliberalism, as an environmental regime whose actions are not standardizing, since the environment (a field of variations) cannot be simply normalized according to preset categories. On the contrary, "environmentality as a mode of power is left no choice but to make do with this abnormally productive 'autonomy' . . . environmentality must work through the 'regulation of effects' rather than of causes. It must remain operationally 'open to unknowns' (imperceptible stirrings) and catch 'transversal phenomena' (nonlinear multiplier effects) before they amplify the stirrings to actual crisis proportions." See Brian Massumi, "National Enterprise Emergency: Steps toward an Ecology of Power," *Theory, Culture and Society* 26, no. 6 (November 2009), 155; and Michel Foucault, *Society Must Be Defended: Lectures at the Collège de France, 1975–76* (New York: Picador, 2003), 243–246. This suggests that the neoliberal architecture of power operates through a topological "government of conduct" involving the control of the rules of the game and the framework. With parameters set up to include infinitesimally large and small numbers, the environmental field of continual variations or extension has become one with power. In other words, the neoliberal system of calculation thus requires inequality as a regulative mechanism, enabling competition and inciting difference as infinitesimal division, which grounds a state of insecurity and fear as indeterminate threats in the environment. For this reason, one may need to agree with Massumi, who echoes Foucault in questioning biopolitics's ability to explain the neoliberal regime of environmental power. (Massumi, "National Enterprise Emergency.")

32. According to Lynn, "A plexus is a multi-linear network of interweavings, intertwinings and intrications; for instance, of nerves or blood vessels. The complications of a plexus—what could best be called complexity—arise from its irreducibility to

any simple organization. A plexus describes a multiplicity of focal connections within a single continuous system that remains open to new motions and fluctuations. Thus, a plexial event cannot occur at any discrete point. A multiply plexed system—a complex—cannot be reduced to mathematical exactitude, it must be described with rigorous probability." Lynn, "Architectural Curvilinearity," 11.

33. For a more detailed discussion of the biogenetic models used in generative software, see Luciana Parisi, "Symbiotic Architecture: Prehending Digitality," *Theory, Culture and Society* 26, nos. 2–3 (March-May 2009), 346–374.

34. Greg Lynn, *Animate Form* (New York: Princeton Architectural Press, 1999), 18.

35. Deleuze, *The Fold*, 23.

36. According to Cache, "In mathematics, what is said to be singular is not a given point, but rather a set of points on a given curve. A point is not singular; it becomes singularized on a continuum. . . . We will retain two types of singularity. On the one hand, there are the extreme, the maximum and the minimum on a given curve. And on the other there are those singular points that, in relation to the extreme, figure as in-betweens. These are points of inflection . . . defined only by themselves." Bernard Cache, *Earth Moves: The Furnishing of Territories* (Cambridge, MA: MIT Press, 1995), 16.

37. Lynn, "Architectural Curvilinearity," 11. In his critique of collage as a technique central to postmodern and deconstructivist approaches to design, Jeffrey Kipnis claims: "From Rowe to Venturi to Eisenman, from PoMo to the Deconstructivists, collage has served as the dominant mode of the architectural graft. There are indications, however, to suggest that collage is not able to sustain the heterogeneity architecture aspires to achieve. . . . First, Post-Modern collage is an extensive practice wholly dependent on effecting incoherent contradictions within and against a dominant frame. . . . The only form collage produces, therefore, is the form of collage." In order to get away from this dominant conception of space, Kipnis suggests that "the key distinction from collage would be that such [new] grafts would seek to produce heterogeneity within an intensive cohesion rather than out of extensive incoherence and contradictions." Kipnis, "Towards a New Architecture," 100–101.

38. For a good introduction to topology in computational design see Giuseppa Di Cristina, "Topological Tendency in Architecture," in Di Cristina, ed., *Architecture and Science* (New York: Wiley, 2001).

39. Gilles Deleuze, "Postscript on Control Societies," in Deleuze, *Negotiations: 1972–1990* (New York: Columbia University Press, 1995).

40. Sanford Kwinter, *Far from Equilibrium: Essays on Technology and Design Culture*, ed. Cynthia Davidson (Barcelona: Actar, 2008), 37.

41. Ibid., 39.

42. Ibid., 51.

43. Ibid., 53.

44. The correspondence between qualitative change, temporality, and movement is evident in the use of computed animation in the design of spatial fields of relations as well as in the design of real-time interactive architectures, where environmental factors and users can become inputs that change the programmed structure of parameters and algorithms. On the notion of timelike architectures, see Lynn, *Animate Form*, 9–41. See also Elizabeth Grosz, *Architecture from the Outside* (Cambridge, MA: MIT Press, 2001); Lars Spuybroek, *Nox: Machinic Architecture* (London: Thames and Hudson, 2004); Mahesh Senagala, "Speed and Relativity: Toward Timelike Architecture," ACSA Annual Meeting Proceedings, Baltimore, 2001, available at www.mahesh.org (last accessed January 2012).

45. For example a line has two parameters—its length and its direction—and altering one of these factors gives you a different form. A polyline has the previous two factors plus the positioning of its vertices, and if any of these are altered a different form is given, and so on.

46. For example a tower that has a vertical rotation of floor plates can be seen in terms of cost: a very twisted form costs more than a not-so-twisted form.

47. Michael Hensel and Achim Menges, "The Heterogeneous Space of Morphoecologies," in Hensel, Hight, and Menges, *Space Reader*, 212.

48. Ibid., 214.

49. Among the most recent experiments with the design of program-evolving architectures, the work of architect-programmer Casey Reas on software processing can be seen as a particularly clear example of engagement with the evolving capacities of variables and of exploring the microdynamics of emergent form derived from complex levels of urban interaction. See "Intensive Fields: New Parametric Techniques in Urbanism," conference, USC, Los Angeles, 12 December 2009, podcast at http://arch-pubs.usc.edu/parasite/intensive-fields/video-archive/ (last accessed January 2012).

50. The Infrasense Laboratory at Imperial College London has recently started a research project called "Smart Infrastructure: Wireless sensor networks for condition assessment and monitoring of civil engineering infrastructure." This project uses smart-infrastructure wireless sensors above all to monitor changes and collect data that software can analyze so as to look for new solutions to emerging problems, such as the flow of water due to pipes leaking. See the documentation of the project at http://www2.imperial.ac.uk/infrasense/SmartInfrastructure.php (last accessed January 2012).

51. This notion of deep relationality also resonates with Lev Manovich's notion of deep remixability, according to which software has become the shared environment

of all media. See Lev Manovich, "Understanding Hybrid Media," in Betti-Sue Hertz, ed., *Animated Paintings* (San Diego: San Diego Museum of Art, 2007), 1–17.

52. For Leach, the first instance of digital architecture was the phase of virtual reality defined by early experimentation of digital forms. In 2002–2003, a second phase of digital design produced an emphasis on the notion of tectonics, as opposed to the earlier phase of form making, because the materials of architecture had become increasingly informed by the worlds of the computer. In particular, Leach refers to the computational programming of the British Museum roof. A third shift in digital design is marked by the current use of computation at an urban scale, defined by the development of parametric techniques in the design of cities. See Neil Leach, introduction to "Intensive Fields: New Parametric Techniques in Urbanism," conference, USC, 12 December 2009, podcast at http://arch-pubs.usc.edu/parasite/intensive-fields/video-archive/ (last accessed January 2012).

53. François Roche, "I've Heard About . . . (A Flat, Fat Growing Urban Experiment): Extracts of Neighborhood Protocols," *Architectural Design* 79, no. 4 (July-August 2009), 40.

54. One can take Zaha Hadid Architects' design of the BMW Central Building as an example of the aesthetics of the curvature, as there the primary organizing strategy of the building lies in the scissor section that connects ground floor and first floor into a continuous field: two sequences of terraced plates (like giant staircases) step up from north to south and from south to north. See http://www.zaha-hadid.com/architecture/bmw-central-building (last accessed January 2012).

55. See www.5subzero.at (last accessed January 2012).

56. At the 2009 Los Angeles conference "Intensive Fields: New Parametric Techniques in Urbanism," Marcos Novak for instance argued that if parametric design had to become autonomous from the master planning of the urban texture, a system of value would have to be created to enable automatic agents to contribute satisfactorily to the design of the city and its interactions. He lamented that such a value system had yet to be invented. The task of urbanism, he argued, is to modify techniques so that they can become platforms for rethinking the question of social values. The problem of parametric architecture, however, may not be resolved simply by the introduction of a value system that could ultimately guarantee the implementation of an alternative form of social urbanism. Under the regime of environmental power, the evolution of a new value system can hardly remain immune from the neoliberal *dispositifs* of continual variations, which precisely feed on the incomplete agency of parameters shared by designers, engineers, and a network of human and nonhuman actors. Since these *dispositifs* include a general process of evaluation involving the indeterminate contingencies encountered by all agents, they foster the evolution of programs tailored to the specificity of changing urban strata. This means that parametric architecture is already creating new systems

of value based on parameters of indetermination, and that it thus makes use of and furthers the advance of a mode of calculation derived from incompleteness.

57. Massumi, "Potential Politics and the Primacy of Pre-emption."

58. This title paraphrases that of Massumi's introduction to *Parables for the Virtual*: "Concrete is as Concrete doesn't."

59. Albert Einstein, *Relativity: The Special and the General Theory*, trans. Robert W. Lawson (London: Routledge, 2001), 61–67. See also Richard Phillips Feynman, *Six Not-So-Easy Pieces: Einstein's Relativity, Symmetry, and Space-Time* (New York: Basic Books, 1998), 68.

60. See Henri Bergson, *Time and Free Will: An Essay on the Immediate State of Consciousness* (London: Alley, 1913), 1–74. See also Whitehead's objection to Bergson's notion of duration, in Alfred North Whitehead, *The Concept of Nature* (Amherst, NY: Prometheus Books, 2004), 53–55; Whitehead, *Adventures of Ideas* (New York: Free Press, 1967), 223; and Whitehead, *Process and Reality*, 321. See also Isabelle Stengers, *Penser avec Whitehead: Une libre et sauvage création de concepts* (Paris: Editions du Seuil, 2002), 71–73, 75, 78–79.

61. Bergson, *Time and Free Will*, 247.

62. Ibid.

63. It has been argued that Bergson did not have a full grasp of Einstein's theory of relativity according to which the twins did not share the same space-time history, and yet were supposed to be interchangeable. Thus no absolutism of time, or absolute spatialization of time, was actually at stake in Einstein's relativity. See Ilya Prigogine and Isabelle Stengers, *Order Out of Chaos: Man's New Dialogue with Nature* (New York: Bantam Books, 1984).

64. Henri Bergson, *Introduction to Metaphysics* (Indianapolis: Hackett, 1999), 31–32.

65. Bergson, *Time and Free Will*, 78–85.

66. Kas Oosterhuis, *Interactive Architecture #1* (Rotterdam: Episode Publishers, 2007), 4.

67. Haque's projects can be visited at http://www.haque.co.uk/ (last accessed January 2012).

68. Usman Haque, "Architecture, Interaction, Systems," in Christine Macy and Sarah Bonnemaison, eds., *Responsive Textile Environments* (Halifax: Tuns Press, 2007), 56–65.

69. Cedric Price argued against the production of permanent, specific spaces for particular functions, stressing instead the need for flexibility and the unpredictability of

the future. His timelike vision of space design was based on the thesis of an "anticipatory architecture" developed through wide-ranging projects in scale, from the urban plans for Strasbourg to Christmas decorations in Oxford Street, London, not to mention the Fun Palace and Potteries Thinkbelt. For Price, architectural design had to become committed to "thinking the unimaginable" and learn to utilize "time" as its most treasured design tool. Samantha Hardingham, *Cedric Price: Opera* (New York: Wiley, 2003). Similarly, Gordon Pask coined the term "new cybernetics" to explain the transfer of information in terms of attractions and repulsions, which laid the grounds for his concepts of conversation and interaction taken from actors' theory. His efforts to define a new cybernetics were then derived from ideas of process. He claimed that the "interaction of actors has no specific beginning or end. It goes on forever." See Gordon Pask, "Heinz von Foerster's Self-Organization, the Progenitor of Conversation and Interaction Theories," *System Research* 13, no. 3 (September 1996), 349–366.

70. Usman Haque's concept of interaction is strongly indebted to Gordon Pask's notion of conversation. As opposed to first-order cybernetics, according to which systems are defined by their activities of input/output feedback interaction, the concept of conversation relied on a view that was closer to learning systems, according to which models could evolve, learn, and change. Pask stated that the principles of agreement, understanding, and consciousness were crucial for the devising of human-to-human, human-to-computer, and computer-to-computer interactions. Interactions like conversation required mutual actions like those performed in dance, where space is offered to the steps of other bodies. In chapter 3 this notion of conversation will be discussed in relation to cognitive models of interaction. For a recent discussion of the use of this notion in interactive architecture, see Usman Haque, "The Architectural Relevance of Gordon Pask," *Architectural Design* 77, no. 4 (July-August 2007), 54–61.

71. *Soft Urbanism* develops a hybrid network space, a fusion of media space and urban space. It emphasizes the role of the public in an increasingly privatized society by occupying the vacuum between the local and the global. The products of this alliance of urban and media networks are "hybrid" spaces, a term that refers to the merging of the analog and the digital, virtual and material, local and global. This project represents a prototype for a new interdisciplinary field of design and planning called "soft urbanism" which looks at the transformations of architectural/urban space in the emerging "information/communication age" by exploring the dynamic interaction of urbanism, the space of mass media, and communication networks. With the notion of soft urbanism this project not only intervenes in the realm of infrastructures, but also aims to change them through the supplementation of networks. It thus addresses the question of urbanism as the creation of new fields of possibilities and frameworks for self-organizational processes. "Soft" strategies are conceived here as involving "bottom-up" practices. Far from first defining the global result of the interaction and then determining the necessary relation between the

elements so as to produce that interaction (a top-down approach), here simple rules for a set of independent elements are developed. What emerges from the interaction of these elements is aleatory. Drawing on biological models, this project sees fields of interaction of plural forces as a reservoir of potentialities for the selection processes that might lead to viable urban transformations. See Elizabeth Sikiaridi and Frans Vogelaar, "Soft Urbanism," in Jorinde Seijdel, ed., *Mobile Space: How Wireless Media Mobilize Public Space* (Rotterdam: NAi, 2006). The *WikiCity* project, developed at the Senseable City Lab at MIT, instead aims at programming a city that is able to perform, and thus that can be actively participated in through real-time control systems. This project implements the dynamic interaction of the inhabitants, who are intelligent actuators pursuing their individual interests in cooperation and competition with one another. The project uses real-time communication platforms, such as mobile phones, GPS devices, web interfaces, and physical interface objects, to allow the inhabitants to become live actuators who trigger the programming and modeling of urban systems. Through location- and time-sensitive platforms for storing and exchanging data, people become distributed intelligent actuators able to differentiate and add new levels of unpredictable variation to the computation of urban systems. See Francesco Calabrese, Kristian Kloeckl, and Carlo Ratti, "WikiCity: Real-Time Urban Environments," *IEEE Pervasive Computing* 6, no. 3 (July-September 2007), 52–53, available at http://senseable.mit.edu/wikicity/

72. Elie During, "Philosophical Twins? Bergson and Whitehead on Langevin's Paradox and the Meaning of 'Space-Time'," in Guillaume Durand and Michel Weber, eds., *Alfred North Whitehead's Principles of Natural Knowledge* (Frankfurt: Ontos, 2007), 9.

73. Whitehead rejects the view that experience is determined by sensory impressions or is composed of aggregate atoms, which constitutes the idea of an absolute space and time. He believes that nature can be divided up into events that successively extend over each other and that are characterized by eternal objects: patterns or "forms" in which "facts" or events participate. Spatiality and duration are thus not to be considered as disconnecting or as a result of the distortion of the world by the intellect, but as intrinsic to physical objects and as being derived from the ways in which things are interconnected. Whitehead, *Process and Reality*, 489–490.

74. According to Whitehead, to describe experience one cannot start from the empiricists' idea of sense data or impressions, but must begin rather from the notion of prehension or prehending entities, which enter and exit relations with one another, and which we are initially aware of through receptive sensations (proprioception or the autonomic response, for instance) associated with the body as a whole (through the muscles, our position, etc.) rather than just through our sense organs, such as those of sight and touch. For Whitehead, to prehend through the whole body is to perceive "in the mode of causal efficacy." In this mode, sensations, including emotional experiences, are subsequently brought to full consciousness and projected back into the "contemporary spatial region" of the world as prehensive

sensations: these constitute a later and higher perception at the conscious level "in the mode of presentational immediacy." Both primary and secondary qualities are thus referred back to a common actual occasion as a prehending entity. Whitehead admits that these sensations may not be veridical, because of the time lag between the two modal stages. Whitehead, *Process and Reality*, 119–123, 169, 171–172.

75. Alfred North Whitehead, with H. W. Carr and R. A. Sampson, "Symposium: The Problem of Simultaneity: Is There a Paradox in the Principle of Relativity in Regard to the Relation of Time Measured and Time Lived?," *Proceedings of the Aristotelian Society*, supplementary volume 3 (1923), 15–41; Whitehead, *An Enquiry Concerning the Principles of Natural Knowledge* (Cambridge: Cambridge University Press, 1919), 81; Whitehead, *The Principle of Relativity, with Applications to Physical Science* (Cambridge: Cambridge University Press, 1922), 67.

76. Minkowski's manifold space showed that there is no space in the world, but many spaces and planes existing in a 4D space. Minkowski conceived of time as a fourth dimension of space. Thus a rotation in time involved a rotation in space. Walter Scott, "Minkowski, Mathematicians, and the Mathematical Theory of Relativity," in H. Goenner, J. Renn, J. Ritter, and T. Sauer, eds., *The Expanding Worlds of General Relativity* (Basel: Birkhäuser, 1999), 45–86. Bergson was particularly concerned with attacking Minkowski's four-dimensional schema of space-time (or the subordination of time to space), together with the notion of the dislocation of simultaneity, the dilatation of time described by the special theory of relativity, and Langevin's paradox (or the twins paradox). As Bergson points out, "The idea of temporal flow can't be derived from relativity theory or Minkowski's model. . . . Real time can be perceived [consciously], not conceived." Henri Bergson, *Duration and Simultaneity: Bergson and the Einsteinian Universe*, ed. Robin Durie (Manchester, UK: Clinamen Press, 1999), 44–46.

77. For a detailed discussion of this Whitehead-Minkowski convergence, see Ronny Desmet, "Whitehead and the British Reception of Einstein's Relativity: An Addendum to Victor Lowe's Whitehead Biography," Centre for Process Studies, Seminars, 2 October 2007, available at http://www.ctr4process.org/publications/SeminarPapers/30_2-DesmetR.pdf (last accessed January 2012). While some have directly related Whitehead's simultaneous spatiotemporalities to the Minkowskian concept of the manifold, others have pointed out that Whitehead's extensive continuum focuses more explicitly on the discrepancy between particular perspectives (or time systems) embedded in the time-space manifold of events.

78. Stengers, *Penser avec Whitehead*, 193–194. On Whitehead's discussion of the special theory of relativity, see also Desmet, "Whitehead and the British Reception of Einstein's Relativity."

79. Whitehead specifies that straight lines have specific properties: (1) completeness: no other line or point defines a line or a point; (2) inclusion of points: the points of B include the points of A; (3) unique definition by any pair of included

points; (4) the possibility of mutual intersection at a single point. Whitehead, *Process and Reality*, 330. Whitehead does not want to exclude the possibility of distant effects, but he stresses that all the forces function via direct contact along a sequence of intermediate regions through a route of successive quanta of extensiveness. These quanta of extensiveness are the basic regions of successive contiguous occasions.

80. Ibid., 77.

81. Whitehead, *The Concept of Nature*, 15.

82. However, the divergence of perspectives and the asymmetry of time systems do not entail a disruption of time. For Whitehead, time extended beyond "now" expresses the advances of nature as a whole. However, against Einstein, he argues that there is no such thing as the slowing down of clocks. Without interfering forces (gravitational or otherwise), all clocks run in the same way and at the same rate throughout spatiotemporal paths. This means that temporal units have to be congruent all along these paths in spite of the discrepancy in the measures of total elapsed time.

83. In his writings on the general theory of relativity, Whitehead replaces the ontological model in which matter has priority over space-time, and space-time over the relatedness of events, with a model in which these priorities are reversed. See Whitehead, *The Principle of Relativity, with Applications to Physical Science*; Whitehead, Carr, and Sampson, "Symposium: The Problem of Simultaneity," 15–41.

84. Whitehead's analysis of parthood relations (*mereology*, from the Greek *mero*, "part") was an ontological alternative to set theory. It dispensed with abstract entities and treated all objects of quantification as individuals. As a formal theory, mereology is an attempt to set out the general principles underlying the relationships between a whole and its constituent parts, as opposed to set theory's search for the principles that underlie the relationships between a class and its constituent members. As is often argued, mereology could not explain by itself, however, the notion of a whole (a self-connected whole, such as a stone or a whistle, as opposed to a scattered entity of disconnected parts, such as a broken glass, an archipelago, or the sum of two distinct cats). Whitehead's early attempts to characterize his ontology of events provide a good exemplification of this mereological dilemma. For Whitehead, a necessary condition for two events to have a sum was that they were at least "joined" to each other, i.e., connected (despite being or not being discrete). These connections, however, concerned spatiotemporal entities, and could not be defined directly in terms of plain mereological primitives. To overcome the bounds of mereology, the microscopic discontinuity of matter (and its atomic composition) had to be overcome. The question of what characterized an object required topological and not mereological analysis. From this standpoint, two distinct events could be perfectly spatiotemporally colocated without occupying the spatiotemporal region at which they were located, and could therefore share the region with other entities. The combination of mereology and topology contributed

to Whitehead's articulation of the notion of the extended continuum. See Roberto Casati and Achille C. Varzi, *Parts and Places: The Structures of Spatial Representation* (Cambridge, MA: MIT Press, 1999), 13–17, 51–54, 76–77; Whitehead, *Process and Reality*, 294–301.

85. An occasion of experience, according to Whitehead, implies a certain unique togetherness in experience. Whitehead, *Process and Reality*, 189–190.

86. Whitehead uses the notion of mereotopology to address the problem of abstraction and spatial measurement without equating abstraction to infinitesimal points. He uses the idea of nonmetrical spatial relations of extensive parts and wholes, thus starting with concrete actualities or occasions of experience. Since all metrical relations involve measurement, and since measurement and quantification are the ultimate methods of abstraction, Whitehead develops the notion of extensive abstraction. This notion is intended to problematize the general theory of relativity and the theory of measurement, which seemingly collapse physics and geometry, thereby ignoring, according to Whitehead, the distinction between the abstract and the concrete. For Whitehead, it is necessary instead to disarticulate the mathematical-geometric order from the physical world so as to be able to explain their relations formally, thus making measurement as determinate as possible. According to Whitehead, the general theory of relativity equates the relational structures of geometry with contingent relations of facts, and thus loses sight of the logical relations that would make cosmological measurement possible. This is why his mereotopological approach insists on the spatialization and temporalization of extension, whereby "physical time is the reflection of genetic divisibility into coordinate divisibility." Whitehead, *Process and Reality*, 289. Whitehead argues that the solution to this problem is to disentangle the necessary relations of geometry from the contingent relations of physics, so that one's theory of space and gravity can be "bimetric," i.e., built from the two metrics of geometry and physics. Ibid., 283–287, 294–301, 327–329.

87. In particular, and contrary to Whitehead, Bergson's theory of time, the qualitative time of the *élan vital,* is opposed to the metric time of scientific epistemology, thus identifying the necessity of abstraction with the imperatives of the scientific enterprise. Whitehead, on the contrary, seeks to distinguish geometrico-mathematical abstraction from physical actualities to propose a more rigorous metaphysical schema of relations. See Henri Bergson, *Creative Evolution* (New York: Modern Library, 1994), 358–365, 374–380.

88. Whitehead, *Process and Reality*, 332–333.

89. Ibid., 328.

90. Ibid., 169.

91. Ibid., 63, 121–125, 206.

92. As Whitehead explains, each actual entity is atomic as it is spatiotemporally extended (ibid., 77).

93. Ibid., 96–97, 294.

94. Ibid., 66.

95. Ibid., 67.

96. As Whitehead observes, actual occasions are the entities that become and thus constitute a continuously extensive world. In other words, whereas extensiveness becomes, "becoming" is not itself extensive but atomic. The ultimate metaphysical truth is atomism. The creatures are atomic. In each cosmic epoch, according to Whitehead, there is a creation of continuity. Ibid., 35, 77.

97. Alfred North Whitehead, "The Relational Theory of Space," ed. P. J. Hurley, *Philosophy Research Archives*, no. 5 (1979), 712–741.

98. In the relational theory, Whitehead discusses the connection between points and objects as a causal action occurring between atomic units not in the spatial dimension but only in the temporal. (Whitehead, *Process and Reality*, 37.) However, the method of extensive abstraction or the extensive continuum maps the interrelated structures of events according to a geometry that deploys the uniform relatedness of nature, especially of spatiotemporal relations: the topological priority of events. Modern topology distinguishes between many different types of connectivity (connected, locally connected, pathways connected, and so on). Whitehead's mereotopological model of the extensive continuum instead specifically concerns the interrelation between the actual occasions that define the spatiotemporal order of nature (ibid., 148).

99. This is how parametric urbanism is designing new cities and anticipating new spaces of relations. Since, according to Whitehead, extensive abstraction is the most general scheme for the transmission of real potentiality, to divide (or to quantify physical variables through parametric software, for instance) is not to reduce qualities to static quantities, but to cut open undivided continuity for the becoming of space events.

100. Multiagent systems are composed of interactive intelligent agents used to solve problems and make rational decisions, spanning from online trading to disaster response and the modeling of social structures. See Ken Binmore, Cristiano Castelfranchi, James Doran, and Michael Wooldridge, "Rationality in Multi-Agent Systems," *Knowledge Engineering Review*, no. 3 (1998), 309–314.

101. The Belief-Desire-Intention (BDI) software model is a program for intelligent agents using the notions of belief, desire, and intention to solve problems in agent programming. Chang-Hyun Jo, "A New Way of Discovery of Belief, Desire, and Intention in the BDI Agent-Based Software Model," *Journal of Advanced Computational*

Intelligence and Intelligent Informatics 7, no. 1 (2004), 1–3. Inspired by Michael Bratman's theory of human practical reasoning, in which intention and desire are considered as pro-attitudes (mental attitudes concerned with action), the model focuses on problem-solving concerned with plans and planning, and does not just allow the programming of intelligent agents. See Michael Bratman, *Intention, Plans, and Practical Reason* (Cambridge, MA: MIT Press, 1999). According to Manuel DeLanda, these multiagent systems develop an attitude toward the meaning of sentences, propositions, and semantic content. For instance, the belief and desire of agents can change and develop a new attitude toward sentences, which leads to a new set of consequences for the workings of the system. BDI agents, as opposed to neural nets that operate on pattern recognition and extraction, are susceptible to language. The field of parametric design, according to DeLanda, needs BDI agents to model complex urban conglomerates, but it can also benefit from cellular automata to model specific and complete levels and scales of spatiotemporal interaction. Hence, it is only through the interaction of a population of models that specific domains and their singular levels and scales of interaction can be fully designed. See Manuel DeLanda, "Theorizing the Parametric," in "Intensive Fields: New Parametric Techniques in Urbanism," conference, USC, 12 December 2009, podcast at http://arch-pubs.usc.edu/parasite/intensive-fields/video-archive/ (last accessed January 2012).

102. Whitehead's notion of a nexus of actual entities may be particularly relevant in describing the architecture of multiagent systems, which is based on the nexus between variable quantities composed by internal relations and external connections. In particular, actual entities are finite units and have an extension in space and time. Whitehead also calls actual entities "microscopic atomic occasions" (*Process and Reality*, 508), by which he means that actual entities enter a process of concrescence moving from an initial status or fact (or for instance an initial variable quantity) coinciding with a macroscopic view, to a final status or fact (or a changed quantity) defining the microscopic view. In other words, an actual occasion reaches a subjective unity, becoming a final fact through its concrescence. Thus actual entities are divisible but undivided. Actual entities perish, terminate, and become complete quantities through a process of internal division and external connection that forms the architecture of a nexus, involving the development of actual entities in time with all their changes. Similarly, multiagent systems can be conceived as a nexus of finite actual entities, variable quantities acquiring a microscopic unity.

103. Whitehead's abstract scheme defines prehension (or relation within actual entities) as marking the genetic division of the extensive continuum. This means that processes are generated by relations within actual entities via the notion of inclusion (or genetic division) and between actual entities via overlapping or external connectivity (coordinate division and strains). Whitehead, *Process and Reality*, 114–115.

104. Ibid., 23.

105. On the categorical distinction between pure and real potentialities, see ibid., 23.

106. Ibid., 161.

107. Ibid., 160.

108. Alfred North Whitehead, *Science and the Modern World* (New York: Free Press, 1967), 171.

109. Ibid., 160.

110. Ibid., 164.

111. Ibid., 170.

112. Ibid., 161.

113. Henri Bergson, *Matter and Memory* (New York: Zone Books, 1991), 133–178.

114. Massumi, "Potential Politics and the Primacy of Pre-emption."

115. Unlike Hume's definition of perception, Whitehead points out that to prehend corresponds to "feeling with the body": "the withness of the body is an ever present element in our perception of presentational immediacy." Whitehead, *Process and Reality*, 190.

116. Ibid., 324.

117. Ibid., 160.

118. Ibid., 286.

119. Ibid., 72.

120. The divergence in the trajectory of a path from its initial conditions characterizes the physics of chaos and complexity theory. While deterministic chaos, like every empirical phenomenon, is entirely determined in principle by linear cause and effect, chaos physics points out that the cause of chaos cannot be traced back in a linear fashion. From the standpoint of far-from-equilibrium dynamics, there is no deterministic efficient causality for all the particles in the universe. As Shaviro points out, such a position violates Whitehead's ontological principle (that everything actual must come from somewhere) and the reformed subjectivist principle (that everything actual must be disclosed in the experience of some actual subject). Hence, even God is not omnipotent, but subjected to restrictions. Steven Shaviro, *Without Criteria: Kant, Whitehead, Deleuze, and Aesthetics* (Cambridge, MA: MIT Press, 2009), 17.

121. Marco Vanucci, "Open Systems: Approaching Novel Parametric Domains," in Michael Meredith, Tomoto Sakamoto, and Albert Ferre, eds., *From Control to Design: Parametric/Algorithmic Architecture* (Barcelona: Actar, 2008), 118.

122. Deleuze and Guattari argue that logic aims to convert concepts into functions and states of affairs. Concepts are events. They are "pure reserve," potentialities and not functions. Gilles Deleuze and Félix Guattari, *What Is Philosophy?* (London: Verso, 1999), 135–140.

123. The protocol describes the collection of physiological data through nanotechnology and the mapping of the four elemental moods revealed by the retrieval of neuromolecular data (dopamine: the pleasure molecule; adrenaline: the energetic molecule; serotonin: the melancholic molecule; cortisone: the anxiety/stress molecule).

124. As R&Sie(n) specifies: "Until now the acquisition of information used in residence protocols has been based exclusively on visible, reductive data. In our research we want to add the corporealities and their own substances. They can provide information about the relationship between bodies and space, and especially about the social relationships of bodies, the relationships between them, of the self to the other, both inside a single housing unit and in terms of the osmosis of vicinity." R&Sie(n) and Caroline Naphegyi "Protocols & Process," available at http://www.new-territories.com/blog/architecturedeshumeurs/?p=14 (last accessed January 2012).

125. Cantor's investigations into the properties of subsets of the linear continuum are presented in six papers published during 1879–1884, *Über unendliche lineare Punktmannigfaltigkeiten* ("On infinite, linear point manifolds"). These papers provide the first accounts of Cantor's theory of infinite sets and its application to the classification of subsets of the linear continuum. Cantor's set theory points at the manipulation and relation of consistent multiplicities, or aggregates. In this theory there is only one founding axiom that existentially asserts the existence of a set. This is the empty set axiom. All the other axioms state how to manipulate sets, which have already been given. In *Being and Event*, Alain Badiou states: "what has to be declared is that the one, which is not, exists solely as operation. In other words: there is no one, there is only the count-for-one." A pure process of naming inconsistent multiplicity marks the ground of all possible systems of related and consistent unities. This pure multiplicity of the set of sets is completely unordered and unorderable, it cannot be taken as a unity or totality; it is therefore inconsistent or incomplete multiplicity. That which can be unified, or counted as one, is consistent multiplicity. What remains central here is the nonrelation between consistent multiplicity (the event) and inconsistent (being). Alain Badiou, *Being and Event* (London: Continuum, 2005), 24. See also Boyer, *A History of Mathematics*, 273.

126. R&Sie(n) describes these functions as the mathematical inputs, which affect physiomorphologies and include cellular relations, neighborhood relations, and transactional relations. The full documentation of these protocols can be found at http://www.new-territories.com/blog/architecturedeshumeurs/?p=88 (last accessed January 2012).

127. At the same time, however, the elimination of common boundaries does not exclude the possibility of accounting for notions such as points, lines, and surfaces. It may be useful to clarify that Whitehead defines notions of points, lines, and surfaces as construing boundary elements for higher-order entities. For instance, points have been understood as sequences, sets or sets of sets or nested regions that converge but do not simply correspond to an object.

128. Whitehead, *Process and Reality*, 299 (Def. 17).

129. Ibid., 300 (Def. 23).

130. It seems clear here that Whitehead intends regions (the relata of extensive connection) to be almost formally identical with events (the relata of extensions). Regions are limited in extent, or bounded, whereas events may be unbounded (as in the case of durations). Ibid., 110.

131. Ibid., 301.

132. Ibid.

133. As Sanford Kwinter reminds us, a volume is composed of individualizing parts. "If A and B are parts of the volume C—for example the room in which you currently find yourself—A may be understood eventually as presenting an aspect of itself to C just as B does. But a specific relation also exists between A and B, again made up of that particular aspect that each volume may be said to have from the standpoint of the other. This relation AB must also be understood as impressing its contour into our volume C. The aspects A, B and AB from the standpoint of C contribute to, or partake of, the essence of C by means of what is called their *modal ingression*. Not every possible aspect of volume A or region B is actually active in C, but the degree to which some of their potential aspects do ingress, or to which they enter into composition with volume C, they may be said to be individualizing entities rather than simply individuated ones." Kwinter, *Far from Equilibrium*, 80–81.

134. Whitehead, *The Concept of Nature*, 59.

135. Ibid., 285.

136. François Roche, "Protocols/Processes," http://www.new-territories.com/blog/architecturedeshumeurs/wpcontent/uploads/2010/pdf/mouvement%20UK%20Une_architecture_des_humeurs_UKlight2.pdf (last accessed January 2012).

137. On mereology, see Casati and Varzi, *Parts and Places*, 44–45, 110–115.

138. According to Whitehead, in modern times a straight line is defined as the shortest distance between two points, whereas in classical geometry the existence of two points is sufficient to define a straight line. Whitehead, *Process and Reality*, 303.

139. Ibid., 307.

140. Whitehead describes a kind of differential structure on the space-time manifold in terms of mereotopology. However, his insistence on flatness is an attempt at arguing that Einstein's space-time could not be curved. For example, Whitehead observes that any two points in space-time are connected by a uniquely determined line.

141. Whitehead, *Process and Reality*, 308.

142. Ibid.

143. Ibid., 468.

144. In metric topology, an open set is defined by an interval on the real line that excludes its end points, such as [0, 1].

145. See Deleuze, *Difference and Repetition*, 219, 274.

146. Alfred North Whitehead, *The Function of Reason* (Boston: Beacon Press, 1929).

147. VBnet (Visual Basics Net) is an object-oriented programming language used for Web services applications. VBnet supports object-oriented programming concepts such as abstraction, inheritance, polymorphism, and aggregation. Like all scripting languages, VBnet is easier and faster to code in than more structured and compiled languages (such as C and C++). However, a script takes longer to run than a compiled program, since each instruction is being handled by another program first (requiring additional instructions) rather than directly by the basic instruction processor.

148. R&Sie(n) explains how the calculation of parameters occurs: inputs are first received through a text file of the morphology (such as VBnet script) running on Grasshopper-Rhino software. The optimization calculation contributes to define the position and diameter of the inhabitable spaces as three-meter clusters through vertical distributions (that are stuck into and absorbed by the structural calculation. The inputs also define the areas of contact between local and overall calculations, i.e., between the inhabitable morphologies and the overall structure. See François Roche, "Mathematical Operators for Structural Optimization," http://www.new-territories.com/blog/architecturedeshumeurs/?p=98 (last accessed January 2012).

149. This algorithm employs two mathematical strategies: the first follows on from function derivatives and the research carried out by Cauchy-Hadamard, the second originates from a procedure for showing complex shapes which mesh and create a topological structure. Roche, "Protocols/Processes," http://www.new-territories.com/blog/ (last accessed January 2012).

150. A software program arranges the data collected from these molecules. Algorithms connect physiomorphological computation to the algorithmic set to build biocement weaving structures through mathematical structural optimizations. The parameters for the positioning of forces are defined by their contact coordinates (given in x, y, and z) on the surface of each "base cube" volume (defining the overall

and local forces). The length of the vector instead defines the parameters for the intensity of forces. See Roche, "Mathematical Operators for Structural Optimization," http://www.new-territories.com/blog/architecturedeshumeurs/?p=98 (last accessed January 2012).

151. Roche, "Protocols/Processes," http://www.new-territories.com/blog/architecturedeshumeurs/wpcontent/uploads/2010/pdf/mouvement%20U%20Une_architecture_des_humeurs_UKlight2.pdf (last accessed January 2012).

152. If algorithms are not simply logical instantiations of procedures based on finite terms but are determined by an assembly of variable data, then it may be difficult to argue that algorithms are parts that can give us the whole of space. Each algorithmic set is, as it were, infected by an empty set of incomputable quantities that are bigger than all the parts put together. An algorithmic set can at once partake of the whole system of relations, but it can also exceed the consistent dynamics of the whole sum of algorithms as its determinacy remains attached to the indeterminate set that constitutes it. Indeterminate parts enter an algorithmic set of finite steps to constitute a discrete unity, a unique duration infected with indeterminate quantities (eternal objects).

153. To put it in another way, an actual set of variables can be part of the set of given data. However, in order to become connected to another set it also has to diverge from inherited data by prehending its own indeterminate set (as seen in the programming of a treelike urban structure that grows at the edges outside its planning routes) and fulfill itself. Therefore, while algorithmic procedures are completed by a finite number of steps, they always remain incomplete from the standpoint of parametric relations. In other words, a set of finite steps cannot contain within itself the infinite number of parametric relations. This is why computational incompleteness is evident in parametric design; each algorithmic set is what it is: a segment of space and a slice of time. Yet it cannot account alone for the total prehensions of random data in the relation between parameters. Similarly, the sum of parametric relations cannot account for the specific partial prehension of random data in each and every set.

154. Fuzzy logic is a logical calculus that defines the capacities of formal systems to compute nonbinary states or degrees of values between 0s and 1s. The logico-mathematical structure thus enables infinite degrees of states to acquire finite states, and thus implies the formalization of vague quantities: the axiomatic determination of indeterminate numbers.

155. François Roche and Natanel Elfassy, "Stuttering," *Log* 19 (Spring-Summer 2010), available at http://www.new-territories.com/blog/?p=457 (last accessed January 2012).

156. The Viab02 secretes biocement while creating a mapping made of braided diagonal stripes. Biocement is an agricultural polymer that can be secreted in real

time to generate these highly complex and fully singular structures, which are determined by the sensitive worlds of molecules. R&Sie(n) "Bio-cement Secretions/Extrusions," available at http://www.new-territories.com/blog/architecturedeshumeurs/?p=108 (last accessed January 2012).

157. The Viab02 is a machine dedicated to the realization of the 3D morphophysiological file. Ibid.

158. In chapter 1, I defined these quantities through the notion of Omega as theorized by information theorist Gregory Chaitin. Gregory Chaitin, *Meta Math! The Quest for Omega* (New York: Pantheon, 2005).

159. Gilles Deleuze and Félix Guattari, *A Thousand Plateaus: Capitalism and Schizophrenia* (London: Athlone Press, 1987), 43–44.

160. Massumi, "The Future Birth of the Affective Fact."

161. Hatherley, "Zaha Hadid Architects and the Neoliberal Avant-Garde," available at http://www.metamute.org/en/articles/zaha_hadid_architects (last accessed January 2012).

162. Ibid.

163. Douglas Spencer argues that integration of Deleuze's affirmative materialism in architecture has effectively contributed to the formation of a new mode of design coinciding with a neoliberal idea of space. Following Deleuze's affirmative materialism, this new mode of design has been able to neutralize issues of control and has rather tamed political tensions by creating an environment that is now dehierarchized, flexible, and multiple. Spencer in particularly wants to question the noncritical design of morphogenetic space of Foreign Office Architects (FOA), Zaha Hadid Architects (ZHA), Reiser + Umemoto, and Greg Lynn. Not only does this design concretize the spirit of capitalism, according to Spencer, but it also works to evacuate any form of politics by reframing—and thus naturalizing—political issues in terms of " a purely environmental matter." Douglas Spencer, "Architectural Deleuzism: Neoliberal Space, Control and the 'Univer-City,'" *Radical Philosophy* 168 (July-August 2011), 14.

164. Owen Hatherley has discussed Zaha Hadid Architects' 2010 design of Evelyn Grace Academy (London) as an example of neoliberalism, not of a political avant-garde. He explicitly argues that parametricism corresponds to "the logic of late neoliberalism" and cannot be associated with the political undertones of the avant-garde. Hatherley's analysis, however, seems to suggest that the Academy does not fully represent the flowing spaces of parametric form and its vocabulary of smooth connection, iterations, continual variation. Nevertheless, he argues that despite its structural absence, parametricism is politically present in this project as a neoliberal expression of power, where "'processes' of a radically inegalitarian capitalism are embodied, displayed, ennobled; we're aiming to create good little neoliberals."

Hatherley, "Zaha Hadid Architects and the Neoliberal Avant-Garde," http://www.metamute.org/editorial/articles/zaha-hadid-architects-and-neoliberal-avant-garde (last accessed January 2012).

165. Spencer, "Architectural Deleuzism," 16.

166. Ibid., 20.

167. Whitehead, *Process and Reality*, 289.

168. Ibid., 279–280.

169. Ibid., 164.

170. Ibid., 279.

171. Ibid., 164, 172, 183.

172. Ibid., 149, 189.

173. Ibid., 111.

174. Ibid., 280.

175. Ibid., 111.

176. Ibid.

177. Ibid., 112.

178. Ibid.

179. Ibid.

180. Ibid., 86.

181. Ibid., 80.

182. According to DeLanda, the aesthetic value of automated algorithms instead depends on the aesthetic capacities of the designer to combine information. As he points out, "architects wishing to use this new tool must not only become hackers (so that they can create the code needed to bring extensive and intensive aspects together) but also be able 'to hack' biology, thermodynamics, mathematics, and other areas of science to tap into the necessary resources." Manuel DeLanda, "Deleuze and the Use of the Genetic Algorithm in Architecture," in Neil Leach, ed., *Designing for a Digital World* (New York: Wiley, 2001), 115–120.

Chapter 3 Architectures of Thought

1. On biological modes of cognition, see Steven Shaviro, *Cognition and Decision in Non-Human Biological Organisms* (Living Books about Life, 2011), available at http://www.livingbooksaboutlife.org/books/Main_Page (last accessed January 2012).

2. Chaitin explains that if a program is left to run according to precise algorithmic instructions based on the evolutionary drive of growth, change, adaptation, and fitness, then the computational limit arrives as the space of incomputable probabilities that reveal how infinite quantities can reprogram axiomatic rules or add new axioms to existing ones. Gregory Chaitin, *Meta Math! The Quest for Omega* (New York: Pantheon, 2005), 130–131, 57.

3. In chapter 1 I made reference to Kittler's suggestion that the end of digital binary computation may well correspond to the end of thought and philosophy. While this is certainly an interesting proposition, I explained that Kittler does not take into account the incomputable algorithms at the limit of digital binary computation, which reveal that within formal thought and philosophy there are blind spots, anomalies, and incomplete axiomatic functions. The issue therefore is not the end of thought but the realization that reason has always had a dark counterpart even in the form of binary digits. I also suggested that Kittler's argument risks reducing the ontological premises of thought and philosophy to binary mathematics, and it also ignores the capacities of algorithms to make decisions beyond those that they were originally programmed for by a philosophical thought. In this respect they thus expose another form of reason, one that challenges thought and philosophy from within. See chapter 1 for further reference.

4. Alfred North Whitehead, *Modes of Thought* (New York: Free Press, 1938), 27–28.

5. Eshel Ben Jacob, Yoash Shapira, and Alfred I. Tauber, "Seeking the Foundations of Cognition in Bacteria: From Schrödinger's Negative Entropy to Latent Information," in Shaviro, *Cognition and Decision in Non-Human Biological Organisms.*

6. Shaviro, *Cognition and Decision in Non-Human Biological Organisms.*

7. The *AlloBrain* project is an interactive, stereographic, 3D-audio, immersive virtual world constructed from fMRI brain data and installed in the *AlloSphere*, which is one of the largest virtual reality spaces in existence. The *AlloBrain* reconstructs an interactive 3D model of a human brain from macroscopic, organic fMRI data sets. The current model contains several layers of tissue and blood flow, in which 12 intelligent agents interactively mine the data set for blood density level and deliver the information to the researchers. 3D electrocardiogram data are superimposed on the model so as to superimpose computational models of synaptic nerve response and to include the nanoscale organic level. The simulation contains several generative audiovisual systems, stereo-optically displayed and controlled by two wireless devices. Two of the devices used to control the model include wireless (Bluetooth) input and feature custom electronics, integrating several MEMs sensor technologies. The first controller allows one to navigate the space using six degrees of freedom. The second contains twelve buttons that control the twelve agents, and also moves the ambient sounds spatially around the sphere. Its shape is based on the hyperdodecahedron, a four-dimensional geometrical polytope, the shadow of which is projected onto three dimensions. The model was developed using procedural model-

ing techniques and was constructed with a 3D printer capable of building solid objects. Using these controls along with the immersive qualities of the *AlloSphere*, neuroscientists have been able to explain the structure of the brain to varied audiences. This virtual interactive prototype also illustrates some of the key research topics undertaken in the *AlloSphere*: multimedia/multimodal computing, interactive immersive environments, and scientific data representation through art. All the documentation about the project can be retrieved at http://www.allosphere.ucsb.edu/research.php (last accessed January 2012).

8. The *AlloSphere* was created by Dr. JoAnn Kuchera-Morin, director of the Allosphere Research Laboratory at the California Nanosystems Institute. For further information about the developments of the AlloSphere project see http://www.mat.ucsb.edu/allosphere and http://www.create.ucsb.edu (last accessed January 2012).

9. fMRI is a scan that measures the change in blood flow related to neural activity in the brains of animals and humans. This scan has also been taken as an example of the "neurological turn" toward analyses of contemporary media such as the Internet, and such technological measuring of intensive changes is at the core of neuropolitics. See Anna Munster, "Nerves of Data: The Neurological Turn in/against Networked Media," *Computational Culture*, no. 1 (December 2011), available at http://computationalculture.net/ (last accessed January 2012).

10. Unlike the small cubicle of the 1990s, this virtual environment accommodates the presence of 2–30 people in the immersive space, allowing a communal experience of their scanned brain.

11. Andrew Pickering points out that the main concern for British cyberneticians, such as Ross Ashby, Grey Walter, Gordon Pask, and Stafford Beer, was the brain, already indicating that thought involved enaction and environmental interaction. The cybernetic concern for the brain was different from computational models of cognition, which emphasized the interior processing of algorithms without interaction with the environment. Andrew Pickering, *The Cybernetic Brain: Sketches of Another Future* (Chicago: University of Chicago Press, 2010), 5–6.

12. Peter M. Asaro, "From Mechanisms of Adaptation to Intelligence Amplifiers: The Philosophy of W. Ross Ashby," in Philip Husbands, Owen Holland, and Michael Wheeler, eds., *The Mechanical Mind in History* (Cambridge, MA: MIT Press, 2008), 154–155.

13. A homeostat is a device first built by W. Ross Ashby to demonstrate that a machine is capable of adapting itself to the environment.

14. For Ashby, the homeostat was also an example of a simulation that could be useful to scientific education, demonstrating that goal-seeking behavior, as a trial-and-error search for equilibrium, presents a fundamentally different kind of mechanical process—negative feedback with step functions—and opens up new possibilities for what machines might be capable of doing. Asaro, "From

Mechanisms of Adaptation to Intelligence Amplifiers," 162. Similarly, according to Pickering the cybernetic brain modeling entailed an external other, thus emphasizing the performative aspect of cognition. Ashby's model of the homeostat did not describe the brain according to a calculable representation, but according to the adaptive activities of its components in the articulation of connections. Pickering, *The Cybernetic Brain*, 27–28.

15. In 1890 William James proposed the concept of plasticity, according to which the experience of the present could actually change the brain's physical structure (its anatomy) and its functional organization (or physiology), challenging the notion that the brain's structure could no longer change after its early years of development. Between 1970 and 1980, neuroscientist Michael Merzenich demonstrated the fact of neuroplasticity (that the brain can and does change), leading to radical improvements in cognitive functioning. Norman Doidge, *The Brain that Changes Itself: Stories of Personal Triumph from the Frontiers of Brain Science* (New York: Viking, 2007).

16. For further discussion on this topic see Munster, "Nerves of Data."

17. This is Thompson's definition of enaction. Evan Thompson, *Mind in Life: Biology, Phenomenology, and the Sciences of the Mind* (Cambridge, MA: Harvard University Press, 2007), 13.

18. Francisco J. Varela, Evan Thompson, and Eleanor Rosch, *The Embodied Mind: Cognitive Science and Human Experience* (Cambridge, MA: MIT Press, 1991), 9.

19. Thompson, *Mind in Life*, 13.

20. Ibid., 14.

21. I am referring to Varela's definition of "phenomenological experience" in the context of what he defines as "neuro-phenomenology." In response to Chalmers's discussion of an existing gap between cognition and experience, Varela argued for a return to cognitive science. In particular he engaged with connectionism, which studied how local rules determine the behavior of global properties of behavior, and carried out large-scale analysis of brain activity and neuropsychology, thereby tackling the experimental relation of cognition and action. For Varela, however, all cognitive science must confront the problem of determining mental phenomena without having direct experience of them: that is, by overcoming the problem of theory—or mental constructs—about what is instead a lived experience. By excluding the findings of quantum mechanics about the superposition of two states of mind at one point, thus actually questioning the position of the observer, Varela provided a chart of methodologies to approach the hard problem of the relation between cognition and experience. Among them we find: Churchland's eliminativism, which according to Varela reduces experience to a neurobiological fact; a new form of functionalism which replaces cognition with intentional states, such as Dennett's "multiple drafts" and Edelman's "neural Darwinism," which rely on a

third-person approach that validates data; the "mysterianists," who argue that the limit of human knowledge renders the gap between cognition and experience unsolvable; and finally Varela's approach, which focuses on the centrality of first-person accounts of experience. Drawing on Husserl, Varela insists that phenomenology looks at experience in a specific gesture of reflection or phenomenological reduction: the transformation of a naive experience into a reflexive or second-order experience. This includes a suspension of belief about what is being examined, a disciplining of habitual discourses, and a bracketing of the set structures that determine the background of everyday life. Varela explicitly argues that the point of reduction is precisely to suspend our habitual thinking: to stop the stream of thought, and to go backward toward the emergence of thoughts themselves. This is defined as the human capacity for reflexivity or reduction, which abolishes the distance between experience and the world. Reflexivity entails no introspection, but rather intuition entangled with reasoning, which leads to an intersubjective validation of the realm of phenomena. Varela proposes a neurophenomenological circular method based on structural invariants such as attention, emotion, fringe, and center, a perceptual filling-in providing constraints on scientific empirical observations. Experience, in other words, needs to be active in the scientific explanation. Similarly, a large-scale integration in the brain should also count as a first-person account of mental contents. Empirical questions are to be guided by first-person evidence (whatever their nature). Thus, disciplined first-person accounts should be an integral element of validating a neurobiological proposal. Rejecting the assumptions of a theory of mere identity between experience and cognition, Varela argues that these two terms are only established by learning, not by a priori theoretical constitutions. Ultimately, for Varela, the world and the mind are mutually structured in an embodied, situated, or enactive cognition. In other words, the study of any mental phenomena is always that of an experiencing person. Neurophenomenology is thus defined by the mutual constraint between the field of phenomena revealed by experience and the correlative field of phenomena established by cognitive sciences. See Francisco Varela, "Phenomenology: A Methodological Remedy for the Hard Problem," *Journal of Consciousness Studies* 3 (June 1996), 330–350.

22. As explained in the previous note, Varela argues that phenomenological reduction is based on the human capacity for reflexivity, which transforms naive experience into a cognitive enaction.

23. See the project's documentation at http://doublenegatives.jp/installations/Corpora/index.htm (last accessed January 2012).

24. Thompson, *Mind in Life*, 15.

25. Whitehead, *Modes of Thought*, 11–18.

26. Alfred North Whitehead, *Science and the Modern World* (Cambridge: Cambridge University Press, 1928), 197.

27. Ibid., 198.

28. Alfred North Whitehead, *Process and Reality: An Essay in Cosmology* (New York: Free Press, 1978), 23.

29. Ibid., 41.

30. Ibid., 41–42.

31. I discussed this example in chapter 1. See Kas Oosterhuis et al., "Interactive Wall: Prototype for an Emotive Wall," available at http://www.bk.tudelft.nl/en/about-faculty/departments/hyperbody/publicity-and-publications/works-commissions/interactivewall-prototype-for-an-emotive-wall (last accessed January 2012).

32. Whitehead, *Process and Reality*, 122–124.

33. In the late 1990s, Rosalind Picard demonstrated that computers could be given capacities to sense and recognize patterns of emotional information, such as spatio-temporal forms that influence the voice, face, posture, but also to sense and reason about other situational variables. Affective Computing is a continuing project at MIT: see http://affect.media.mit.edu/ (last accessed January 2012). See also Rosalind W. Picard, *Affective Computing* (Cambridge, MA: MIT Press, 2007).

34. James Bradley, "The Speculative Generalization of the Function: A Key to Whitehead," *Tijdschrift voor Filosofie* 64 (2002), 231–252. Also available at *Inflexions*, no. 2 (December 2008), www.inflexions.org (last accessed January 2012).

35. Nigel Thrift, "Movement-Space: The Changing Domain of Thinking Resulting from the Development of New Kinds of Spatial Awareness," *Economy and Society* 33, no. 4 (2004), 582–604.

36. Ibid., 594.

37. Ibid.

38. Ibid., 596.

39. Warren S. McCulloch and Walter Pitts's paper "A Logical Calculus of the Ideas Immanent in Nervous Activity" was written to demonstrate that a Turing machine program could be implemented in a finite network of formal neurons and thus that the neuron (or the mathematically abstracted neural function) was indeed the base logic unit of the brain. Their artificial neuron (abstracted from the neurophysiological structure of the brain) strongly contributed to the development of neural network theory, but more significantly contributed to the development of a cybernetic view of computation, which eventually led to ideas of self-organization defined by adaptation and learning. This paper therefore reveals the impact of cybernetics on computation as being concerned not with symbolic manipulation of data, but with the architectural form of the brain. See James A. Anderson and Edward Rosenfeld, eds., *Neurocomputing*, vol. 1, *Foundations of Research* (Cambridge, MA: MIT Press, 1989),

15–18. Pask's cybernetic brain experimentation further contributed to the artificial development of biological neurons. The *MusiColour* machine, for instance, used banks of lights as biological neurons, which would be activated when and if the output exceeded a certain threshold value that changed over time. See Pickering, *The Cybernetic Brain*, 316.

40. See John Hamilton Frazer, "The Cybernetics of Architecture: A Tribute to the Contribution of Gordon Pask," *Kybernetes* 30, nos. 5–6 (2001), 641–651. The article discusses Pask's contribution to the development of environmentally responsive architectural theory.

41. R. A. Brooks, M. Coen, D. Dang, J. DeBonet, J. Kramer, T. Lozano-Pérez, J. Mellor, P. Pook, C. Stauffer, L. Stein, M. Torrance, and M. Wessler, "The Intelligent Room Project," Proceedings of the Second International Cognitive Conference (CT 1997), Aizu, Japan, August 1997, available at http://www.ai.mit.edu/projects/aire.orig/publications/ (last accessed January 2012).

42. On the MIT *Intelligent Room* project, see Michael Coen, "The Future of Human-Computer Interaction or How I Learned to Stop Worrying and Love My Intelligent Room," *IEEE Intelligent Systems* (March-April 1999), available at http://people.csail.mit.edu/mhcoen/Papers/stopworrying.pdf (last accessed January 2012).

43. See Usman Haque, "The Architectural Relevance of Gordon Pask," *Architectural Design* 77, no. 4 (July-August), 54–61. In this context, the stealing or reappropriation of software, for instance, may also count as a way of developing tools of interaction that build new data environments through a veritable conversation between distinct software structures. On the aesthetics of interaction as the reappropriation of distinct software, see the work of digital media artist Cory Arcangel. In particular, see projects such as the *Infinite Fill Show*, 2004. See "Columbia University Art and Technology Lectures," December 16, 2006, available at http://www.columbia.edu/itc/soa/dmc/cory_arcangel/ (last accessed January 2012).

44. For a more detailed discussion of Pask's pioneering views of interaction see Peter Cariani, "Pask's Ear and Biological Creativity," available at http://www.maverickmachines.com/WordPress/wp-content/uploads/2007/07/petercariani.pdf (last accessed January 2012); Peter Cariani, "To Evolve an Ear: Epistemological Implications of Gordon Pask's Electrochemical Devices," *Systems Research* 10, no. 3 (1993), 19–33.

45. This exhibition was held at Atelier Farbergasse, Vienna, 26 March–4 April 2008. Details of the exhibition can be found at http://paskpresent.com/exhibition/ (last accessed January 2012).

46. Roberts's installation consists of two steel plates that are physically attached to loudspeakers, one acting as a microphone, the other as a driver. An amplifier and monitoring system create an audio feedback loop with the environment. The movement of people around the device triggers the acoustic properties of the space, which

change through differing oscillations. For a more detailed description of *Hearing a Reality*, see http://paskpresent.com/exhibition/?page_id=15 (last accessed January 2012).

47. KRD's project *Responsive Space* was designed for the Machine Exhibition at the Kelvingrove Gallery, Glasgow, in 1999. Documentation of this project is available at http://www.lucybullivant.net/html/showcase/publications/rogers.html (last accessed June 2012).

48. Humberto R. Maturana and Francisco J. Varela, *Autopoiesis and Cognition: The Realization of the Living* (Dordrecht: D. Reidel, 1980), 13.

49. James J. Gibson, *The Ecological Approach to Visual Perception* (Boston: Houghton Mifflin, 1979), 243.

50. Cognition can only start as an activity of perception, as deployed by the flowing array of the observer who walks from one vista to another, moves around an object and thus extracts from it the invariants that underlie a changing perspective, unearthing the connections between hidden and unhidden surfaces. Ibid., 303.

51. Gibson explained that nothing is copied in the light to the eye of an observer, not the shape of a thing, the surface of it, its substance, color, or motion, but all these things are specified in the light itself. Ibid., 305.

52. Gibson's notion of affordance entails a certain type of direct perception. For instance, images are not mediated by retinal, neural, or mental pictures. Direct perception instead gets information from the ambient array of light. Direct perception results from the exploration of what lies around things, leading vision to perceive a continuous background surface. Ibid., 35.

53. Ibid., 202.

54. Ibid., 86.

55. Brian Massumi argues for a notion of lived abstraction to explain the operations of concrete experience. In particular, he puts forward the notion of semblance to explain how events imply the experience of passing and how what passes corresponds to a lived abstraction. Brian Massumi, *Semblance and Event: Activist Philosophy and the Occurrent Arts* (Cambridge, MA: MIT Press, 2011).

56. Whitehead, *Modes of Thought*, 26.

57. Ibid.

58. Alva Noe, *Action in Perception* (Cambridge, MA: MIT Press, 2005), 1–2.

59. Ibid., 8–9.

60. This does not mean, however, that perception guides action, but mainly that sensorimotor knowledge constitutes perception and action. Ibid., 12.

61. Ibid., 15.

62. *Ada—The Intelligent Space* was an interactive pavilion at the Swiss national exposition Expo.02, designed by the Institute of Neuroinformatics at the University of Zurich and ETH Zurich. The interactive designer Paul Verschure considers this neuromorphic architecture to be an affective-cognitive space that differs from projects such as MIT's *Intelligent Room* project, which in his view still applies a functionalist model of interaction. For further details about the project, see "Ada: Constructing a Synthetic Organism," available at www.ini.ethz.ch/~tobi/papers/ada-iros.pdf *(last* accessed January 2012).

63. Noe, *Action in Perception*, 25.

64. Ibid., 31.

65. As Noe claims, "For the world as a domain of facts is given to us thanks to the fact that we inhabit the world as a domain of activity." Ibid., 179.

66. Ibid., 183.

67. Ibid., 184.

68. As Noe points out, "we can tell by looking that a thing is red even if we do not articulate the reasons why." Ibid., 186.

69. Ibid., 188.

70. Ibid., 189.

71. Ibid., 193.

72. Ibid., 198.

73. Ibid., 199.

74. Ibid., 200.

75. Ibid., 207.

76. Noe observes that it is yet to be proved that the experience of red actually matches with neural activities. Ibid., 210.

77. Ibid., 222.

78. Ibid., 227.

79. Ibid., 229–230.

80. Whitehead, *Modes of Thought*, 23.

81. Ibid., 28.

82. Whitehead clarifies this point even more precisely: "In order to understand the essence of thought we must study its relations to the ripples amid which it emerges." Ibid., 36.

83. I am referring here to Parmenidean absolutism, according to which there can be no thinking without being: the eternal, unmovable, unchangeable whole that subsumes thought. Against the experience of a continuously changing world, Parmenides claims an undivided, infinite, and changeless Being.

84. See Andy Clark and David J. Chalmers, "The Extended Mind," 1998, available at http://www.cogs.indiana.edu/andy/TheExtendedMind.pdf (last accessed January 2012).

85. Ibid., 20.

86. Ibid., 25.

87. Ibid., 26.

88. Ibid.

89. Andy Clark, "Where Brain, Body and World Collide," *Daedalus* 127, no. 2 (Spring 1998), 257–280.

90. Andy Clark, "Embodiment and the Philosophy of Mind," in Anthony O'Hear, ed., *Current Issues in Philosophy of Mind* (Cambridge: Cambridge University Press, 1998), 35–52.

91. Connectionism defines cognition in terms of the synaptic links that constitute the neural architecture, which includes units, layers, and connections, but also learning rules and computational representations emerging from the activity of the network. NETtalk is a neural network that has learned to read. It takes strings of characters forming English text and converts them into strings of phonemes, which are used as input to a speech synthesizer. NETtalk demonstrates that a relatively small network can capture most common and uncommon regularities in English phonetics. By using a learning algorithm, the system discovers combinations of letters and phonemes. Terrence J. Sejnowski and Charles R. Rosenberg, "NETtalk: A Parallel Network that Learns to Read Aloud," Johns Hopkins University Electrical Engineering and Computer Science Technical Report, JUH/EECS-86/01, in Anderson and Rosenfeld, *Neurocomputing*, vol. 1, 663–672. For a historical overview of philosophical debates about connectionism, see Terence Horgan and John Tienson, *Connectionism and the Philosophy of Mind* (Dordrecht: Kluwer Academic Publishers, 1991).

92. Recently Manuel DeLanda has argued that the study of neural nets in a space that can affect and be affected by its parts shows how creatures behave in an intentional way as "oriented toward external opportunities and risks." Manuel DeLanda, *Philosophy and Simulation* (London: Continuum, 2011), 91.

93. Clark, "Embodiment and the Philosophy of Mind," 39.

94. The "connectionist crab" is a hypothesis that explores the application of artificial neural networks to the problem of creating efficient point-to-point linkages between deformed topographic maps. Paul M. Churchland, *A Neurocomputational*

Perspective: The Nature of Mind and the Structure of Science (Cambridge, MA: MIT Press, 1989). Churchland's conception of neurocomputational cognition will be discussed in the next section.

95. Ibid., 42.

96. See Ruth Millikan, "Biosemantics," *Journal of Philosophy* 86, no. 6 (1989), 281–297; reprinted in Cynthia MacDonald and Graham MacDonald, eds., *Philosophy of Psychology: Debates on Psychological Explanation* (Oxford: Blackwell, 1995).

97. Clark, "Embodiment and the Philosophy of Mind," 44.

98. Ibid., 46.

99. This notion is discussed in chapter 1 in the context of genetic or generative models of architecture. See Richard Dawkins, *The Extended Phenotype: The Long Reach of the Gene* (Oxford: Oxford University Press, 1999).

100. Clark uses this notion of wideware to refer to an intuitive notion of the external environment, which he uses in conjunction to notions of mindware and wetware. For instance, wideware is represented by notebooks or calculators, which are understood by Clark as being extended structures of cognition. Similarly, this notion is used to describe the functional role of these structures or the fact that they promote a cognitive adaptation to the external environment. Thus the notion of wideware is used to address those cognitive processes of storage, search, and transformation which are not carried out by the internal structure of the brain, but are realized by means of bodily action and a variety of external media. See Clark, "Where Brain, Body and World Collide," 268.

101. Clark, "Embodiment and the Philosophy of Mind," 50.

102. Andy Clark, *Natural-Born Cyborgs: Minds, Technologies, and the Future of Human Intelligence* (Oxford: Oxford University Press, 2004), 4.

103. Ibid.

104. Ibid., 5.

105. Ibid., 6.

106. Ibid., 27.

107. Ibid., 33.

108. Ibid., 78.

109. It may be worth adding here that DeLanda's recent explanation of emergentism precisely points out how this historical and philosophical notion has acquired scientific relevance in the context of ideas of self-generation and morphogenesis that are rooted in the biological sciences. DeLanda, *Philosophy and Simulation*, 1–7.

110. Ibid., 136.

111. Ibid., 141–142.

112. Dennis Bray, *Wetware: A Computer in Every Living Cell* (New Haven: Yale University Press, 2009), 194.

113. These chemical reactions include "the transformations of small molecules familiar in energy metabolism and synthetic reactions to make larger molecules; the modifications of the structure of proteins by addition of phosphate and methyl groups; the assembly of protein into large complexes; the turning on and off of genes; the transport of ions and small molecules across membranes; the generation of mechanical force and directed motion." Ibid., 226.

114. Ibid., 227.

115. Ibid., 235.

116. Bray quotes Nathalie Balaban's experiment with *E. coli* bacteria. This experiment demonstrated that these bacteria contain a small number of cells that grow much more slowly than the rest, and are therefore resistant to antibiotics that target fast-growing cells. "By coercing a few cells to grow slowly the bacterial culture as a whole takes out an insurance policy. The organism pays a small premium in terms of material and energy in order to protect itself against future cathartic experiences." In other words, cells deliberately produce variations as a way to anticipate future changes. Ibid., 236.

117. Shaviro, *Cognition and Decision in Non-Human Biological Organisms.*

118. Andy Clark, *Mindware: An Introduction to the Philosophy of Cognitive Science* (Oxford: Oxford University Press, 2001), 7.

119. Ibid., 8.

120. Whitehead, *Modes of Thought*, 20.

121. Ibid.

122. According to Clark, the very activity of bodily spatiotemporal orientation is what drives the development and evolution of inner states of cognition: additional memory and new capacities of symbol manipulation, new forms of communication, interaction, and digital computation. Here the architecture of thought is no longer internal to the human brain, but has become spatially extended onto the world. Such a global brain derives, in Clark's view, from the coevolutionary relation between brain and environment, where the technoextension of cognition determines what thought can do beyond the confines of the skin.

123. Deborah Aschheim's *Neural Architecture* includes a series of site-specific installations that investigate the biological aspects of architecture and the architectural qualities of biology. In particular, the installation at the Laguna Art Museum features

a network of luminous neural clusters based on the neural columns of the cerebral cortex. When the movement of visitors activates the darkened space of the cortex, its neural dendrites light up. The clusters also contain mini spy cameras, which transmit images of the visitors to mini televisions embedded in the cells. For more details, see http://www.deborahaschheim.com/projects/neural-architecture/3 (last accessed January 2012). For a review of Aschheim's work see Tyler Stallings, "Deborah Aschheim: Neural Architecture (a Smart Building Is a Nervous Building)," Laguna Art Museum, 2004. The article is also available at http://www.tylerstallings.com/WritingContents/Aschheim/AschheimEssayScan.htm (last accessed January 2012).

124. In neuroscience, a neural network describes a population of physically interconnected neurons or a group of disparate neurons, the inputs—or signaling targets—of which define a recognizable circuit. The history of neural networks started with Marvin Minsky and Seymour Papert's book *Perceptrons* (1969), which is famous for the devastating effect it had on neural networks as a topic for research in brain models. In particular, Minsky and Papert's book discussed the theoretical limitations of perceptrons as computational models used to demonstrate that certain things cannot be computed. These limitations included "the requirement for linear separability of the data for perfect classification by an output unit," but also whether "too much generalization was required." (See Anderson and Rosenfeld, *Neurocomputing*, vol. 1, 157.) One of the most famous mathematical results of the book, however, came from the discussion of the geometric predicate of connectedness, where it was demonstrated that perceptrons could not compute connectedness. Contrary to what was predicted in *Perceptrons*, the construction of more advanced neural networks demonstrates that the latter are in fact capable of computing some logical predicates more efficiently than perceptrons could. In particular, the contemporary resurrection of neural networks research is also linked to the research on how these nets learn and can be taken as models for psychological studies. (Ibid.,159–160; see also "Marvin Minsky and Seymour Papert, Perceptrons (MIT, 1969)," in ibid., 161–173.) However, it is widely recognized in the literature on neurcomputation that the modern era of research on neural networks was demarcated by John Hopefield's paper on emergent computational abilities, which explained the usefulness of neural networks to engineering, and in particular to the development of neural net chips. Whereas standard approaches to neural networks were based on a learning rule, defined by synaptic modifications that eventually led to emergent properties of cognition, Hopefield pointed out that the nervous system developed a number of locally stable points in state space. In particular, attractors had the capacity to transform the space flow into stable points. The task of these attractors was to correct errors and reconstruct missing information. Hopefield therefore considered the evolution of the system in terms of physical energy, whereby a random element looked at its inputs and changed its state, thus implying an increase or decrease of energy until an energy minimum was reached. (Ibid., 457–459, 460–464.)

125. Paul Churchland, *The Engine of Reason, the Seat of the Soul: A Philosophical Journey into the Brain* (Cambridge, MA: MIT Press, 1995), 3.

126. Ibid., 6.

127. Ibid., 11.

128. Ibid., 17.

129. Paul Churchland, *Neurophilosophy at Work* (Cambridge: Cambridge University Press, 2007), 2.

130. Ibid.

131. Ibid.

132. As Churchland points out, "The familiar feedforward pathways are called 'ascending' pathways. The feedbackward pathways are called 'descending' or 'recurrent' pathways." Churchland, *The Engine of Reason, the Seat of the Soul*, 99.

133. Synaptic weights define the strength of connections between neurons. These weights are responsible for the patterns of activations in a network.

134. Churchland, *The Engine of Reason, the Seat of the Soul*, 95.

135. Churchland, *Neurophilosophy at Work*, 8.

136. Churchland is here referring to von Neumann machines. Against Dennett, Churchland argues that these machines do not need to download a memetic program in order to work: "a vN machine is not a piece of 'software' fit for downloading." Instead he argues that the material configuration of a recurrent network "already delivers the desired capacity for recognizing, manipulating, and generating serial structures in time." Ibid., 9.

137. NETtalk is a neural network that has learned to read. It takes strings of characters forming English text and converts them into strings of phonemes, which are used as input to a speech synthesizer. NETtalk demonstrates that a relatively small network can capture the most common and also the most uncommon regularities in English phonetics. By using a learning algorithm, the system discovers combinations of letters and phonemes. Sejnowski and Rosenberg, "NETtalk," 663–672.

138. As Churchland explains: "the sequence in which the outputs appear is owed not to any computation within the network itself, but entirely to the spatial order in which they are presented to the network. Present them to the network in reverse order, and the net will respond by talking backwards. It doesn't know anything about temporal order." Churchland, *The Engine of Reason, the Seat of the Soul*, 98.

139. Alfred North Whitehead, *Adventures of Ideas* (New York: Free Press, 1967), 91.

140. Churchland, *The Engine of Reason, the Seat of the Soul*, 98.

141. Ibid., 103.

142. Ibid.

143. Ibid., 104.

144. However, Churchland also points out that the simplest architectures or artificial neural networks are for instance unable to represent the unfolding of time. Ibid., 98.

145. Ibid., 134–135.

146. Ibid., 150.

147. Ibid., 104.

148. Ibid., 106.

149. Ibid.

150. Ibid., 10–11.

151. Ibid., 235.

152. Ibid., 243.

153. Ibid., 245.

154. Ibid., 250.

155. For more specific examples of intelligence defined by the language capacities of neural networks, which can be developed as forms of learning in humans, animals, and machines, see ibid., 264–268.

156. Ibid., 286.

157. Churchland, *Neurophilosophy at Work*, 33.

158. Ibid.

159. Churchland, *The Engine of Reason, the Seat of the Soul*, 251.

160. In his 1981 article "Eliminative Materialism and the Propositional Attitudes," Churchland proposed several arguments to challenge and eliminate commonsense psychology. In particular, he claimed that folk psychology challenged the scientific understanding of thought, seen as being simply based on ordinary notions such as belief. Similarly, Patricia Churchland in *Neurophilosophy* also argued that the increasing developments in neuroscience research would finally make the commonsensical notions of mental states disappear. See Patricia Smith Churchland, *Neurophilosophy: Toward a Unified Science of the Mind-Brain* (Cambridge, MA: MIT Press, 1989), 1–10.

161. Propositional attitudes are, for instance, beliefs, desire, fear, and hope, which constitute a commonsense understanding of the mind that is not scientifically

grounded in material or empirical evidence and not supported by scientific explanations. Churchland, *Neurophilosophy*, 383.

162. Churchland, *The Engine of Reason, the Seat of the Soul*, 232.

163. Churchland, however, specifies that the conceptual framework should be identified with the partitions that the synaptic weights effectuate across the activation space of the assembled neurons to which they connect. Ibid.

164. Churchland, *A Neurocomputational Perspective*, 219.

165. Ibid., 241.

166. For a detailed discussion of the idealism of Churchland's material eliminativism, see Ray Brassier, *Nihil Unbound: Enlightenment and Extinction* (London: Palgrave Macmillan, 2007), 29–40.

167. Ibid., 37.

168. Ibid., 38, 40.

169. Ibid., 21.

170. Ibid., 59.

171. Churchland, *The Engine of Reason, the Seat of the Soul*, 243.

172. Chaitin, *Meta Math!*, 130–131, 57.

173. I articulated this notion of speculative computation in chapter 1.

174. In particular, one central question in William James's radical empiricism is: How are changes felt? Are they really felt after they are produced by the sensory nerves of the organs, which would then report back to the brain the modifications that have occurred? Or are these felt before they are produced, by our being conscious of the outgoing nerve currents as they start their way down toward the parts that they are to excite? According to Antonio Damasio, James believed they were felt after. Thus in this case James's view on emotional cognition seems to support Damasio's statement that the cognition of emotions occurs after the physiological registering of perceived data. Damasio argues that despite the lack of neurophysiological knowledge, James pointed out the existence of a cortex that carries out the semantic perception of feelings or emotions. Nevertheless, James could only emphasize the centrality of perceiving the stimulus, the physiological feeling of a changing state within a body, and not the appraisal of the stimulus. According to Damasio, the specific physiological response to a stimulus depends on the context. Bad news in a happy context does not have the same affect as bad news in an already sad context. Similarly, Damasio suggests, James could not define the specific location in the brain responsible for triggering an action and did not acknowledge the importance of internal stimulation in the generation of emotions. See William James, "What Is an Emotion?," *Mind* 9 (1884), 188–205, footnotes 1 and 4; and Antonio

Damasio, *Looking for Spinoza: Joy, Sorrow, and the Feeling Brain* (Orlando, FL: Harcourt, 2003), 60–65.

175. Whitehead, *Adventures of Ideas,* 180–181.

176. Nonsensuous or conceptual prehensions are neither sensory responses nor cognitive reflections, but expose the activities of thought at all levels of nature.

177. Damasio, *Looking for Spinoza,* 86. In this book, Damasio draws on Baruch Spinoza's axiom that thinking is an idea of the body. Although there is not enough space here to engage with Damasio's reading of Spinoza, I do want to stress that Damasio's neurophysiological reading completely ignores Spinoza's metaphysical enterprise, and ends up identifying the body with thought. In Spinoza, extension and thought are attributes of substance, which defines the existence of parallel yet distinguishable modes of being. In this chapter, I have chosen not to focus on Spinoza but rather on James, so as to address the problem of immanent experience more directly.

178. Ibid., 148.

179. Damasio's research points out that some types of frontal lobe damage have been seen to produce two main effects. In the first place, there is evidence that this sort of impairment leads to the loss of certain kinds of secondary emotional reactions, or to the loss of care about existing matters, such as physical pain. In the second place, Damasio has found evidence that this impairment diminishes creativity and the abilities of decision making and planning. As a result, the loss of secondary emotional reactions induces a loss of the ability to manage the normal functions of perception, memory, motor control, language, intelligence, and circumstantial knowledge. Ibid., 174–175.

180. Damasio maintains that James had not envisaged the importance of simulation, the thinking of feeling. Instead, James turns to the notion of simulation when he argues that the sole thought of an emotion without its actual sensorial content does indeed incite a feeling-thought. As James points out, the sight of a blade give rises to nonsensory (or affective) bodily effects, and the thought of yearning can equally produce real yearning. James, "What Is an Emotion?," 205. Similarly the point just made about the capacity of thought to become self-abstracted and yet to incite feeling without content refers to the importance of simulation in computation. Simulation therefore is not an abstraction but corresponds to the reality of felt thoughts: not a representation of what an external agent is feeling or thinking, but of the algorithmic mode of feeling-thinking itself.

181. James, "What Is an Emotion?," 202.

182. This expression refers to Antonio Damasio, *The Feeling of What Happens: Body, Emotion and the Making of Consciousness* (New York: Harcourt, 2000).

183. The definition of an "aesthetic cogito" is borrowed here from Brian Massumi, "Deleuze, Guattari and the Philosophy of Expression (Involutionary Afterword)," *Canadian Review of Comparative Literature* 24, no. 3 (1998).

184. For instance, the aesthetics of the digital accident has implied that codes are modes of thought to the extent that they do things. They are engines of production, government, and control as they exist not in isolation but bear upon structures, from data structures to hardware to physicalities. These perfomative aspects of coding, which imply an operative mode of thinking in and through matter, do however leave us an important question. If the digital code is more than a mental form or idea, then we may have to agree with the affective approach, according to which novelty in digital computation can only ever arise from aesthetic qualities. In other words, if novelty can only be derived from perfomativity, then codes, it is assumed, do not think, but only execute thought. Instead, it is argued here that the novelty of soft thought has to be found in its process of division of potential quantities: mathematical ideas that Whitehead calls eternal objects. These quantities are "felt" by the entities that they operate without being summed up into a finite cipher or being counted as infinities. Rather than having to go through their qualitative transduction into colors, sounds, and numbers, I want to argue, as suggested elsewhere, that quantities "are indirectly felt as conceptual contagions . . . conceptually felt but not directly sensed." Luciana Parisi, "Symbiotic Architecture: Prehending Digitality," *Theory, Culture and Society* 26, nos. 2–3 (March-May 2009), 346–374.

185. All the documentation for this project can be found at http://b.durandin.free.fr/iveheardabout/iha.htm (scroll down, go script 2, click on numbers 1–8) (last accessed January 2012).

186. Whitehead defines a subjective aim as an ongoing process, which results from the activities of prehensions, from the selection of data that constitute an actual entity according to its subjective aim. The process of concrescence of an actual entity is therefore defined by a subjective aim driving the entity to become a unity, to reach satisfaction and then to perish (i.e., the actual entity then becomes objective data that can be prehended by another entity). Whitehead, *Process and Reality*, 22, 104.

187. From this point of view, *I've Heard About . . .* is symptomatic of another kind of thought architecture developed from the uncertainties of formal systems, which add new contrasts, tensions, and evaluations of form and matter, and of planning and implementation. Automated procedures imply the ingression of new ideas that change what can be empirically experienced.

188. The animation of the Viab machine can be found at http://b.durandin.free.fr/iveheardabout/viab.htm (last accessed January 2012).

189. See the contour-crafting video at http://b.durandin.free.fr/iveheardabout/contourcrafting.htm (last accessed January 2012).

190. For a short video on the final structure, see http://b.durandin.free.fr/iveheardabout/model1.htm (last accessed January 2012).

191. The notion of temporal continuity has been problematized in chapter 2.

192. According to Shulgin, this video-sequencing installation shows how a machine aesthetic is not a mere reflection of its functionality. There is instead an aesthetic of the machine interface, which is self-sufficient and which is not simply mediated by the relation between the creator and the created. The *Nirvana Transitions* project addresses such an aesthetic from inside the machine, beyond the mediations of the creator and user. For more detail on this project and on Shulgin's works, see "Electroboutique," available at http://www.electroboutique.com (last accessed January 2012).

193. Whitehead, *Adventures of Ideas*, 186.

194. Stephen Jay Gould argues that consciousness is but a cosmic accident and not the progressive evolution of the brain. He points out that there is no reason to believe that mammals prevailed because of their warm-bloodedness, their bearing of live young, or their large brains. The survival of mammals can only be attributed to their size (i.e., to their small size at certain key points in earth's history), since only small creatures survived the impacts of comets or asteroids. See Stephen Jay Gould, "Challenges to Neo-Darwinism and Their Meaning for a Revised View of Human Consciousness," Tanner Lectures on Human Values, delivered at Clare Hall, Cambridge University, 30 April and 1 May 1984, available at http://www.tannerlectures.utah.edu/lectures/documents/gould85.pdf (last accessed January 2012).

195. In *Nirvana Transitions*, this deep space is extended to 30 seconds to amplify the ungraspable briefness of algorithmic prehensions.

196. William James, *The Principles of Psychology*, vol. 1 (Cambridge, MA: Harvard University Press, 1983), 239.

197. Whitehead's atomic theory of time has been discussed in chapter 2. It may suffice here to remind the reader that Whitehead argues that the becoming of continuity is only conceivable by means of the atomization of temporal continuity between the past and the present. This atomization is defined by the composition of actual occasions, which defines an event with determinate duration.

198. James, *The Principles of Psychology*, vol. 1, 244.

199. Graham Harman has objected to Whitehead's internal system of prehended relations, arguing that such a system only guarantees infinite series in a house of mirrors. Hence interiority exists because it is prehended by another and not because it is objectively there with its internal architecture. For Harman, internal relations cannot therefore be explained by prehensions, since the latter seem to act mainly as external conjunctions between the same interiorities. Conceived in these terms,

prehensions are unable to account for the qualitative elements that compose the interiority of an object. I have discussed this argument in chapter 1.

200. Whitehead, *Science and the Modern World*, 101–106.

201. Whitehead, *Process and Reality*, 85, 130.

202. As James clarifies, "the relations that connect experiences must themselves be experienced relations, and any kind of relation experienced must be accounted as 'real' as anything else in the system." James continues: "Elements may indeed be redistributed, the original placing of things getting connected, but a real place must be found for every kind of thing experienced, whether term or relation, in the final philosophical arrangement." William James, *Essays in Radical Empiricism* (Lincoln: University of Nebraska Press, 1996), 42.

203. Whitehead, *Process and Reality*, 44.

204. James, *Essays in Radical Empiricism*, 49.

205. Ibid., 50.

Glossary

1. Humberto Maturana and Francisco Varela, *The Tree of Knowledge: The Biological Roots of Human Understanding* (Boston: Shambhala, 1992).

2. Christian S. Calude and Gregory Chaitin, "Randomness Everywhere," *Nature* 400 (1999), 319–320.

3. Michael Meredith, "Never Enough (Transform, Repeat ad Nausea)," in Tomoko Sakamoto and Albert Ferre, eds., *From Control to Design: Parametric/Algorithmic Architecture* (Barcelona: Actar, 2008), 7–9.

4. Brian Massumi, "Potential Politics and the Primacy of Preemption," *Theory and Event* 10, no. 2 (2007).

5. Gregory J. Chaitin, *Exploring Randomness* (London: Springer-Verlag, 2001), 22.

6. Alfred North Whitehead, *Process and Reality: An Essay in Cosmology* (New York: Free Press, 1978), 3.

References

Anderson, James J., and Edward Rosenfeld, eds. *Neurocomputing*. Vol. 1, *Foundations of Research*. Cambridge, MA: MIT Press, 1989.

Armstrong, Rachel. "Designer Material for Architecture." *Architectural Design* 78, no. 6 (October 2008), 86–89.

Asaro, Peter M. "From Mechanisms of Adaptation to Intelligence Amplifiers: The Philosophy of W. Ross Ashby." In Philip Husbands, Owen Holland, and Michael Wheeler, eds., *The Mechanical Mind in History*, 149–184. Cambridge, MA: MIT Press, 2008.

Bachelard, Gaston. *The New Scientific Spirit*. Trans. Arthur Goldhammer. Boston: Beacon Press, 1984.

Badiou, Alain. *Being and Event*. London: Continuum, 2005.

Badiou, Alain. *The Clamor of Being*. Minneapolis: University of Minnesota Press, 1999.

Barad, Karen. *Meeting the Universe Halfway: Quantum Physics and the Entanglement of Matter and Meaning*. Durham: Duke University Press, 2007.

Becher, Veronica, and Gregory Chaitin. "Another Example of Higher Order Randomness." *Fundamenta Informaticae* 51, no. 4 (2002), 325–338.

Becher, V., S. Daicz, and G. Chaitin. "A Highly Random Number." In C. S. Calude, M. J. Dinneen, and S. Sburlan, eds., *Combinatorics, Computability and Logic*, 55–68. London: Springer, 2001.

Bennet, Jane. *Vibrant Matter: A Political Ecology of Things*. Durham: Duke University Press, 2010.

Bergson, Henri. *Creative Evolution*. New York: Modern Library, 1994.

Bergson, Henri. *Duration and Simultaneity: Bergson and the Einsteinian Universe*. Ed. Robin Durie. Manchester, UK: Clinamen Press, 1999.

Bergson, Henri. *Introduction to Metaphysics*. Indianapolis: Hackett, 1999.

Bergson, Henri. *Matter and Memory*. New York: Zone Books, 1991.

Bergson, Henri. *Time and Free Will: An Essay on the Immediate State of Consciousness*. London: Alley, 1913.

Berlinski, David. *The Advent of the Algorithm: The Ideas that Rule the World*. New York: Harcourt, 2000.

Binmore, Ken, Cristiano Castelfranchi, James Doran, and Michael Wooldridge. "Rationality in Multi-Agent Systems." *Knowledge Engineering Review*, no. 3 (1998), 309–314.

Bowman, Clarke L. "Individuals and Points." *Notre Dame Journal of Formal Logic* 26, no. 1 (January 1985).

Boyer, Carl B. *A History of Mathematics*. 2nd ed. New York: Wiley, 1989.

Bradley, James. "The Speculative Generalization of the Function: A Key to Whitehead." *Tijdschrift voor Filosofie* 64 (2002), 231–252. Also at *Inflexions* no. 2 (December 2008). http://www.inflexions.org.

Brassier, Ray. *Nihil Unbound: Enlightenment and Extinction*. London: Palgrave Macmillan, 2007.

Bratman, Michael. *Intention, Plans, and Practical Reason*. Cambridge, MA: MIT Press, 1999.

Bray, Dennis. *Wetware: A Computer in Every Living Cell*. New Haven: Yale University Press, 2009.

Bryant, Levi. "Being Is Flat: The Strange Mereology of Object-Oriented Ontology." Paper presented at the symposium "Object-Oriented Ontology," Georgia Tech, 23 April 2010. http://ooo.gatech.edu/?listen.

Bullivant, Lucy. "Alice in the Technoland." *Architectural Design* 77, no. 4 (July-August 2007), 7–10.

Bullivant, Lucy. "Playing with Art." *Architectural Design* 77, no. 4 (July-August 2007), 32–43.

Bullivant, Lucy. *Responsive Environments: Architecture, Art and Design*. London: V&A, 2006.

Bullivant, Lucy. "Shadow Play: The Participative Art of Scott Snibbe." *Architectural Design* 77, no. 4 (July-August 2007), 68–77.

Cache, Bernard. *Earth Moves: The Furnishing of Territories*. Cambridge, MA: MIT Press, 1995.

Calabrese, Francesco, Kristian Kloeckl, and Carlo Ratti. "WikiCity: Real-Time Urban Environments." *IEEE Pervasive Computing* 6, no. 3 (July-September 2007), 52–53.

Calude, Christian, and Gregory Chaitin. "Randomness Everywhere." *Nature* 400 (1999), 319–320.

Cariani, Peter. "Pask's Ear and Biological Creativity." http://homepage.mac.com/cariani/CarianiWebsite/PaskDevice93.pdf.

Cariani, Peter. "To Evolve an Ear: Epistemological Implications of Gordon Pask's Electrochemical Devices." *Systems Research* 10, no. 3 (1993), 19–33.

Casati, Roberto, and Achille C. Varzi. *Parts and Places: The Structures of Spatial Representation.* Cambridge, MA: MIT Press, 1999.

Chaitin, Gregory J. "Evolution of Mutating Software." *Bulletin of the European Association for Theoretical Computer Science*, no. 97 (February 2009), 157–164.

Chaitin, Gregory J. *Exploring Randomness.* London: Springer, 2001.

Chaitin, Gregory J. "The Limits of Reason." *Scientific American* 294, no. 3 (2006), 74–81.

Chaitin, Gregory. *Meta Math! The Quest for Omega.* New York: Pantheon, 2005.

Chaitin, Gregory J. "Metaphysics, Metamathematics and Metabiology." In Hector Zenil, ed., *Randomness through Computation: Some Answers, More Questions*, 93–103. Singapore: World Scientific Publishing, 2011.

Chown, Marcus. "The Omega Man." *New Scientist* (March 2001). http://www-2.dc.uba.ar/profesores/becher/ns.html.

Chu, Karl. "Metaphysics of Genetic Architecture and Computation." *Architectural Design* 76, no. 4 (July-August 2006), 38–45.

Chun, Wendy. *Control and Freedom: Power and Paranoia in the Age of Fiber Optics.* Cambridge, MA: MIT Press, 2006.

Churchland, Patricia Smith. *Neurophilosophy: Toward a Unified Science of the Mind-Brain.* Cambridge, MA: MIT Press, 1989.

Churchland, Paul M. *The Engine of Reason, the Seat of the Soul: A Philosophical Journey into the Brain.* Cambridge, MA: MIT Press, 1995.

Churchland, Paul M. *A Neurocomputational Perspective: The Nature of the Mind and the Structure of Science.* Cambridge, MA: MIT Press, 1989.

Churchland, Paul M. *Neurophilosophy at Work.* Cambridge: Cambridge University Press, 2007.

Clark, Andy. "Embodiment and the Philosophy of Mind." In Anthony O'Hear, ed., *Current Issues in Philosophy of Mind*, 35–52. Cambridge: Cambridge University Press, 1998.

Clark, Andy. *Mindware: An Introduction to the Philosophy of Cognitive Science*. Oxford: Oxford University Press, 2001.

Clark, Andy. *Natural-Born Cyborgs: Minds, Technologies, and the Future of Human Intelligence*. Oxford: Oxford University Press, 2004.

Clark, Andy. "Where Brain, Body and World Collide." *Daedalus* 127, no. 2 (Spring 1998), 257–280.

Clark, Andy, and David J. Chalmers. "The Extended Mind." 1998. http://www.cogs.indiana.edu/andy/TheExtendedMind.pdf.

Coen, Michael. "The Future of Human-Computer Interaction or How I Learned to Stop Worrying and Love My Intelligent Room." *IEEE Intelligent Systems* (March-April 1999). http://people.csail.mit.edu/mhcoen/Papers/stopworrying.pdf.

Crutzen, Cecile, and Erna Kotkamp. "Object Orientation." In Matthew Fuller, ed., *Software Studies: A Lexicon*, 200–205. Cambridge, MA: MIT Press, 2008.

Damasio, Antonio. *The Feeling of What Happens: Body, Emotion and the Making of Consciousness*. New York: Harcourt, 2000.

Damasio, Antonio. *Looking for Spinoza: Joy, Sorrow, and the Feeling Brain*. Orlando, FL: Harcourt, 2003.

Davis, Martin. *The Universal Computer: The Road from Leibniz to Turing*. New York: W. W. Norton, 2000.

Dawkins, Richard. *The Blind Watchmaker*. New York: W. W. Norton, 1986.

Dawkins, Richard. *The Extended Phenotype: The Long Reach of the Gene*. Oxford: Oxford University Press, 1999.

DeLanda, Manuel. "Deleuze and the Use of the Genetic Algorithm in Architecture." In Neil Leach, ed., *Designing for a Digital World*, 115–120. New York: Wiley, 2001.

DeLanda, Manuel. *Philosophy and Simulation*. London: Continuum, 2011.

DeLanda, Manuel. *War in the Age of Intelligent Machines*. New York: Zone Books, 1991.

Deleuze, Gilles. *Difference and Repetition*. Trans. Paul Patton. London: Continuum, 2004.

Deleuze, Gilles. *The Fold: Leibniz and the Baroque*. Minneapolis: University of Minnesota Press, 1993.

Deleuze, Gilles. "Postscript on Control Societies." In *Negotiations: 1972–1990*. New York: Columbia University Press, 1995.

Deleuze, Gilles, and Félix Guattari. *A Thousand Plateaus: Capitalism and Schizophrenia*. London: Athlone Press, 1987.

Deleuze, Gilles, and Félix Guattari. *What Is Philosophy?* London: Verso, 1999.

Desmet, Ronny. "Whitehead and the British Reception of Einstein's Relativity: An Addendum to Victor Lowe's Whitehead Biography." Centre for Process Studies, seminars, 2 October 2007. http://www.ctr4process.org/publications/SeminarPapers/30_2-DesmetR.pdf.

Di Cristina, Giuseppa. "Topological Tendency in Architecture." In Di Cristina, ed., *Architecture and Science*, 6–14. New York: Wiley, 2001.

Doidge, Norman. *The Brain that Changes Itself: Stories of Personal Triumph from the Frontiers of Brain Science*. New York: Viking, 2007.

During, Elie. "Philosophical Twins? Bergson and Whitehead on Langevin's Paradox and the Meaning of 'Space-Time.'" In Guillaume Durand and Michel Weber, eds., *Alfred North Whitehead's Principles of Natural Knowledge*. Frankfurt: Ontos, 2007.

Einstein, Albert. *Relativity: The Special and the General Theory*. Trans. Robert W. Lawson. London: Routledge, 2001.

Feynman, Richard Phillips. *Six Not-So-Easy Pieces: Einstein's Relativity, Symmetry, and Space-Time*. New York: Basic Books, 1998.

Fishwick, Paul. *Aesthetic Computing*. Cambridge, MA: MIT Press, 2005.

Fletcher, Peter. "Non-standard Set Theory." *Journal of Symbolic Logic* 54, no. 3 (September 1989), 1000–1008.

Foucault, Michel. *Society Must Be Defended: Lectures at the Collège de France, 1975–76*. New York: Picador, 2003.

Frazer, John Hamilton. "The Cybernetics of Architecture: A Tribute to the Contribution of Gordon Pask." *Kybernetes* 30, nos. 5–6 (2001), 641–651.

Fredkin, Edward. "Finite Nature." Proceedings of the XXVIIth Rencontre de Moriond, 1992. http://www.digitalphilosophy.org/Home/Papers/FiniteNature/tabid/106/Default.aspx.

Fuller, Matthew. *Behind the Blip: Essays on the Culture of Software*. Brooklyn, NY: Autonomedia, 2003.

Fuller, Matthew. "Elegance." In Matthew Fuller, ed., *Software Studies: A Lexicon*, 87–91. Cambridge, MA: MIT Press, 2008.

Galloway, Alexander. *Protocol: How Control Exists after Decentralization*. Cambridge, MA: MIT Press, 2004.

Garcia, Mark. "Otherwise Engaged: New Projects in Interactive Design." *Architectural Design* 77, no. 4 (2007), 48–49.

Gardner, Martin. "Mathematical Games: The Fantastic Combination of John Conway's New Solitary Game 'Life'." *Scientific American* 223 (October 1970), 120–123.

Gelernter, David. *The Aesthetics of Computing*. London: Weidenfeld & Nicholson, 1998.

Gibson, James J. *The Ecological Approach to Visual Perception*. Boston: Houghton Mifflin, 1979.

Gödel, Kurt. "Some Basic Theorems on the Foundations of Mathematics and Their Implications." In Gödel, *Collected Works*, ed. Solomon Feferman et al., vol. 3, 304–323. Oxford: Oxford University Press, 1995.

Goffey, Andrew. "Algorithm." In Matthew Fuller, ed., *Software Studies: A Lexicon*. Cambridge, MA: MIT Press, 2008.

Goldstein, Rebecca. *Incompleteness: The Proof and Paradox of Kurt Gödel*. New York: W. W. Norton, 2005.

Goodman, Steve. *Sonic Warfare: Sound, Affect and the Ecology of Fear*. Cambridge, MA: MIT Press, 2010.

Gould, Stephen Jay. "Challenges to Neo- Darwinism and Their Meaning for a Revised View of Human Consciousness." Tanner Lectures on Human Values, Clare Hall, Cambridge University, 30 April and 1 May 1984. http://www.tannerlectures.utah.edu/lectures/documents/gould85.pdf.

Greenfield, Adam. *Everyware: The Dawning Age of Ubiquitous Computing*. Berkeley: New Riders, 2006.

Grosz, Elizabeth. *Architecture from the Outside*. Cambridge, MA: MIT Press, 2001.

Guattari, Félix. *Chaosmosis: An Ethico-Aesthetic Paradigm*. Trans. Paul Bains and Julian Pefanis. Bloomington: Indiana University Press, 1995.

Guattari, Félix. *The Guattari Reader*. Ed. Gary Genosko. Oxford, UK: Blackwell, 1996.

Guattari, Félix. *Molecular Revolution: Psychiatry and Politics*. Trans. Rosemary Sheed. Harmondsworth, UK: Penguin, 1984.

Hansen, Mark. *Bodies in Code: Interfaces with Digital Media*. London: Routledge, 2006.

Haque, Usman. "The Architectural Relevance of Gordon Pask." *Architectural Design* 77, no. 4 (July-August 2007), 54–61.

Haque, Usman. "Architecture, Interaction, Systems." In Christine Macy and Sarah Bonnemaison, eds., *Responsive Textile Environments*, 56–65. Halifax: Tuns Press, 2007.

Hardingham, Samantha. *Cedric Price: Opera*. New York: Wiley, 2003.

Harman, Graham. *Guerrilla Metaphysics: Phenomenology and the Carpentry of Things*. Chicago: Open Court, 2005.

Harman, Graham. *Prince of Networks: Bruno Latour and Metaphysics*. Prahran, Australia: re.press, 2009.

Hatherley, Owen. "Zaha Hadid Architects and the Neoliberal Avant-Garde." *Mute: Culture and Politics after the Net,* 2010. http://www.metamute.org/editorial/articles/zaha-hadid-architects-and-neoliberal-avant-garde.

Hawking, Stephen, and Leonard Mlodinow. "The Elusive Theory of Everything." *Scientific American* (September 2010). http://www.scientificamerican.com/author.cfm?id=2536.

Hayles, N. Katherine. *How We Became Posthuman.* Chicago: University of Chicago Press, 1999.

Hayles, N. Katherine. *My Mother Was a Computer: Digital Subjects and Literary Texts.* Chicago: University of Chicago Press, 2005.

Hensel, Michael, and Achim Menges. "The Heterogeneous Space of Morpho-ecologies." In Michael Hensel, Christian Hight, and Achim Menges, eds., *Space Reader: Heterogeneous Space in Architecture,* 182–201. London: Wiley, 2009.

Hilbert, David. "The New Grounding of Mathematics: First Report." In W. B. Ewald, ed., *From Kant to Hilbert: A Source Book in the Foundations of Mathematics,* vol. 2, 1115–1133. New York: Oxford University Press, 1996.

Ho Mae-Wan. "What Is (Schrödinger's) Negentropy?" *Modern Trends in BioThermo-Kinetics,* no. 3 (1994), 50–61.

Holland, John. *Adaptation in Natural and Artificial Systems.* Ann Arbor: University of Michigan Press, 1975.

Hookway, Branden, and Chris Perry. "Responsive Systems/Appliance Architectures." *Architectural Design* 76, no. 5 (2006), 74–79.

Horgan, Terence, and John Tienson. *Connectionism and the Philosophy of Mind.* Dordrecht: Kluwer Academic Publishers, 1991.

Jacob, Eshel Ben, Yoash Shapira, and Alfred I. Tauber. "Seeking the Foundations of Cognition in Bacteria: From Schrödinger's Negative Entropy to Latent Information." In Steven Shaviro, ed., *Cognition and Decision in Non-Human Biological Organisms.* Living Books about Life, 2011. http://www.livingbooksaboutlife.org/books/Main_Page.

James, William. *Essays in Radical Empiricism.* Lincoln: University of Nebraska Press, 1996.

James, William. *The Principles of Psychology.* Vol. 1. Cambridge, MA: Harvard University Press, 1983.

James, William. "What Is an Emotion?" *Mind* 9 (1884), 188–205.

Jo, Chang-Hyun. "A New Way of Discovery of Belief, Desire, and Intention in the BDI Agent-Based Software Model." *Journal of Advanced Computational Intelligence and Intelligent Informatics* 7, no. 1 (2004), 1–3.

Johansen, John M. *Nanoarchitecture: A New Species of Architecture*. New York: Princeton Architectural Press, 2002.

Kay, Alan. "The Reactive Engine." Doctoral thesis, Electrical Engineering and Computer Science, University of Utah, 1969.

Kipnis, Jeffrey. "Towards a New Architecture." In Michael Hensel, Christopher Hight, and Achim Menges, eds., *Space Reader: Heterogeneous Space in Architecture*, 97–117. New York: Wiley, 2009.

Kittler, Friedrich. "The History of Communication Media." *Ctheory*, ga114 (1996). http://www.ctheory.net/articles.aspx?id=45.

Kittler, Friedrich. *Literature, Media and Information Systems*. Ed. John Johnston. Amsterdam: Overseas Publishers Association, 1997.

Kittler, Friedrich. "Towards an Ontology of Media." Public lecture, symposium "A Topological Approach to Cultural Dynamics," University of Amsterdam, 29–30 November 2007.

Knuth, Donald. *The Art of Computer Programming*. 3 vols. 3rd ed. Reading, MA: Addison Wesley, 1997.

Kwinter, Sanford. *Far from Equilibrium: Essays on Technology and Design Culture*. Ed. Cynthia Davidson. Barcelona: Actar, 2008.

Leach, Neil. "Swarm Urbanism." *Architectural Design* 79, no. 4 (July-August 2009), 50–56.

Leibniz, Gottfried Wilhelm. *Discourse on Metaphysics and Related Writings*. Ed. R. N. D. Martin and Stuart Brown. New York: St. Martin's Press, 1988.

Leibniz, Gottfried Wilhelm. *The Labyrinth of the Continuum: Writings on the Continuum Problem, 1672–1686*. Trans. Richard T. W. Arthur. New Haven: Yale University Press, 2001.

Leibniz, Gottfried Wilhelm. *New Essays on Human Understanding*. Trans. Peter Remnant and Jonathan Bennett. Cambridge: Cambridge University Press, 1981.

Lobell, John. "The Milgo Experiment: An Interview with Haresh Lalvani." *Architectural Design* 76, no. 4 (July-August 2006), 52–61.

Lynn, Greg. *Animate Form*. New York: Princeton Architectural Press, 1999.

Lynn, Greg. "Architectural Curvilinearity: The Folded, the Pliant and the Supple." *Architectural Design* 63, nos. 3–4 (March-April 1993), 22–29.

Lynn, Greg. *Folds, Bodies and Blobs: Collected Essays*. Brussels: Bibliothèque Royale de Belgique, 2004.

Maeda, John. *Creative Code: Aesthetics and Computation.* London: Thames and Hudson, 2004.

Manovich, Lev. "Alan Kay's Universal Media Machine." *Northern Lights* 5 (2007), 39–56.

Manovich, Lev. *The Language of New Media.* Cambridge, MA: MIT Press, 2001.

Manovich, Lev. *Software Takes Command,* 2008. http://lab.softwarestudies.com/2008/11/softbook.html.

Manovich, Lev. "Understanding Hybrid Media." In Betti-Sue Hertz, ed., *Animated Paintings,* 1–17. San Diego: San Diego Museum of Art, 2007.

Massumi, Brian. "Deleuze, Guattari and the Philosophy of Expression (Involutionary Afterword)." *Canadian Review of Comparative Literature* 24, no. 3 (1998).

Massumi, Brian. "'Everywhere You Want to Be': Introduction to Fear." In Massumi, ed., *The Politics of Everyday Fear,* 3–38. Minneapolis: University of Minnesota Press, 1993.

Massumi, Brian. "The Future Birth of the Affective Fact: The Political Ontology of Threat." In Melissa Gregg and Gregory J. Seigworth, eds., *The Affect Theory Reader,* 52–70. Durham: Duke University Press, 2010.

Massumi, Brian. "National Enterprise Emergency: Steps Toward an Ecology of Power." *Theory, Culture and Society* 26, no. 6 (November 2009), 153–185.

Massumi, Brian. *Parables for the Virtual.* Durham: Duke University Press, 2002.

Massumi, Brian. "Potential Politics and the Primacy of Pre-emption." *Theory and Event* 10, no. 2 (2007).

Massumi, Brian. *Semblance and Event: Activist Philosophy and the Occurrent Arts.* Cambridge, MA: MIT Press, 2011.

Maturana, Humberto R., and Francisco J. Varela. *Autopoiesis and Cognition: The Realization of the Living.* Dordrecht: D. Reidel, 1980.

Maturana, Humberto R., and Francisco J. Varela. *The Tree of Knowledge: The Biological Roots of Human Understanding.* Boston: Shambhala, 1992.

Meredith, Michael. "Never Enough (Transform, Repeat ad Nausea)." In Tomoko Sakamoto and Albert Ferre, eds., *From Control to Design: Parametric/Algorithmic Architecture,* 7–9. Barcelona: Actar, 2008.

Millikan, Ruth. "Biosemantics." *Journal of Philosophy* 86, no. 6 (1989), 281–297. Reprinted in Cynthia MacDonald and Graham MacDonald, eds., *Philosophy of Psychology: Debates on Psychological Explanation.* Oxford: Blackwell, 1995.

Mitchell, William J. "After the Revolution: Instruments of Displacement." In Georg Flachbart and Peter Weibel, eds., *Disappearing Architecture: From Real to Virtual to Quantum*, 13–24. Basel: Birkhäuser, 2005.

Munster, Anna. "Nerves of Data: The Neurological Turn in/against Networked Media." *Computational Culture*, no. 1 (December 2011). http://computationalculture.net/.

Nielsen, Michael, and Isaac Chuang. 2000. *Quantum Computation and Quantum Information*. Cambridge: Cambridge University Press.

Noe, Alva. *Action in Perception*. Cambridge, MA: MIT Press, 2005.

Ochoa, Gabriela. "An Introduction to Lindenmayer Systems." http://www.biologie.uni-hamburg.de/b-online/e28_3/lsys.html.

ONL. "Digital Pavilion Korea, Sampang-dong, Seoul, South Korea, 2006." *Architectural Design* 77, no. 4 (2007), 48–49.

Oosterhuis, Kas. *Interactive Architecture #1*. Rotterdam: Episode Publishers, 2007.

Oosterhuis, Kas, Mark David Hosale, Chris Kievid, Veronika Laszlo, and Remko Siemerink. "InteractiveWall: Prototype for an Emotive Wall." 2009. http://bk.tudelft.nl/index.php?id=16045&L=1/.

Parasuraman, Raja. "Neuroergonomics: Research and Practice." *Theoretical Issues in Ergonomics Science* 4 (2003), 5–20.

Parasuraman, Raja, and Matthew Rizzo. *Neuroergonomics: The Brain at Work*. Oxford: Oxford University Press, 2007.

Parisi, Luciana. "Symbiotic Architecture: Prehending Digitality." *Theory, Culture and Society* 26, nos. 2–3 (March-May 2009), 346–374.

Pask, Gordon. "Heinz von Foerster's Self-Organization, the Progenitor of Conversation and Interaction Theories." *Systems Research* 13, no. 3 (September 1996), 349–366.

Picard, Rosalind W. *Affective Computing*. Cambridge, MA: MIT Press, 2007.

Pickering, Andrew. *The Cybernetic Brain: Sketches of Another Future*. Chicago: University of Chicago Press, 2010.

Pike, Steve. "Manipulation and Control of Micro-Organic Matter in Architecture." *Architectural Design* 78, no. 6 (October 2008), 16–24.

Prigogine, Ilya, and Isabelle Stengers. *Order Out of Chaos: Man's New Dialogue with Nature*. New York: Bantam Books, 1984.

Prusinkiewicz, Przemyslaw, and Aristid Lindenmayer. 1990. *The Algorithmic Beauty of Plants*. New York: Springer.

Roche, François. "I've Heard About . . . (A Flat, Fat Growing Urban Experiment): Extracts of Neighborhood Protocols." *Architectural Design* 79, no. 4 (July-August 2009).

Roche, François. "Mathematical Operators for Structural Optimization." http://www.new-territories.com/blog/architecturedeshumeurs/?p=98.

Roche, François. "Protocols/Processes." Interview by Caroline Naphegyi. http://www.new-territories.com/blog/architecturedeshumeurs/wpcontent/uploads/2010/pdf/mouvement%20UK%20Une_architecture_des_humeurs_UKlight2.pdf.

Roche, François, and Natanel Elfassy. "Stuttering." *Log* 19 (Spring-Summer 2010). http://www.new-territories.com/blog/?p=457.

Rocker, Ingeborg M. "Apropos Parametricism: If, in What Style Should We Build?" *Log*, no. 21 (March 2011).

Rocker, M. Ingeborg. "When Code Matters." *Architectural Design* 76, no. 4 (July-August 2006), 16–25.

Schmidhuber, Jürgen. "Low-Complexity Art." *Leonardo* 30, no. 2 (1997), 97–103.

Schmidhuber, Jürgen. "Simple Algorithmic Principles of Discovery, Subjective Beauty, Selective Attention, Curiosity and Creativity." In Vincent Corruble, Masayuki Takeda, and Einoshin Suzuki, eds., *Discovery Science: 10th International Conference*, 26–38. Berlin: Springer, 2007.

Schmidhuber, Jürgen. "Theory of Beauty and Low-Complexity Art." http://www.idsia.ch/~juergen/beauty.html.

Schumacher, Patrick. "Parametricism: A New Global Style for Architecture and Urban Design." *Architectural Design* 79, no. 4 (July-August 2009), 14–24.

Scott, Walter. "Minkowski, Mathematicians, and the Mathematical Theory of Relativity." In H. Goenner, J. Renn, J. Ritter, and T. Sauer, eds., *The Expanding Worlds of General Relativity*, 45–86. Basel: Birkhäuser, 1999.

Sejnowski, Terrence J., and Charles R. Rosenberg. "NETtalk: a Parallel Network that Learns to Read Aloud." John Hopkins University Electrical Engineering and Computer Science Technical Report, JUH/EECS-86/01. In James A. Anderson and Edward Rosenfeld, eds., *Neurocomputing*, 663–672. Cambridge, MA: MIT Press, 1989.

Senagala, Mahesh. "Speed and Relativity: Toward Time-like Architecture." ACSA Annual Meeting Proceedings, Baltimore, 2001. http://www.mahesh.org.

Shaviro, Steven. *Without Criteria: Kant, Whitehead, Deleuze, and Aesthetics*. Cambridge, MA: MIT Press, 2009.

Shaviro, Steven. "The 'Wrenching' Duality of Aesthetics: Kant, Deleuze and the 'Theory of the Sensible'," 2007. http://www.shaviro.com/Othertexts/SPEP.pdf.

Sikiaridi, Elizabeth, and Frans Vogelaar. "Soft Urbanism." In Jorinde Seijdel, ed., *Mobile Space: How Wireless Media Mobilize Public Space*. Rotterdam: NAi, 2006.

Spencer, Douglas. "Architectural Deleuzism: Neoliberal Space, Control and the 'Univer-City." *Radical Philosophy* 168 (July-August 2011), 9–21.

Spuybroek, Lars. *Nox: Machinic Architecture*. London: Thames and Hudson, 2004.

Stengers, Isabelle. *Penser avec Whitehead: Une libre et sauvage création de concepts*. Paris: Editions du Seuil, 2002.

Terzidis, Kostas. *Algorithmic Architecture*. Oxford: Architectural Press, 2006.

Terzidis, Kostas. *Expressive Form: A Conceptual Approach to Computational Design*. London: Spon Press, 2003.

Thompson, Evan. *Mind in Life: Biology, Phenomenology, and the Sciences of the Mind*. Cambridge, MA: Harvard University Press, 2007.

Thrift, Nigel. "Movement-Space: The Changing Domain of Thinking Resulting from the Development of New Kinds of Spatial Awareness." *Economy and Society* 33, no. 4 (2004), 582–604.

Turing, Alan M. "On Computable Numbers, with an Application to the *Entscheidungsproblem*." *Proceedings of the London Mathematical Society*, 2nd ser., 42 (1936), 230–265.

Vanucci, Marco. "Open Systems: Approaching Novel Parametric Domains." In Michael Meredith, Tomoto Sakamoto, and Albert Ferre, eds., *From Control to Design: Parametric/Algorithmic Architecture*, 118–121. Barcelona: Actar, 2008.

Varela, Francisco. "Phenomenology: A Methodological Remedy for the Hard Problem." *Journal of Consciousness Studies* 3 (June 1996), 330–350.

Varela, Francisco J., Evan Thompson, and Eleanor Rosch. *The Embodied Mind: Cognitive Science and Human Experience*. Cambridge, MA: MIT Press, 1991.

Virilio, Paul. *The Information Bomb*. London: Verso, 2000.

Virilio, Paul. *War and Cinema: The Logistics of Perception*. London: Verso, 1989.

Watson, Janell. *Guattari's Diagrammatic Thought: Writing between Lacan and Deleuze*. London: Continuum, 2009.

Watson, Janell. "Schizoanalysis and Metamodeling." *Fibreculture Journal*, no. 12 (2008). http://twelve.fibreculturejournal.org.

Weiser, Mark. "Some Computer Design Issues in Ubiquitous Computing." *Communications of the ACM* 36, no. 7 (July 1993), 75–84.

Weiser, Mark, and John Seely Brown. "Designing Calm Technology." Xerox PARC (21 December 1995). http://www.ubiq.com/hypertext/weiser/calmtech/calmtech.htm.

Whitehead, Alfred North. *Adventures of Ideas*. New York: Free Press, 1967.

Whitehead, Alfred North. *The Concept of Nature*. Amherst, NY: Prometheus Books, 2004.

Whitehead, Alfred North. *An Enquiry Concerning the Principles of Natural Knowledge*. Cambridge: Cambridge University Press, 1919.

Whitehead, Alfred North. *The Function of Reason*. Boston: Beacon Press, 1929.

Whitehead, Alfred North. *Modes of Thought*. New York: Free Press, 1938.

Whitehead, Alfred North. *The Principle of Relativity, with Applications to Physical Science*. Cambridge: Cambridge University Press, 1922.

Whitehead, Alfred North. *Process and Reality: An Essay in Cosmology*. New York: Free Press, 1978.

Whitehead, Alfred North. "The Relational Theory of Space." Ed. P. J. Hurley. *Philosophy Research Archives*, no. 5 (1979), 712–741.

Whitehead, Alfred North. *Science and the Modern World*. Cambridge: Cambridge University Press, 1928.

Whitehead, Alfred North, with H. W. Carr and R. A. Sampson. "Symposium: The Problem of Simultaneity: Is There a Paradox in the Principle of Relativity in Regard to the Relation of Time Measured and Time Lived?" *Proceedings of the Aristotelian Society*, supplementary vol. 3 (1923), 15–41.

Wiener, Norbert. *Cybernetics, or Control and Communication in the Animal and the Machine*. Cambridge, MA: MIT Press, 1965.

Wolfram, Stephen. "How Do Simple Programs Behave?" *Architectural Design* 76, no. 4 (July-August 2006), 34–37.

Wolfram, Stephen. *A New Kind of Science*. Champaign, IL: Wolfram Media, 2002.

Zadeh, Lofti. "Fuzzy Sets and Systems." In J. Fox, ed., *System Theory*, 29–39. Brooklyn, NY: Polytechnic Press, 1965.

Index